All about the ITERS-R

Environment Rating Scales

ECERS–R

Early Childhood
Environment Rating Scale
Revised edition

ITERS–R

Infant-Toddler
Environment Rating Scale
Revised edition

FDCRS

Family Day Care Rating Scale

SACERS

School-Age Care
Environment Rating Scale

UNC
FRANK PORTER GRAHAM
CHILD DEVELOPMENT
INSTITUTE

All about the ITERS–R

A detailed guide
in words and pictures
to be used with the ITERS-R

Debby Cryer | Thelma Harms | Cathy Riley
FPG Child Development Institute

Cover design by Thelma Harms
Production manager: Pat Conte
Book design by Michael Brady
Printed in China

Contents

Acknowledgements

All About the ITERS-R is a book prompted by many questions asked by observers as they use the environment rating scale in real life situations. The great challenge of meeting the highly individual needs of infants and toddlers in a group setting, and the diversity of solutions used to meet these needs, has raised many questions about interpreting the meaning of the indicators, and will no doubt continue to raise questions in the future. We have appreciated all these comments and questions because they have stimulated so much thought on our part. We would like to take this opportunity to recognize the valuable contributions all of our colleagues who cared enough to present us with their questions, concerns and ideas. All of them are represented in this work.

We would like to express our appreciation first to the many early childhood programs who allowed us to photograph their settings and practices. In order to illustrate both strengths and weaknesses, they even allowed us to set up examples that did not show best practices. It takes a lot of courage to show what you do when it is good, but even more so when it is not perfect. Also, we thank the parents of children in the classrooms for trusting us to photograph their children; and especially the infants and toddlers, for being what they so naturally are—completely authentic, amazing, and wonderful, each and every one of them.

The authors of this book were greatly supported by our colleagues, who helped with the many tasks required to put together this undertaking. This work would not have been possible if we had not had the benefit of our dedicated team at the Frank Porter Graham Child Development Institute at the University of North Carolina at Chapel Hill. All of our team members work closely together on many projects, and this book represents only one of them. While some of us have been working on this book, others have been taking responsibility for the other things all of us must do, ensuring that everything is completed.

It is difficult to specify any one team-member as being responsible for any one part of this book. There has been lots of sharing of tasks, but we especially want to recognize the contributions of the following people:

Kristina Spence Lee, who was important in ensuring that we had the photographs to illustrate the necessary points. Kris not only provided us with many of the photographs, but she also worked behind the scenes to ensure that situations were set up to capture the essence of the text, necessary permission was obtained, and coordinated our work with child care programs. Her organizational skills became especially valuable as we created easy-to-access data files from our slide archives, and added to them as needed.

Kim Winton, who was significant in obtaining many photographs to illustrate the points covered in the text. In addition, she organized photos into computer files for use in the final publication, communicated with numerous centers, obtained consent for the photos, and ensured that the photographs we needed were acquired, even taking pictures of her nephew, Jett, to fill our needs. Thanks to Kim's efficiency, the final stages of photo selection went smoothly. Kim was also helpful in reviewing and editing the text.

Acknowledgements

Tracy Link provided help with reviewing and editing the text, and helped with taking photographs. Tracy was also valuable in reading the text to ensure that we were being reasonably dependable in what we were saying, and frequently was able to help us rethink our inconsistencies.

Elisa Allen was invaluable to the authors in reviewing and editing the text. Elisa represented the viewpoint of a less experienced scale user (she now qualifies as "more experienced") who helped us understand when we needed to add further information or to clarify points. Everyone involved in the writing process appreciated Elisa's dependability and competence. In addition to helping with the text, she was involved in taking some of the photographs.

Left to right: Kim Winton, Mary Baldwin, Elisa Allen, Kris Lee, Tracy Link, Debby Cryer, Thelma Harms, Cathy Riley, Vanessa Loiselle, Lisa Waller

Lisa Waller provided help with reviewing and editing the text, and also helped with acquiring photographs. Over the past few years, Lisa has provided input into the interpretations of the ITERS-R that are given in this book. In many ways Lisa has helped most by keeping the rest of our projects on course as we devoted time to this book.

Also, we thank additional members of our team, Vanessa Loiselle, Rebecca Decker, and Mary Baldwin. They helped with this book too or with tasks that allowed the work to continue. Our work would have been far more difficult and time consuming without their support.

Our book designer, Michael Brady, also of the Frank Porter Graham Child Development Institute at the University of North Carolina at Chapel Hill, has worked closely with us on the format of the book, contributed ideas that make the book user-friendly and pleasant to read, and completed all the work under a difficult timeline.

We especially wish to thank the Winston-Salem Foundation, provided by the Leon and Renee Kaplan Fund, that partially supported this work.

Finally, we want to acknowledge the cooperation and support provided by our publisher, the PACT group of the Kaplan Early Learning Company. Hal Kaplan is a fine partner, trusting us to do what we are so eager to do, and magically making it possible for us to move forward towards our shared goals of encouraging positive experiences for young children in early childhood programs. We would also like to thank Pat Conte, who worked closely and patiently with us to ensure that this book is everything we wanted it to be.

We are fortunate to have many friends in our work, those who work directly with us on a daily basis, and those who help us in many other ways. We could not have done this alone, so we are glad to have all of you!

DEBBY CRYER
THELMA HARMS
CATHY RILEY
Frank Porter Graham Child Development Institute
University of North Carolina at Chapel Hill

September, 2004

About this book

This book is to be used as a resource guide to the ***Infant/Toddler Environment Rating Scale-Revised Edition*** (ITERS-R, 2003), by Thelma Harms, Debby Cryer, and Richard M. Clifford, published by Teacher's College Press, Columbia University, New York.

When using this book, have a copy of the ITERS-R accessible so the resource guide and the scale can be used side-by-side. The information in this book is not particularly useful without the ITERS-R book because it applies only to the requirements within that scale. This resource guide defines what the requirements in the scale mean, in terms of assigning scores to any classroom. Definitions of words used in the scale are provided, with descriptions of what to look for and the rules that are used to score.

Before using the ITERS-R scale and this resource guide, it is recommended that basic introductory training be completed, using the ITERS-R video training package. The package consists of an interactive video, a *Video Guide and Training Workbook* for use with the video, and an instructor's guide.

About the photographs in this book

Information in this guide is provided as text, with photographs to support meanings. The photographs in this book have been taken over many years, in many early childhood programs. Almost all represent real situations that we have been allowed to document and use as we explain quality practices. There are many positive examples of practices shown.

In showing examples of less positive practices, we have sometimes used situations that were arranged for us to photograph. *Therefore, the photographs used in this book do not always represent the actual practices used in the classrooms where we have been allowed to photograph.*

It is important to remember that there is a lot of flexibility in how the requirements of the ITERS-R can be met. Things can be done very differently in different classrooms, and the same requirement may still be met in each. This is why all classrooms that score high do not look the same. For example, cozy areas can differ substantially from one classroom to another but they still might meet the ITERS-R requirements as long as they provide a substantial amount of softness, and are accessible to the children. Or two teachers with different personalities and styles might both meet the requirements for positive interactions with children even though they may be quite different in how they talk with and relate to the children.

In some cases we have used the same photograph several times in this book to show that different aspects of quality can be observed while looking at the same scene. The same photograph, therefore, might be shown as an example for several different items. For example, one photograph is used to show something about interactions and also about the toys that can be used for sand play. This is because as observers collect information in a classroom, one single instance might give information for several aspects of early childhood care and education. Observers should be able to apply the complex information collected in a classroom to the appropriate requirements of the scale. Sometimes information observed will be simple, and apply to only one requirement, but in many other cases, one observed instance will give information that should be considered in scoring several items. It should be remembered, however, that it would be unusual for one instance to carry the power to determine a score, but that scores are usually based on many pieces of information collected during the entire observation period.

We are not able to represent all the possibilities for how requirements can be met through the photographs we have included in this book. There will be many other options. However, the photographs we have included should be used to help the reader understand certain important aspects of evaluating whether the requirement is met.

Who should use this book?

People in many different early childhood professions use the ITERS-R to see how well a program is meeting children's needs--to see whether children receive the protection, learning opportunities, and positive relationships they need for successful development. Practitioners (teachers, administrators) who provide programs for infants and toddlers frequently use the ITERS-R to ensure the quality of the program they are creating. Program monitors use the ITERS-R when evaluating programs for licensing or other quality assurance systems (accreditation, credentialing). Researchers use the scale to collect data on the quality of early childhood programs.

For ITERS-R scores to be meaningful and truly representative of the quality of an early childhood program, the scale must be completed accurately, with a clear understanding of what each indicator requires. Although the ITERS-R words appear to be clear upon reading, there is actually great variation in interpretation across scale users. This creates problems if the user's interpretations are either too demanding or too accepting. Observers who are too demanding give very low scores even though a classroom might be meeting the requirements properly. Observers who are not demanding enough--who give credit for the slightest evidence of any indicator, provide scores that are too high. Neither makes appropriate use of the scale.

For scale scores to be useful, they must be accurate enough to maintain the proven relationship between ITERS-R program quality and children's positive development. This relationship is not supported if scale scores are systematically too high, too low, or inconsistent across classrooms.

This book will be helpful to everyone who wants to use the ITERS-R accurately, towards the end result of clearly understanding early childhood programs, so improvements can be implemented. It will be helpful to the practitioner who is using the ITERS-R in self-assessment, and needs to know what to do to meet a requirement. It will be useful also to those who provide technical assistance in program quality enhancement efforts, so that the guidance provided is based on accurate interpretations. It will be especially useful to those who evaluate program quality for monitoring or research, by increasing reliability among observers.

Using the book will not necessarily create an observer who is considered "reliable," which means a person who would score items very similarly to another reliable observer. This is because reliability must be developed within any group of observers who train to be "reliable." They must go out and observe together, and score independently, then correct differences in scoring until they score similarly enough to meet the standards of the group in question.

However, *consistent use of the information in the book will encourage the development of the observation skills and the common context of meaning needed for a group of observers to become reliable* with one another. In addition, the reliability of the group will be more consistent with that of the ITERS-R authors.

How this book is organized

Subscales, items and indicators

This guide follows the organization of the ITERS-R, with subscales that contain a number of items. Each item consists of numbered indicators at four quality levels. The subscales and the items within each one are listed on page 9 of the ITERS-R.

The *subscales* are organized primarily to help the observer collect information that is likely to be found under similar circumstances. They provide a practical, and conceptual, organization for the items, which makes the scale easier to use. For example, items in the first subscale require that the observer look at the space and furnishings for the children. Many of the requirements in these items are relatively easy to see at the beginning of an observation, so they are placed together at the beginning of the scale. Also, the items represent issues that are often thought of at the same time, for example, when setting up or making plans to change a classroom.

There are 39 *items*, organized into 7 *subscales* in the ITERS-R. Each of the numbered *items* represents a dimension found in any early childhood program.

Most of the items (1-32) allow the observer to examine the quality of what children actually experience in a program. These items are considered most directly related to how children develop. In research, a relationship has been shown between higher scores on the scale and better child development outcomes in a wide range of areas. The outcomes include those that are usually thought to be important for later success in school and in our society, namely, cognitive development, language, and social/emotional skills.

The items in the last subscale (items 33-39) look at the quality of provisions for the adults involved in the program--the parents and staff. The items about parents and staff are supportive of the other items. They deal with providing a comfortable and convenient work environment for staff, as well as professional development opportunities to encourage staff competence. Communication with parents is also considered to help balance the child's life in the two settings of home and the early childhood program.

Each item is presented as a 7-point scale with descriptions of what is required under 1 (inadequate), 3 (minimal), 5 (good), and 7 (excellent). Each description is made up of one or more numbered *indicators* that must be scored when completing an observation and evaluation of a classroom. An *indicator* is a specific requirement that must be scored "Yes," "No," or (where indicated) "NA."

This book provides a "General Information" section about each item in the ITERS-R. This general information is followed by a section called "A Closer Look at Each Indicator," which gives specific information about each requirement. This will help in understanding what each indicator means, what to look for in deciding whether or not it is true, and how to score it.

Understanding the meaning of ITERS-R scores

Many things will affect the care and education that teachers provide for the children in infant/toddler programs. The cultural preferences or other beliefs of the adults involved, the curriculum approach used, the physical conditions of the building, finances or staffing issues, are only some examples of variables that affect what a program is able to provide in terms of quality reflected in the scores on *the Infant/Toddler Environment Rating Scale-Revised Edition*. Because of these variables, it is unlikely that programs will score uniformly high on *all* the requirements of the scale. Instead, programs will have both strengths and weaknesses in their scores, which give program staff an opportunity to consider where change is needed, and to determine how to create desired improvement.

About this book

The important thing to remember, when considering ITERS-R scores, is that the individual requirements of the scales are far less important than the average total score for any classroom. *It is the average total score that is related to positive child development, but not any of the single requirements by themselves.*

The scales are weighted, through repetition of important requirements, to ensure that key aspects for positive development are more heavily represented than single less significant details. This provides some flexibility with regard to how and when requirements are met while ensuring that the larger concepts within the scales, of *protection, learning,* and *positive relati*onships, are adequately measured.

Flexibility is possible to some extent in how a program wishes to provide high quality. As long as the classroom's average total score meets enough of the requirements of the scale, a center can consider which indicators they will provide to improve chances for better child development, while recognizing that they are not providing others. Having a few relative weaknesses in a program will not harm children's development substantially, *unless too many requirements are not met,* causing the average total score to be too low.

Here are some examples of how this works.

- The staff in a program decide that sets of fine motor materials with multiple pieces, such as pop beads, large beads with strings, or puzzles, should not be accessible to older toddlers without intense supervision. They believe there would be too much mess because the toddlers would throw these all over the room. So sets of fine motor materials are only used with the whole group, under close teacher supervision. Such appropriate materials are not accessible at any other times, limiting children's opportunities. This decision would cause the classroom to score below a 5 (good) on the ITERS-R Fine motor item.

  The score on this one item, in itself, would not be likely to affect the children's overall development significantly. However, if the children were denied access to using many other materials as well, such as books, blocks, music toys, or dramatic play toys, this would create a lower average total score, because many item scores would be low. Since access to a variety of materials that children can learn from is important to children's development, this requirement is weighted in the scale through repetition in various items.

- Teachers in a room think that manners are very important for toddlers to learn during meals and snacks. They believe that the children should wait until food is served to everyone before eating anything from the plate that is placed in front of them. They enforce the no-eating rule with no flexibility and punish children for eating ahead of time by taking their food from them.

  This action by the teachers would cause low scores on several items (e.g., Meals/snacks, Discipline, Staff-child interactions), decreasing the chances for a high average total score. If this type of practice, which has been shown to be associated with negative child development, is continued through the day, then other items would also be affected, making the chance for a high average total score impossible.

- The teachers are concerned because the building has some limitations that will cause the program to get several low scores. For example, the facility is not handicapped accessible, the playground must be reached by going through other classrooms, or space in the rooms is limited. When the staff members first read the scale, they became discouraged because they feel that these things are not under their control and they will be penalized even though they are providing a good program.

However, by doing the best they can to improve the many items that are under their control (such as the 3 language items, the 6 personal care routine items, the 10 activities items, the 4 interaction items, and the 4 program structure items, and several of the space and furnishing items) they can maximize higher scores, while minimizing the effects of the lower scores they will receive because of the things they can not control at the time. Then, the resulting average classroom score should be relatively high and meet children's developmental needs.

A higher average score will reflect the high quality of the program which provides lots of stimulating activities and warm staff interactions with children and parents. Classrooms can get a high average score even if there are some limitations in the facility that cannot be changed, if the program is providing high quality experiences in other areas.

It is important for program staff to understand what they are choosing to do or not to do, and to balance these choices in terms of what is possible. The ITERS-R assists program staff to make *well-informed* choices as to which areas the staff might emphasize in program improvement. It is not required that all things be perfect for a high average total score on the scales. But early childhood staff who wish to provide children with what they need for present well-being and future success need to be well informed about the choices they are making, and to minimize low scores whenever possible.

How to use this book

This guide is to be used whenever an ITERS-R user wants to know:

- Why an item or indicator is important, because the rationale for each item is presented

- What the words or terms in an item or indicator mean, according to the authors of the scale

- How much and what kind of evidence must be found to give credit for any indicator

- How to look for, and document, the evidence needed to score

Since the guide is organized by subscale, then items within the subscale, and then indicators within the item, the user only needs to go to the item of interest, read the general information, and then the specifics about the indicators.

For example, if two observers were having a disagreement about what sanitary conditions are required at meal/snack times, they would only have to turn to Item 7, Meals/snacks, and look at the indicators related to this issue (1.3 and 3.3). Or if a teacher wanted to improve her block area, but did not know whether the mixed group of blocks she used could count as 1 "set" (Indicator 3.1) or "2 sets" (Indicator 5.1), she would find Item 19, Blocks, then read the General Information section, and then read the information provided in the two indicators of interest.

The whole book can be used as a comprehensive introduction to the scale. People who want to improve their scoring accuracy can study the ITERS-R by using this book, so that their understanding of what is required is vastly improved. But it is more likely that the book will be used as a reference, like a dictionary or encyclopedia, to look up information on an "as needed" basis.

About this book

Observing classrooms with the ITERS-R

To use the ITERS-R *accurately*, an *observation period* of at least 3 hours must be completed in the classroom being evaluated, followed by an interview with the classroom's teacher (20-30 minutes). As indicated in the scale, the observation must be done during the time of day when children are most active and when most children are present, and it must include both play/learning times and routines, such as a feeding, toileting, and nap time. For a classroom with infants on individual schedules, it is possible to complete the observation in either the morning or afternoon, because those two times of day should not differ significantly. However in infant or toddler classrooms where there is a regular afternoon naptime, it is best to complete the observation during the morning.

The scale should be used to assess one classroom at a time. Multiple observations should not be completed in different classrooms during the same observation time period. Too much valuable information is lost while the observer is in the other room, such as the types of materials children are allowed to use, the kinds of interactions that occur, or whether certain routines are carried out so that they meet requirements.

The specific period of the observation (3 or more hours) is required, to allow the observer to sample enough of what is needed to score all observable items accurately. (Additional time of 20-30 minutes will be needed to ask classroom teachers questions about indicators that were not observed.) A shorter time cannot be used to observe in the classroom, because many important aspects of care and learning will be missed and the observer will not be given sufficient opportunity to discover the scope and variation in practices used. For example:

- In some items, the observer must actually observe one or more instances of a behavior during the observation. When the observation is shortened, there is less chance that the behavior will be seen, and the score will not be a fair representation of what actually occurs. (The inverse is also true--more than 3 hours cannot be allowed to observe required behaviors. This would give credit for a behavior that is not likely to happen frequently enough.)

- Classrooms change dramatically over the day, with periods of greater stress occurring at different times. The observer must be present to see what happens during both the more relaxed and the more stressful times in order to give balanced scores.

- Indoor and outdoor times vary greatly, and both should be observed sufficiently.

- Changes in staffing and the children in the group can occur throughout the day. A good sample of who is usually present and how that affects scores is needed. As children enter or leave the classroom, changes in practice may occur. As teaching staff come and go, a reasonable sample of the impact of these changes must be considered in scoring.

Often we are told that a director of a program knows her classrooms so well, that she can complete the scale on classrooms in the center without actually doing a formal observation, but rather by sitting in the office, and scoring from memory. This leads to unreliable scores that are usually inflated because the scores are based on assumptions, rather than on a systematic continuous observation of the required length.

We are also told that some observers can complete scoring the items without actually having the scale present during the observation. This also leads to inaccurate scores because the observer does not have the scale to read, to be sure that each of the large number of indicators is properly considered.

Completing the scale accurately requires that the observer be in the classroom, constantly referring to the scale, while searching for the evidence needed to score the indicators. All items should be completed and scored before leaving the facility in which the classroom is located, so that if any information is forgotten or was not collected, the observer can still access the classroom.

Being a good ITERS-R observer

When completing the ITERS-R, it is necessary for observers to *minimize* their impact on the classroom environment. Therefore, an accurate ITERS-R observation requires that the observer *not participate or interfere* in classroom activities at all under usual circumstances.

If the observers talk to the children, this takes away the chance to see how the teacher would have interacted with them (or not) at that time, under those conditions. If observers talk to the teacher, the teacher will not be able to do what she would have normally been doing at that time. If observers help with tasks then they cannot see how these tasks are handled without their help. If they make suggestions to the staff about how to improve what they are doing, this changes things as well.

Observers must arrange for the visit before arriving at any program. Permission is needed to observe, teachers must be notified, and a clear explanation of what to expect should be provided. The age-range of children in the program's classrooms must be known so that the classroom observed with the ITERS-R will be one with children from birth to 30 months of age. The observation must be scheduled to take place on a regular day, for example with no fieldtrip planned, or other activity that would prevent observation of the typical operation of the classroom. A time will have to be set when a classroom staff member is free of caregiving responsibilities and can answer questions about things that were not observed. Usually all these requirements are arranged with program administrative staff before the visit.

Observer guidelines have been established to help observers minimize their effect on a classroom. These guidelines should be followed throughout the observation:

- Upon arrival at the facility, have everything you need to complete the observation--an ITERS-R book, score sheet, any materials that should have been put into the scale (such as Playground Safety Guidelines, Meal Requirements, Additional Notes), pencils, and other materials such as a tape measure. However, do not bring extra materials into the room, such as purses, back packs, tote bags, because these are often put down and forgotten resulting in things being lost or misused by others. They can also contain things that are dangerous to very young children.

- Be sure to introduce yourself to the person in charge of the facility, and wear a name tag (or the program's visitor tag if provided). Unless arrangements for the observation have been made ahead of time, do not go into a classroom until you are shown where to go by a responsible staff member.

- Observe only in the classroom that you are evaluating. Use all your observation time with this group of children, rather than looking at other places or classrooms in the building.

- Upon entering the classroom, introduce yourself to the classroom staff, briefly telling about what you will be doing. Be sure to explain that you cannot participate in the classroom in any way--that you will be working the whole time to see what children's experiences are during the observation. However, you will need to ask about the information required to complete the top of the score sheet--about numbers of children and staff, ages of children, and any disabilities among the children in the group. Do this with as little disruption as possible, allowing the staff to take care of the children whenever necessary.

About this book

- Stay with the children in the class, as they are taken from one place to another. If they are indoors, you should be observing indoors also. If they move to another place in the building or go outside, you should follow along.

- Do not interfere with classroom activities in any way. Station yourself around the perimeter of the classroom as unobtrusively as possible. You may move around the perimeter to get a better vantage point during the observation and move into areas for a closer look when it is obvious that children will not be needing to access those areas.

- Move, if you are in the way of teachers or children. Remain sensitive to what is happening around you in the classroom.

- If it does not interfere with the ongoing program, sit in a chair or on the floor so that children are not intimidated by your height. This can be difficult in classrooms with mobile children because sitting on the floor is often a signal that you are there to play with the children. So more standing may be required than in observations of older groups. However, do not sit on other furniture, such as shelves, tables, the children's chairs near an activity table, or on play equipment.

- If you are observing with someone else, refrain from talking with the other person while you are in the classroom.

- Take notes on a pad and/or on your score sheet to help in scoring and forming questions that you may need to ask staff later during the prearranged interview.

- Never leave your materials. (Infants and toddlers may try to eat them!) Keep them with you throughout the observation.

- Try to keep a relaxed, neutral facial expression so that children and/or staff are neither drawn to you nor concerned about your response to them.

- Teachers will be involved with the children during your visit and should not be asked to talk with you or answer questions. This holds true even if teachers are not very involved with the children, and want to talk to you.

- Acknowledge children if they approach you. If they are able to ask, you can tell them that you are watching them play today or that you have to finish your work. Do not otherwise take part in classroom activity or encourage children to interact with you in any way. If children continually approach you because you are sitting at their level, stand up and move away, but in a nice way.

- Look at materials that are in plain view on open shelves or on the floor, if you can do so without disturbing the group. However, a close inspection of these materials is best done when the children are not in the area.

- Do not look through drawers, in cabinets, or in other closed spaces without the permission of the classroom staff. If the class is out of the room and you have gotten the teacher's permission, you may take a few minutes to look in storage spaces.

- Score as much as possible before the end of the observation, so that all items will be scored after interviewing the classroom staff.

- Upon completion of the observation, be sure to thank classroom staff (and say goodbye to both children and adults).

Improving accuracy in scoring

Specific strategies can be used to improve efficiency in collecting information and ensuring accurate scoring. The strategies provided here can be used in collecting information for many items in the ITERS-R.

Observing the right things at the right times

When completing the ITERS-R, some things that need to be observed happen only at certain times of the day, while others can be observed at almost any time. When observers are aware of the *special* things to look for at certain times, they can focus attention on these when they happen and collect all other information at the other times.

Examples of items containing indicators that must be observed at special times include:

Item 2, Furniture for routine care, play and learning:
Whether tables and chairs are "child-sized" for toddlers must be observed while most children are sitting at tables, for example at lunchtime.

Item 6, Greeting/departing:
Must be observed as children/parents enter the classroom or depart.

Item 7, Meals/snacks:
Must be observed as soon as preparation for the feeding process begins to see whether appropriate procedures, such as disinfecting tables and proper handwashing, are carried out; observation must continue until the end of the feeding. For children who are fed on individual schedules, a sample of all feedings must be observed, from beginning to end.

Item 8, Nap:
Set-up of nap area must be observed, as well as a sample of the supervision that occurs during this time. For children who sleep on individual schedules, a sample of all naps must be observed.

Item 9, Diapering/toileting:
Must be observed as it occurs, with a sample of instances that indicate the general practice.

Item 10, Health practices:
Certain circumstances require observation. For example, whether noses are wiped and hands washed as needed or if "spit-up" is cleaned and sanitized properly.

Detailed explanations of what to look for and when to look are provided in this book for each item. The experienced and accurate observer knows when to pay attention as needed.

Tracking practices of handwashing, greeting and other daily events:

To accurately score some ITERS-R items, it is necessary to observe a sample of practice and count to see whether certain requirements have been sufficiently met. Simple charts help to keep a fairly accurate count of certain ongoing events, such as greeting or handwashing. Examples of informal charts you can keep on your notepad or on the score sheet are provided in the sections for each specific item in this book.

Space and Furnishings

1 Indoor space

General information about this item

When we score the item, Indoor space, we consider primarily the room used by the group being observed most of the day. The primary space will carry most of the weight in deciding the score for the item. If multiple rooms are used for approximately the same amounts of time, consider both as the indoor space being evaluated. If toilets or a sleep room are part of the indoor space normally used, then count that as part of the indoor space also, but give its characteristics less weight. Additional spaces that are also used occasionally by the children in the group, such as an indoor gross motor room, a multi-purpose room where they eat or nap, or another room where they spend relatively small amounts of time during the early morning or late afternoon hours, are not considered in this item.

This item covers the amount of space, the basic amenities such as light, temperature, ventilation and noise level, as well as the state of repair and maintenance, and the accessibility to children and adults with disabilities. The amount of space in the room where the children are cared for most of the day is important because it affects both the efficiency of the staff as they try to meet the many routine care needs of infants and toddlers, and the number and types of play activities the children can engage in at the same time. Routine care furnishings, such as cribs, feeding tables, a diaper-changing area separated from the food preparation area, and individual storage for children's possessions, take up a lot of room. In addition, accommodation must be made for open play space for children, furniture to store and provide access to the many toys and materials needed to keep them happily occupied, and appropriate play furnishings, such as infant seats, gross motor equipment, tables and chairs, or child-sized pretend play furniture. Insufficient space can lead to conflicts among children due to crowding, and can also create safety hazards from the cluttered conditions. It can also cause limitations in the program because materials easily become disorganized or must be minimized if the space in which they are used is cramped.

In order to decide whether there is ***enough space***, scoring should be based on observation of how the space functions when in use, not on the square footage. The observer needs to consider the areas used for routines such as meals/snacks, sleeping and diaper changing, as well as those areas where the necessities for play activities, such as infant seats, crawling space, push or pull toys, musical toys, blocks, and books, are found.

Scores should be based on the observer's judgment of how well the space would work if the largest number of children allowed in the group at one time were attending, even if the observation takes place on a day when fewer children are present. The observer must also keep in mind the age range of the children currently enrolled in the group, since the needs of infants and toddlers change greatly during this rapid growth period. Therefore, if a non-mobile baby or an older toddler is enrolled but not present during the observation, the observer must take that child's space needs into account. In evaluating the adequacy of indoor space, consider:

- the maximum number of children and adults who may use the space on any day,
- whether there is enough space for the furnishings and materials required for basic care,
- whether there is enough space for the furnishings and materials needed for play, and
- the total amount of space that may be used in the room.

Space may appear to be adequate because the basic furnishings and materials for routines or play are lacking, or because very few children are present on the observation day, but it must be considered in terms of how it would work if the basic materials required for appropriate care were included and the maximum number of children allowed to attend were present.

The condition of the space is also important because it affects the comfort, health and safety, as well as the self-image of the children and the adults who spend many hours daily in the room. Space that is in poor repair or poorly maintained encourages rough and neglectful behavior towards the surroundings and materials, and can also be depressing and dangerous to both the children and staff.

A closer look at each indicator

1.1 *Not enough space* means that there is an insufficient amount of space in the room used by the children most of the day to accommodate the largest number of children allowed to attend at one time, the staff needed to care for them and the basic furnishings required to meet the children's needs for both care and play. Common signs of not enough space in an infant/toddler room are:

- Crawling infants have so little open space to move around in that they crawl under the cribs or other furnishings that take up most of the room.
- Toddlers play between and under the cribs or feeding tables because there is so little open play space that is cleared of furniture.
- Staff must move the highchairs used for feeding infants out into the hallway after each use to provide space for play and move them back into the room for the next feeding.
- There is no room to make toys accessible to the children on open shelves near the small open area, so toys are stored in boxes under the cribs.
- It is difficult to walk from one area of the room to another without having to consciously avoid furniture or move it out of the way.
- The room appears spacious at first glance, until you imagine what it would be like with sufficient furnishings.
- Cribs must be crowded together to free up space for play.

Score 1.1 "Yes" only if the room is extremely crowded. (See photos 1.1.1a-f.) If a class is located in a very large room but staff are allowed to use only a small part, base the score on the amount of space they may use. If the staff are allowed to use the entire space and choose to use only a small portion, credit can be given only for the total amount of space used.

1.1.1 a

1.1.1 b

1.1.1a-b In this sparsely furnished room, cribs/playpens take up most of the space, leaving very little open space for crawling, walking, or play and no room to store toys so they are accessible to children. Children are kept in the cribs/playpens much of the day.

1.1.1 c

1.1.1 d

1.1.1c-d Routine care furniture for diapering, feeding, and sleeping take up most of the space, leaving insufficient open space for children to move around and play. Mobile infants often crawl under the cribs or into the routine care area where they are under foot, and non-mobile babies are held or placed in confining play equipment. There is no provision for accessible toy storage.

1.1.1 e

1.1.1 f

1.1.1e-f This room is crowded with routine care furniture, open shelves for toys, and play furnishings, and does not have enough space for children to play with the toys.

1 Indoor space

1.2 This indicator assesses the basic amenities needed for children and adults to use the space comfortably.

Lacks adequate lighting means much of the room is too dark to use materials comfortably that require close attention, such as reading, working with pegs and pegboards or putting together pop-beads. The room may seem gloomy or dim and it may be difficult for staff to supervise children visually, for example by glancing over to see if a sleeping baby is breathing, or seeing what the toddler is putting into her mouth.

Lacks adequate temperature control means that the space is too cold or too warm for the adults and children in the group, and nothing is done to correct this problem in a timely fashion during the observation. It must be obvious to the observer that many of the children or staff are uncomfortable. Observers should not judge the adequacy of temperature control based on their own comfort level, but should look and listen for signs that staff or children are uncomfortable.

Lacks adequate sound-absorbing materials means that the noise level is so high that staff and children have to raise their voices to be heard. A room that lacks sound-absorbing materials (e.g., rugs or ceiling tiles) reflects and magnifies the unavoidable sounds of human voices and the process of using materials. Noise pollution hinders good language development because it interferes with children's attention to adult speech and makes it hard for children to hear the subtleties of spoken language. It also creates tension and over-excitement, which are distracting and prevent children from sustained involvement in constructive play and learning.

Noise that travels from another classroom is considered in scoring if it adversely affects the observed classroom.

1.1.2 The temperature control in this room is inadequate, requiring children and staff to dress inappropriately indoors to keep warm.

Since a reasonable amount of noise is to be expected in a program where very young children are active and vocalizing, and staff are responding, this indicator is marked "Yes" only when the noise level becomes detrimental to the program. For example if staff cannot hear a baby's whimpers or have to raise their voices to be heard, then ***lacks inadequate sound absorbing materials*** would be true. Score 1.2 "Yes" if any of the listed basic amenities are lacking. (See photo 1.1.2.)

1.3 ***Poor repair*** means that there are one or more major repair problems which present health and safety risks, such as substantial damage to the walls, ceiling, floors, floor covering, or other aspects of the space. Common problems include missing or detached ceiling tiles, torn carpeting, holes in the walls, damaged or missing floor tiles, or peeling paint on the walls. Such repairs usually require facility maintenance skills that go beyond what staff can do in daily clean-up.

Rooms that are in ***poor repair*** can cause health problems (e.g., exposed asbestos, lead in peeling paint) or pose safety hazards (e.g., tripping, splinters). If this is true, score 1.3 "Yes." Repair problems that can cause accidents can also be counted under Item 11, Safety practices. If there are one or a few minor problems, such as a small place on the wall where paint is chipped or a small worn place on a rug, do not score "Yes." (See photo 1.1.3.)

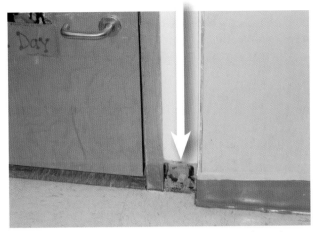

1.1.3 One minor problem such as this missing piece of baseboard does not in itself qualify as poor repair. However, if there are many minor problems or one major repair needed, the indoor space would be considered in poor repair.

1.1.4 a

1.4   ***Poorly maintained*** means that there is evidence that the room is not cleaned or kept up routinely. Floors may not be washed thoroughly after eating or messy play, chairs have ingrained dirt, padded high chairs have food lodged in crevices, trash cans are over-flowing even in early morning, sinks are dirty, rugs or floors have dried on stains, or evidence of previous art activities, such as paint drips, is dried on the table edges or floors.

A ***poorly maintained*** room adversely affects the health of the children as well as the sense of organization and peacefulness in the space. If there is clear evidence that the room is poorly maintained, score Indicator 1.4, "Yes." (See photos 1.1.4a-b.)

1.1.4 b

1.1.4a-b Ongoing maintenance is needed to keep the indoor space clean and usable. If messes are not cleaned up in a reasonable amount of time before they cause problems, the space is considered to be poorly maintained.

3.1   ***Enough indoor space*** is defined in the "Note for Clarification" for this item on page 11 of the ITERS-R.

A space that is not crowded due to a lack of basic furnishings and materials cannot be considered to have enough space if the addition of the needed furnishings and materials would result in crowding. Remember, this indicator is at the minimal level, so "enough" space means only that the classroom can function adequately. This includes:

- space for the staff to move around to meet children's routine needs, for example, easy access to children in cribs,
- separation between diapering and food preparation areas,
- space for children to play without being crowded,
- open space for play,
- space to accommodate furniture needed for accessible toy storage (e.g., open shelves, containers for toys),
- room to arrange cribs to meet the sanitation space requirements for nap (in Item 8, Nap, indicator 3.2) without sacrificing too much play space.

1 Indoor space

1.3.1a This room has enough space to accommodate the care and play needs of the infants enrolled. Open play space for mobile infants is separated from space for non-mobile infants to play. Note the blanket on which a non-mobile baby can play in the area behind the gate. There is also enough space for additional toy shelves and active play equipment.

1.3.1a

1.3.1b

1.3.1c

1.3.1d

1.3.1b-d This long, narrow room has enough space to provide accessible storage for play materials and open space to play for the small group enrolled, as well as for the routine care furniture needed. Staff can circulate freely as they assist with routine care and supervise play. If problems with the room arrangement or safety issues are observed, they should be handled in the respective items.

1.3.1e

1.3.1f

1.3.1e-f This toddler room has enough space for routine care furniture, play furniture for various activities, and space for children and staff to circulate freely during both routine and play activities.

In some cases, one space might meet the requirements of this indicator, while another that is the same size, or even larger, will not. This is because one space might be used more efficiently than the other. For example, it is possible to make a relatively small space function adequately by using proportionally smaller furniture rather than larger furniture that serves the same purpose. In a small room, the size of the routine care furniture, such as the cribs, feeding tables, and chairs, and furniture for play, including open shelves used for accessible toy storage, can make the difference between being "crowded" and having "enough" space. For example, cribs with solid ends require less space than cribs with non-solid sides, which require 36" of space between them to meet the sanitary guidelines for nap (see Item 8, Nap). Similarly a few high chairs take less space than large feeding tables.

Space can also be "stretched" by leaving just enough furniture and materials out in the room for use in routine care and play, and storing excess materials in an easily accessible place. Often, infant classrooms leave every crib they own set up in the infant room, even if they have only half their enrollment. These unused cribs take up space and may cause additional clutter by being used for storing routine care and play materials that have no immediate use. The fact that a smaller space might sometimes be used more efficiently than a larger space means that it is not only the size of the classroom that impacts the scoring decision for this indicator. The way in which the space is used has an effect as well. If a classroom is located in a very large room but staff are allowed to use only a small part of the room, base the score on the amount of space they may use. If the staff are allowed to use the entire space and choose to use only a small portion, credit can be given only for the amount of space used.

Score this indicator "Yes" if there is enough space used to run the classroom without crowding. (See photos 1.3.1a-f.)

3.2   *Adequate lighting* means that there is enough light, either natural light from windows or skylights, or artificial light from lamps or lighting fixtures, so that staff and children can read and use toys that have small pieces without eyestrain and so that staff can adequately supervise the children. The room should have enough light overall so that it looks bright and cheerful. Light can be dimmed at naptime, but children should remain easily visible to staff throughout nap.

Adequate temperature control means that the room is kept at a comfortable temperature for children and staff. If needed, a source of cooling in summer and heat in winter is present so that children and adults seem comfortable. Since sensitivity to room temperature varies greatly, judge the adequacy of the room temperature based on how the children and adults are reacting. If staff are flushed and perspiring, or, at the other extreme, are dressed very warmly indoors and are putting sweaters or jackets on the children, then there is inadequate temperature control, even though the observer may not be uncomfortable.

Adequate sound-absorbing materials means that the sound in the room is at a level where people can hear one another speak without raising their voices or shouting. The usual sounds of play, such as the noise of the wheels of toys running on the floor and musical toys being used or the voices of excited children, are not magnified to an uncomfortable level, where they become disruptive noise. The classroom has sufficient *sound-absorbing materials,* such as ceiling tiles, carpets and soft furnishings, and there is a sound barrier between classrooms. A reasonable level of sound is maintained that permits children and adults to hear and be heard without constantly raising their voices.

1 Indoor space

1.3.4a

1.3.4b

1.3.4a-b   Spills are cleaned up promptly, before additional problems occur. If proper sanitary procedures are not followed, do not consider in scoring this indicator, but rather in Item 10. Health practices.

1.3.4c

1.3.4d

1.3.4c-d   Larger maintenance jobs are done regularly so that the room is basically clean and daily messes can be cleaned up relatively easily.

Score this indicator "Yes" if all requirements are met. If even one requirement is lacking, score this indicator, "No."

3.3   ***Space in good repair*** means that there are no major repair problems and relatively few minor problems observed. Major problems include: hanging or missing ceiling tiles, holes in doors and walls, large accessible areas of peeling paint, broken window panes, and gouged, splintery floors. Examples of minor problems include: frayed spots on the rugs that might cause tripping accidents, a little peeling paint that is not accessible to children, and unpainted areas on walls.

Score this indicator "Yes" if there are no major and only 2 or 3 minor problems observed.

3.4   ***Space is reasonably clean and well-maintained*** means that messiness from the usual routine care and play activities of an infant/toddler program are cleaned up thoroughly after the activities are completed, and the room looks as if it is being cared for regularly. For example, daily maintenance is done, such as emptying wastepaper baskets, sweeping floors, vacuuming the rugs, emptying diaper receptacles and cleaning dry paint off the easel. Larger jobs, such as cleaning carpets or bleaching sinks, are done often enough so that the room is basically clean, and

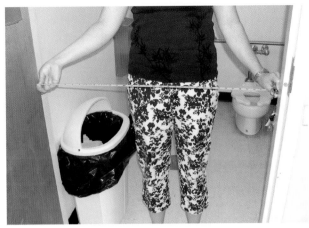

1.3.5a This doorway meets the width requirement for handicapped accessibility (32"). Do not consider items which can easily be moved, such as the trash can.

1.3.5b This door handle can be operated with limited use of the hands and is therefore accessible.

1.3.5c A round door knob cannot be operated with limited use of the hands and makes this door inaccessible.

the predictable messes resulting from ongoing activities, such as an art project or feeding children, are cleaned up relatively quickly. (See photos 1.3.4a-d.)

Score "Yes" if space is generally clean and gives the overall impression of being well-maintained.

3.5 This indicator requires that the space is ***accessible*** to all children and adults ***currently using*** the classroom. A score of "NA" (Not Applicable) is permitted if there are no children or adults with physical disabilities requiring adaptations to the environment currently using the classroom.

To meet the requirements for accessibility, the building, classroom and the bathroom (including toilet stalls) must be accessible to individuals with disabilities, including those using wheelchairs. All doorways regularly used by both children and adults currently using the class to enter the building, the toileting areas, and the gross motor areas must be at least 32" wide. The door handles must be operable with limited use of hands, which is not possible with round doorknobs. The entrance door threshold should be ½" high or less and, if over ¼", must be beveled to make it easier to roll over.

If there are two or more restrooms regularly used by the children in the classroom, only one of them must be accessible. A child with a disability should be able to use the same restroom as his/her classmates. Therefore, even if there is an accessible restroom in another part of the facility, it cannot be counted if it is not usually used by the rest of the group. A staff member or other adult with physical disabilities, who is responsible for supervising children, will also need access to the children's restroom to help them.

Access to the building, the floor on which the classroom is located, the classroom and the children's restroom is considered in this item, under Indicators 3.5 and 5.3. (See photos 1.3.5a-d.)

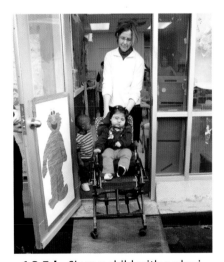

1.3.5d Since a child with a physical disability is enrolled in this class, this indicator must be scored "Yes" or "No" and cannot be scored "NA." This doorway leading to the playground is wide enough, and there is a ramp to modify the door sill, but the round door knob prevents the door from being accessible.

1 Indoor space

Score 3.5 "NA" if no child or adult currently using the classroom needs accessible accommodation. Please note that access to the various play areas in the room is considered under Item 4, Room arrangement, and not in this item. Adaptations to toilets (e.g., bars to help with stability) are considered in Item 2, Furniture for routine care and play, Indicators 3.4 and 5.3. Access to restrooms for adults is considered in Item 34, Provisions for personal needs of staff, Indicators 3.5 and 5.5.

5.1   *Ample indoor space* means that there is a lot of space in the room for different types of activities. Consider both the areas used for routines such as diapering, meals/snacks and nap/rest, as well as the play spaces used for activities with various materials, including books, music and sound making toys, fine motor toys, gross motor toys, blocks, and dramatic play materials. (See photos 1.5.1 a-e.)

1.5.1a This infant room has ample space to play with a variety of different toys. It has open shelves so that children can have easy access to safe toys and books.

The observer should look at the room as it is being used to assure that there is plenty of space for the maximum number of children allowed in the group at one time to crawl and move around freely, and a spacious open area to use the materials, as well as for the materials and furniture needed in almost all of the activity areas. If a classroom is located in a large room but staff are allowed to use only a small part of the room, base the score on the amount of space they may use. If the staff are allowed to use the entire space and choose to use only a small portion, credit can be given only for the amount of space used.

Staff should be able to move around freely and not have to move furniture out of their way to assist the children during routines such as meals and snacks while the children are seated at the table, or when a child needs to be gotten out of a crib. If a child with physical disabilities is enrolled in the program, there should be enough space to comfortably accommodate any special equipment needed by the child without crowding other children or limiting activities.

1.5.1b

5.2   *Good ventilation* requires effective air circulation resulting in a fresh, pleasant odor throughout the observation. This can be provided by windows that open (with screens if bneeded), exhaust fans, or an air circulation system. *Good ventilation* means that there is enough air circulation so that there are no unpleasant or strong odors in the room for any length of time. Odors from soiled diapers, the bathroom, or from cleaning products should either not be present at all or dissipate very quickly. Odors from air fresheners are apparent only very briefly or not at all to meet this requirement.

1.5.1c

1.5.1b-c This toddler room has ample space to meet the children's need for routine care and a variety of activities. (Note also the ventilating fans, and window that can be opened by the staff, which meet Indicator 7.2.)

Natural lighting requires that daylight directly enters the room through windows or skylights to some degree. Artificial lighting may also be used to provide the total amount of light needed, but does not count as natural lighting.

Score "Yes" if both ventilation and natural lighting requirements are met.

1.5.1d

1.5.1e

1.5.1d-e There is ample space to include a variety of activities in which all the children, including the child who needs special equipment, can participate.

5.3 To meet the requirements of this indicator, the space must be ***accessible*** for all children and adults with disabilities that require such provisions, regardless of whether anyone with a disability uses the room or is currently enrolled in the program. Accessibility is legally required in all public facilities so that everyone can have equal opportunity to use the service, and is therefore required at the good level for all centers. For the definition of "accessible" see Indicator 3.5. on page 11.

7.1 Staff should be able to ***control the natural light*** coming through windows, skylights, or doors. Natural light can be too bright at times, causing glare that can interfere with classroom activities. Adjustable blinds, curtains, or other provisions should be present and adequate to prevent any problems with natural lighting. (See photos 1.7.1a-b.) It is not required that staff can adjust all natural lighting. For example, a very small window that allows little natural light, and never any glare, would not require additional means of controlling the light.

Score "Yes" if the staff have a way to control any source of natural light that could cause a problem due to glare or extreme brightness.

1.7.1a

1.7.1b

1.7.1a-b Natural light can be controlled by the staff to cut down on glare and manage the amount of light coming in from windows, doors, or skylights.

1 Indoor space

1.7.2a Windows with screens such as this one can be opened safely to ventilate the room. The staff can decide when additional ventilation is needed.

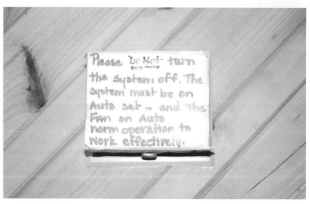

1.7.2b When the control of the ventilation system is not obvious, staff must be asked if they can control ventilation in their room. In this case, staff have no control.

7.2   *Ventilation can be controlled* means that the staff in the room can control the ventilation. If a door or a window needs to be opened for ventilation, it must have safeguards such as screens or a locking gate, so that children's health and safety are protected, to be given credit. If a ventilating fan is used in the room or a central air circulation system for the building, ask the teacher whether she can control it herself. A fan that moves air (but does not ventilate from the room) will not count to meet this requirement. A thermostat that does not regulate air circulation, does not serve as ventilation. To score "Yes" for this indicator the staff need to have control of safe ventilation for the room. (See photos 1.7.2a-b.)

1.7.3 Messy activities such as art projects and eating are done on an easy-to-clean floor.

7.3   *Built-in surfaces* are those that are a permanent part of the room, such as the floors, walls, counters and cabinets. *Easy-to-clean* materials are those that can withstand frequent washing and disinfecting without harm. Since infants, toddlers, and young twos are very vulnerable to infectious diseases, frequent washing and disinfecting of counter tops and other built-in surfaces are needed to protect their health. (See photo 1.7.3.) This indicator addresses only the built-in surfaces in the room. Other surfaces, such as removable pads used in diapering, high chair trays or table tops used for feeding, and cribs, cots, or mats used for napping, are included under the appropriate item in the Personal Care Routines subscale. To score this indicator "Yes," all built-in surfaces must be easy to clean.

2 Furniture for routine care and play

General information about this item

This item looks at the furniture used by and with the children for routine care and play activities. Basic furniture for routine care considered in this item includes all tables and seating provisions for meals and snacks, including infant seats and highchairs as well as small tables and chairs; cribs, cots, mats for rest or nap; diapering table and storage for diapering supplies; and cubbies for storage of children's personal items and creative work. Basic furniture for play includes infant seats, small tables and chairs where children can use materials, and open shelves or dishpans and other containers for materials, which children can access independently. Additional furniture to facilitate specific types of play, such as an easel for art activities, sand/water table, or furniture for dramatic play, or furniture for infant play, such as swings or play table seats, are also considered in this item. Gross motor equipment is not considered in this item, even if it is located in the classroom or other spaces used indoors. All gross motor equipment is considered in Item 16, Active physical play.

Furniture in the classroom should support the children's independence in meeting their routine care needs and in conducting their play and learning activities. There are two important reasons for encouraging children's independent use of furnishings, even for these very young children. First, being able to handle their surroundings independently as much as safely possible helps children feel competent and secure. Second, staff working with groups of young children need to make the best use of their time and energy to help children learn good self-help skills. Therefore, staff should not spend time reinforcing children's dependence by lifting older toddlers and twos into highchairs when they can seat themselves on small chairs at low tables, or by opening tight container lids that prevent children from accessing safe toys themselves for independent use.

Furniture should also be safe, appropriately sized, and available in sufficient quantity for the total number of children enrolled in the group. Unless all children are fed at the same time, a separate feeding arrangement for each child is not required. Low, open shelves help in the organization of learning materials offered to children and give children opportunities to make independent choices about the materials they want to use. Low tables and chairs are useful for working with puzzles and other table top toys, as well as for serving meals and snacks.

A closer look at each indicator

1.1 *Not enough furniture for routine care* means that there are not enough feeding tables or small tables and chairs, cubbies, cribs/cots/mats, or a suitable diapering arrangement with storage for supplies, to meet each child's routine care needs in a timely fashion. For example, each child does not have his own crib, cot

2 Furniture for routine care and play

or mat for sleeping or personal space to help keep his belongings. If a program for young twos has meals and snacks as a whole group, score "Yes" if there are not enough tables and chairs for the highest number of children attending at any time to be seated. For infants and toddlers on a flexible schedule, only enough feeding places are required so children do not have to wait unnecessarily.

1.2 ***Not enough furniture for play*** means that there are not enough low, open shelves, or other open storage used to make play materials easily accessible to the children, or enough tables and chairs to use for activities. There must be enough low open shelf space to store the toys/materials required for at least a minimal level of quality for the total number of children allowed to attend on any day. Open storage shelves must not be overcrowded, making independent choice impossible or dangerous.

2.1.2 There are not enough open storage shelves to make toys accessible to the children so toys are randomly piled in a box.

Large toy boxes and crates are not acceptable substitutes as furniture to store play and learning materials in place of low open shelves, because it is impossible to sort and store materials in an organized way for independent use in such boxes. For example, if dolls, rattles, music toys, blocks, and cars are stored together in a large box, children cannot see the different materials that have been heaped randomly on top of one another in the box. In contrast, when toys are sorted and stored separately on open shelves, children can easily see the different types of toys and thus make informed choices about what they want to play with.

Smaller boxes or other containers used to separate and store different toys can be put on open shelves to offer materials to children. However, the containers are not considered storage furniture. If there are a sizable number of open shelves for storage of materials and only a few boxes, do not give a score of "Yes" on Indicator 1.2. However, if most of the toys are stored in crates or toy boxes and there are very few open shelves, a score of "Yes" is appropriate. (See photo 2.1.2.) In some cases so few toys and materials are accessible that very little storage is required. If there is ***enough storage*** because there are too few toys and materials, then 1.2 must be scored "Yes" because the available storage would not be sufficient if there were enough toys and materials to store.

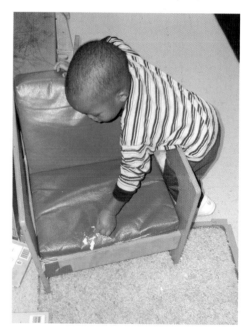

2.1.3 This child-sized upholstered chair is in poor repair with exposed padding that could be a choking hazard.

1.3 ***Poor repair*** means that the furniture being used presents safety problems for the children and needs repair or replacement. Examples include chair seats with splinters or protruding nails, tables with broken legs, torn highchair padding, and diapering pads or sleeping mats with exposed interior padding that children could choke on. The observer should look at all furniture used by the children to determine the general or overall condition, and document any safety concerns. However, score Indicator 1.3 "Yes" only if the furniture used by the children has several serious problems that could cause injury. Do not count furniture that children do not use, such as a desk

Indicator

2.3.1 The children's possessions are stored in the bags hanging from the hooks, the two high chairs are used for feeding the infants and the low tables and small chairs are used for the toddlers. Since only one crib is observed in the classroom, the staff will need to be asked about the sleeping arrangements for the other children and watch to see where children are diapered to make sure that all the requirements for enough routine care furniture are met.

and chair meant only for the teacher, or chairs that have been put into storage. Safety problems due to furniture being in poor repair are also considered in Item 11, Safety practice. (See photo 2.1.3.)

3.1   *Enough furniture for routine care* means that there is a sufficient number of pieces of furniture for use in diapering/toileting, nap, meals/snacks, and storing children's possessions for the total number of children allowed to attend at one time. This indicator looks only at the quantity and not the size, state of repair, or other properties, of the furniture. However, to be counted to meet the requirement, the piece of furniture must be usable for its intended purpose. Score "Yes" if there are enough pieces of furniture for feeding children, enough cribs/cots/mats for sleeping, and enough cubbies to store personal belongings for the maximum number of children permitted to attend at one time. Cubbies can be shared by children if this does not cause crowding of materials and if the personal possessions of the children do not touch, so that there is no possibility for the spread of disease or nuisance infestations, such as lice. (See photo 2.3.1.)

3.2   *Enough furniture for play* means that the children have the developmentally appropriate seating needed to use play materials and that there are suitable ways of making play materials accessible to the children on open storage shelves. Seating arrangements, such as infants seats or highchairs, are needed to support infants in a sitting position so that they can play with hanging objects put in front of them or into their hands. Other seating arrangements can be used for older infants who can sit independently while they play with toys that are on, or attached to, a table-like surface, such as bouncing chairs or a baby stander on a broad base with toys fixed to the ledge around the seat. Infants who are not yet able to move around on their own (non-mobile infants) must have toys brought to them (or be taken to the toys) in order to have independent access. Small- to medium-sized containers or baskets are useful to store such toys on open shelves where they can be easily brought by staff to non-mobile babies.

Toddlers and twos, who can select toys independently, should have access to materials on low, open shelves. Appropriate seating on small chairs near very low tables is also needed to encourage more sustained play with toys. Score Indicator 3.2 "Yes" if there is enough appropriate open storage and seating and table space for play for the maximum number of children allowed to attend at one time. (See photos 2.3.2a-g.)

2.3.2a Furniture for play includes enough low, open shelves for accessible toy storage. This non-mobile infant has been brought to the shelves where he can select toys.

2.3.2b This infant who is not yet mobile is appropriately supported and has toys nearby for easy access.

2.3.2c Non-mobile infants may have additional furniture for independent play.

2.3.2d Mobile infants and toddlers need to have access to safe toys.

3.3 *All furniture* means that each piece of furniture used by or with the children is in *good repair,* so that when used there are *no* serious concerns for any child's safety or health. If there are any repairs needed that may cause serious harm to the children, then score this indicator "No." However, if there are one or two minor repairs needed and they do not pose a safety threat to children, then this would not affect the score. For example, in a classroom where only one chair or table is slightly wobbly but will not cause a child to fall off, or one vinyl covered mat or couch is worn but the padding is not exposed, and all other furniture is in good repair, these small problems would not affect the score.

Besides being in good repair, this indicator requires that the furniture is sturdy. Sturdy means that the furniture will not break, fall over, or collapse when used appropriately. If furniture falls over, look to see why that happened. For example, if a toy storage shelf is placed where it is easily knocked over or put on an uneven surface and it falls during the observation, this may not be due to the sturdiness of the furniture itself, but rather to its placement. In contrast, an open storage unit is not sturdy if the shelves collapse when children remove toys from them. If any of the furniture is not sturdy, then this is considered in scoring. However, do not consider safety concerns due to the placement of the furniture in this indicator. Such issues should be addressed in Item 11, Safety practices. This indicator is scored "No" if any furniture used by or with the children is not sturdy or is not in good repair, as discussed above.

2.3.2e

2.3.2f

2.3.2e-f If many toys are stored on the tops of shelves creating a safety hazard, or shelves are too crowded so that children cannot access toys easily, more accessible storage may be needed.

3.4 When seats are ***comfortable and supportive*** children are not in danger of falling or slipping out of them or tipping over while they are seated. Children should also feel secure when they move around in the seats. For example, if infants and young toddlers are seated in slippery plastic seats with their legs dangling and no foot rest, then the seats cannot be considered to be comfortable and supportive. In contrast, young infants whose short legs are supported by the seat in a padded highchair may not need a foot rest because their legs are not dangling. The term "comfortable and supportive" should not be confused with "child-sized," found in Indicators 5.2 and 7.2 of this item. As stated in the "Note for Clarification" for this indicator in the ITERS-R, this indicator can be scored "Yes" if the vast majority of children are comfortable in the feeding chairs, even if one child is not as comfortable as the others. (See photos 2.3.4a-b, here, and 2.3.4c, next page.)

2.3.2g The lid on this container may prevent easy access to the toys inside if it hard to remove.

2.3.4a The seats in this group feeding table are not comfortable and supportive because the infants' legs are dangling and the plastic seats are slippery; therefore no credit would be given for Indicator 3.4.

2.3.4b These chairs are comfortable and supportive because they prevent the children from slipping out or falling, so they can be given credit for 3.4. They are also suitable for individual care, and meet the requirements of 5.1. However, they are not child-sized because the children's feet do not reach the floor. The table is also too tall to permit the children's elbows to rest on the table. Therefore credit cannot be given for 5.2 because the table and chairs are not child-sized.

2.3.4c These chairs are comfortable and supportive, and they and the table are also child-sized. This table and chairs meet Indicators 3.4, 5.2, and 7.2.

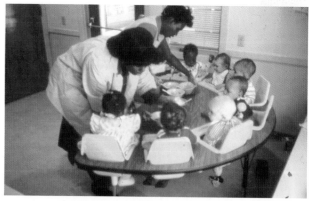

2.5.1a This group feeding table is not suitable for the individual care of infants.

5.1 *Suitable for individual care* means that the furniture used for the care of infants and toddlers encourages and supports staff's attention to individual children during feeding and other care activities. Free standing highchairs permit infants to have an individual tray all to themselves, a seat far enough away from other infants to prevent interruptions and sharing of food, and most important, an adult who does not have to be shared with many others. Feeding time is a prime opportunity for staff to interact individually with very young children, timing their feeding and verbal interaction in response to each child's needs and interests. In contrast, group infant feeding tables with multiple seats placed close together encourage group feeding practices. One staff member can feed as many as 6 babies, without having the time to interact with any of them, and the chances of spreading germs from one child to another are multiplied dramatically. Using small chairs around small low tables for toddlers helps to continue this individualized approach by permitting staff to adjust the distance between children, the size of the group, and have children face one another in a social grouping, instead of all children facing the staff like patrons at a fast food counter. (See photos 2.5.1a-b.)

Individual storage of children's possessions is important because it prevents confusion for the parents who must store and retrieve their children's things, and also prevents health problems through the spread of germs. (See photo 2.5.1c-d.)

Score Indicator 5.1 "Yes" if all furniture used for the routine care of infants and toddlers encourages appropriate individual care. Small tables and chairs can be used with toddlers and count towards meeting the requirement.

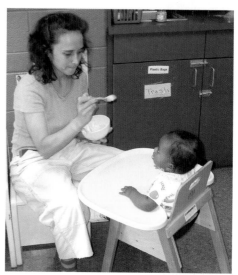

2.5.1b Any individual high chair for infants or table with individual, movable chairs is considered suitable for the individual care of infants/toddlers.

2.5.1c Each young toddler in this program has an individual cubby.

Indicator

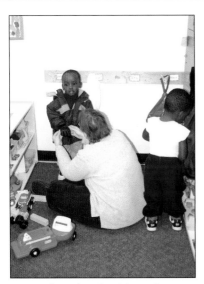

2.5.1d A hook with each child's name is a place to hang clothing and other possessions.

2.5.2a

2.5.2b

2.5.2a-b Child-sized furniture in the dramatic play area meets the requirements of this indicator, even if the chairs and/or table used for routine care are not child sized.

5.2   This indicator should be scored "NA" (Not Applicable) if no toddlers are enrolled in the group being observed. See "Explanation of Terms Used Throughout the Scale" on page 7 of the ITERS-R for the definition of infants/toddlers and for more information on when to give a score of "NA." If an older child with a disability is enrolled, and all the other children are infants, the appropriateness of this indicator will depend on the child's abilities, not necessarily on the child's age.

Child-sized means that toddler's feet are able to touch the floor, but not necessarily rest flat on the floor, while they are seated, and that tables are an appropriate height so that children can rest their elbows on the top of the table, while their legs fit comfortably underneath the table. Children should not have to perch on the edge of the chair to touch the floor because this can cause the chair to slip out from under them, increasing the possibility of injuries from falls. Highchairs, group feeding tables, or any other type of chair that toddlers must be put into by an adult are not considered child-sized.

Some child-sized chairs and tables used with toddlers means that children from 12 to 30 months of age have access to at least one seating arrangement where there are at least two child-sized chairs at an appropriately sized table. For example, this may be in the dramatic play area or where children use art or other table toys; it does not necessarily have to be where they are fed. (See photos 2.5.2a-b.) Score this indicator "Yes" if these requirements are met.

This indicator only addresses the size of tables and chairs for children. If cubbies or other furnishings present a problem due to size, consider this under Indicator 7.1.

5.3   *Promotes self help* means that as children become ready to be more independent in both care and play activities, furniture is added to encourage and support their growth in independence. For example, placing steps or a sturdy platform near the sink where the staff wash the children's hands helps young toddlers become more actively involved in washing their own hands. Older infants and toddlers who are

2.5.3a

2.5.3b

2.5.3a-b A safe step that permits an infant to be more involved in handwashinig and an older toddler to be more independent in the same task, is an example of promoting self-help in routines.

mobile can reach and select toys by themselves if the toys are placed on low open shelves. Children with physical disabilities can participate more independently in both care and play activities if they have the appropriate furniture they need to join the group. Infant seats that support young infants in a semi-sitting position allow babies to see more of what is going on around them. At least two different provisions to support independence, one in routines and one in play, are required to give credit for this indicator. (See photos 2.5.3a-g.)

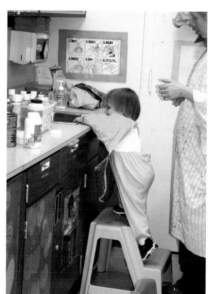

2.5.3c-e Although these steps promote self help and therefore meet this indicator, there are safety issues to be considered in Item 11, Safety practices.

Indicator

2.5.3f Low, open shelves that offer easily accessible toys promote self-help and independence in play.

2.5.3g Special furniture is available for the child with disabilities enrolled in the group so that she can participate in the program as fully as possible.

5.4 The **storage** required in this indicator is for **extra toys and supplies** that are not currently accessible to children or adults for immediate use in the classroom. Having a place to store extra supplies for routine care, such as packages of diapers, paper plates and napkins, and extra clothing, prevents running out of needed supplies. Having storage for extra play materials such as additional books, art materials, puzzles, musical instruments, and fine and gross motor toys, helps staff exchange currently accessible materials with less familiar ones, thus keeping the children interested. Since the infant/toddler years are periods of very rapid growth, stored materials will need to be brought into the classroom as children's needs change, and materials that are no longer suitable will need to be stored. The storage required in this indicator does not have to be in the room or available at a moment's notice, but it must be on-site storage that is not too difficult to access. Score Indicator 5.4 "Yes" if there is at least one on-site storage provision for routine care supplies and one on-site storage provision for play materials. (See photos 2.5.4a-b.)

2.5.4a [above] Frequently used extra toys and materials are stored in this on-site storeroom that is accessible to all staff in the center.

2.5.4b [right] This off-site storage shed contains extra supplies for the entire center, and is difficult for the staff to access. The things stored in the shed are not needed very often. Credit would not be given in this indicator for materials stored in this shed.

2.5.4b

2 Furniture for routine care and play

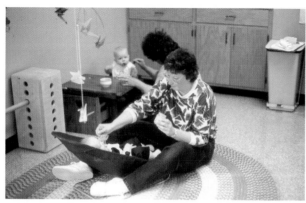

2.5.5a If staff sit on the floor while providing routine care, credit is not given for this indicator. Sitting on the floor while feeding children is not acceptable because staff members' hands are likely to become contaminated when they sit down or stand up.

2.5.5b This staff member is sitting on the floor while he is supervising the toddlers' lunch. Credit would not be given for 5.5.

2.5.5c In contrast, this staff member uses a block as a seat while she supervises the mealtime. Credit can be given for 5.5, even though the block is a makeshift seating arrangement. However, credit would not be given for comfortable adult seating in 7.4.

2.5.5d Credit can be given for some adult seating for use in routine care in Indicator 5.5, but not for Indicator 7.4.

5.5   *Adult seating* means something that staff can use to sit on while they are providing *routine care* for the children, such as bottle-feeding infants, spoon-feeding babies in a highchair or sitting with toddlers at a very low table during meals, or rocking a baby to sleep. Sitting on the floor while feeding children is not acceptable because the staff members' hands are likely to become contaminated when they sit down or stand up. Anything a staff member uses to sit on that is large enough and seems to work well for that staff member can be given credit in this indicator, including preschool-sized chairs, large cubes or stools. Such makeshift adult seating can be given credit in this indicator as long as it is currently being used as part of routine care. For example, a preschool-sized chair will meet the requirement if staff sit on it while helping children with eating. A rocking chair meets the requirement in a class where it is used to rock children to sleep or to feed babies. However, the rocking chair would not count if not regularly used in routine care. The furniture credited must meet the needs of what staff must do while they are engaged in routine care activities. Score "Yes" if any adult seating is provided in the room and is appropriate for use by staff in the routine care tasks they do. (See photos 2.5.5a-d.)

2.5.3a

2.5.3b

2.7.1a-b These mats and cots are conveniently stored in the children's room where they will be used during nap time.

2.7.1c Having cubbies in the room makes it easy for the staff to supervise the children's use. Parents also have easy access to the cubbies without disturbing the entire group because the cubbies are near the door.

2.7.1d The children's diapering supplies are stored in the bags and containers in the sleep area, far from the diapering table. This is inconvenient for the staff.

7.1 *Routine care furniture* means all furniture used to meet children's needs for feeding, diapering/toileting, nap/rest, and storing of their personal possessions. To be *accessible and convenient* for the staff to use, the furniture must be placed so that staff are not required to leave the children or interrupt their supervision. For example, diapering supplies should be stored near the diapering table and the diapering table should be placed in the room; cots and/or mats should be stored in the room for easy access when preparing for nap time; cubbies should be placed for easy access by parents and staff, and if older toddlers and young twos are permitted access to their cubbies they must be placed in the room so that the children can be adequately supervised while using them.

2.7.1e [right] In contrast, in this classroom, each child's diapering supplies are stored near the diapering table for easy access by staff.

2.7.1e

25

2 Furniture for routine care and play

Since infants will most likely be on individual schedules, routine care activities such as feeding, diapering, and napping will be ongoing throughout the day. If the furniture needed to conduct these routines is placed conveniently in the room, fewer interruptions in supervision are required.

Older toddlers and twos may be starting to have naps and meals in small groups. Such major transitions in the schedule involving groups of children are very busy times. For example, preparing for feeding a group of toddlers requires hand washing, getting children seated at the table, putting on bibs, serving food and beverages; preparing for naps means setting the mats or cots in each toddler's special place, putting on the bedding, changing diapers, while soothing tired, impatient children. Having all the necessary furniture close at hand in the room helps to accomplish an efficient and smooth transition. To score "Yes" no furniture used for routine care can be difficult to access or to use in completing required tasks smoothly. (See photos 2.7.1a-e, preceding page.)

7.2 This indicator should be scored "NA" (Not Applicable) if no toddlers are enrolled in the group being observed. (See "Explanation of Terms Used Throughout the Scale" on page 7 of the ITERS-R for the definition of infants/toddlers and for more information on when to give a score of "NA.") ***Most of the tables and chairs*** means that, based on the ages of the largest number allowed to attend on any day, 75% of the toddlers use *child-sized* chairs and tables. ***Child-sized*** chairs allow children to sit back in the chair with feet touching the floor (not necessarily flat on the floor). Children should not have to perch on edge of the chair for their feet to touch the floor. A ***child-sized*** table allows children's knees to fit under the table while their elbows are comfortably above the table surface. Highchairs or group feeding tables that ***toddlers*** must be put into by an adult are not considered child-sized. To help determine how many tables and chairs are child-sized, observers should check at those times in the schedule when as many children as possible are sitting at the tables, for example, during lunch or snack. It also helps to use a recording system to determine whether the 75% requirement is met. Such a chart should include all toddlers present in the group during the observation. Below is an example of a simple chart for scoring whether chairs and tables are child-sized.

Child	Child-sized?
1	yes
2	no (chair too high, legs dangle)
3	yes
4	yes
5	yes
6	no (chair OK, table too high)

In this example, the table and chairs are child-sized for 4 out of 6 children, or 67% of the children. Therefore credit would not be given for the indicator.

7.3 ***Convenient*** storage for extra toys means that it is easy for the staff to access materials in storage with only a momentary interruption of visual supervision of children. Examples of convenient storage for extra toys are:

- a built-in closet or cupboard in the room,
- a high shelf in the room that only adults can reach,
- a closed cabinet that is added to the room to provide extra storage.

2.5.3a

2.5.3b

2.7.3a-b These well organized storage closets are located in the classroom. Materials can be accessed quickly because of their convenient location. Even if the storage closets were not so perfectly neat, credit would still be given if the materials were easy to access.

Organized storage means that the extra toys have been sorted by type and are stored in such a way that they can be easily accessed for rotation into the classroom. The organization should be judged on how well it functions, i.e., can staff easily see where things are and can they get what they need quickly. Absolute neatness is not expected in order to score this indicator "Yes." (See photos 2.7.3a-b.)

7.4 ***Comfortable*** seating for adults while working with children means that the seating arrangement is of suitable size and design for the intended use. For example, the seat is wider than that used for preschoolers, and provides back support. An adult-sized rocking chair or upholstered armchair is a comfortable seating arrangement for a staff member who is bottle-feeding an infant, but it may not be comfortable seating when assisting toddlers eating lunch at a low table. Makeshift seating arrangements such as preschool-sized chairs, large blocks or cubes made for children to play with can be given credit in Indicator 5.4 but cannot be given credit in this indicator. Even if teachers say they prefer to sit or kneel on the floor while feeding children, or say that they are comfortable using smaller than adult-sized chairs/cubes/blocks, credit cannot be given for this indicator since the requirement is for ***comfortable adult-sized furniture.*** Score this indicator "Yes" if appropriate adult seating is available for each staff member when assisting with routines or play activities that require being seated. (See photos 2.7.4a-b.)

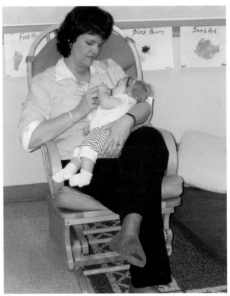

2.7.4a This rocking chair provides comfortable adult seating for feeding the baby. (See photo 2.5.5d on page 24 as a contrast).

2.7.4b [right] A comfortable adult-sized chair is used by the staff member as she supervises the activity.

2.7.4b

3 Furnishings for relaxation and comfort

General information about this item

Children need softness in their physical surroundings and in their playthings. It helps them relax and feel comfortable. Softness is provided through furnishings, such as wall-to-wall carpeting, rug areas, cushions, padded chairs and couches. Including soft toys, such as soft, fuzzy balls, plush puppets, soft dolls, or stuffed animals of various sizes, also provides softness.

This item looks at the amount of softness the children have access to during play, and not at the condition of the soft furnishings and toys. Any health or safety concerns about the soft furnishings and toys observed in this item should be considered when scoring Item 10, Health practice and Item 11, Safety practice.

This item considers only the softness accessible to infants and toddlers during play. Softness provided during personal care routines, such as blankets, crib mattresses or mats for nap or rest, padding in highchairs and feeding tables, on diapering tables, or in playpens are not given credit in this item. Since softness is intended to help children relax, the extent to which the accommodations encourage quiet play, rather than active, is also considered.

3.1.1a There are no soft furnishings in this classroom. The surfaces are all hard and easy to clean.

A closer look at each indicator

1.1 In order to score this indicator "Yes," there can be **no softness provided** in the indoor space where the children spend most of the day to **play**. Examples of **softness for children who are playing include** furnishings such as wall-to-wall carpeting, rugs, mats, soft couches or chairs (both upholstered furniture and beanbag chairs), mattresses, futons, and cushions to use during play, as well as soft toys of any size or type. Soft furnishings provided during personal care routines, such as crib mattresses and mats for nap, or padding in highchairs, are not given credit in this item. However, even if there is only one soft toy or furnishing provided for children to use during play, or if softness is only accessible for a short period, this indicator is scored "No." (See photos 3.1.1a-b, here, and 3.1.1c, next page.)

3.1 *Some soft rug or other furnishing* means that there is at least one soft furnishing in the room being

3.1.1b The padding in the high chair is not given credit for softness at play.

3 Provisions for relaxation and and comfort

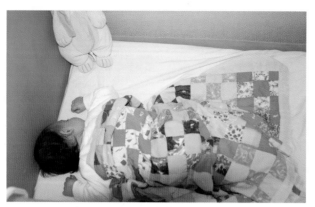

3.1.1c Softness found in cribs is not given credit for softness at play. In fact, the soft toy and quilt in this crib create a suffocation hazard which is assessed in Item 11, Safety.

observed that the children may use while they play. This can include any soft floor covering, such as wall-to-wall carpeting or rug, or furniture such as an upholstered couch or chair, or something else that provides similar softness for the children, such as a quilt or mat placed on the floor.

In order to give credit for being a rug, the rug must be large enough to permit at least one child to stretch out and lounge comfortably or play with toys on the rug. Therefore, one carpet square (1 ft. x 1 ft.), of the type that is sometimes used for each child in a group to sit on in circle time, is too small to give credit as a rug to play on.

In order to give credit for being a *soft* floor covering, there is no requirement for minimum thickness or softness. Any type of large carpet that is put on top of a bare floor (made of concrete, tile, wood, or linoleum), even indoor-outdoor carpeting, is considered a soft floor covering because it is softer and usually warmer than the uncovered floor. To be given credit as *some* soft furniture at this minimal level, the furniture must be large enough for at least one child to use, for example, two cushions whose combined size is equal to a bed pillow, a child-sized padded chair, a padded backrest cushion, or a beanbag chair. Large soft animals or toys that children can sit or lie on are counted as soft toys rather than furnishings, and are considered in Indicator 3.2. (See photos 3.3.1a-c.)

If *either* some soft floor covering *or* soft furniture is accessible to children, score Indicator 3.1 "Yes."

3.2   *Accessible* means at least three soft toys are within children's reach and that children are allowed to play

3.3.1a   This child has a carpet and a bean bag chair, which provide some soft furnishings as he plays. (The mattress in the crib is not given credit for softness at play.)

3.3.1b   The two pillows and the carpet can be given credit for some soft furnishings.

3.3.1c   The wall-to-wall carpeting and the soft mats provide some soft furnishings for these infants.

3.3.2a If this bear is the only soft toy accessible for play, then credit cannot be given for "some soft toys accessible."

3.3.2b Credit can be given for some soft toys because there are at least three soft toys accessible for play.

with them. The toys must be accessible to children for ***much of the day*** (defined in "Explanations of Terms Used Throughout the Scale" on page 7 of the ITERS-R). Examples of soft toys are listed in the "Notes for Clarification" (ITERS-R, page 14) for this indicator and include cloth dolls and puppets and stuffed animals. To count as soft toys, puppets must be completely soft and be made of a plush material, not thin cloth with hard plastic body parts. Dolls can be completely soft or have soft bodies with plastic heads, arms, and legs. Soft toy animals can be of all sizes, from those that can be held in one hand to large animals children can sit or lie on. Also counted are soft stuffed toys in other shapes such as trucks or boats and soft cloth or vinyl covered blocks. Cloth or vinyl books are not counted as soft toys, but counted as books in Item 14, Using books. Only accessible soft toys that children can reach and are allowed to play with are given credit. If soft toys are located in children's cribs, and are not accessible for play much of the day, then they are not counted here. If soft toys are used to decorate the room and are not accessible for children to use, they are not given credit in this item. (See photos 3.3.2a-b.)

Score this indicator "Yes" if at least three soft toys are accessible to the children in the group being observed daily, for much of the day.

5.1 A ***cozy area*** is defined in the "Notes for Clarification" for this indicator (on page 14 of the ITERS-R). It is space set up in the room where a substantial amount of softness is provided in one place for the children to use. (See photos 3.5.1a-d, next page.) The soft furnishings in the cozy area must allow a child to relax, completely escaping the hardness of the typical early childhood classroom. One *small* soft thing by itself does not create a *cozy area*. Thus, a small padded chair, a small child-sized beanbag chair, a few small stuffed pillows, a thin mat, or a carpeted corner by itself is not enough. However, credit can be given for a combination of such furnishings that are gathered together in an area.

Since the cozy area is meant for relaxing, it cannot be an active play area that is equipped with some soft materials. For example, a climber with a slide may be surrounded with a mat or cushions to protect children from injury if they fall. Although softness is present, the area is not counted as a cozy area. Similarly, large vinyl covered shapes, used for climbing, or mats used for active play, would not be considered cozy areas.

3 Provisions for relaxation and and comfort

3.5.1a

3.5.1b

3.5.1c

3.5.1d

3.5.1a-d   A cozy area has a substantial amount of softness.

Large furnishings, such as a mattress, adult-sized couch, or adult-sized beanbag chair, might be given credit if they provide the required substantial amount of softness, by allowing the child to completely escape the hardness of the floor and wall. Judgment of whether a soft area can be given credit as a ***cozy area*** should be based on the amount of softness provided, not on whether the area is aesthetically appealing.

Accessible means that the children are permitted to use the cozy area for lounging, looking at books, being read to, and other quiet activities. A cozy area must be accessible to children ***for much of the day*** (defined in "Explanations of Terms Used Throughout the Scale" in the ITERS-R, page 7), meaning throughout the day with few exceptions. Since infants and young toddlers are often on individual or flexible schedules, with some children sleeping while others are being fed or playing, a cozy area is required to be accessible throughout the day so that most of the children can have a chance to use it.

If there are two or more ***cozy areas*** in the main classroom for the group being observed, each cozy area does not have to meet all the requirements of Indicators 5.1 and 5.2. However, there must always be one area providing a substantial amount of softness, where children can depend on being able to relax safely, which is *not* used for active physical play. It must be obvious that a child, who wants to use a cozy area, is not constantly in danger of being interrupted by active play.

A combination of accessibility to all cozy areas in the room can be used to judge whether a cozy area is accessible for much of the day to score this indicator "Yes."

3.5.2a The cozy area is protected from active play by being placed far from the gross motor area and other active play such as blocks and housekeeping.

3.5.2b Non-mobile infants who are placed in a cozy area must be supervised carefully to see that more mobile children do not climb on or disturb the child in any other way.

3.5.2c The close proximity of active play materials invites active play into the cozy area.

3.5.2d

5.2 The cozy area must be **protected** from active play for most of the day, although it may be used for short periods as an active play space (e.g., for dancing). **Protected** is defined in the "Notes for Clarification" for this indicator in the ITERS-R. A cozy area should be placed away from any active play equipment, such as climbers, riding or wheeled toys, and have protection from active children through its placement in the room or by means of a physical barrier. Staff should be diligent to ensure that children engaged in active play do not interfere with a child in the **cozy area** by jumping on or running into the child who is relaxing. If active physical play occurs in the **cozy area,** staff must be observed stopping and redirecting such play. (See photos 3.5.2a-g.)

3.5.2e

3.5.2d-f [right] Children playing with blocks, music, and transportation toys make quiet play impossible in an unprotected cozy area.

3.5.2f

3.5.2g This boat, which is meant for children to use for active dramatic play, is not counted as a cozy area, even though it contains soft cushions.

If the cozy area is adequately protected in some way, and if no active physical play is allowed in the **cozy area,** score this indicator "Yes."

3.5.3a

3.5.3b

3.5.3a-b In order to be given credit, the required number of soft toys must be accessible to the children for much of the day. Non-mobile babies need a variety of soft toys brought to them to make the toys accessible.

5.3 **Many**, as stated in the "Notes for Clarification" for this indicator, means at least 10 soft toys for a group of five children or fewer, and at least two per child in groups of more than five children. This number is meant to provide enough toys to ensure that children do not have to compete over them. See Indicator 3.2 for examples of soft toys. As in the other indicators, **accessible** means that the children can reach and use to the toys. The observer should give credit in this indicator only for those soft toys that children can reach and are allowed to play with. (See photos 3.5.3a-b.) Toys used as decorations do not count as being accessible to the children, nor do soft toys that can be used only while a child is in a crib.

Older infants and toddlers who are able to crawl or walk around are able to select soft toys from accessible storage by themselves. However, non-mobile babies, or other children who cannot move around to access toys independently, must have toys made accessible to them by the staff. See "Explanation of Terms Used Throughout the Scale," on page 7 of the ITERS-R, for the meanings of **accessible** and **much of the day**. Remember that for toys to be accessible to non-mobile babies, the toys need to be brought to the babies or the babies moved near the toys. The staff need to rotate the toys made accessible to the babies so that they can also have **many** toys accessible to them, but not necessarily all at once. In order to score this indicator "Yes," many soft toys need to be **accessible** to all the children, including non-mobile infants and other children who are not mobile throughout the day. If there are many soft toys, but they are not accessible throughout the day, score this indicator "No."

7.1 In order to give credit for **softness in several other areas** of the room **in addition to the special cozy area,** rug areas, wall-to-wall carpeting, cushions or padded furniture of any size in other areas can be given credit. Give credit only for additional soft furnishings that can be used during play, not for soft toys that may be in other parts of the room. (See photos 3.7.1a-b.) If there is a carpet under

3.7.1a

3.7.1b

3.7.1a-b   In addition to a cozy area, these rooms have softness in several other areas. (a) A large bean bag chair and an upholstered adult-sized chair are accessible in addition to the cozy area. (b) The protected cozy area is supplemented by wall-to-wall carpeting and several cushions.

3.7.2a

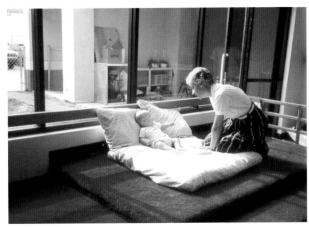

3.7.2b

3.7.2a-c   Non-mobile infants should be placed in the cozy area so that they can enjoy the relaxing atmosphere.

tables that cannot be used to sit or play on, it cannot be given credit for soft furnishings. However, indoor/outdoor carpeting that is accessible for play can be given credit, even though it is not very thick, since it is softer than the bare floor. Additional soft furnishings may include cushions or padded furniture in the housekeeping area, a rug or cushions in the book area, or rugs in the block or fine motor areas. Soft furnishings must be observed in at least two areas other than the special cozy area in order to score this indicator "Yes."

3.7.2c

7.2   This indicator is scored "NA" if there are no non-mobile infants enrolled in the group. Otherwise, it must be scored. ***Non-mobile infants*** means any children who are not yet able to move around the room by themselves and are therefore dependent on the staff to change their location. If there are children of toddler age as defined in this scale (12–30 months of age) but who are not yet mobile, they need to be included in scoring this indicator. ***Placed*** in cozy area means that staff bring

3 Provisions for relaxation and and comfort

3.7.3a

3.7.3b

3.7.3c

3.7.3a-d After many pleasant experiences of having books read to them in the cozy area, older infants and toddlers go to the area by themselves to look at books or play with puppets or other quiet toys.

3.7.3d

non-mobile children into the cozy area so that they can also experience the soft, relaxing atmosphere and the quiet activities possible there. (See photos 3.7.2a-c. preceding page.)

As stated in the "Note for Clarification" for this indicator, to give a score of "Yes," at least one instance of a non-mobile child being placed in the cozy area must be observed. This must be observed during a normal 3-hour observation. If no instance is observed within that time, score "No," even if an instance is observed later. This is because the practice must happen often enough to make a difference to the children. The score cannot be based on information reported by the staff.

7.3 The cozy area is particularly conducive to being used for ***reading or other quiet play*** because it is a soft, relaxing area and is protected from active play. Activities suitable for the cozy area are quiet ones, such as being read to, looking at books, daydreaming, relaxing, listening to soft music, and playing quietly with a toy. (See photos 3.7.3a-d.) Credit can be given for quiet play that is initiated by staff with individuals or groups or self-selected by children. As stated in the "Note for Clarification," in order to give credit, at least one instance must be observed. The score cannot be based on information reported by staff. This must be observed during a normal 3-hour observation. If no instance is observed within that time, score "No" even if an instance is observed later, if an observation of more than three hours has been completed.

4 Room arrangement

General information about this item

The arrangement of space in an infant/toddler classroom affects how well the staff can supervise the children to protect their health and safety, meet their routine care needs in a timely manner, and enhance their play and learning experiences. Since infant and toddler care requires many pieces of routine care furniture as well as play furniture, it can be very challenging to create a room arrangement that leaves enough open space for play. Moreover, the extreme vulnerability of very young children to illness, accidents, and injuries makes it necessary for staff to maintain close visual supervision of the group at all times.

During the years covered in the ITERS-R, from birth to 30 months, children grow and develop at a more rapid pace than at any other time in their lives. This means that it is possible to have non-mobile babies and fast-moving toddlers in the same group. Infants who need many feedings and diaper changes may be sharing a room with older toddlers whose messy art activities, fine motor materials, and story groups require close supervision. The room arrangement has to support and facilitate the overlapping staff roles of protector, nurturer, and educator.

This item requires examination of room arrangement in terms of the general layout of the space(s) used for children, and how furniture and materials are placed in that space. Issues related to the effects of room arrangement on supervision, children's play opportunities, and the ease with which staff can function are considered in scoring the item.

A closer look at each indicator

1.1 *Furnishings* refer to the many pieces of furniture necessary to meet children's needs for both routine care (diapering, feeding, naps, storage of children's possessions) and play (open shelves for toys, gross motor equipment, tables and chairs). See Item 2, Furniture for routine care and play, beginning on page 15 of this book, for further detail about requirements for furniture.

Often routine care needs are emphasized in infant/toddler classrooms, so the care furniture is given priority over the play needs of the children. The room is arranged so that cribs, cots or mats for sleeping, a diapering area, and highchairs, infant seats or tables and chairs for feeding arrangements take up most of the space. This leaves very little open space, and children have to find small, often unsafe spaces between or under cribs, chairs and tables to play. Sometimes children must even be kept in their cribs, or in swings or playpens, because there is too little safe, open space to play.

In other cases, there is simply too much furniture in too small a space, leaving little space for play. The furniture might be necessary for the operation of the program,

4 Room arrangement

4.1.1a The placement of the cribs in this room leaves little space for play.

4.1.1b

4.1.1c
4.1.1b-c Furnishings take up most of the space so children have to play between cribs and in other small spaces between furniture.

but the classroom is simply too small to accommodate all that is needed. In other cases, there is more furniture than is really needed for the children in the group. For example, the room may contain duplicates of furniture that are not needed or used. When there is little space for children to move about and play without being crowded because furnishings take up most of the room, children are limited, preventing them from getting the sensory-motor or gross motor experiences they need in order to properly develop intellectually, physically, and emotionally.

If the room is crowded with furniture and there is very little open space to play, score 1.1 "Yes." (See photos 4.1.1a-c.)

1.2 This indicator considers whether there are major problems with **supervision.** **Supervision** means easy **visual supervision,** since such deadly silent killers as Sudden Infant Death Syndrome (SIDS), suffocation, or strangulation do not allow children to give warning cries. As stated in the "Note for Clarification" for this indicator (ITERS-R, page 15), if there are more than one staff with the group at all times, then each person does not have to be able to see all the children at a glance. However, all children must be within view of one of the staff members at all times. If not observed, the staff must be asked if there is ever a time when there is only one person with the group (e.g., early or late in the day). If at any time there is only one staff member supervising, then this needs to be considered in scoring.

A major problem with room arrangement, related to supervision, means that the design of the space and placement of furniture and equipment within that space create a barrier that may hide one or more children from view. (See photos 4.1.2a-b.)

The term **major problems with room arrangement** means more than one major problem that might prevent adequate supervision. Examples are provided in the indicator, but other examples include:

- a separate sleep room without a supervising staff member in the room;
- a room that is L-shaped or one that has alcoves that create "blind" areas;
- high toy shelves or room dividers that create hidden areas where children cannot be seen;

Indicator

4.1.2a An "L-shaped" room may not appear to cause major supervision problems when two staff members are present.

4.1.2b When there is only one staff member present, or when both are busy in the same part of the room major problems with supervision exist.

- simultaneous use of the main room and an adjacent semi-shelter or another room;

- a loft or two-story dramatic play structure that creates hidden areas in, under, or behind the structure;

- two separate classrooms joined by an open, shared walk-through diapering area, that permits children to wander into the other classroom unnoticed;

- toileting areas that are out of view, or that require staff to accompany a child into toileting area, leaving the other children in the classroom unattended;

- playhouses, tents or large boxes used for dramatic play that are hard to see into; and

- diaper changing or food warming area in a separate room, or one that is situated in such as way that the rest of the children are not in view when a staff member is taking care of one child or preparing food.

Since **major problems** is used as a plural, more than one major problem must be observed. If during the observation it is obvious that there is more than one major problem with the room arrangement, score 1.2 "Yes." (See photos 4.1.2c-d.)

3.1 **Some open space for play** means that there is adequate space for children to move around and play with the toys and materials made accessible to them without undue crowding. Children are not forced by crowding to find play space between or under cribs or in the area used by the staff for diaper changing or food preparation. If they are exploring and occasionally wander into these areas, chil-

4.1.2c Food preparation room [arrow]

4.1.2d Diaper changing room [arrow]
4.1.2c-d If separate rooms are used for food preparation, diapering, or as a sleep room, it is impossible for one staff member alone to supervise all areas adequately.

4 Room arrangement

4.3.1a

4.3.1b

4.3.1a-b   In these infant rooms, the routine care furnishings are placed to provide some open space for play.

dren can easily be helped to find other more suitable play spaces. If furnishings are placed so that there is a clearly designated, adequate open play space, score 3.1 "Yes." (See photos 4.3.1a-c.)

3.2   ***Visual supervision*** means that staff can see and monitor all the children in the indoor space. Being able to see the entire room, including being able to see into the play area when staff are working in routine care areas, as well as having a view of the routine care areas while supervising the play area, helps to avoid safety problems and to prevent conflicts among children. It also keeps the staff in touch with the children's play so that they can take full advantage of "teachable

4.3.1c   Space to play is provided in many areas in this toddler room.

moments." For example, if several children are playing with small trucks, a staff member could bring over a book about trucks to read or look at with them. Such timely extensions of learning cannot happen if the staff cannot see what children are doing.

In order to score this indicator "Yes," it must be clear that there are no ***major difficulties*** with room arrangement that prevent staff from providing continuous careful visual supervision. ***Major difficulties*** means "major problems" and is discussed under Indicator 1.2. For example, if there is a separate sleep room there must be a staff member supervising the sleep room when it is being used. If one staff member is working in a separate room for diapering or food preparation, another staff member needs to be in the main room actively supervising the rest of the children. A few minor difficulties are acceptable at this level of quality. For example, if children are partially hidden behind a low shelf while playing, or if a mirror must be used over a diapering table placed against a wall, providing a less clear view of children behind the caregiver, then this indicator could be scored "Yes," as long as no major problems were observed. (See photos 4.3.2a-f.)

3.3   If there are no children with disabilities enrolled in the group, this indicator should be scored "NA." However, if a child with any type of disability is enrolled in the group, observe to see whether ***most*** spaces for play have been made accessible by accommodating the needs of the child. For example, a child who is visually impaired may need modifications, such as a rope mounted on the wall to lead him to particular areas and clear pathways to get there. A child using a walker or wheelchair needs

4.3.2a

4.3.2b

4.3.2a-b Devices used to separate areas should not prevent visual supervision.

4.3.2c

4.3.2d

4.3.2c-d Tall shelves and play furniture can create difficulties in visual supervision.

4.3.2e Since there are always two staff members in this group, and all areas except the rear right corner are easy to supervise, the requirements for 3.2 are met.

4.3.2f While one staff member diapers a child, which places her back to the group, the other staff supervises the rest of the children.

pathways that are wide enough to accommodate the equipment and a suitable play space at a table to use materials. Note that at this quality level, it is not required that all spaces be accessible; but ***most spaces*** need to be accessible (with only a few exceptions) if there is a child enrolled who needs such accommodations. (See photos 4.3.3a-b, next page.)

4 Room arrangement

4.3.3a   **4.3.3b**

4.3.3a-b   This room has been arranged so that the child with a physical disability can access all areas and freely interact with the other children.

5.1   *Routine care areas* are those where diapering/toileting, meals and snacks, and naps are provided. ***Conveniently arranged*** means that these areas have been arranged for the convenience of the adults, so that the staff can carry out their caregiving duties efficiently. For example:

- the diapering area should have a diapering table or surface and all the needed supplies at hand, for example, paper to cover the table, diapers, receptacle for diaper disposal, and handwashing sink;

- cribs/cots/mats should be placed so that it is easy for the staff to access a child without having to navigate between crowds of sleeping children;

- feeding tables should be placed on an easy-to-clean surface;

- warm, running water should be accessible where it is needed for various types of clean up; and

- if cots or mats are used for toddlers, they should be stored in the room for easy access during the difficult transition to nap time.

If most of the routine care areas are conveniently arranged, with only one or two minor exceptions, give 5.1 a score of "Yes." (See photos 4.5.1a-d.)

5.2   Staff can see ***all children at a glance*** means that the room is arranged so that it is very easy to supervise all children visually throughout the day, even when staff are involved in diapering or preparing food. In other words, neither major nor minor problems are observed. The room arrangement must be clear of any full or partial obstructions to visual supervision. If the diapering table is facing the wall, causing the adult's back to be turned toward the rest of the group when she is diapering a child, this makes it impossible for this staff member to supervise the rest of the group visually even if a mirror is placed over the diapering area. This can be counteracted if there are always two staff members present with a relatively small group of children in a classroom without any additional major room arrangement problems. During the observation, notice whether the staff can see children all over the room from various viewing points, especially while staff are seated. Remember that all the children need to be within easy view of at least one staff member at all times to score "Yes" on this indicator. (See photos 4.5.2a-d.)

5.3   *Quiet play* is play that requires children to sit and concentrate or pay close attention, such as when they are using fine motor toys, listening to a story, looking at a book by themselves, putting a puzzle together, scribbling on a piece of paper, painting a picture, or relaxing in the cozy area. ***Active play*** is play that requires

4.5.1a This feeding area in the room makes food storage, preparation, service, and clean-up convenient for staff.

4.5.1b A diapering area with a cabinet to store diaper changing supplies and a separate sink for handwashing makes following sanitary procedures easier.

4.5.1c These toddlers eat their meals and snacks in an area where all surfaces are easy to clean and the sink is nearby.

4.5.1d Cots are stored in the room for easy access.

4.5.2a

4.5.2b

4.5.2a-b While one staff member diapers a toddler on a changing table that causes her to turn her back to the room, another staff member supervises the rest of the children. The need for a second staff to supervise the rest of the group would be true during food preparation in photo 4.5.2b when one staff prepares to serve meals.

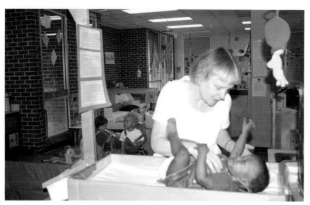

4.5.2c Even though only three children are present before the second staff arrives, it is impossible for one person to see all children at a glance while she is changing the baby.

4.5.2d This diaper changing table juts out into the room, permitting the staff member who is changing one baby to help in visually supervising the rest of the children.

gross motor activity such as crawling, walking, climbing, riding or pushing wheel toys, dancing, or throwing a ball.

Quiet-play materials should be separated from active-play materials by a physical barrier and by placing each type of play as far from the other as possible. In infant/toddler rooms it is also important to protect less mobile children, who may be using materials in quiet play as they recline in an infant seat, sit up on their own, or lie on their stomach, from more active children who can crawl, walk, climb, or run. It is a common occurrence in infant and toddler classrooms for more active children to run into, fall on, or stumble over less mobile children or those engaged in quiet activities. Young children still have not developed the ability to think far enough ahead to avoid such problems. Therefore, having clear, physical barriers and sufficient distance separating quiet and active areas is helpful in avoiding problems and interruptions.

Score this indicator "Yes" if separation of quiet and active play is clear in the arrangement of space and is enforced by the staff. (See photos 4.5.3a-d and 4.7.2, on page 47.)

5.4 The *toys* referred to in this indicator are those that have been placed in the room by the staff for the children to reach and use. *Stored* means made available on open shelves or in open containers, ready for children to use when they want to. If toys are simply left out, all over the floor, and not cleaned up and stored or replaced on shelves or in containers for use by children at least daily, credit cannot be given for this indicator.

Easy access means that the children can reach the toys by themselves. Mobile children can select the toys, books, or materials from the open shelves or

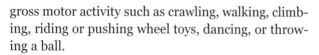

4.5.3a This room is arranged so that areas for quiet activities such as reading, drawing, or puzzles are placed as far away as possible from active play areas such as gross motor, blocks, and dramatic play.

4.5.3b The cozy area for reading and playing with soft toys contains open storage shelves with musical instruments for dancing. Children are also permitted to play with transportation toys and blocks in this area. Thus, there is no separation of quiet and active play.

Indicator

Book area   **Cozy area**

4.5.3c   **4.5.3d**

4.5.3c-d   Quiet and active play areas are not sufficiently separated to protect quiet play from active play.

containers by moving over to them. Non-mobile children need to be moved over close to the toys by staff, or the staff need to move the toys close to the children so they can reach them.

Easy access to toys can be discouraged in many ways, for example by storing toys

- high on shelves,
- in closed cabinets,
- in bins with lids that are hard to remove,
- on shelves that are too crowded,
- in toy chests or boxes with many toys underneath other toys, or
- behind barriers that prevent children from approaching toys, such as a rocking chair in front of the book shelf or a table pushed against the shelf with fine motor toys

Score this indicator "Yes" if the vast majority (almost all) of the toys are stored so that children can easily access them. (See photos 4.5.4a-f, next page.)

7.1   ***Suitable space*** needs to be provided to help children experience success with a variety of different activities. Examples of such spaces are provided in the indicator. Others include:

- adequate cushioning surface under the climber with a big space around it in case of falls;
- a big, smooth place free of things to bump into or trip on for riding, pulling, or pushing wheel toys;
- a steady, level surface such as a flat rug that allows children to build with blocks successfully, but deadens the noise when the blocks fall;
- an easy-to-clean surface, preferably near water, for art materials such as paint, play dough, and crayons;
- a big space to move around in for dancing to music and playing instruments;
- a quiet place with something soft to sit on and lean against, for books and stories; or
- a clear space at a table or on a rug to sit and work with manipulatives.

To give credit (score "Yes") a minimum of three different types of play spaces must be provided for *toddlers* indoors: an active play area, a quiet play area, and a messy materials play area. (See photo 4.7.1a, on page 47.) More specific areas (interest areas, see 7.2) can be used, such as areas for books, fine motor play, dramatic

4 Room arrangement

4.5.4a These young toddlers can get the blocks from the low self by themselves. When they have finished playing with them, staff help them replace the blocks on the shelf to keep the blocks from cluttering the play space.

4.5.4b

4.5.4b-d In order to provide access to toys, non-mobile children need to be moved close to the toys or different toys must be brought to them. This is true for both very young children and those with disabilities.

4.5.4c

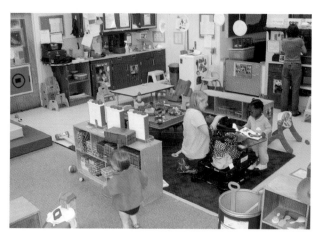

4.5.4d

4.5.4e

4.5.4e-f Easy access to toys is sometimes unintentionally prevented by leaving a tight lid on a container or placing materials too high to reach. If materials are not meant to be accessed by children, they should not be left out on open shelves in children's view and reach.

4.5.4f

Quiet area   Messy activities   Active play

4.7.1a To meet the requirements of this indicator, at least three different types of play spaces are required: quiet, messy, and active.

4.7.1b Art activities are done near the sink and on a washable floor, blocks and transportation toys are in an area with lot of open shelves and a flat rug, and the dramatic play area has suitable play materials on a washable floor in a separate area.

play, blocks, nature/science, art, or sand/water, but at a minimum, the three types of play must be represented – active, quiet, and messy. *Infants* need less defined areas, but they also need safe space to play with different types of toys and space in which they can move freely. Three areas are needed, although an area for especially messy play is not required.

7.2 An ***interest area*** is a place where materials with similar use are placed together and suitable play space is provided nearby. Young infants need fewer interest areas, mainly one for crawling and moving around and another for exploring with smaller, but safe, objects, such as rattles, textured toys, toys to reach for, and books. As children grow older, more areas are needed in response to their increasing abilities. Toddlers need more interest areas, such as for musical and noise-making toys, gross motor toys to ride, push, pull, or climb on; blocks, manipulatives, simple art materials, and simple dramatic play materials. Mobile infants will need more areas than very young infants, but less than toddlers. (See photos 4.7.1b-c.)

By having materials with similar use organized together, children gradually learn about order in their world. They develop a sense of where to access materials, where it is appropriate to use them, and where they can be put back to find next time. Score this indicator "Yes" if most materials accessible to children have a clearly defined place in the room, are organized by type, and are replaced by staff to restore the organization. (See photo 4.7.2.)

7.3 ***Traffic patterns*** are pathways adults and children use to move around the room. The placement of furniture in a room helps to determine traffic patterns, along with the fixed features of the room, such as

4.7.1c The gross motor area has a padded surface, blocks and accessories are in a rug area with lots of shelves, and fine motor materials are used on the table with a raised edge to prevent pieces from falling on the floor.

4.7.2 This toddler room has clear traffic pathways and many interest areas, including a soft, cozy area with books, and areas for blocks, table toys, a sensory table, messy art, gross motor, and dramatic play behind the block area. The arrangement also meets the requirements for 5.3 because quiet and active areas are separated.

4 Room arrangement

where the entry and exit doors are, where the bathroom is, and where closets or storage areas are.

Traffic patterns **interfere with activities** when people walk (or crawl, toddle, run, etc.) through a child's play. Examples include:

- A staff member carries a baby to the changing table, stepping over a child working with stacking rings, distracting the child from play.
- A parent has to step through the babies' primary play area to reach his child's cubby.
- Another class walks through the block area to reach the door to the playground.
- A child walks through the dramatic play area to reach the bathroom.

High traffic areas, such as the space near doorways and the bathroom, should be kept free of activities because of the possibility of constant interruptions. Whenever possible, furniture should be used to direct traffic around activity areas. In infant/toddler classrooms, children need to be kept away from areas of potential danger, such as doors that open inward, and areas where play is not allowed, including under cribs or in the diapering or food-preparation areas. Keeping children within the play area is easier if enough suitable space and activities are readily available to maintain their interest and if there are clear physical boundaries and barriers.

Within the play area, traffic patterns need to be clearly established in order to minimize conflicts among the children. By using the open storage shelves as protective barriers for the various play areas, traffic patterns can be directed around areas where children play instead of through them.

It is acceptable for slight traffic problems to exist, such as:

- staff must go through a play area while children are playing in the space to access a toy storage closet that is not used often, or
- an interest area is in path to playground door, but the door is never used during indoor play.

However, such slight problems should not be observed to interrupt children's play. To score "Yes," all traffic patterns within the space must be arranged to prevent interference with activities. (See photos 4.7.2, 4.7.3a-d.)

4.7.3c-d This long, narrow room has two doors. The door to the outdoor play area, which is less frequently used has the major open play area directly in front of it. Even more disruptive is the fact that the major traffic pathways used frequently by the staff as they feed, diaper, and put children down for nap and pick them up, cross over the mats where non-mobile infants are placed when they play. The play areas are frequently disrupted as staff must step over playing children.

4.7.3a The play area is directly in the path of the door leading into the room. Space in front of frequently used doors should not be used as open play areas.

4.7.3b The block building area and gross motor structure interfere with one another because neither area has a clear traffic pathway around it.

4.7.3c

4.7.3d

5 Display for Children

General information about this item

Infants and toddlers are remarkable observers. They pay wide-eyed attention to everything in their environment that they can explore with their senses. Knowing this, staff need to be aware of what the children are able to see from every area they use, in order to make the display space in the classroom a valuable learning experience. When young children are sitting in their highchairs, crawling on the floor, having their diapers changed, getting up from a nap, cruising around the room and steadying themselves by putting their hands against the wall, or walking around and actively exploring every nook and cranny, materials should be displayed for them to see at their eye-level. Putting both two-dimensional and three-dimensional objects where they can easily be seen by the children makes the surroundings more varied, interesting and instructive.

Two-dimensional or flat work, such as photographs, paintings, drawings, collages, and posters, can be displayed on any solid surface where they are easy for infants and toddlers to see, including:

- on low bulletin boards,
- visible places low on walls,
- on the backs and sides of low, open shelves, and
- on the floor.

All displayed items that are within the children's reach will need to be protected and made safe for the children to touch and explore, for example, by using transparent plastic covering. Thumbtacks, staples and exposed tape should not be used to attach two-dimensional display because young children can easily pick them off and put them in their mouths.

Three-dimensional objects that have height, width, and depth, such as plants, mobiles, light-weight textured objects, can be displayed by hanging them at various heights, either for visual display only or for seeing and touching. Objects of a size or material that could cause choking, such as balloons or small objects, should not be within children's reach. (If observed, consider this in Item 11, Safety practices.)

This item considers only the display contained in the classroom where the children in the group spend the majority of the day. Although many programs also use the hallways for display, this does not count in scoring the item because the children are usually in the halls only to go from one place to another and barely have time to see what is displayed. Also, this item gives credit only for the display provided for the children, not the display meant for the staff or parents.

The display in the classroom, both two-dimensional and three-dimensional, needs to be changed frequently, because young children respond to novelty and pay more

5 Display for children

attention to new things than to familiar ones. If the display is rarely changed it becomes a familiar, expected background that is taken for granted and is no longer noticed.

The content of the display is also considered in this item. It is especially important that the items selected for display are carefully chosen to be meaningful to these very young children. Familiar people, animals they see often, objects in daily use, and everyday events can be used by staff to initiate conversations, because they are common experiences for the children.

Two-dimensional display includes:

- photographs of the children engaged in various classroom activities, including both routines and play;
- photographs of their families and their pets in familiar surroundings;
- pictures showing children using familiar objects in daily living;
- pictures of children using toys;
- posters showing children and adults of various races, ethnic and cultural groups, ages, and differing levels of abilities, engaged in a variety of activities;
- scribble pictures done by the toddlers in the group;
- photographs of characters children see in books or on TV; and
- cloth pieces and objects of different textures that are pleasant to touch.

Three-dimensional display includes:

- light-weight safe objects of different textures that hang, some of which can be touched or moved by the children;
- mobiles that move, some that also make sounds, to look at and listen to;
- hanging plants; and
- bright objects hanging in space to look at, that are of different sizes and shapes, some higher and some lower.

What is displayed and how the display is used by the staff can provide information useful in scoring several other items as well, including Item 12, Helping children use language, Item 22, Nature/science, and Item 24, Promoting acceptance of diversity.

A closer look at each indicator

1.1   ***Displayed*** means put up intentionally by the staff for children to look at and experience visually or through touch. ***No pictures or other materials*** displayed for children means that there are neither two- nor three-dimensional objects displayed in the classroom for children to look at or touch. Stored toys on open shelves meant for children to access and drying art work are not considered display because they are present not for display but for another purpose. Count only the display in the classroom where the children spend most of the day, and that they can see easily. This does not mean that all counted display must be on the child's eye level, but it must be clearly visible. Do not give credit for displayed materials meant for staff or parents, such as the daily schedule or materials on a parent bulletin-board.

In some cases, there may be no materials displayed initially, but staff put up something during the observation. If displaying materials for the children is obviously not a regular practice, do not count the item that has been put up during the observation. (See photo 5.1.1.)

Score "Yes" only if there are no materials at all displayed that the children can see easily. For examples of materials that might be displayed, see the "General Information" section for this item.

1.2 Displayed materials are considered ***inappropriate for the predominant age group*** if over 50% of the materials are not meaningful for over 50% of the children in the group. Appropriate means that the materials match children's abilities and interests. For example, in a group of infants, toddlers or young twos, if the displayed materials consist of letter and number cards placed around the room, the alphabet posted up high near the ceiling, and one poster of a teddy bear, the displayed materials would be considered inappropriate because most of the children would not know what the number and letter symbols meant. They are abstract symbols that carry no meaning for the children, while photographs and pictures of real objects and scribble pictures a toddler made, displayed in their classroom, are full of meaning for the children. Although the poster of the teddy bear was appropriate, it made up less than 50% of the display.

Materials that show violence, give negative messages about any racial or cultural group, or are frightening to children are considered inappropriate and harmful.

Score Indicator 1.2 "Yes" only if more than 50% of the display is inappropriate for more than 50% of the group or if ***any*** of the displayed materials shows violence or prejudice. It is not necessary to count materials to score and try to calculate the percentage. Instead, consider what is visible and how apparent it is to the children (the placement, size, clarity), and then determine the relative weight of appropriate and non-appropriate materials. If the general impression is one of "appropriate," then score "No" even if some less appropriate materials, such as alphabet letters or numbers, may be displayed. (See photos 5.1.2a-b.)

3.1 This indicator requires that at least three things be displayed for children. They may be two-dimensional pictures, three-dimensional objects, or a combination of the two. ***Where children can easily see them*** means that the display must be in the children's path

5.1.2a

5.1.2b
5.1.2a-b If most of the display consists of numbers, letters, shapes and other academic material suited to older fours and kindergarteners, the display would not be considered appropriate for infants and toddlers.

5.1.1 A room without any display has a bland, cold feeling. Both two-dimensional and three-dimensional display can add interesting things for the children to see and interact with.

5 Display for children

5.3.1a This display would not get credit because it is behind furniture so the children cannot easily see the pictures.

5.3.1b This picture is too high to be easily seen by the children and would not be given credit.

5.3.1c Although there are more than three pictures displayed, credit cannot be given for this indicator because only one picture can be easily seen by the children. The others are hidden by the clothes hanging on the hooks or too high for the toddlers to see

5.3.1d Credit can be given for some display because there are five children's drawings in the book area that can be easily seen by the children.

of vision as they participate in daily routines such as eating, being diapered or using the toilet, and resting, as well as while they move around to explore and play. Observe the display, keeping the children's size, mobility level, and activity patterns in mind. Also consider size (large or small) and clarity of the displayed material. For example, a small blurry or complicated photograph would be less easily seen than a large simple colorful poster, even if the poster were displayed farther from the child's eye level. Score 3.1 "Yes" if at least three colorful pictures or objects are displayed where they can easily be seen by the children. It is not required that the materials be displayed on the child's eye-level as long as children can easily see. Even colorful pictures on wallpaper or a mural painted on the wall can be given credit in this indicator. (See photos 5.3.1a-f.)

3.2 The term ***appropriate*** is defined in Indicator 1.2. Generally ***appropriate*** means that at least 75% of the display is meaningful to the children because it is age and developmentally suitable, and that none of the display is violent, frightening, or gives negative messages about any group of people (race, gender, culture, etc.). For examples of appropriate display see the "General Information" section for this item.

5.3.1e Credit can be given for some display because photographs and children's work are displayed low where the children can see them.

5.3.1f Credit can be given for some display because there are three hanging objects (three-dimensional display). The bunnies on the bulletin board alone would not be given credit because they are too hard for the infants to see.

Score 3.2 "Yes" if almost all displayed materials are appropriate and none is violent or prejudicial. See Indicator 1.2 for information on how to judge the percentage of appropriate display. (See photo 5.3.2a-b.)

5.1 This indicator focuses on the two-dimensional or flat work that is displayed in the classroom, specifically the ***pictures, posters and/or photographs. Many*** means that there are pictures, posters or photographs displayed in most of the areas that children come into contact with in the course of routine care, exploration and play. No specific number of items is required for "many" because many small items, especially if grouped together, may not have as great an impact as fewer clear, large items. For example, a group of many small photographs that are harder to see clearly might have less impact than fewer (but still many) large posters or pictures. ***Throughout the room*** requires that the two-dimensional materials are not gathered in only one place, such as on a bulletin board or the back of a cabinet, but rather are dispersed in a number of areas in the room commonly used daily by the children, such as where they are diapered and fed, take naps, crawl or walk around, and play. The content of the materials on display should be ***simple,*** that is easy for these very young children to recognize and relate to. They are also required to be ***colorful,*** that is using color to attract the children's attention. As noted in the "Notes for Clarification" for Indicator 3.1, a large single display, such as wallpaper, a mural or one large bulletin board would not meet these requirements. (See photos 5.5.1a-c, next page.)

Score "Yes" if all requirements of this indicator are met.

5.3.2a

5.3.2b
5.3.2a-b The content of these two displays are appropriate for infants and toddlers because they show pictures that are meaningful to these very young children.

5 Display for children

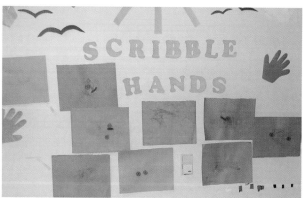

5.5.1a This bulletin board is the only display in the room. Therefore, no credit can be given because the indicator calls for pictures displayed throughout the room.

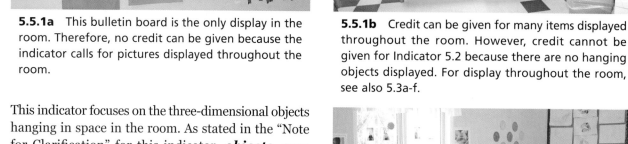

5.5.1b Credit can be given for many items displayed throughout the room. However, credit cannot be given for Indicator 5.2 because there are no hanging objects displayed. For display throughout the room, see also 5.3a-f.

5.2 This indicator focuses on the three-dimensional objects hanging in space in the room. As stated in the "Note for Clarification" for this indicator, **objects,** even those that are three-dimensional, which hang against or on a wall, such as a quilt or a puppet, are not given credit in this indicator because they are not perceived as being surrounded by space. **Mobiles** are hanging objects that have moving parts. For further information on three-dimensional objects see the "General Information" section on this item. In order to be given credit, the mobiles or other colorful objects hanging in space must be visible at some time to all the children. Therefore, a cradle gym or mobile located on one crib would not count for this item because it is clearly seen by only one child. Infants should not be left in their cribs when they are awake, so there would be little time to look at mobiles in cribs. On the other hand, a mobile over the diapering table is meant to be used by all children while they are awake, and is given credit. (See photos 5.5.2a-b.)

5.5.1c This display can be given credit for 5.1 because there are many pictures displayed throughout the room. However, credit cannot be given for 5.2 or 5.3.

5.5.2a Only hanging objects that are visible at some time to all the children are given credit in this indicator. Mobiles on cribs, which are meant for one child, are not given credit. Babies should not be left in their cribs when they are awake to watch the mobiles.

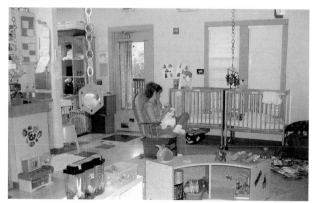

5.5.2b There are hanging objects all the infants can see in this room as well as cradle mobiles. Credit is given only for the hanging objects all the children can see.

In many cases, materials cannot be hung from ceilings due to fire hazard regulations. In these circumstances, hanging objects should be displayed in other areas, for example, hanging in a window or from a bracket on the wall or shelf.

To score this indicator "Yes" there must be at least 2 three-dimensional hanging objects in the room for use by all the children most of the day.

5.3   ***Many items*** means that the vast majority of the items on display, at least 75%, including both two- and three-dimensional objects, are displayed where children ***can easily see them*** without additional assistance during the usual activities of the day.

Displayed items that are easily seen by children without additional assistance include those in routine care areas (eating, sleeping, diapering/toileting), located on the floor where children crawl or walk, hung on the lower portion of walls and cabinets in the room near areas where children play, and in clear view in the play area. Items on display that children must be held up to see are not counted in this indicator.

Some within easy reach means that at least 50% of the displayed items that can be easily seen also can be touched by mobile children without additional assistance as they crawl, walk and move around the room. Non-mobile infants may need to be moved into close proximity by staff in order to reach the displayed items. (See photos 5.5.3a-g, below and on next page.)

See Indicator 1.2 for information on determining percentage of materials. To score "Yes," both parts of this indicator must be true: "many" where children can see them, and of those, "some" within easy reach.

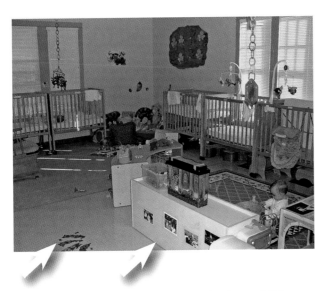

5.5.3a Many items are displayed where children can easily see them, some on the floor and on the backs of low shelves within easy reach.

5.5.3b

5.5.3c

5.5.3b-c Display on the floor is easy for crawlers and walkers to look at and reach.

5 Display for children

5.5.3d

5.5.3e

5.5.3f
5.5.3d-f Display placed on low walls in interest areas and on cabinets are within easy reach.

5.4   **Staff** refers to the adults who care for the children daily or almost daily for much of the day. Interactions with adults who are not in the classroom on a consistent basis, who are there only briefly, are not counted unless their interaction is extremely negative. Unfortunately, a negative interaction makes a much bigger impression than a positive one because of the threatening emotional context. The **talk** given credit in this indicator must be about the content of displayed material, and it has to be positive in nature. Talking about the displayed items helps children link spoken language to what they are seeing, hearing, or touching, and helps in both their language and concept development. Give credit for talk that is initiated by the staff pointing out displayed materials as well as in response to a child's interest in the display.

Examples of helpful things staff can talk about while children are looking at, touching, or interacting with displayed materials are:

- identifying familiar people in the picture ("Yes, that's a picture of you with your friend Ellen. What other friends are in this picture?" "That's a little boy just like you.");

- identifying familiar animals or objects commonly used by children ("That's a big dog, and this one is a little dog." "This looks like your cup and plate, doesn't it? Is yours yellow like this?");

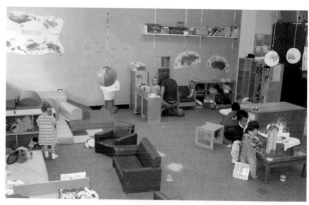

5.5.3g Credit cannot be given for 5.3 because all displayed items are too high for children to reach. However, credit can be given for Indicators 5.1 and 5.2.

- describing actions shown in the picture ("What is this girl doing? Is she jumping? See, her feet go way up when she jumps, and her hands are in the air like this." – staff member demonstrates); and

- talking about what the child is seeing, touching, or hearing as he or she interacts with three-dimensional objects hanging in space ("Look at the birds flying on the mobile – round and round. Can you hear them singing?" "The ball hanging on the long string is very soft. Can you make it swing?" "Look at the pretty plant up there. It has pink flowers.").

Indicator

5.5.4a

5.5.4b

5.5.4c

5.5.4a-c When staff talk to the children about displayed items, children's learning is enhanced. The interaction with the displayed item may be initiated by the child or the staff member.

5.7.1a-b [right] Family pictures are endlessly fascinating, especially when they are of the child's own family. These family display boards are covered with plastic to protect the photographs and can be given credit also in Indicator 7.2.

In order to score this indicator "Yes," at least one instance of staff talking to the children about the displayed materials must be observed within the typical 3-hour observation. Do not give credit if observed after the first three hours in a longer observation. (See photos 5.5.4a-c.)

5.7.1a

7.1 Having **photographs,** which are realistic representations of **familiar** people (of themselves, their classmates, their families and their pets) not only helps children become comfortable with the concept of two-dimensional representations of real life experiences, but keeps them interested in looking at the display because it is meaningful to them. **Child's eye level means** where mobile children can easily see the displayed photographs without additional assistance as they participate in the daily personal care routines and play activities, and as they move around the room. Non-mobile infants may need to be brought into close proximity with the displayed photographs in order to see them and, if necessary, there must be evidence observed that this would occur. To give credit for this indicator, the photographs must be of the children currently in the group or things familiar to them, and most of the group must be represented. At least two photographs that meet these requirements must be observed where all children can easily see them. A photograph or even several photographs in each child's crib, or out of view in cubbies, would not meet the requirements because only one child would be able to view them clearly. (See photos 5.7.1a-b.)

7.2 When very young children look at pictures, they usually want to touch and explore them, much as they would the real object. Therefore it is necessary to **protect** the pictures from being torn while the children are permitted to see and touch them. (See photos 5.7.1a-b and 5.7.2, on next page.) Putting a clear plastic covering on photographs or using a display board that has a

5.7.1b

5 Display for children

built-in transparent cover protects the pictures while allowing the children to have a full experience. ***Most*** pictures means that at least 75% of pictures displayed should be protected to give credit for this indicator. (See Indicator 1.2 for information on how to calculate percentages.)

7.3 Since ***new materials*** that are displayed receive more attention than familiar ones, it is important for the staff to add to the display or change it at least monthly. This indicator refers to both the two-dimensional and three-dimensional materials on display. Pictures can be rotated from a collection that the staff has or new pictures showing recent activities can be added. The entire display does not have to be changed monthly but at least 30% of the display should be changed or rotated monthly to give credit for this indicator.

Information to score this indicator usually requires the observer to ask a staff member the question given in the ITERS-R on page 16. If there are dates posted on displayed photographs of children's activities or art work, this information can also be used to score this indicator. (See photos 5.7.3a-b.)

7.4 ***Art work*** refers to any work done by the toddlers in the group using crayons, felt pens, play dough or other creative materials displayed or put up to be seen in the room. The quality of the art experience is not considered in this indicator, but rather the fact that what children have done is valued and displayed. The appropriateness, safety of the art materials, and the opportunity for individual expression are assessed in Item 17, Art.

Toddlers are defined in this scale as children from 12 to 30 months of age. Mark this indicator "NA" if all children in the group are infants younger than 12 months of age. However, if one child in the group is more than one month over the age cut-off, or there are two or more children who are 12 months of age, then this indicator must be scored. If an older child with a disability is enrolled, and all the other children are infants, the appropriateness of this indicator will depend on the child's abilities, not necessarily on the child's age. For further age and ability information concerning when "NA" is applicable, see "Explanation of Terms Used Throughout the Scale," page 7 in the ITERS-R booklet under the definition of infants and toddlers. (See photos 5.7.4a-e.)

Score this indicator "Yes" if there is artwork made by toddlers in the display, if children of eligible age and ability are included in the program.

5.7.2 The photos can be changed in this commercially produced display board.

5.7.3a

5.7.3b

5.7.3a-b Display should be added to or changed at least monthly. Children enjoy seeing their work being put up.

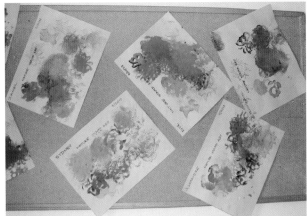

5.7.4a

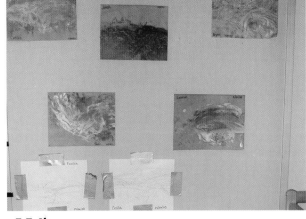

5.7.4b

5.7.4c

5.7.4d

5.7.4a-e Artwork done by the toddlers is displayed. Any work done by toddlers, whether it is creative or imitative, can be counted. See Item 17, Art for assessment of individual expression using art materials.

5.7.4e

Personal Care Routines

6 Greeting/departing

General information about this item

There are three major topics considered in this item: infants' and toddlers' social/ emotional needs, ensuring children's safety, and providing for communication among adults that is necessary for each child's well-being.

With regard to social/emotional needs, greeting children in a positive way helps them feel welcome in the classroom and sets the tone for the whole day. Warm, affectionate greetings from staff remind children that they are valued in their early childhood program. In addition, during the infant/toddler years, children experience heightened separation and stranger anxieties that must be handled sensitively, with patience and understanding, to protect the child's developing sense of self. Children's caring adults—the parents (or others who have primary responsibility for caring for a child) and child care program classroom staff can work together to help very young children with the frequent difficult transitions from home to school.

Similarly, pleasant, organized departures help the children move smoothly from the child care program to home. When things are relaxed and orderly, frantic searches for important possessions are minimized. When parents and staff calmly exchange child-related information, the children get the message that they will be well cared for.

From the safety point of view, greeting and departing helps all adults, both staff and parents, to formally transfer responsibility for the child. (See photo 6A.) Through greeting, staff register in their minds each child who is present. At departure, staff know who picked up a child and when the child left.

6A. Greeting helps staff and parents to formally transfer responsibility for the child.

Greeting of parents helps to build the relationship of trust that allows them to leave their children in the care of others. Greeting also provides the opportunity for parents and staff to share required information about the child. The exchange of information between parents and the staff who directly care for the children is extremely important with this age group. Infants and toddlers are vulnerable to problems in a wide range of health, safety, and developmental issues. Unlike older children, they cannot clearly explain why things are going wrong. When they cry or show discomfort during change of caregivers, adults often misinterpret the reason for their distress. To maximize understanding of each child, staff and parents must participate in frequent two-way conversations to become well informed about the child's status.

In this item, there is a strong emphasis on having parents bring their child into the classroom. This reduces the danger of a child becoming "lost" between home and school, and also gives parents opportunities to monitor their child's care set-

6 Greeting/departing

ting and learn about how the child is being cared for away from home. A friendly atmosphere helps parents feel at ease so they can linger to see what happens in the classroom.

Observation of greeting and departure for each child in the class is not required to score the item. Scores can be based on the number of greetings and departures observed, and information may be generalized to come to a scoring decision. In some situations where only one or two greetings are observed, even this small sample may be used to score this item. However, to get as much information as possible through observation and to depend less on staff reports, it helps to learn, before the observation, the time when most parents and children arrive and to begin observing early enough to see some children arriving.

If some greetings, but no departures, are observed, base the score on what is observed, and ask questions to collect information about how departures are handled. Do not consider answers to questions that are not supported by what was observed. For example, if it is observed that greeting procedures are chaotic, or staff seem detached, it is unlikely that departure procedures will differ substantially, even if the staff report that they are.

A closer look at each indicator

1.1   For this indicator, ***greeting*** requires that the children entering the classroom upon arrival at the center, or when entering a new classroom if they have been cared for in another, be acknowledged in some way—in other words, welcomed to the classroom. The requirement for a greeting is meant to help children make the change from home to the center, from the care of the parent (or other responsible adult) to classroom staff, or from one classroom to another, so they feel more comfortable. It also assures that staff know the child has entered their area of responsibility.

Greetings can vary in intensity and content. The requirements of the greeting for this item become more demanding as the quality level increases. At the lower quality levels, it is only required that children entering the classroom be acknowledged by the classroom staff in some way that is either positive or neutral, but *not* negative.

To give credit for the greeting of infants and toddlers:

- The staff member must be located close enough to the child and communicate directly to the child so the child can perceive the greeting as a communication. Young children have difficulty perceiving interaction from someone who is across the room. A mother will probably feel greeted if the staff member waves to her and makes eye contact from across the room, but the baby will likely need the staff member to come close and make direct contact in order to tune into the interaction. As children become older the greeting can be done from farther away, because older toddlers and 2-year-olds have learned how to intercept communications more successfully from previous experience and have the expectation for an interaction upon arrival in the classroom.

- The child must obviously perceive the greeting. Watch the child in addition to noting what the staff member does. If the child does not notice or pay attention, do not give credit for a greeting.

- Greetings must be positive (warm with some enthusiasm) or neutral (acknowledging the child in a routine manner) in their message, not negative. Negative messages that are given make a child feel unwelcome in the class, and are not considered "greetings." For example, the following would not be counted as greetings:

  - "I thought you would be sick again. That diarrhea better be gone!"

  - "Are you going to cry today? Crying is not going to get your mom to stay."

  - "You are late. You missed breakfast. Tell your mom to get you here on time. I hope you are not hungry."

  - "Are you going to be nice today or are you going to bite your friends again?"

- Greeting of a child must take place when the child enters the classroom, and if delayed, it must happen before the parent leaves the child. If the child is ignored by the staff for an unreasonable amount of time, no credit for greeting can be given. Of course, there will be times when a staff member is busy with another child or task and cannot give a newcomer immediate attention. But the greeting must be completed before the child is left by the parent. If a child is asleep upon entry into the classroom, arrival of the sleeping child should be acknowledged to the parent, and the child should be greeted upon awakening.

To determine if greeting is neglected, it is best to keep track of arrivals, noting specifics. See Chart 1 for a sample of a tracking system.

Greeting is *often neglected* and Indicator 1.1 is scored "Yes" if the majority (more than 50%) of children are *not* greeted by staff upon entering the classroom, or very soon after their arrival and before the parent leaves. If the child is sleeping upon arrival, his or her arrival must be acknowledged to the parent (or other adult who leaves the child), and the child must be greeted upon awakening.

Chart 1

Child Arrived	Child greeted / other interactions
1	No, parent left sleeping child in crib; teacher did not notice
2	Yes, teacher holds child and says Hello, Billy; talked to parent
3	No, teacher takes child but talked only to parent
4	No, never saw child enter
5	No, child put on floor to play, by parent; greeted after parent left

This chart shows that 4 of the 5 children (80%) were not greeted. In this case, 1.1 would be scored "Yes."

1.2 **Departure** is the time when children change from the care of the classroom staff back to that of their parent or other responsible caregiver (such as grandparent, foster parent or other responsible adult designated by the parent). Most often children will be going home, but departure may also be followed by such activities as shopping with the parent, going out to eat, or a visit to the doctor. Departure usually happens close to the time a center closes at the end of the day, but some departures occur at irregular times, and sometimes the child even returns to the classroom at a later time that day.

Since the parent is taking responsibility for the child at departure, staff must acknowledge the parent and know that the child is leaving. This assures that the child will not go unsupervised because each adult (parent and staff member) thinks the child is the other's responsibility. Either staff must continue to supervise or the parent must assume supervision, or both must do so together, for departure to be considered *organized*.

It is important for parents and children to have a familiar routine regarding departure from the center or classroom. If departure is well organized, children and parents have an easier time making the change from center to home. For example, there will be less time spent in searching for and gathering up the child's belongings or putting play materials away. In addition, staff and parents are assured that the transfer of responsibility for the child has been handled carefully, and children do not become "lost" or "forgotten." Parents, children, and staff are usually tired out by the time departure comes. An organized departure eliminates confusion at this stressful time.

Score 1.2 "Yes" if there is evidence that departure is *not well organized,* such as:

- During the observation, a parent enters the classroom, picks up the child, and leaves without being noticed or acknowledged by staff.
- Parents must search for their children's belongings before they can leave with their children because there is no obvious place for parents to find their children's belongings, or the belongings are not routinely placed in children's cubbies during the observation.
- There is no routine to ensure the safe exchange of responsibility for the child (e.g., sign-out list indicating who picked up the child and when, or another system).
- Parents have difficulty finding where their children are, and no one can easily tell them.
- Staff assume that a child has been picked up when the child is actually still present.
- Inadequate supervision is provided at pick-up time, so things are chaotic, and children might wander away unsupervised.
- There is no communication between parents and staff.

1.3 It is important for the parents of infants and toddlers to **enter the area used for their child's care at greeting and departure times** for several reasons. First, parents are considered to be the primary monitors of what happens to their children in early childhood programs. If they do not experience the classroom on a regular basis, they will not be adequately informed to make judgements about whether the program is meeting their children's needs. Parents should be able to go into the classroom to see what their children are able to experience during the day in terms of materials, display, space, staff, or friends. Parents should have the opportunity to become familiar with everything that their children have access to while they are in the program.

Second, the safety of the children is best ensured when the parent turns over responsibility for the child directly to the child's teachers. Possibilities for the child becoming "lost" are minimized when parents bring the child directly into the classroom. For example, a sleeping baby, dropped off in a car-seat at the center's reception area, may be forgotten in the early morning rush and never reach the classroom until he wakes up and cries. A toddler, who is dropped off and expected to find her own class, might wander away with no one ever knowing she is not absent.

Third, parents can learn from and profit by seeing what happens in the classroom and hearing what staff have to say, while staff can learn from the information and suggestions offered by parents.

Fourth, when parents do not come into the classroom, they have less to share with their children about what the child has been doing while in care. Shared experiences between child and parent are minimized, and the child never gets the message that the parent knows about the classroom and thinks it is okay.

And finally, when parents rarely enter the classroom, the natural interactions that should occur between parents and staff are restricted to communication by phone, notes, formal conferences, or other less naturally occurring methods. Parents might be less aware of important information, such as their child needing a new supply of diapers or clean clothing, developmental problems, or the presence of new children and staff. If a teacher must relay this information through several people, there is no guarantee that the information will get to the parent. With the responsibility of many children, information can easily get misplaced or forgotten along the way. For these significant reasons, the requirement that parents bring their very young children into the caregiving area daily is required.

In some programs, such as Early Head Start or centers that provide transportation for children as a service to parents, children are not brought to the center by a parent. In this case, parents do not usually enter the child's classroom, as is required by Indicators 1.3 and 3.3. Although providing transportation may be of significant benefit to both the children and their parents, because some children might not be able to attend without this support, the requirements of the indicators still apply, and should be scored as written. (See "About This Book," page ix, for "Understanding the Meaning of ITERS-R Scores.")

Enter area used for child's care means that the parent comes into the classroom where the child will be cared for most of the day. The following are not counted to meet the requirement of the indicator:

- handing a child to the classroom staff or receiving the child from the room, across a gate or other barrier, without entering the room. (See photo 6.1.3.);

- having a staff member take the child from (or deliver to) the parent sitting in a car;

- delivering the child to (or receiving from) a receptionist or other staff member without visiting the child's room;

- dropping the child off (or picking up) in a room that is not used for care most of the day, such as a multi-purpose room or cafeteria, or another class where groups are mixed at the beginning and end of the day, unless the parent routinely goes into the child's regular room to access the child's cubby or for another purpose; and

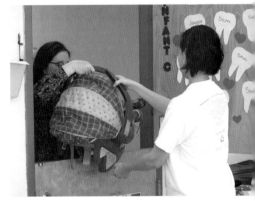

6.1.3 Parents who do not enter the area used for their child's care when dropping off or picking up their child miss opportunities to learn about what children experience throughout the day.

- dropping the child off (or picking him up) on the playground without going to the child's regular room either before or after pick up.

Rarely means less than 50% of the time. The 50% can be based on the number of parents who do not transport their children to the program themselves. For example, if some children are transported to the center in vans as a service provided by the program, and fewer than 50 % of the parents transport their own children, Indicator 1.3 would be scored "Yes." The 50% can also be based on the number of parents who do not enter the classroom even though they routinely bring their children to the center. For example, if all parents bring their own children to the center, but fewer than half enter the classroom when dropping off the child, this indicator would also be scored "Yes." Score 1.3 "Yes" if parents rarely enter their children's classroom at greeting/departing times as a part of the daily routine.

3.1   For the definition of **greeting**, see Indicator 1.1. **Greeted warmly** means that staff acknowledge the child's arrival and are positive rather than negative or neutral in tone of voice, non-verbal communication, and verbal content of greeting. (See photos 6.3.1a-b.) The greeting can be verbal ("Hello." "Hi there." "How are you?" "I see you brought Teddy with you this morning."), or non-verbal (eye contact with a hug, or picking up the child and making eye contact with a big smile), or a combination of both. The child's name may be used in the warm greeting, but it is not required at this level of quality, as long as the greeting is positive. Warm greetings do not have to be filled with enthusiastic excitement; calm, reassuring greetings are also considered warm. The most important thing is that a staff member positively recognizes the child's arrival in the classroom and does not reject or ignore the child. In addition, the greeting must be provided in a way that the child perceives directly and notices. Warm greetings that a child cannot recognize, such as from across the room, are not credited. The children should be able to tell that the staff member realizes they are there and is happy to see them. If two or more staff are in the classroom during arrival, then it is not necessary for all staff to greet children, but at least one staff member must be observed greeting children warmly.

Sometimes a group of children is being supervised by one person who has already greeted them, and then a new staff member joins the group either to take over or to share in responsibility for the children. In this case, the new staff member must greet the children in some way, but not necessarily individually. It is sufficient for the new person to acknowledge some, but not necessarily all, of the children. However, the greeting should also be warm.

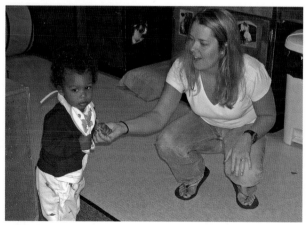 

6.3.1.a   **6.3.1.b**
6.3.1.a-b A warm greeting helps an uncertain toddler to feel secure when entering the room.

Children can include other children not enrolled in the classroom. For example, if toddlers are being transitioned into the classroom being observed, even for a short period of time, staff should greet each child warmly.

To determine whether ***most*** of the children are greeted warmly, as is required in this indicator, it helps to keep track of each child as he or she enters the room and to note whether each is warmly greeted or not. See Chart 2 for a sample of a tracking system.

Chart 2

Child arrived	Child greeted / other interactions
1	No
2	Yes, with hug
3	No, said hi from across room; child did not notice
4	Yes, took child's hand and used child's name
5	Yes, smiles, child's name
6	Yes, child's name
	Assistant arrived; and did not greet children

Most requires that at least 75% of the children are greeted warmly, and any new staff member greets the children as well. In this example, two of the six children (33%) observed entering the class were not warmly greeted. In addition, the assistant did not greet the children upon her arrival in the classroom. All opportunities for required greetings should be considered when scoring this indicator. Since at least 75% is required for ***most***, credit cannot be given for the indicator.

3.2   See Indicator 1.2 for a definition of ***departure*** and what is required at this time. A departure that is ***well organized*** requires the following:

- The child is transferred safely to parent (or other authorized person). This means that there is a system working that ensures both parents and staff know who has picked up each child, every day. Staff must be aware of parents and acknowledge them. Often there is a sign-out system in place and used, with a list of the people who are authorized by the parents to pick up their child.

- Parents can immediately locate their children.

- Children are adequately supervised until they leave the classroom or center.

- The child's personal belongings are collected together in an individual space, so things do not usually have to be found at the last moment.

- Children are ready to be picked up (e.g., diapers recently changed).

- A staff member is present who can speak knowledgeably to the parent, or other authorized adult who is picking the child up, about the child's day. That staff member has been involved in caring for the child or has been given the information by another staff member.

To score Indicator 3.2 "Yes," the departure must be well organized for most of the children. A few lapses are acceptable, such as having to look for a child's blanket or pacifier when the parent arrives, or a parent having to change a child's diaper before leaving. However, departure cannot be so chaotic that a child is left unsupervised,

6 Greeting/departing

or it is assumed that the child was picked up when actually the child is still present. If such examples are observed, score 3.2 "No."

3.3 This indicator requires that *all* parents (or other responsible adults) bring their children into the classroom used for most of the child's care, or access that classroom, even if they do not leave the child in that space. They must come into the room with their child and feel free to move around the room. (See photo 6.3.3.) If some parents bring their children early in the morning and are expected to take them into another classroom, such as the cafeteria, and the classroom regularly used is locked or the door is closed with no lights, then score this indicator "No."

6.3.3 Parents, children and staff all benefit when parents bring their children directly into the classroom.

The importance of allowing parents to enter the classroom is described in Indicator 1.3 of this item.

3.4 This indicator requires that parents and staff ***share information*** with one another about the child for whom they share responsibility. Since the indicator is part of the Greeting/departing item, the sharing should be observed at those times. This can occur through verbal or written communication. Verbal communication can be observed as parents and staff talk to one another during drop-off and pick-up times. (See photo 6.3.4a.) If parents are reluctant to talk or are in a hurry, staff must make an attempt to engage the parent briefly so necessary information can be transferred. Written information is usually conveyed on forms that are easily completed. For example, on arrival a parent will complete a form to show when the child woke up and was fed or to list special concerns. Similarly, staff will complete forms documenting the child's routine care and other experiences throughout the childcare day. In some cases a longer narrative is completed that is more personal than what is provided on a generic form. All are credited as information sharing. (See photo 6.3.4b.)

The sharing of information must be understandable by both parents and staff. For example, if parents and staff do not speak the same language, a process for translating must be in place and used. If a parent has a hearing disability, a form of communication that both parents and staff understand must be available.

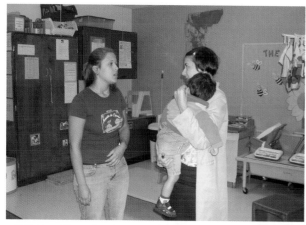

6.3.4a The sharing of child-related information between parents and staff helps to ensure the well-being of the child.

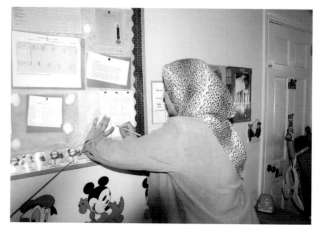

6.3.4b Parents and staff can share written information, for example by completing forms about the child's routine care that both can use.

Long, detailed conversations are not required for each parent on a daily basis, but it must be observed that some communication with staff, beyond the social, occurs for *each* parent. This makes it easier for the caring adults to correctly interpret the very young child's communications and needs and to respond appropriately.

The content of the conversation must relate at a minimum to the child's **health or safety**. Examples of such content are provided in the example for the indicator. Other examples include:

- a change in child's health status (e.g., child did not sleep well that night);
- results of a visit to the child's health practitioner;
- development of an ability (such as walking or opening doors) that might alert adults to new safety concerns;
- what the child ate, or introduction of new foods;
- when the last diaper change occurred; or
- requests for any health-related supplies needed for the child, such as formula, food, diapers, clean clothing.

Score Indicator 3.4 "Yes" if all parents and staff are observed sharing information about the child's health or safety. To give credit, the communication can be limited with some parents (for example, "He did fine today.") as long as it is more detailed with the majority (for example, "She finished all of her 4:00 feeding."). Specific information provided on a form is given credit here.

5.1 Since this indicator requires that each child and parent is greeted by staff, no lapses in practice can be observed or reported to give credit for this indicator. (See photo 6.5.1.) In addition, organized departure is required for every child, with no lapses allowed.

As with earlier indicators, it helps to keep track of each child and parent as they enter the room and to note whether *each* was individually greeted or not. Use the same tracking system shown in Charts 1 and 2, but add notes on whether the parent was greeted as well.

5.2 Infants and toddlers frequently have problems with **separation from their parents** upon arrival at the child care center. They go through normally occurring stages when separation may be more difficult, especially at about six months, and again at one year of age, but also at other times throughout the early childhood years. There is significant variation among children, with some showing the pain of separation more strongly than others. Separation issues may be seen at unexpected times, when they are not a part of a developmental stage. For example, children often show separation anxiety when they are becoming sick, after they have been away due to illness or vacation, when something has changed in their home life, or when they have changed classrooms or teachers. Whatever the cause of separation problems, staff and parents should take the child's reactions seriously, understanding the real pain the child is feeling, and responding **sensitively**. It helps to understand how the child is feeling when the adults remember how they feel when having to leave someone they love, not knowing when they will see them again.

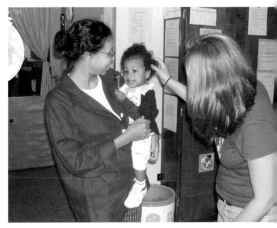

6.5.1 In good infant/toddler programs, every parent and child can expect a greeting.

6 Greeting/departing

6.5.2a When parents leave, it is natural for some children to become upset.

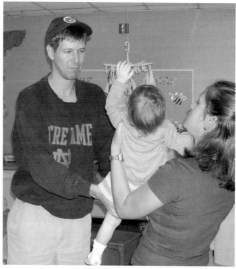

6.5.2b Sensitive handling of these painful separations are needed.

6.5.2c Providing affection and comfort helps the child through the unhappy time.

6.5.2d The best results come with patience. Comforting takes time.

6.5.2e Once the child's emotional needs have been fully met, play becomes possible.

To ***handle separation sensitively*** means that adults are patient with the child and allow the separation to happen gradually, giving the child the time and support needed to adjust and become involved in the ongoing program. (See photos 6.5.2a-e.) Sensitive handling of separation does *not* include:

- the "cold turkey" approach, where the parent hands over the child who is upset, and leaves as quickly as possible;
- the parent sneaking out when the child is not looking;
- staff ignoring children who are upset after their parents leave;
- a parent leaving and then coming back, giving the child a mixed message; or
- staff responding negatively to the child in any way, such as shaming the child, punishing the child for crying, putting the child in time out.

Look for signs of *sensitive handling* of separation, such as those provided in the example for this indicator, or other examples, such as staff:

- providing affectionate physical comfort to the child by holding or rocking;

- reassuring the child through quiet, personal talking or singing;

- helping the child to become involved in an interesting activity;

- providing the child with something that comforts him or her, such as a special blanket, a pacifier, or a photo or possession of the parent;

- encouraging a regular routine for being dropped off that the child can depend on (arrival at the same time every day, following same steps in leave-taking), rather than unpredictable events each day;

- encouraging parents to stay longer and help their child to become involved in classroom activity; or

- making sure parents say good-bye to the child once they must leave (even if the child cries), and not giving the child double messages about whether they are leaving or not.

In some cases, children will have trouble separating from the classroom at pick-up time. These times require the same sensitive handling required for separation problems at arrival.

To score this indicator, observe arrivals and departures, paying special attention to children who show separation difficulties. If no arrivals, departures or separation problems are observed, ask the question for Indicator 5.2 provided in the item. Obviously, however, if staff do not show sensitivity to children as part of their normal interactions throughout the day, there is no reason to believe staff might change their behavior in this one instance. In that case, score the indicator based on the regular interactions with children observed, and do not ask the question.

5.3 This indicator is scored "NA" when no infants (less than 12 months of age) are enrolled in the group being observed. However, if one child is under 12 months of age, then this indicator applies to the infant only: it is not required for children 12 months or over.

A *written record* shows the times that routines are completed with each child, and provides information about the important facts that parents should be made aware of to provide continuity between home and child care. The record must include information on:

- when a child was fed, what was served, and if bottle fed, how much was consumed;

- when a child's diaper was changed, whether the child was dry, wet, or had a bowel movement; and

- when a child went to sleep and woke up.

In addition, any special concerns or comments, such as signs of discomfort or illness should be included.

To give credit, the record must be:

- written,

- easily accessible for parents to look at,

- accurate, and

- contain individual information for each child.

6 Greeting/departing

6.5.3a

6.5.3b

6.5.3a-b Throughout the day staff frequently add information to the infants' daily record. The records are posted in the classroom where they can be easily seen by the staff and parents.

The record may consist of a form that staff complete throughout the day or be a narrative that staff write for parents. (See photos 6.5.3a-b.) The observer must watch to be aware of whether a record is kept accurately for each child. This normally requires that information be filled in as the various routines occur. (See photo 6.5.3c.) If staff wait until midday to fill in all records at once, or if they fill in a child's record long after routines have been completed, it is unlikely that the record will be accurate.

To score "Yes," it is not necessary that the record be given to parents to take home. This will be required in the excellent (7.3) level of quality.

Score Indicator 5.3 "Yes" if written records are kept accurately for each child, and parents can easily access the information being provided. The indicator can also be scored "Yes" if written records are provided for the parents of older children, but this is not required.

6.5.3c To ensure accurate information for parents, staff document routine care for each child as it is completed.

7.1 A *friendly, relaxed atmosphere* is one in which parents feel at ease and welcome to remain in the classroom, interacting with children, staff, and one another without feeling uncomfortable or pressured to leave. (See photo 6.7.1.) Staff can create such an atmosphere by smiling and showing interest in parents, by encouraging them to stay if they have time, and by being calm or enthusiastic, and pleasant. It is easiest to observe this atmosphere by watching how parents act when bringing in or picking up their children. If pleasant communication is obviously part of the greeting/departing routine, and parents feel free to linger if they have time to do so, then such an atmosphere exists. But if parents more often drop off their children and rush off, even trying to avoid calling attention to themselves, then such an atmosphere is not likely to be present.

6.7.1 This father knows he is welcome in the classroom and enjoys spending the extra time with his child, giving the message that the classroom is a good place.

To give credit, not all parents have to be observed taking advantage of the positive atmosphere—there will be differences among parents in their wish to do so and their time constraints. However, at least some parents should be observed to be relaxed in the classroom, and no parents should appear to be uncomfortable, without the staff attempting to be welcoming. If any parent is ignored by staff or treated in a manner that implies dislike, score this indicator "No."

This indicator should usually be scored based on observation. However, when no greeting or departing has been observed, a question is provided in the ITERS-R item to obtain the information needed to score.

Score "Yes" if a positive atmosphere, as described above, exists for parents in the classroom during greeting/departing.

7.2　***Providing information about care routines*** includes sharing information with parents related to the child's health and safety (see Indicator 3.4), as well as giving parents access to the written record of their child's diapering, feeding, and nap (see Indicator 5.3). The requirement for this indicator goes beyond such basic information and requires that a wider range of information be shared with parents.

Since the indicator requires that staff ***talk with parents*** about the information, the exchange must be verbal. The sharing of information must be in a form that the parents and staff can both understand. For example, if parents and staff do not speak the same language, a process for translating must be in place and used. If a parent has a hearing disability, a form of communication that both parents and staff understand must be used.

To give credit, staff must exchange information with parents that goes beyond the generalities that are often used to tell parents how a child did while in care. In other words, they must share information about ***specific things their child did during the day***. Credit cannot be given if the staff talk in a non-specific manner, for example by saying, "He did fine today" or "She had such a good day" or "She played a lot today." Instead, details for specific children must be provided. Several examples of the types of information required are provided in the indicator. Other examples might include:

- "She has learned to roll the ball and follow it."
- "We read his favorite book about puppies together, and he pointed to the dogs on every page."
- "She waved Bye-bye to me when I went to lunch. She has never done that before!"
- "You might need to bring in some boots for him to wear outdoors. The grass is wet, but he loves going outdoors."
- "Here's a scribble picture she did today. She likes using the markers. Does she use markers at home?"
- "He and LaToya were very involved with stacking the big blocks together. They are getting to be such good friends."
- "Beth is adjusting well to the new group she is being transitioned into. She's starting to play with some of the children."
- "We put out some more difficult puzzles today. The others were too easy for her. She spent at least 10 minutes working on this one, and finally figured it out."

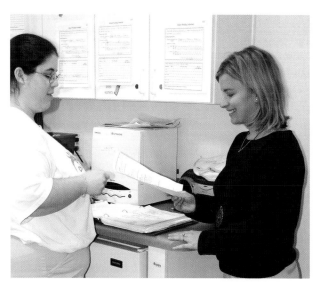

6.7.3a

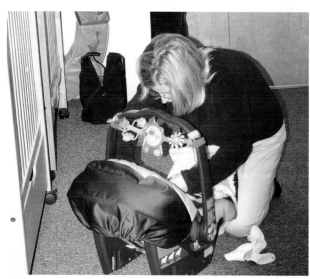

6.7.3b

6.7.3a-b   When parents pick up their infants, staff ensure they have the written information they need for a smooth transition from school to home.

Remember that the specific information cannot be about the child's routine care or health and safety, considered in earlier indicators.

To give credit, in-depth information need not be shared with every parent observed at drop-off or pick-up times, but it must be obvious that this verbal sharing is a regular occurrence with each parent at some time.

7.3   The ***individual written record about the child's day*** is described in Indicator 5.3. To give credit for this indicator, the written record (or a copy) must be provided for parents to take home with them. (See photo 6.7.3a-b.) Information in addition to that on routines can be part of the record, but is not required.

This indicator should be scored "NA" if no infants under 12 months of age are enrolled in the classroom. The indicator can be scored "Yes" if individual written records are provided to the parents of older children, but it is not required.

General information about this item

The feeding of infants and toddlers requires a combination of specialized information about each child's nutritional and developmental needs, along with an emphasis on the essential sanitary procedures that help protect young children's health in group care. In infant and toddler programs, feeding times must be designed to meet the children's widely varying physical needs for healthful foods, while providing the social/emotional support that is attached to feeding. In addition, there is an educational component during feeding times, since language is introduced and, as children progress, self-help skills are encouraged.

To adequately meet the feeding needs of infants, each child must be handled individually in terms of schedule, foods served, and responding to the child appropriately. This requires that the staff caring for infants work in a setting that facilitates appropriate practices, with convenient equipment and supplies at hand, plenty of administrative support, access to specialized training, and responsibility for only a few children, so personalized care can be provided. Although toddlers are less dependent and more able to handle some of their own feeding needs, meal/snack times remain extremely demanding for staff, but for different reasons. Toddlers' meals and snacks are frequently handled similarly to those of preschoolers—they are fed as a group, provided with the foods that older children eat, and expected to feed themselves. However, young toddlers are not developmentally ready to handle meals independently. They have very immature social skills and are therefore not good at sitting next to a peer without problems. They have limited fine motor skills, but excellent gross motor skills so they excel at running away and throwing things. Usually they still require individualized attention. Thus, staff caring for infants and toddlers need similar support and well-defined systems for handling feeding times, if meals and snacks are to go well.

If an infant is being breast-fed, and the mother can come into the classroom on a fixed schedule to feed her child, the program should encourage and support this practice. A comfortable chair will need to be available, and if possible a private place where the mother will not be disturbed. If there is no suitable private place, and the mother decides to breast feed her baby in the classroom, this should be allowed.

In some cases, babies will be fed breast milk in bottles prepared at home by the mother. The bottles should be clearly labeled with the infant's full name and the date the breast milk was pumped. Proper sanitary storage in a refrigerator kept at the required temperature is required, and the same bottle-feeding procedures should be followed as for other infants. Unused bottles should be returned to the parent at the end of the day.

All infants and toddlers who eat solid food should be offered drinking water between feedings. This is because water is required to help move solids through the digestive system. Juice should not be used for this purpose between meals/snacks because it adds unnecessary calories and children may learn to prefer sweet foods. Milk cannot be used for this purpose because it contains many solids.

This item must be observed to score and the observer should be present for one or more meals/snacks. If infants are bottle-fed, information obtained through careful observation of the practices used across a sample of children is required to score.

A closer look at each indicator

1.1   For this indicator, the ***meal/snack schedule*** is judged by observing when children are actually served meals and snacks. A written schedule should not be used as evidence to determine whether meals/snacks are served at the correct times, unless the schedule is consistent with what has been observed.

A meal/snack schedule that ***meets individual needs*** is one in which each child is fed according to the standards of the U.S. Department of Agriculture (USDA) Child and Adult Care Food Program (CACFP) Meal Guidelines, or national standards adopted by a particular country if the scale is being used outside the U.S. These standards are to be used whether or not the program is participating in the USDA Child and Adult Care Food Program (or alternative in another country). According to the USDA Meal Guidelines, which represents the minimum basic requirements, children should be given nutritious food, meals and/or snacks often, (i.e., every 2 to 3 hours), unless they are sleeping. This means that programs of up to 4 hours in length are required to provide one meal or snack; of 4-6 hours require one meal; of 6-12 hours require one meal and two snacks or two meals and one snack; of more than 12 hours require two meals and two snacks. Any supplementary foods served in addition to the required meals/snacks do not have to conform to the required food group components. In addition, infants must be fed on demand. Toddlers can be fed on a group schedule as long as it is flexible enough to meet each child's needs.

An *infant* ***meal/snack schedule does not meet individual needs*** when, during the observation, any child is not fed as required by USDA Meal Guidelines or ***within a few minutes of indicating hunger or thirst,*** for example by crying, or making sounds or gestures signifying hunger or thirst. (See photo 7.1.1a-b.) This does not mean that that infants should be fed every time they cry, because

7.1.1a   When infants are fed as a group, their individual needs are ignored, causing undue stress.

7.1.1b   Babies who are treated as individuals face less stress in child care.

infants cry for many reasons. The observer must watch to see whether staff feed a child when feeding is what a child needs to be satisfied. The schedule also **does not meet individual needs** when an ongoing attempt is made to feed a child who is obviously not interested, for example, the child who prefers to play or needs to sleep. If, during the observation, any child is not fed within a few moments of clearly showing hunger or thirst, or if they are encouraged to eat when obviously not interested, score 1.1 "Yes."

A *toddler* meal/snack **schedule does not meet individual needs** when children are not offered meals/snacks as required by USDA Meal Guidelines or when they indicate strong hunger or thirst, either verbally or non-verbally. Toddlers can usually wait for the next meal or snack if the wait is not too long, and staff need to ensure that when meals and snacks are served, the children will be interested in eating. When judging the meal/snack schedule, observers should watch for signs that toddlers are *so* hungry that they are not able to become involved in interesting activities, or that they are too tired or sleepy to eat when food is served.

Toddlers have different appetites and food interests, so flexibility in the schedule is essential. One child might be going through a growth spurt and will require more calories, while another might be going through a slower growth period and be less interested in meals and snacks. A more active child will need to eat more to make up for all of the calories he/she has expended. If there is no flexibility in the meal/snack schedule, and one or more children show obvious signs of distress (such as hunger or fatigue), then the indicator should be scored "Yes."

1.2   The term **nutrition guidelines** refers to the USDA Meal Guidelines for infants and children up to 2 1/2 years of age. These guidelines allow the observer to determine whether or not a program's meals/snacks are nutritionally adequate for the children.

A copy of these guidelines can be found in on page 80 and should be inserted into the front or back cover of the ITERS-R so observers can easily reference it during an observation.

Personal dietary preferences of the observer (e.g., home-made vs. commercially prepared baby food, breast milk vs. formula) are not to be used in determining the quality of the foods served. It should be noted, however, that the program is not required to *supply* the food for the meals or snacks, but is required to make sure the required food is offered to the children. Often parents supply food for their own children or take turns providing snacks. However, in scoring the indicator, the observer must make sure that any meals or snacks served meet the USDA guidelines for nutritional adequacy. (See photo 7.1.2.) Staff are responsible for ensuring that children's nutritional needs are met, even if the program has to provide the required foods by adding to what the parent sends.

Although the major judgment about this indicator is based on observation of the foods and beverages served at meals and snacks, menus for the classroom for one week should also be examined to ensure that the observed meals and snacks are similar in nutritional adequacy to others served.

Not appropriate means that children are not developmentally ready to handle what they are fed, or need something more chal-

7.1.2 A snack of marshmallows and water does not meet the nutritional requirements for these children (1.2), nor should the marshmallows be served on the table surface (1.3).

Meal Guidelines – Ages 1-12

Source: Child and Adult Care Food Program, USDA Food and Nutrition Service *Updated 9/25/00*
www.nal.usda.gov/childcare/Cacfp/index.html

BREAKFAST

Food Components	Ages 1-2	Ages 3-5	Ages 6-12[1]
1 serving milk fluid milk...............	½ cup.............	¾ cup.............	1 cup
1 serving fruit/vegetable juice[2], fruit and/or vegetable....	¼ cup.............	½ cup.............	½ cup
1 serving grains/bread[3]			
bread or.............	½ slice.............	½ slice..........	1 slice
Cornbread, biscuit, roll or muffin, or......................	½ serving........	½ serving.......	1 serving
Cold dry cereal or.............	¼ cup.............	1/3 cup...........	¾ cup
Hot cooked cereal or.............	¼ cup.............	¼ cup.............	½ cup
Pasta, noodles or grains.............	¼ cup.............	¼ cup.............	½ cup

LUNCH OR SUPPER

	Ages 1-2	Ages 3-5	Ages 6-12[1]
1 serving milk fluid milk...............	½ cup.............	¾ cup.............	1 cup
2 servings fruit/vegetable juice[2], fruit and/or vegetable...	¼ cup.............	½ cup.............	¾ cup
1 serving grains/bread[3]			
bread or.............	½ slice.............	½ slice.............	1 slice
Cornbread, biscuit, roll or muffin, or......................	½ serving........	½ serving........	1 serving
Cold dry cereal or.............	¼ cup.............	1/3 cup...........	¾ cup
Hot cooked cereal or.............	¼ cup.............	¼ cup.............	½ cup
Pasta, noodles or grains.............	¼ cup.............	¼ cup.............	½ cup
1 serving meat/meat alternative			
meat, poultry or fish[4], or.............	1 oz.	1½ oz.	2 oz.
alternate protein product or.............	1 oz.	1½ oz.	2 oz.
cheese or.............	1 oz.	1½ oz.	2 oz.
egg or.............	½.	¾.	1
cooked dry beans or peas, or.............	¼ cup	3/8 cup	½ cup
nuts and/or seeds[5], or.............	½ oz.	¾ oz.	1 oz.
Peanut or other nut or seed butters, or.............	2 tablespoons...	3 tablespoons...	4 tablespoons
Yogurt[6]	4 oz.	6 oz.............	8 oz.

SNACK: *Choose 2 of the 4 components*

	Ages 1-2	Ages 3-5	Ages 6-12[1]
1 serving milk fluid milk...............	½ cup.............	½ cup.............	1 cup
1 serving fruit/vegetable juice[2], fruit and/or vegetable...	½ cup.............	½ cup.............	¾ cup
1 serving grains/bread[3]			
bread or.............	½ slice.............	½ slice.............	1 slice
Cornbread, biscuit, roll or muffin, or......................	½ serving.......	½ serving.......	1 serving
cold dry cereal or.............	¼ cup.............	1/3 cup..........	¾ cup
hot cooked cereal or.............	¼ cup.............	¼ cup.............	½ cup
pasta, noodles or grains.............	¼ cup.............	¼ cup.............	½ cup
1 serving meat/meat alternative			
meat, poultry or fish[4], or.............	½ oz.	½ oz.............	1 oz.
alternate protein product.............	½ oz.	½ oz.	1 oz.
cheese or.............	½ oz.	½ oz.	1 oz.
egg or.............	½.	½.	½
cooked dry beans or peas, or.............	1/8 cup	1/8 cup	¼ cup
nuts and/or seeds, or.............	½ oz.	½ oz.	1 oz.
peanut or other nut or seed butters, or.............	1 tablespoon....	1 tablespoon....	2 tablespoons
yogurt[6].............	2 oz.............	2 oz.............	4 oz.

Footnotes

1 Children age 12 and older may be served larger portions based on their greater food needs. They may not be served less than the minimum quantities listed in this column.
2 Fruit or vegetable juice must be full-strength. Juice cannot be counted as the second snack-item if the other snack-item is milk.
3 Breads and grains must be made from whole-grain or enriched meal or flour. Cereal must be whole-grain or enriched or fortified.
4 A serving consists of the edible portion of cooked lean meat or poultry or fish.
5 Nuts and seeds may comprise only half of a meat/meat alternative serving and must be combined with another meat/meat alternative to fulfill the lunch or supper requirement.
6 Yogurt may be plain or flavored, unsweetened or sweetened.

lenging for a meal or snack. Examples of inappropriate foods are provided in the examples for the item in the ITERS-R. Other examples include:

- babies fed formula mixed with cereal from a bottle, or diluted so it is not full strength;
- infants fed solid foods before they are 6 months of age, or introduction of solid foods is arbitrarily delayed well past 6 months, unless a health care provider has recommended either for a child;
- foods that children cannot manage are fed to them, such as hot soup in a bowl to be eaten with a spoon, very tough foods, or food in big pieces that children cannot chew; or
- foods or beverages that are too hot, such as those that have been warmed in a microwave oven or in water warmer than 120 degrees.

If the proper components required by the USDA Guidelines are *not* served at observed meals/snacks or if any inappropriate foods are served to children, score Indicator 1.2 "Yes."

1.3 Many illnesses, such as diarrhea or other gastrointestinal diseases, are spread in group care and education settings. Infants and toddlers, who have immature immune systems, are at risk of complications when made ill by such diseases. Gastrointestinal illnesses can be reduced substantially by consistent use of ***basic sanitary procedures*** before, during, and after meals/snacks.

To score this indicator, *careful* observation of feeding practices, including bottle-feeding and solid food for infants, and meals/snacks for toddlers is required. The complete feeding procedure must be tracked, including preparation, feeding, and clean-up. During an observation, there will be only a limited number of chances to watch how feeding procedures are handled. While the teacher is preparing for bottle feeding or a meal or snack, close attention must be given to the preparation of the food and feeding area, such as the cleaning and sanitizing of tables or highchairs, and the washing of both children's and adults' hands. Collecting information on play materials or looking at the display should be avoided by the observer during the feeding preparation because without careful observation, very important information will be missed.

To score this indicator, there are three ***basic sanitary procedures*** that must be considered, namely, handwashing, eating surfaces, and uncontaminated foods. Information to be remembered when considering the adequacy of sanitary procedures is:

1. Handwashing of adults' and children's hands:

Handwashing is the most important way to reduce the spread of intestinal infections. Studies have shown that unwashed or improperly washed hands are the primary carriers of disease. Handwashing for children and staff requires that both hands be washed with liquid soap and rinsed thoroughly under warm running water for about 10 seconds (sing "Row, Row, Row Your Boat" once). Hands should be dried with individual paper towels that are not shared, or air-dried with a blower. Using gloves, wipes, or antiseptic waterless washes does not count as a substitute for handwashing.

Care must be taken so that hands (or gloves) are not recontaminated before handling or eating food. For example, children should not be allowed to touch the floor or play with toys between handwashing and eating. Staff with washed hands, with or without gloves, should keep from touching children, toys, materials, the floor, and other things that would contaminate their hands or the gloves. Faucets that can be turned off without the use of hands (e.g., with a foot pedal or automatic sensor) are helpful because they prevent the recontamination of hands. If these are not available, to prevent recontamination a disposable paper towel should be used to turn the water off.

If children touch food or finger-feed themselves during meals, then they must have their hands washed before and after eating to prevent contamination of the foods eaten, and the many surfaces around the classroom from the food and saliva on their hands after eating. Faces should also be wiped.

To determine whether there are lapses in handwashing, it helps to keep track of each child and adult, and to note whether each person washes hands as required or if significant recontamination takes place after hands are clean. Handwashing should be documented separately for adults and children. The following is an example of an easy way to keep track on the score sheet.

Child	Hands washed?	Recontaminated?
1	yes	no
2	yes	no
3	yes	yes, played with toy
4	yes	no
5	no, held own bottle	
6	yes	no
7	yes	no
8	yes	no

Adult	Hands washed?	Recontaminated?
1	yes	yes, picked up child
2	yes	yes, hands on floor
3	yes	yes, wiped child's face
4	no, bottle feeding	
5	yes	yes, fed 2 children with fingers

In this example, handwashing without recontamination is clearly a successful part of the program for the children but not for the staff. Children's handwashing without recontamination was practiced in 75% of the instances observed. However, there were significant lapses in proper handwashing by adults, caused by recontamination without subsequent rewashing.

The score for Indicators 1.3, 3.3 and 5.3 is determined partially by the percent of proper handwashing required. However, other measures must be considered when determining the score for these indicators. As stated in the notes for the indicator in the ITERS-R, these include the requirement that the children's and teachers' hands are washed in a separate sink from that used for diapering or toileting. If the same sink is used for both diapering/toileting and food-related handwashing,

7.1.3a Food that has fallen onto the floor needs to be cleaned up before children can eat it.

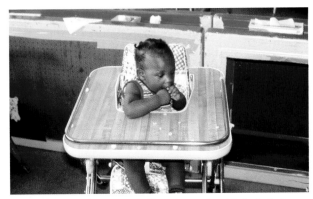

7.1.3b Serving cereal directly on the highchair tray does not meet sanitation requirements unless the tray is sanitized in the same way as plates and other eating utensils.

the sink and faucets must be disinfected with a bleach and water solution before use for food-related purposes.

2. Eating surface:

Eating equipment and surfaces must be kept clean and sanitized to avoid the spread of disease. Tables and highchair trays should be washed with a soap/water solution to remove gross soil, dried with a paper towel, and then sanitized with a bleach-water solution before and after being used for meals and snacks. To allow the bleach-water solution to do its job to kill the germs it should be allowed to sit for at least 10 seconds before being wiped dry. (Allowing the solution to sit for at least 2 minutes before wiping dry is preferable, or the table can be allowed to air dry.)

Sponges should not be used for sanitizing tables because they soak bacteria away from the surface of the sponge, which then cannot easily be reached in the interior of the sponge by a sanitizing agent. If wet cloths are used, a separate cloth is required for each table and highchair tray, and cloths cannot be returned to soak in a bleach-water solution. Food spills on the floor should also be cleaned up promptly and completely. Food should not be put directly on the table or highchair tray because eating surfaces are more likely to be contaminated than disposable plates or washed and sanitized dishes. If highchair trays are used as eating surfaces, the trays should be washed and sanitized in the same way as plates and other food service utensils. (See photo 7.1.3a.)

3. Uncontaminated foods:

Food and beverages should be served only under sanitary and safe conditions. They should be served using sanitary containers and utensils. Clean dishes, cups, utensils, and napkins should be used for eating. Reusable plates, cups, utensils, etc. must be washed and sanitized before reuse. Disposable supplies should not be reused. Foods should not be served directly onto the tabletop. Generally, foods should not be served directly onto highchair trays. (See photo 7.1.3b.) However, if trays are used as plates, with food served directly onto the tray surface, they must be made of plastic, in good repair, and sanitized between use as non-disposable plates would be, for example in a sanitizing dishwasher or in a three-compartment sink dishwashing area, following an approved procedure. Simply spraying the surface with a bleach and water solution and wiping dry is not sufficient. No contaminated foods should be served, such as food that can spoil which has been un-refrigerated for more than an hour or not kept hot enough, or foods that have been dropped on the floor.

7 Meals/snacks

To score Indicator 1.3 "Yes" it must be observed that very little attention is given to all three of these requirements (handwashing, eating surfaces, and uncontaminated foods). Staff rarely attend to the three requirements so that sanitary conditions are met for less than half of the time. Score "No" if staff sometimes properly complete each of the three requirements, even if they do not properly meet the requirements half of the time or if at least one requirement is properly carried out consistently.

7.1.5a

If meal or snack times are flexible and children come and go throughout a period of time, the same sanitary conditions are required (e.g., table sanitized between children using same places, children's hands washed, etc.)

1.4   ***Inappropriate feeding practices*** are those that do not meet the developmental, health and safety needs of the children. Examples of such practices are provided on page 18 of the ITERS-R. Other examples include:

- foods used as rewards for certain behaviors, or foods withheld as punishment;

- meals/snacks that are stressful because children are expected to use skills that they have not yet developed, such as eating with a spoon rather than fingers, never spilling milk, not eating until everyone is served, eating without getting messy;

- feeding of breast milk discouraged by the program and not adequately supported even if parents persist;

7.1.5b

- staff member bottle-feeding more than one infant at a time, even if this seems to work well, because of the possibility of contamination between children and inadequate attention given to each child;

7.1.5a-b Children's food allergies are clearly displayed in the area where children eat.

- children being allowed to take food/bottles from one another; or

- children being expected to feed themselves; and if they do not do so, staff assuming that they are not interested in eating (so little help is given to ensure that children eat what they might be interested in eating, if they were helped to do so).

If any inappropriate feeding practices are observed being used during the observation, score Indicator 1.4 "Yes."

1.5   To score this indicator, look for a list of children with their ***food allergies*** specified. (See photos 7.1.5a-b.) This may be posted in the classroom or in another space used for eating. If there are children with food allergies listed, but proper food substitutions are not made as needed, credit cannot be given.

If no list is observed, during the interview time, ask staff the questions listed in the ITERS-R to collect the information needed to score this indicator. Then ask if they make any accommodations for those children.

If a child with food allergies is enrolled in the group, the observer must find out whether ***accommodations*** are made to meet the child's nutritional needs. Accommodation means that substitutions are provided to adequately replace the food the child cannot consume. A food or beverage substitution made because of allergies must meet the primary nutrient contribution of the food or beverage it replaces, according to the USDA Meal Guidelines. For example, in the case of milk, the substitute beverage needs to be equal in calcium and protein, and not be just something else to drink. Therefore, water, juice, or even calcium-enriched juice is not a milk substitute (unless approved in writing by child's health care provider), since it does not replace the protein, but a vegetarian milk, such as soy milk, is a suitable substitute. To collect additional information about whether substitutes can be credited, ask staff, "How are substitutions made for foods/beverages children cannot eat?"

If *no* children in the program have food allergies, this indicator should be scored "NA."

3.1 See Indicator 1.1 for information needed to score whether the meal/snack schedule *meets each child's needs*.

Score this indicator "Yes" if observed meals/snacks schedule meets each child's needs, no children seem unduly hungry or tired and infants are fed on their own schedules. (See photos 7.3.1a-b.)

3.2 Use the USDA Meal Guidelines (see Indicator 1.2) to determine whether meals/snacks are *well-balanced*. The personal preferences of the observer cannot be used when assessing the quality of the food. Consider only the guidelines when determining the score. (See photo 7.3.2.) To give credit, no meal or snack served to children can be out of compliance with the guidelines. It should be noted that the guidelines represent the minimum requirements for children, and that larger servings or more food choices are permissible, in addition to the minimum requirements.

Any additional food/beverage served after the program has met the USDA requirements does not need to have the required components. For example, if children are given a cupcake because of a birthday in the class, it does not have to meet any nutritional guidelines as long as the requirements have already been met in the other meals/snacks.

In addition, to give credit, all foods and beverages served to the children must be appropriate, meaning that they are right for each child's developmental level.

7.3.1a Babies should be fed when hungry, on their own individual schedules.

7.3.1b These toddlers are offered water between meals/snacks because it helps them digest the solid foods they eat.

7.3.2 [right] This lunch of tortilla with meat and cheese, corn, carrots, and milk meets the USDA nutrition guidelines.

7.3.2

7.3.3a

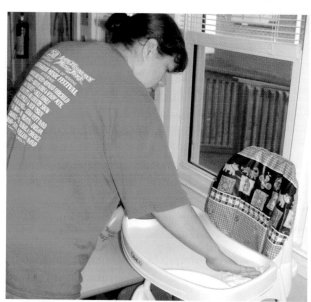

7.3.3b

7.3.3a-b After washing the table and highchair trays, the bleach and water solution is sprayed on and not wiped dry until at least 2 minutes have passed.

If the proper components required by the USDA Meal Guidelines are served at observed meals/snacks and if all foods and beverages served to children are appropriate, score Indicator 3.2 "Yes."

3.3 For information on the ***sanitary procedures required*** for meals/snacks, see the "Notes for Clarification" for this indicator, provided in the ITERS-R on page 19, and refer to the information provided in this section for Indicator 1.3.

To determine whether the proper sanitary procedures are practiced ***at least half of the time,*** at least one meal or snack should be observed (preferably one of each), and if children are bottle-fed, a sample of bottle feedings should be observed. If possible, make sure to observe all staff who handle the meal/snack routines when collecting information. (See photos 7.3.3a-b.)

When deciding on whether to give credit for ***at least half***, be sure to consider what was done properly as well as what was not. To score, collect information on the three sanitary requirements listed in Indicator 1.3, handwashing of adults' and children's hands, eating surfaces and uncontaminated foods. To score this indicator "Yes," no requirement can be ignored by staff, and each requirement must be successfully carried out at least half of the time.

3.4 ***Adequate supervision*** for infants and toddlers during meals and snacks (including bottle feeding) means that children are closely supervised to protect their health and safety. Feeding is considered a "high risk" activity for young children because they can aspirate or choke on foods. Close supervision allows staff to prevent problems before they occur and to act quickly when necessary. The type of supervision needed will vary according to the ages and abilities of the children. For example, adequate supervision of small babies means that the children are held and bottle-fed one at a time. Bottles are not propped. For children who can feed themselves, adequate supervision means that a staff member is within arm's reach of the children and paying attention to them. If children are being fed in groups, there must be enough staff supervising so that each child is within easy reach of an adult. (See photos 7.3.4a-c.)

Indicator

7.3.4a Staff are not positioned to provide adequate supervision.

7.3.4b Adequate supervision requires that staff stay within arm's reach of toddlers who feed themselves.

If any child is observed being fed without the type of supervision described above, no credit can be given for Indicator 3.4 (score "No").

3.5 "NA" is permitted if there are no children in the program with a food allergy. See information for Indicator 1.5 to score this indicator.

5.1 The intent of this indicator is to ensure that children are fed under conditions that allow personalized care while encouraging positive, appropriate social interaction. The "Notes for Clarification" provided for this indicator in the ITERS-R, page 19, give information on the number of children who comprise ***very small groups***. (See photos 7.5.1a-c.) The numbers provided

7.3.4c Sitting with toddlers who are eating helps to ensure their safety.

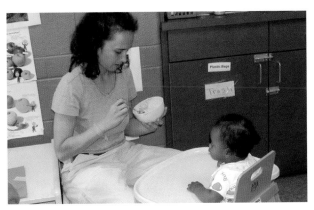

7.5.1a

7.5.1a [above] Personalized care means that this baby is the center of the teacher's attention.

7.5.1b [above right] A small group of four allows each toddler to receive personal attention.

7.5.1c [right] These toddlers receive personalized care, with two teachers paying close attention to each child's needs.

7.5.1b

7.5.1c

in the Note can vary somewhat, as long as the group size allows the positive interaction and support required by the children. However groups of children that are significantly larger than the size recommended in the Note would never be considered appropriate, even if the children might appear to be able to handle the situation. Similarly, smaller groups might be needed for children who have unusual difficulties with the size of group in which they participate.

Generally, the size of the group considered here refers to the number of children who are eating close together, for example at one table or in a group of highchairs. However, in some circumstances, the actual "table" group size may be appropriate, while the numbers of groups in close proximity within a room may not be. For example, many children eat at small tables but all in a huge cafeteria or lunchroom. This issue is mentioned in the ITERS-R Note, where it says "infants and toddlers should never be fed in a setting where many groups of children come together to eat." In this case, the individual table group size might be very small, but the overall group size in the room would prevent giving credit for Indicator 5.1.

5.2 Meals/snacks with infants and toddlers can be the most hectic time of the day for both children and staff. To provide ***relaxed and pleasant*** meals/snacks requires organization, great sensitivity to each child, and adults who are patient and able to deal with children on an individual basis. (See photo 7.5.2.) In addition, staff who provide meals and snacks need the right supports, such as having food delivered on time, someone who can help during the most demanding times, or a physical setting that works for, not against, staff. Many other indicators in this item (and in other items as well) are meant to assess whether the prerequisites for relaxed and pleasant meals/snacks are present. This indicator assesses whether the children are receiving such an experience.

Examples of things to look for in relaxed and pleasant meals/snacks are provided in the ITERS-R indicator. Additional examples include:

- Children are generally content during meals/snacks observed. Some upset might be observed with very young children, but this should be handled sympathetically by staff and quickly resolved.

- No child is hurried or interrupted while eating so that staff can attend to other matters. For example, a baby who is being bottle-fed should not be interrupted so the staff member can attend to another child who is crying; another staff member needs to be responsible for the rest of the children.

7.5.1d A teacher may need to take attention away from the toddler being fed, but for personalized care, she quickly returns to the child in the highchair.

7.5.2 Snack for these toddlers is well organized so everyone can be relaxed.

- Staff expectations of children are appropriate for the age and ability of each child. Staff are patient and not punitive with children who spill, drop or throw foods, while encouraging appropriate behaviors.

- While they are eating, children are not bothered by others. For example, their food is protected from being taken by others and they are not physically hassled while eating, such as being pulled on or hit by another child.

- For toddlers, manners are practiced and modeled by staff but not strictly enforced. Staff are patient and understand that it takes a long time to develop manners, and that the best way for children to learn is to watch adults model manners. They gently and politely guide children to use good manners, without over-emphasizing this aspect of meals/snacks.

Score 5.2 "Yes" if meals and snacks are pleasant and relaxed for each child. Do not give credit if eating times are hectic, rushed, or a negative experience for any child.

5.3 For information on the ***sanitary procedures required*** for meals/snacks, see the "Notes for Clarification" for this indicator, in the ITERS-R on page 19 and refer to the information provided in this section for Indicator 1.3.

Usually, as defined in the ITERS-R on page 8, means "the common or prevalent practice observed, that is, carried out with only a few lapses." To determine whether the proper sanitary procedures are ***usually practiced,*** at least one meal or snack should be observed (preferably one of each), and if children are bottle-fed, a sample of bottle feedings should be observed. If possible, observe all staff who handle the meal/snack routines when collecting information.

Track the three requirements (handwashing, eating surfaces, and uncontaminated foods) as described in the information provided for Indicator 1.3. When deciding on whether to give credit for ***usually***, be sure to consider what was done properly as well as what was not. (See photos 7.5.3a-k.) If only a ***few lapses*** are observed so that the three requirements are each completed at least 75% of the time, credit can be given for 5.3 (score "Yes"). Score "No" if any one of the three requirements has more lapses and is not met at least 75% of the time.

5.4 Talk during meal/snack time allows staff to incorporate learning of many kinds into a routine care activity. With infants and toddlers, the responsibility for the vast majority of talking will usually be on the staff, but children should be encouraged to take part in any way that they are able. ***Staff talk with the children*** requires some two-way communication, with one person initiating the interaction and the other responding. Talk with the children, at this level of quality, means that staff use talk not only to direct children with their words, but that the interaction is reciprocal. The child should have opportunities to initiate the interaction, with the staff responding, and the staff should also initiate the communication at times. Turn-taking should be observed. Children who are unable to talk can participate in conversations by using non-verbal communication, as well as early verbalizations, such as coos, babbling and other sounds. Staff responding verbally to such communications should be observed.

To give credit for ***staff talk with children*** during meals/snacks, staff must be close enough to the children so that children are able to perceive the interaction and respond to it if they wish. For babies, who tune in best to interactions that

To usually practice sanitary procedures requires...

7.5.3a washing and sanitizing table before food is served.

7.5.3b handwashing after sanitizing table and before serving food.

7.5.3c avoiding contamination of hands by turning off water with a paper towel.

7.5.3d washing children's hands and being sure they do not become dirty again before eating begins.

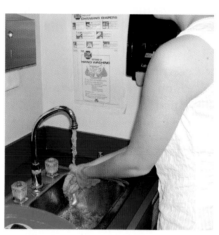

7.5.3e washing hands before serving foods and after helping children wash.

7.5.3f serving of foods with clean utensils; if gloves become contaminated, they must be discarded and hands washed.

are face-to-face, the adult must be close to the child. Babies being held for bottle-feeding will naturally be close enough to the adult who is speaking to the child. Babies in highchairs or at feeding tables will need to have the adult who is talking close to them, to give credit for talking. Many toddlers can interact across greater distances, and credit can be given for talking with the children if the children show that they understand the interaction, for example, by making eye contact with the staff member, through the child's facial expression or verbal communication.

To give credit, it is not necessary for staff to talk with children constantly, throughout the whole meal/snack, but it should be obvious that talking with the children is a regular and frequent part of the daily practice. Obviously, if there are long periods with no talking, or if staff discourage children from communicating, credit should not be given.

*A **pleasant time*** means that the staff interact positively with the children and help the children interact positively with one another. (See photo 7.5.4.) When children are eating together, the staff act as the social host, encouraging positive interac-

7.5.3g quickly cleaning up spills, not reusing utensils that have become contaminated.

7.5.3h washing contaminated hands (again!).

7.5.3i washing and sanitizing table.

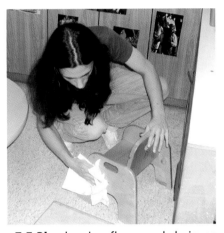

7.5.3j cleaning floors and chairs as needed.

7.5.3k more handwashing (both adults and children).

tions among the children by guiding and protecting as needed. In addition, they help with the tasks that children might find difficult, such as using a spoon, keeping from knocking things over, or serving themselves. Score this indicator "Yes" if all staff talk is either positive or neutral and none is negative in tone.

5.5   *Menus* list the foods children are served each day, for each meal/snack. Menus can consist of information on an infant's individual daily or weekly feeding, or a document that shows what the group of children is served. To give credit, the menu must be an accurate reflection of what the children are actually served; it cannot differ substantially from what was served. For example, if the menu on the day of the observation shows that children are being served oatmeal, milk, and peaches for breakfast, and they are actually given peanut butter on toast and orange juice, then, unless the

7.5.4 Staff and children enjoy talking with one another at this pleasant mealtime.

menu shows the change, credit cannot be given. This is because parents need to be well informed about what their child eats while the child is not in their own care. (See photo 7.5.5.) Some parents, for example, need to check menus to be sure that no foods that could cause allergic reactions are being served to their child. Others may want to provide variety in their child's diet and need to know what the child ate so that something different can be offered at home.

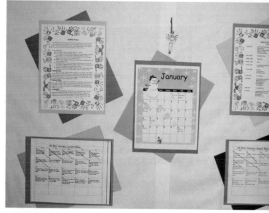

7.5.5 Parents find the menu for their children's meals and snacks on their classroom bulletin board.

To count as being ***posted for parents***, the menu must be in an easily observed place in the classroom or included as part of a parents' information display in the center where parents can easily see it. If infants and toddlers are served foods that differ from what is served to older children, the menu that applies to the younger children must also be shown.

7.1   Having ***staff sit with the child(ren) during meals/snacks*** provides benefits that go beyond supervising only for safety. Eating times provide naturally occurring opportunities to encourage learning for infants and toddlers informally.

To encourage learning means that staff actively interact with the children who are eating and provide input that promotes developmental progress. Many areas of development can be encouraged during meals and snacks, including social skills, language and cognitive development, and self-help skills. For example, staff who are pleasant and polite act as good role models for social interaction. The children watch, listen, and learn how one is supposed to act when eating. Acceptance of healthful foods is encouraged if the staff eat with the children and enjoy the foods the children are eating, or show enthusiasm for healthful foods.

- "Yummmmm. Broccoli! They look like little trees."
- "You like yogurt. I like yogurt too."
- "I never tried asparagus, but now I will. I like it. I'll take another one."

Conversations initiated by staff can expose children to many new words that will later be echoed in what the children say, as well as in using proper grammatical structures. (See photo 7.7.1.) For example, early exposure to numbers often takes place when staff talk about amounts, sizes, and numbers of foods.

- "Wow, you ate four peas! If you eat another that will be five peas!"
- "Do you want the other half of the banana?"
- "Oh, you took a big bite."
- "You have two spoons. Where did the second spoon come from?"
- "The milk is almost gone. There is only a little more milk in the bottle."

Self-help skills are encouraged as staff model how to do things that children will learn by copying, such as using a napkin, cup, or spoon. Staff can also actively help children to do these things independently, as they are able. By example, staff expose children to the tasks they will be able to do during the preschool years, such as using a fork, pouring, serving, or cleaning up spills.

To give credit for this indicator, at least one staff member must sit with any child who is eating and go beyond supervising only for health and safety by talking with the child about things related to the eating experience. If the whole group is

7.7.1 When the child says "More," the teacher asks "More cereal?" The child then says "More cereal."

7.7.2 Conversations between parents and staff help ensure similar feeding practices for the child at home and child care.

eating together, all staff should be sitting with the children and involved with them throughout most of the meal or snack. It may be necessary for staff to get up, for example, to get more food or to help a child, but for the most part, they should be sitting with the children, not standing and watching or attending to other tasks.

If children are eating together in groups, but there are not enough staff members to sit at each table, then the staff should arrange eating areas so that a staff member sitting at one table will be close enough to interact with children at another table.

7.2 During the infant/toddler years, children are encouraged to progress rapidly in their eating abilities, both in terms of what they consume (liquids to solid foods) and the extent to which they manage their eating independently (bottle to cup, fingers to spoon). It is during these early years that major health habits are established, such as enjoying healthful foods, eating the right amounts for good health, and avoiding contamination of foods. Parents and staff must cooperate in efforts to maintain a consistent message that encourages good food habits that children may carry throughout their lives.

Staff cooperate with parents means that:

- There is an exchange of information between the parents and staff as partners, so that each knows what the other is thinking about food-related topics. This can be done through the informal daily verbal exchanges that occur at greeting and departing times; but for infants it is required that the foods they eat and their feeding schedules are worked out in a formal way. For example parents need to furnish an individual feeding schedule for their child in writing, which the staff can follow.

- Staff carry out the parents' instructions; if there is any disagreement or concern about the child's meals/snacks, it is resolved. This can be done through parent-staff conversations, with both partners providing information, or with the advice of a health care practitioner. Staff need to keep careful records to share with parents about how things are coming along.

- Follow-up feedback occurs as the child makes changes, so that both parents and staff can make further plans together and use consistent practices.

Try to obtain the information required to score this indicator from observation. Listen for conversations between parents and staff about meals/snacks during greeting/departing or other times. (See photo 7.7.2.) Look for evidence such as forms where parents record instructions for or information about feeding done at home and staff record food-related information for parents. If the information needed to score is not observed, ask the question provided for the indicator and score based on what the staff report.

General information about this item

Infants vary greatly in their sleep patterns, some sleeping for long periods at a time and others taking many short "cat naps" throughout the day and night. Some sleep through the night, while others awaken and are alert and ready to play, often stressing parents who must be up with the baby at night. Some infants go to sleep independently, while others need to be rocked and soothed to sleep. In infant programs, children's sleep schedules should be individualized for each child.

Although toddlers usually become more regular and similar in their sleep patterns, there are still substantial differences among children, just as there are among adults. For example, some toddlers require a morning nap while others are able to wait until the afternoon to sleep. In high quality infant classrooms, individual sleep patterns are recognized and respected, and accommodations made for each child's needs. However, quite frequently, it is expected that all toddlers will be on the same sleep schedule. This is observed to cause undue stress in some of the children, especially when they have recently made the transition to the older class. It is equally important that staff remain sensitive to the individual sleep pattern of each toddler and ensure that toddlers' naps are handled according to their needs.

This item considers aspects of nap that go beyond the schedule and includes evaluating the measures required for the protection of the children's health, safety, and comfort while sleeping, the type of adult supervision provided, and the extent to which nap is personalized. The health requirements may appear stringent, especially with regard to placement of children's cribs, cots, or mats to avoid the spread of germs. Many people ask why this is necessary, since the children are in such close contact throughout the rest of the day. The reason has to do with limiting children's exposure to germs from others whenever the opportunity allows. When children are sleeping, adults can take advantage of the fact that they are non-mobile and reduce their total daily exposure to germs, making it less likely for them to contract some illnesses. Obviously, staff cannot completely protect children from germs, but responsible adults will try to protect children when they can, taking advantage of the opportunities as they arise.

To score this item, it is best to observe how nap is handled. During the observation, when infants sleep according to individual schedules, the provisions for nap are quite apparent to the observer. With toddlers, however, who usually are provided a group nap time only in the afternoon, the observer should, at a minimum, observe the beginning of that routine. If nap/rest time is not observed at all, the observer should ask the questions provided for the item during the staff interview time.

In some cases, in a part-day program of less than 4 hours, this item may be scored "NA." However, it cannot be assumed that the item does not apply to all programs of less than 4 hours for these very young children. The "Note for Clarification" for the item on page 21 in the ITERS-R gives guidance for determining whether a score of "NA" can be used. The item must be scored in all programs of 4 or more hours in duration.

A closer look at each indicator

1.1 ***Provisions for nap not appropriate*** means that the conditions under which nap takes place do not meet each child's needs for safe, healthful, and comfortable sleep. When determining the score for 1.1, consider the nap schedule, health conditions, any safety hazards present, and information provided in the "Note for Clarification" for the indicator (page 21 of the ITERS-R). If the nap schedule is inappropriate for any child, 1.1 should be scored "Yes." Signs of an inappropriate schedule might include:

- Nap time is too late for any child. Evidence would be that the child is tired and cranky for a long period and unable to become positively engaged in activities. Children may rub their eyes or fall asleep on the floor or while sitting at a table. (See photo 8.1.1a.) If any child is yawning constantly, tired and cranky, or is falling asleep, but staff do not arrange for them to nap, score this indicator "Yes."

- Nap time is too early for any child. Evidence would be that the child is put down for nap even though obviously he is not tired enough to settle down and rest. Even after 15-20 minutes, the child remains actively awake, does not appear to be able to relax, or complains about having to rest. A certain amount of settling down is to be expected as a child begins to go to sleep. (See photo 8.1.1b.) Some children cry for short periods, stand up in the crib, or wiggle and rearrange their sleeping position for a while. However, if any child remains alert or upset after a reasonable "settling down" time has passed and appears not to be tired, score 1.1 "Yes." No child should be left crying for more than 3 minutes at nap without either the staff attempting to help the child go to sleep or taking the child out of the sleeping place. The attempt to help a child should be positive and more than just a short verbal statement to the child, such as "time for nap" or "you're really fighting sleep." The attempt must be effective and comforting to the child.

8.1.1a For these toddlers, nap is too late.

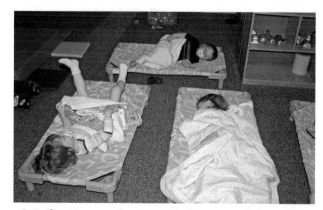

8.1.1b Nap may be too early for some of these children. It is necessary to observe to see if everyone goes to sleep.

- Nap time is too long. Upon awakening, infants and toddlers should be gotten up and involved in other routines or in play. If any child is forced to continue to rest or sleep after awakening, and is not allowed to get up and leave the crib, cot or mat within a reasonable amount of time (within 2-3 minutes if unhappy or 15 minutes if content), score 1.1 "Yes." When nap is not observed, the observer must determine the actual length of nap time. Use the written schedule as evidence only if it is an accurate depiction of what has been observed throughout the observation. If needed, ask staff questions during the interview time.

- Nap time is too short. Sometimes infants and toddlers are awakened by staff or other children before they have gotten the sleep they need. For example, a crib might be within reach of a child who annoys the sleeping child, thereby prematurely awakening him or her. Or staff might wake a child in order to accommodate the needs of the rest of the children to do a group activity or to go outside. When a child has had plenty of sleep, it is sometimes permissible to waken a child as long as the child does not show distress. Toddlers can be wakened if nap time goes beyond 2 hours. Babies can be wakened if their feeding time is long past, or if they have fallen asleep in an inappropriate place and need to be moved to their cribs. However, if any child is awakened from a nap and shows substantial distress or a lack of sufficient sleep, score 1.1 "Yes."

- Nap time is not dependable. For infants, this means that their signals indicating that they need sleep are not clearly recognized by staff. Thus their sleep needs may be recognized and met sometimes, but not at others. For example, if there are different staff caring for the child, one might be more responsive to the child's sleep needs while another may try to force the child into a set schedule. Or it might be that staff cannot read the child's signals that show tiredness and respond inconsistently, making errors in interpreting what the child is trying to communicate. Thus, the child will be assumed to need sleep and placed in the crib, when he or she is actually bored or hungry, or the opposite may be true.

For toddlers, not dependable means that there is no regular time in the daily schedule when toddlers know they will be napping or resting. Nap does not come at a particular place in the sequence of events that toddlers experience in the program. For example, nap might be at 11:30 one day and 1:00 the next, or nap may follow lunch one day and follow outdoor play the next day.

If any child cannot count on having nap handled consistently, score 1.1 "Yes."

There are safety hazards associated with naps for infants that put them at risk of smothering. A child's breathing may be obstructed by soft sleeping surfaces or soft blankets, pillows or toys that could cover the child's face. Children less than 1 year of age should be placed on their backs to sleep, and if able, allowed to assume another sleeping position by themselves. The space between the mattress and crib should not allow two fingers to fit. No hanging objects in which children might become entrapped should be used.

There are other hazards associated with nap that are not related to dangers of smothering. For example, no child should have access to any hazards, such as the cords to window blinds, small objects, or uncovered outlets. When cribs are located in the play spaces of mobile children, other hazards become apparent, such

8.1.1c Infants must be placed on their backs to sleep, but allowed to assume a favorite position by themselves.

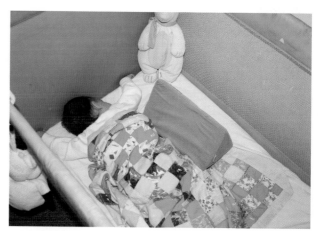

8.1.1d Soft toys and blankets create additional safety hazards for this sleeping infant.

as children being able to reach into a crib or throw things on a sleeping child. Crib sides must be latched securely, but easy for an adult to open to remove a child in an emergency. Sufficient space must exist between sleeping children for easy access by adults. The observer should closely inspect the areas used for sleeping and make sure that no hazards exist within the space. (See photos 8.1.1c-e.) If any hazard is found, score 1.1 "Yes."

When evaluating whether the sleeping conditions are sanitary and healthful for the children, the observer should consider what he or she would expect in a hotel. The following are required as healthful nap provisions for each child:

- All children sleep on a special, clean nap surface, such as a crib mattress, cot, or mat, and do not rest directly on the floor. Bed linens, such as blankets or sheets, cannot be used as a substitute for a cot or mat. However, mattresses, cots and mats must be covered with a clean sheet.

- Children are not allowed to sleep in shared places, such as infant seats, strollers, swings, cozy areas, or on tables. If a child falls asleep in such a shared place, he or she should be moved without delay to a sanitary individual sleeping place.

- The nap area is not crowded, with cribs, cots, or mats at least 36" apart or separated by a solid barrier. Even if children sleep head-to-toe, so their faces are not close, the sleeping surfaces must still be placed 36" apart. (See photos 8.1.1f-g.)

8.1.1e This sleeping area has many safety hazards – the area is too crowded to easily access children, mattresses do not fit cribs properly, and infants are not placed on their backs to sleep.

8.1.1f Nap areas are too crowded when cribs or cots are less than 36" apart, unless separated by a solid barrier.

8.1.1g Separation by solid crib ends is required when cribs are placed less than 36″ apart.

8.1.2 When even one infant sleeps in this separate nap room, an adult must be in the room to supervise.

- Children are provided with clean, individual bedding and do not share the same bedding or sleep surface (e.g., cot or mat, blankets, sheets, pillows) with another child. If the same bedding is used by two or more children, it must be washed between use by each child. There are no visible signs of toileting accidents, saliva, mucus, food, or dirt on the sleeping surfaces.

- Each child's bedding is stored separately, so that personal items are not touching those of another child. In addition, sleeping surfaces of cots or mats are kept clean; they are not touching one another, not touching the floor, nor touching the floor-side of other children's sleeping surfaces.

- Sleeping surfaces are covered with material that makes them easy to wash and sanitize. They must be sanitized after they have been contaminated (such as by vomit, mucus, blood, or toileting accidents).

1.2 Since sleeping infants under the age of one year are at heightened risk of Sudden Infant Death Syndrome (SIDS), supervision of sleeping infants requires that the children are within the view of the staff, and visually checked regularly when sleeping. Children who sleep in a separate nap room must be supervised by an adult in that room. (See photo 8.1.2.) Electronic forms of surveillance cannot be used in place of this requirement unless the TV system used allows clear and close supervision of each child to ensure that every child is breathing and not distressed. Otherwise each sleeping child must be in easy view of the staff, with no obstructions that prevent staff from clearly seeing him or her.

Napping toddlers also need to be within sight and hearing of at least one supervising adult. An adult needs to be there in case some children are awake, an emergency occurs, or a child suddenly wakes up and is frightened or feeling sick. In addition, sufficient staff must be present to help in case of an emergency, such as an evacuation due to fire.

Little or no supervision is true (score "Yes") when there is *not* a staff member actively supervising in the room during the time that any child is napping. If regular, required staff-child ratios are not maintained for toddlers during nap times, at least one staff member must be in the room with the children, and additional staff to meet ratio requirements must be immediately available, in case of emergencies or if children wake up and need attention. Regular ratios are required with infants throughout the day since it is expected that some children will be sleeping and

8.1.3a Since children spend most of the day in cribs, 1.3 would be scored "Yes."

8.1.3b When babies wake up and are happily involved in an activity, staff can wait a few minutes before taking them from the crib.

some awake at the same time. Another teacher who is solely responsible for watching her own group of children cannot serve as the additional staff available for emergencies. When groups of children are combined for nap (for example, all children from several classrooms nap together in one big nap room), more than one staff member is required to supervise the increased number of children.

The staff members must remain in the room with the children at all times, and not go out into the hall, attend meetings that are not in the room, or leave the room for personal reasons unless someone else takes over the supervision in the nap room. Supervising staff must be awake and alert, with primary interest in ensuring the safety and comfort of the napping or resting children. There can be *no* lapses in supervision, and infants must be in easy view and regularly checked, to score Indicator 1.2 "No."

8.1.3c Babies who want to get up should not have to wait for attention.

1.3 In some cases, children are put into cribs or forced to remain on cots, mats or in playpens that are used for sleeping, for reasons other than for napping. (See photos 8.1.3a-c.) For example, a non-mobile baby might be kept in her crib to protect her from other more active children, or a mobile child might be placed in a crib to prevent him from harming the non-mobile children who are in a play space on the floor. Toddlers might be told to sit on their mats while the diaper of each child in the group is changed. Each of these examples shows ***children left in cribs (or on cots, mats, and so forth) inappropriately.***

The examples provided in the item for this indicator suggest maximum times that children should remain confined in a sleeping place. However, since these examples are not firm statements of requirements, the observer must watch carefully to see the response of the child. If a child is extremely upset, it would be inappropriate to leave the child confined for the 3 minutes suggested as the upper limit in the example, and even 1 minute without response from the staff might be too long. In contrast, if a child remains happily involved in a worthwhile activity while in the crib or on the cot or mat and seems to be enjoying the time, a period of more than 15 minutes might be acceptable. However, allowing children to remain in cribs or on cots for long periods, as a regular practice would be considered inappropriate.

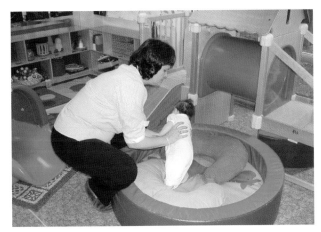

8.3.1a

8.3.1a-c Staff are sensitive, and know when this infant needs a nap, so she is moved to her crib.

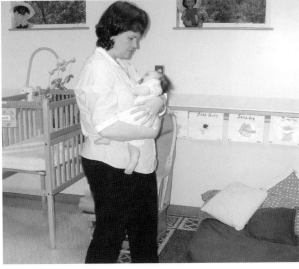

8.3.1b

If any child is confined to the sleeping place inappropriately, score Indicator 1.3 "Yes."

3.1 ***Scheduled appropriately*** means that the nap is not too early, too late, too long, too short, or not dependable from day to day. See Indicator 1.1 for more information on each.

For this young age group, the minimal (3) level of quality requires that the nap schedule experienced by the children meets the needs of ***each child***. (See photos 8.3.1a-e.) Therefore, to score 3.1 "Yes," the schedule must provide nap when needed by each individual child. If even one child's needs for sleep are not met appropriately, score Indicator 3.1 "No."

8.3.1c

8.3.1d

8.3.1

8.3.1d-e Staff remove babies from cribs as soon as they wake up and give affection before settling them into play or routine care.

8.3.2a

8.3.2b

8.3.2a-b   Cots and mats are stored to ensure clean bedding and sleeping surfaces.

8.3.2c   The cots of these toddlers are placed to minimize the spread of germs while children sleep.

8.3.3   The staff remain in the room and frequently glance at children who are sleeping.

3.2   The term ***healthful provisions*** requires that all cribs, cots, mats, or other sleeping places are at least 36" apart, unless separated by a solid barrier. Solid barriers include the wall, storage shelves, solid ends of cribs, or other solid dividers placed between sleeping places. In addition, bedding and sleep surfaces (e.g., cot, mat, blankets, sheets) must be clean, meeting the requirements discussed in Indicator 1.1. (See photos 8.3.2a-c.)

3.3   ***Sufficient supervision*** means that enough staff are present in the room to protect the children's safety in case of an emergency and to handle children who may be awake. At least one alert staff member must always be in the room where any child is sleeping, actively supervising the child(ren) with no lapses. If any children sleep in a separate sleep room, an alert adult must be present in that room to supervise. In cases of very large groups of children sharing a nap room, more staff are required. More staff may also be required when the needs of one or several children require most of the attention of the staff present. Sleeping infants must be frequently checked visually. (See photo 8.3.3.)

See Indicator 1.2 for more information on ***supervision.*** Score Indicator 3.3 "Yes" if sufficient supervision is present.

3.4   Score Indicator 3.4 "No" if any child is left in a sleeping place inappropriately, for too long or for the wrong reason, as described in Indicator 1.3.

5.1   ***Nap is personalized*** means that the nap routine is carried out with each child's preferences in mind, ensuring the comfort and security of every child. Examples of personalizing are provided as part of the indicator. Other examples might include:

- Pictures of familiar people are placed where the child can see them.
- Infant is placed to face the same direction each time she sleeps.
- Child's cot is placed near the same friend each day.
- Same music box is played for child at every nap time.
- Same individual routine is used each day to get infant settled. Staff may rock one baby to sleep, feed another and then place in the crib, and leave another who prefers to go to sleep independently; but in each case, the same thing is done each day for each child.

If any such practices are used, Indicator 5.1 is true and can be scored "Yes."

5.2   Requiring a child to move from an individual nap schedule to a schedule that is used with a group of children is a more difficult adjustment for some children than for others. Sometimes, when a child has been moved from the infant room to the toddler room, the child is expected to make this adjustment overnight. Needless to say, if the child has not been well prepared, or simply is not ready, there is a clash between what the child is expected to do and what is really possible. This can result in an adult who becomes irritated with having to care for a child whose schedule does not match those of the other children (and usually the adult's lunch break), a child who is required to be alert when he is too tired, or another expected to sleep when he is not ready.

It can be difficult for an observer to tell if toddlers have been eased into the group schedule unless the observed experience of a specific child provides the information needed to score. If the observer sees examples of children having problems adjusting, then this indicator should be scored "No," but it will be more likely that Indicator 3.1 would have already been scored "No." For example, if the observer sees staff trying to get a child to eat lunch and the child falls asleep at the table and cannot eat much because he is too tired, this would indicate that the toddler has not been eased into the group schedule.

If all children are able to deal with the nap schedule during the observation, the observer will usually not know whether this is because they were gradually eased into this schedule or were forced. Children can be prepared for the group schedule before they enter the toddler class, for example by gradually being moved to sleep on the toddler schedule while still in the infant class. If a child enters the toddler class without having experienced this gradual transition before the move, then it is up to the staff in the toddler room to ease the child into the schedule of the group. For example, staff might allow a tired child to have a morning nap while the rest of the children play, or serve the child an earlier lunch if she is tired so she can start her nap without missing the meal. In no case should the observer see a tired child encouraged to stay awake beyond his or her limits so that the child will sleep well at the group nap time. (See photo 8.5.2.)

8.5.2 Sometimes toddlers who are tired must be provided with an extra nap in a protected place.

8.5.3 As soon as the staff member notices the child is awake, she talks to her, waiting for a sign that the child wants to be picked up.

8.7.1 The teacher knows that singing softly while patting the child's back will help this toddler fall asleep.

If it is observed that the group nap schedule suits each child's needs for sleep, the observer will still need to ask staff about how this came to be. The question provided for Indicator 5.2 (on page 21 of the ITERS-R) can be asked of staff during the staff interview. Further questions might be required to find out how children are helped to make the transition from individual sleep schedules to a group schedule.

This indicator does not apply (score "NA") to classrooms where only infants on individual schedules are enrolled or if toddlers remain on individual schedules that do not conform to the nap times of all others.

5.3 Supervision that is ***pleasant, responsive and warm*** gives children the message that they are valuable and loved. ***Pleasant*** means that staff supervision is reassuring and accepting of the children. ***Responsive*** means that the staff take seriously the messages given by the children and act to meet the children's needs. ***Warm*** means that the supervision is not detached or harsh. All three of these characteristics are required to give credit. No negative supervision can occur with any child to score this indicator "Yes." (See photo 7.5.3.)

A "Note for Clarification" for this indicator (page 21 of the ITERS-R), provides instruction on how to score when nap is not observed. However, the most accurate score is one based on observation of at least some of nap time.

7.1 Examples of how staff can ***help children relax*** for nap are provided in the indicator. (See photo 8.7.1.) In a program that handles nap at the highest levels of quality, accommodations are made to meet the needs of each child. Other examples include:

- A baby is rocked to sleep or fed until he sleeps and then moved to crib.
- A staff member sits next to toddler who has trouble settling down and talks quietly to her.
- A staff member sings a lullaby to the children.
- A book is read to older toddlers.
- Lights are turned down or blinds are closed to dim the room. However, the room must remain light enough to permit appropriate supervision.
- Cots or mats of more active children are separated from those who sleep, and more active children are also separated from one another.

- The room is quiet.
- Problems are handled very calmly and gently by staff.
- Toddlers are allowed to have a soft toy or special blanket for sleep (as long as it does not pose any safety hazards).
- Toddlers are allowed to read a book or play quietly with a toy while on their cots or mats until they are ready to sleep.

To score Indicator 7.1 "Yes," the staff must accommodate each child's individual needs, giving each child what is needed to fall asleep or rest quietly. Not all children may need help with relaxing, and if it is observed that children readily fall asleep without help from staff, credit can be given, as long as those children who need it are helped to relax.

7.2 In classrooms where toddlers follow a group nap schedule, there may well be early risers or occasionally a child who does not nap at all (a non-napper). In classrooms where children are on individual nap schedules, it is likely that some children will be awake while others are sleeping.

8.7.2 Children who wake up early are allowed to get up for quiet play until everyone else is ready.

Programs that handle nap at the highest levels of quality make **provisions** for these children who are awake, even if this requires extra staff to be on hand. (See photo 8.7.2.) Rather than making early risers or non-nappers stay quietly on their cots or mats with nothing to do, staff provide a way for the children to be appropriately involved and supervised while others are sleeping. To score Indicator 7.2 "Yes," the observer should look for evidence of provisions, such as the following:

- Toddlers are encouraged to read books quietly or play with toys on their mats or cots.
- Infants who are awake are routinely taken out of their cribs and involved in play or routines.
- Children are allowed to go to another room where non-nappers or early risers can participate in interesting activities, with the necessary supervision.
- Children can go outside where they can participate in either free play or specific activities, supervised by staff.

If no situation involving early risers or non-nappers is observed, then questions about how this is handled should be asked during the staff interview, using the suggested questions in the scale.

9 Diapering/toileting

General information about this item

Maintaining sanitary conditions during diapering/toileting routines is especially important to minimize the spread of germs in the infant/toddler classroom. Having so many children sharing space, equipment, and materials for a large part of the day makes it easy to spread germs among both children and adults. In terms of diapering/toileting, the diseases spread most frequently are those that are passed from contaminated hands to the mouth, especially intestinal diseases that cause diarrhea.

For children between about 6-24 months, preventing gastrointestinal illness is of heightened concern because all prenatal immunity from their mother is gone and their own immune system is still immature. Children of this age have more trouble fighting off diseases that older children could more readily deal with. Infants and toddlers with diarrhea are more likely to become dehydrated quickly and require medical attention or hospitalization than are older children with the same disease. Of course, everyone gets diseases throughout life, thereby building up valuable immunities to certain diseases. However, it is better if children get fewer diseases during the infant/toddler years when they are less able to easily fight them off.

A vast amount of contamination is known to occur in classrooms where children are in diapers. First, the diapers, even modern disposable types, do not completely prevent leakage. Germs are spread around the areas used by children, although that may not be obvious to staff. Second, the diapering procedures, even when done according to the best known practices, only minimize but do not eliminate the spread of germs, and when not carried out carefully according to stringent standards, substantially spread contamination.

Early childhood programs, especially those enrolling children in diapers, are often considered places into which germs are carried, transferred to others, and then spread out into the community. However, studies have shown that infections can be reduced by half when proper sanitary procedures are used. Such procedures help prevent the spread of disease within a program and limit the spread outside the program as well. So it is important that sanitary procedures be carried out consistently and correctly to protect the health of the staff, the children, their families, and the greater community.

In addition to basic health concerns, this item examines the social-emotional and learning aspects of diapering/toileting: how well children are supervised, whether these routine care times are pleasant for the children, and whether children are helped to learn the skills needed for independence.

9 Diapering / toileting

A closer look at each indicator

1.1 ***Sanitary conditions*** for this item include those aspects of cleaning and sanitizing that are required to minimize the spread of germs associated with diapering and toileting, and include washing and sanitizing diapering and toileting surfaces and preventing contamination of other surfaces within the child care space. ***Sanitary conditions of the area*** means proper procedures to care for the space, and equipment within that space, used for diapering or toileting of the children in the group. The area may be located within the classroom or elsewhere in the building in which the classroom is housed, for example, down a hallway or within another classroom. More than one area might be used, and the requirements for "sanitary conditions" must be met in all diapering and toileting areas used by the children.

Maintaining ***sanitary conditions*** requires the following:

- Ideally, a separate sink should be used only for handwashing after diapering/toileting to prevent the spread of infectious agents in the feces and urine. If staff or children touch sink faucet handles while washing their hands after they have used the toilet or taken part in diapering, germs from feces or urine will get on the faucets and in the sink. Therefore, a separate sink should be used only for diapering/toileting and not for any other purpose. (See photos 9.1.1a-b.) If it is possible to designate sinks for specific purposes, then this should be done. For example, the sink near the diapering table or toilet should be used only for handwashing after diapering/toileting, while the other sink in the classroom should be used for all other handwashing. If the same sink is used by either children or adults for both diapering/toileting and food-related routines (including brushing teeth) or for other purposes (for example, to wash toys, pacifiers, or other classroom equipment), it must be sanitized after diaper/toileting use by spraying the sink and faucet handles with a bleach solution that is left on the surface to work for several seconds. All use of the sink for one purpose can be completed before the sink needs to be sanitized for another use. For example, shortly after morning arrival staff diaper several children and wash their hands and the children's hands using the only sink located in the classroom. Staff spray both the sink and faucets with a bleach-water solution after use for diapering so it is ready for other uses. It is not required that the sink be sanitized before diapering/toileting use. However, the sink should be sanitized after use for diapering/toileting, before using the same sink for other purposes.

- Toilets must be flushed after use, sanitized and cleaned daily or more frequently, if needed. Since some 2-year-olds may be allowed to handle toileting independently, observe periodically to see if toilets are flushed as needed and clean.

- If potty chairs are used, required sanitary procedures must occur immediately after each use. The contents of potty chairs must be disposed of in the toilet, which is flushed. After emptying, the potty chairs must be rinsed and washed in a special sink designated for that use only, and sanitized.

- Diapering/toileting area(s) must be kept clean. Diapering surfaces, floors, doors, and walls should be well maintained and obviously clean. No trash (paper towels, toilet paper), built-up grime, or spills should be on the floor. The area should not be dominated by the smell of urine, or feces, or covered up by air fresheners. If an area is obviously old and more difficult to maintain, the requirements for cleanliness must still be met.

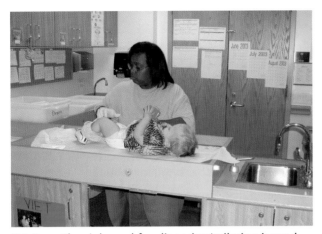

9.1.1a The sink used for diapering/toileting is used for no other purpose.

9.1.1b If a sink must be used for diapering/toileting and other purposes, it must be sanitized between uses.

- Trash, including paper towels and diapers, must be disposed of properly in a hands-free trash can (touching the trash can lid recontaminates hands). In addition, diapers must be disposed of in a covered container separate from the trash can used by the children.

Also, **sanitary** conditions to avoid contamination during diapering require following the diapering procedure shown in the chart on page 110. (See photos of diapering procedure 9.1.1a-t above and on pages 111–113.)

If the sanitary requirements listed above are not completed in at least half the cases observed, score Indicator 1.1 "Yes."

To determine whether the appropriate sanitizing procedures are used less than half of the time, a sufficient sample of diaper changes must be observed to represent the usual practices. If there is more than one staff member diapering children, the observer should be sure to document the work of all staff who change diapers. For example, if teachers provide primary care to their own small groups, and each changes the diapers of the children assigned to them, each teacher must be similarly represented in the sample of diaper changes observed. Or if the class has one teacher in the early morning and is assisted by another staff member later, then diaper changes of both staff members should be observed.

To gather the evidence needed to score this indicator, keep a chart as diapering of children is observed so it is clear at the end of the observation what was or was not done to maintain sanitary conditions.

It is not necessary to observe every diaper change if many take place throughout the observation. A sample can be used, as long as it represents the regular practice of each staff member. Track diapering until a clearly representative sample is observed. After that point, any diapering that represents new information should be added to the sample. For example, new cases would be needed in the sample when a new teacher arrives in the classroom who was not observed changing diapers earlier.

When tracking the procedures used to minimize the spread of germs associated with diapering, use a chart such as the one shown. Give a check (√) if the step was done correctly, and an X if not done correctly. Each item on the chart represents a

Continued on page 114.

9 Diapering / toileting

I. Preparing for Diapering

To minimize contamination outside of the diapering area, prepare for a diaper change *before* bringing the child to diapering area, for example, by having ready:

- Changing table paper (if used) to cover the table from the child's shoulders to heels (in case it becomes soiled and must be folded over to give a clean surface during the change)

- Enough wipes for the diaper change (including wiping the bottom and hands after taking the soiled diaper away from the child's skin)

- A clean diaper, plastic bag for soiled clothes, and clean clothes if soiled clothing is anticipated

- Non-porous gloves if they will be used, and a dab of diaper cream on a disposable piece of paper or tissue if cream is being used

Supplies should have been removed from their containers and placed near, but not directly on, the diapering surface before starting the diaper change.

II. Diapering Procedure

1. Prepare for diapering as indicated above.

2. Place child on diapering table. Remove clothing to access diaper. If soiled, place clothes into plastic bag.

3. Remove soiled diaper and place into lined, hands-free trash container. (To limit odor, seal in a plastic bag before placing into trash container.)

4. Use wipes to clean child's bottom from front to back.

5. Use a wipe to remove soil from adult's hands.

6. Use another wipe to remove soil from child's hands.

7. Throw soiled wipes into lined, hands-free trash container.

8. Put on clean diaper and redress child.

9. Place child at sink and wash hands following the "handwashing procedure." [See page 117.]

10. Spray diapering surface with bleach-water solution and wait more than 10 seconds before wiping with disposable towel or allow to air dry. It should be noted that the recommended practice is to wait for 2 minutes to allow the solution to kill germs. However, if there is a delay of at least 10 seconds before the solution is wiped from the surface, this will be considered adequate. The surface cannot be sprayed and immediately wiped.

11. Adult washes hands using the "handwashing procedure," without contaminating any other surfaces.

Additional Precautions

- The diapering surface must be sanitized after each diaper change with a bleach-water or other approved sanitizing solution (all surfaces must be able to be sanitized—e.g., no quilted pads or safety straps, no containers that are stored on the diapering surface). The bleach-water solution must be allowed to stay on the surface for more than 10 seconds, and ideally 2 minutes, to kill the germs. So it is best for staff to spray the surface as the last step of the diapering procedure before washing their own hands. After the time lapse, the surface can be dried (no additional handwashing required at this time) or allowed to air dry (and wiped dry if still damp) before use with another child.

- Diapers are disposed of in a hands-free covered can (usually one that has a step pedal that lifts the lid) to prevent further contamination of surfaces.

- Toys that are played with or objects that are touched, while children's diapers are changed, must be put aside to be sanitized.

- Note: Both child's and staff's hands must be washed after the diapering procedure is completed (see 1.3 for information).

The Diapering Procedure in Photos

9.1.1c Prepares supplies.

9.1.1d Puts clean diaper with enough wipes near (but not on) changing surface.

9.1.1e Adds plastic bag in case of soiled diaper/ clothing.

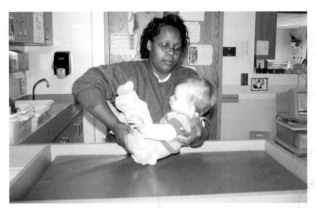

9.1.1f When preparation is complete, places child on changing surface. (Height of protective edge around diapering area is considered in Item 11, Safety.)

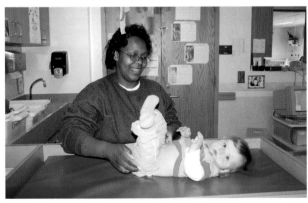

9.1.1g Removes clothing.

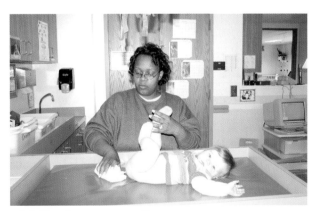

9.1.1h Removes wet diaper.

The Diapering Procedure in Photos (continued)

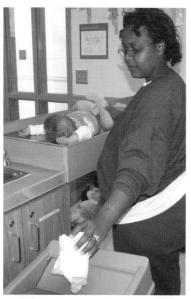

9.1.1i Places diaper in hands-free trash can (weight of diaper allows it to fall through opening).

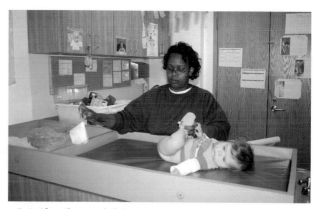

9.1.1j Cleans child with wipe.

9.1.1k Wipes own hands.

9.1.1l Wipes child's hands.

9.1.1m Puts on clean diaper and dresses child.

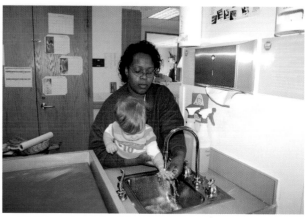

9.1.1n Washes child's hands.

The Diapering Procedure in Photos (continued)

9.1.1o Returns child to play, without touching anything else in room.

9.1.1p Soap and bleach solutions to be used in cleaning surface.

9.1.1q Washes diapering surface with soap/water solution and dries with paper towel.

9.1.1r Sprays surface with bleach/water solution and allows to air dry.

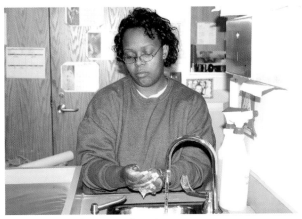

9.1.1s Washes own hands.

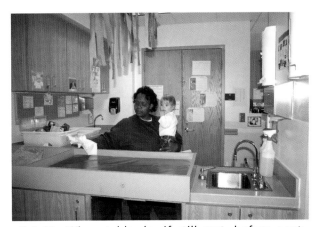

9.1.1t Wipes table dry if still wet, before next change.

9 Diapering / toileting

Continued from page 109.

part of the process required to reduce the spread of germs. Credit is given for what is done successfully and not given when a step is missed or not done as required. If fewer than 50% of the boxes on the tracking chart are scored with checks (√), then Indicator 1.1 is scored "Yes."

Chart 1:
Tracking diapering procedures used to minimize spread of germs

Diapering observed	1	2	3	4	5	6	7	8	9
Preparation of supplies (wipes, diaper, etc.)	✓	✓	✓	✓	✓	✓	X		
Disposal of diaper in hands-free trash can	✓	✓	✓	✓	✓	✓	✓		
Child's hands cleaned with wipe	X	X	✓	✓	X	X	X		
Adults hands cleaned with wipe	X	X	✓	✓	X	X	X		
Diapering surface cleaned and sanitized (2 minutes, or at least 10 seconds)	✓	✓	✓	✓	✓	✓	X		
Sink not used for other purpose without being sanitized	✓	X	✓	✓	✓	X	X		

In this example, seven diaper changes were observed, each with six steps needed to minimize contamination of the area. Some of the steps were completed and others were not. The checks represent the completed steps. To determine whether the sanitary conditions of the area were maintained during diapering, calculate whether the checks make up 50% or more of all steps required in the seven diaper changes. The observer noted that 27 of the total of 42 required steps were successfully completed to minimize contamination during the diapering times. Twenty-seven represents 64% of 42, so in this case the correct steps were completed more than half of the time. Even though in this example there was some variation in the diaper changing procedures, Indicator 1.1 would be scored "No."

Results from tracking diapering is not the only information that might be needed in deciding on a score. If children use toilets, it must be observed that sanitary procedures are followed. If there are major problems with any procedure associated with toileting that lead to substantial contamination (such as the same sink being used both for toileting and for other purposes without being sanitized; potty chairs not being cleaned and sanitized properly; toilets being flushed less than half the time after each use; floor contaminated around toilet without being cleaned and sanitized) then this indicator would be scored "Yes."

If there is a combination of toileting and diapering used, sanitary conditions must be maintained at least half the time for both procedures to score Indicator 1.1

"No." If diapering is done more than toileting, factor diapering more heavily than toileting in determining the score. The converse would be true if toileting is done more frequently.

1.2 Examples of *major problems with meeting diapering/toileting needs* are provided in the indicator. From a more general perspective, the term *diapering/toileting needs* relates to two areas:

1. Whether children are handled in a way that matches their developmental level, with appropriate expectation for toilet training, toileting accidents, individual personalities of children.

   Only in the oldest ITERS-R age groups, (children between the ages of about 24 to 30 months), should toilet training be a regular part of diapering/toileting routines. In addition, toilet training should never be forced on any child, even if the child seems to be old enough or ready. If a younger child shows interest in using the toilet rather than wearing diapers, then accommodations should be made to meet the child's needs. Parents may request that toilet training be started with younger, less ready children, but the staff should explain to parents the toilet training practices used in the program, and suggest that they postpone the toilet training challenge if the child is not ready for and receptive to this change in his or her life. Any negative toilet training methods, such as punishing a child, making a child sit on the toilet for long periods, or toileting of large groups of children at the same time, would be considered *major problems*.

   Practices that represent an overly permissive approach to diapering/toileting may also be considered major problems. Allowing a child to refuse to have her diaper changed when obviously needed, allowing children routinely to go without diapers or to wear training pants that leak, or allowing children to urinate on the playground, pose serious health hazards for children being cared for in groups.

2. Whether there are basic provisions for diapering/toileting, such as a diapering table to use for children either in diapers or with soiled clothing, or clean diapers and clean clothing available so children can be changed when needed.

   Provisions for diapering include the equipment and supplies needed to change children properly, including a diapering surface that can be sanitized, a sink with warm running water, liquid soap, wipes, bleach and water (or other approved sanitizing solution), diapers, plastic bags for soiled clothes, and individual or disposable towels. Children in wet or soiled training pants (disposable or cloth) or with wet or soiled clothing must be changed only on the diapering surface, not on the floor, even if it is in the toileting area. *Provisions* for toileting include a toilet (or less desirable, potty chair), toilet paper, a sink with warm running water, liquid soap, plastic bags for wet or soiled clothes, and individual or disposable towels. (See photo 9.1.2.)

   Supplies needed for staff and children in the toileting or diapering areas must be within easy reach to encourage proper personal hygiene and to minimize the spread of disease. If supplies are not readily accessible, children and staff will be less likely to use them. Also, if staff and children must move from one area to another to reach needed supplies, they

9.1.2 The lack of toilet paper is a sign that basic provisions for toileting are not present, unless the problem is quickly fixed by staff.

are more likely to spread contamination to other areas of the classroom. It is not a major problem if a supply runs out and is immediately replaced by staff. However, if the problem is not remedied before the supply is needed again, this would be counted as a major problem. For example, if there is no soap and the teacher quickly notices and then replaces the soap, this is not a major problem. But if hours go by and the soap is still not replaced, then the problem would grow in its impact, and be considered major.

Score Indicator 1.2 "Yes" if two or more **major problems** with meeting the diapering or toileting needs of any child are observed, or if a single problem applies to the group of children (such as all children being made to sit on toilet for too long, or the floor not being cleaned and sanitized around the toilet when needed).

1.3   *Handwashing* is the most important way to reduce the spread of gastrointestinal diseases. Studies have shown that unwashed or improperly washed hands are the primary carriers of such disease.

Handwashing is defined in the "Notes for Clarification" for this item, on page 23 of the ITERS-R. (See "Handwashing Procedure," below.)

Note that handwashing does not have to be timed by observers. Rather, the observer should watch to see that the proper handwashing steps have taken place, including wetting hands, applying liquid soap, rubbing fronts and backs of hands and between fingers, and rinsing thoroughly. (If staff have long fingernails, they should be cleaned with a nail brush.) Then the hands should be dried with a disposable paper towel.

Handwashing Procedure

The handwashing procedure should be completed immediately after toileting and/or diapering and before touching other objects in the room. Handwashing at the sink should be conducted individually. For example, each child should wash hands, not having to share the sink and water, and the teacher should not consider that her hands have been washed because she washes the hands of a child. The teacher, as well as the child, should independently wash hands using the following procedure:

1. Moisten hands with warm water and use liquid soap.

2. Rub hands together for 10 seconds (sing 1 verse of "Row, Row, Row Your Boat").

3. Rinse hands free of soap under running water.

4. Dry hands with a clean, disposable paper towel or air dry with a blower.

5. Throw the used paper towel into a hands-free trash container.

Using wipes or antiseptic waterless washes does not count as a substitute for handwashing, except, as stated in the "Note for Clarification" (page 27 of the ITERS-R), with very young infants who do not have the head or body control to be safely held at the sink. (See photo 9.1.3a.)

9.1.3a Wiping the child's hands is required during the diapering procedure, and the child's hands must be washed when the change is complete.

Gloves do not take the place of handwashing. Teachers are not required to wear gloves, but gloves may reduce soil on caregivers' hands and underneath fingernails. Teachers who wear gloves during diapering/toileting must remove their gloves, dispose of them properly, and wash their hands to reduce the spread of germs. Gloves must be changed after use with each child.

Children who are diapered require the same handwashing procedure as children who use the toilet, because their hands become contaminated in the diapering area or during play. Washing at diapering time reduces the amount of all types of germs on a regular basis. Staff who assist children in toileting or diapering, or who check diapers, also need to follow correct handwashing procedures after helping each child. (See photos 9.1.3b-c.)

The handwashing procedure must minimize recontamination of hands from diapering/toileting germs that are on the sinks and faucets. Faucets that can be turned off without the use of hands (e.g., with a foot pedal or automatic sensor) are best because they minimize the recontamination of hands. If these are not available, faucets should be turned off with a disposable paper towel.

If children have their hands washed after diapering/ toileting and then immediately sit down for meals or snacks, contamination of children's hands at the toileting sink must be minimized by having children turn off the faucets with a paper towel or having adults turn off the faucets. Children do not have to wash their hands twice, once at the toileting sink and once at the food sink if one of these measures is taken to prevent the recontamination of their hands by touching the faucets.

Handwashing for this item is considered ***often neglected*** when adults' and children's hands are washed less than 50% of the time when needed. Score 1.3 "Yes"

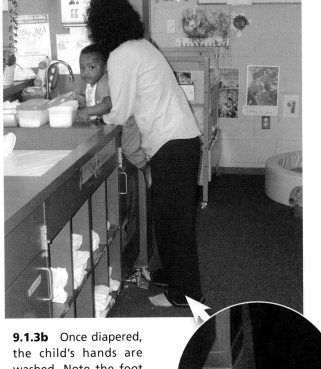

9.1.3b Once diapered, the child's hands are washed. Note the foot pedal that helps prevent spread of germs.

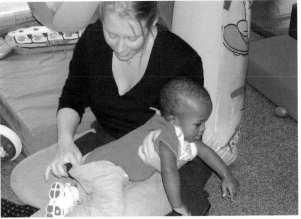

9.1.3c The staff member must wash her hands after checking the child's diaper.

9 Diapering / toileting

when most (more than 50%) of adult or child hands are not washed when required for diapering/toileting.

To gather the evidence needed to score this indicator, keep a chart as you observe handwashing by children and staff so it is clear at the end of the observation how many children and staff washed their hands properly. Handwashing is not considered properly completed if the child or adult touches objects, such as toys, furniture, door knobs, or people after diapering/toileting, but before handwashing.

It is not necessary to observe every handwashing instance if many take place throughout the observation. A sample can be used, as long as it represents the regular practice of each staff member and of the children. Watch the handwashing until a clearly representative sample is observed. After that point, any handwashing that represents new information should be added to the sample. For example, new cases would be added to the sample when a new teacher or additional children arrive in the classroom who were not observed earlier, or if children use the toilet independently, whereas they had been supervised earlier in the day.

Handwashing for adults should be observed and tallied separately from handwashing for children. To determine whether the number of proper handwashings observed is less than 50%, divide the number of handwashings completed by the number that were required. In the following chart, a check mark (√) represents proper handwashing and an X represents improper handwashing.

Chart 2:
Tracking handwashing

Diaper change, check, or toileting

	1	2	3	4	5	6	7	8	9	10	11	12	13	14	15	16
Child	√	√	√	√		X	X	X	√	√	X	√		√		
Adult	√	√	√	X	√	√	√	X	√	√	√	√	√	√		

In this example, 11 instances where children needed to have their hands washed were observed. Of these, proper handwashing was done in 7 of the cases, which is 64% of the time (7 divided by 11). For the adults, there were 14 instances observed when handwashing was required, and of these, it was completed properly in 12 cases, or 86% of the time (12 divided by 14). Note that there were some times when adults needed to wash their hands but this was not required for the children (e.g., after checking diapers), so the "Child" boxes in the chart were left blank.

In this example, because both adults' and children's hands were washed more than 50% of the time when needed, Indicator 1.3 would be scored "No."

1.4   *Inadequate supervision,* as defined in the "Notes for Clarification" for this item on page 23 of the ITERS-R, means that staff do not monitor to protect the children or ensure that sanitary procedures (e.g., handwashing) are carried out. For diapering, inadequate supervision means that staff do not pay sufficient attention to the child, for example, by leaving a child on the diapering table alone for any amount of time, or by not cleaning the child adequately to minimize the spread of germs. For toileting/toilet training, staff do not keep close watch on children using the toilet to ensure that the child is secure, toilet paper is used, toilets are flushed, or hands are washed as needed; or staff do not notice when children are using the toileting area inappropriately (such as splashing water, unrolling all the toilet paper, playing in the toilet, or rough-housing) when they should be using the toilet, or not be in the area at all.

Close supervision is required for all children in the ITERS-R age groups, even for any 2-year-olds who may be able to complete the toileting procedure somewhat independently. The closeness of the required supervision will depend on the ages and abilities of the children being observed, with closer, more helpful supervision required for younger or less able children. If any child is inadequately supervised during the observation, Indicator 1.4 must be scored "Yes."

To score whether the supervision is **unpleasant** requires close observation of diapering/toileting, with an emphasis on what the adult does and the child's response. However, it must be noted that in some cases a child's response to diapering/toileting might be negative, even though the adult is being gentle and appropriately responsive. Infants and toddlers have greatly varying personalities, and these normal differences often show themselves in the child's response to diapering, toilet training, and toileting. For example, one very young baby might cry and show distress when placed on the diapering table, obviously disliking the removal of the diaper. Another baby might show delight at the same experience, using the time when free of the diaper to flex the legs and practice gross motor skills. Some toddlers may not care at all who changes their diaper, while a particular child may refuse to be changed except by her favorite teacher. Some children are eager to become toilet trained, while others fight the idea.

Pleasant supervision means that staff accept these differences, responding sensitively to the child's preferences to the extent possible, handling children gently, reassuring them when needed, and taking advantage of the personal time associated with working with one child at a time. If a child dislikes diapering or toileting, the adult completes what is needed without prolonging the child's distress and by remaining calm and accepting throughout.

Unpleasant supervision means that staff are observed using any of the following:

- responding in a harsh or negative manner verbally or physically to any child about diapering, toilet training, or toileting;

- using rigid control or harsh treatment to manage the children during diapering/toileting routines, such as embarrassing or teasing children, yelling at them, handling them roughly, or using any physical punishment;

- not providing help when children request or obviously need it, but rather belittling children and making them feel incompetent because they need help;

- responding to children's diapering/toileting needs or experiences in a way that the children would interpret negatively, such as complaining about lifting a child to the diapering table or commenting negatively about a soiled diaper; or

- putting undue pressure on children to be toilet-trained, such as forcing children to use the toilet when they do not want to or making them sit on the toilet and "try" for a long time.

Any unpleasant treatment of any child or lapses in supervision that endanger a child in any way require that Indicator 1.4 be scored "Yes."

9 Diapering / toileting

3.1 When staff complete the diapering/toileting procedure consistently, it is easier to maintain the necessary sanitary conditions for both the children and the staff. Following the same procedures correctly, over and over again, turns good practices into a habit. Staff should not complete diapering on their own unless they have been trained in the proper procedure to use.

For information on the requirements of **sanitary conditions** see Indicator 1.1.

To score this indicator, track diapering as described in Indicator 1.1. If 50% or more of the boxes on the tracking chart are scored with checks (√), then 3.1 is scored "Yes."

The observer should keep track of toileting to ensure that specific procedures are practiced. It is important for observers to check the children's toileting area several times during the observation to be sure sanitary conditions are maintained, such as toilets flushed, spills cleaned up, trash removed from floors, and sinks cleaned. If there are major problems with any procedure that lead to inadequate sanitary procedures being followed more than half of the time (such as the same sink usually being used for toileting as for other purposes, without being sanitized; potty chairs rarely being cleaned and sanitized properly; toilets being flushed less than half the time after each use; floor left contaminated around toilet without being cleaned and sanitized), then this indicator would be scored "No." If some lapses are observed but constitute less than 50% of the sanitary procedures for toileting, score Indicator 3.1 "Yes."

If there is a combination of toileting and diapering used, sanitary conditions must be maintained, at least half the time. If diapering is done more than toileting, consider diapering more heavily than toileting in determining the score. The converse would be true if toileting is done most frequently.

3.2 See Indicator 1.2 for the requirements of **diapering/toileting needs. Met in an appropriate manner** means that expectations are appropriate for all children in the group, and necessary provisions are available and used.

Score Indicator 3.2 "Yes" if no major problems with meeting diapering/toileting needs are observed. If a single problem applies to the group of children (such as all children being made to sit on toilet for too long; floor not cleaned and sanitized around toilet when needed), 3.2 would be scored "No." If there are no major problems affecting the group of children and, in at least 75% of the instances observed, expectations are appropriate and necessary provisions are available and used, score 3.2 "Yes."

3.3 Watch carefully during diapering/toileting times to make sure that children and staff wash their hands properly. If less than 75% of children or staff wash their hands when needed, credit cannot be given (score Indicator 3.3 "No"). Keep track of how many handwashings are needed and the number completed properly, as shown in Chart 2 on page 118. The observer should watch a sample of the times when handwashing is needed until evidence is obtained to document the usual practice (as explained in 1.3). If more than one staff member handles diapering/toileting during the observation, collect evidence on all staff. Consider adults' and children's handwashings separately when calculating percentages. Both must complete handwashing at least 75% of the time when needed. For example, if adults wash hands 80% of the time and children wash hand 50%, then this indicator should be scored "No."

3.4 *Adequate supervision* means that staff monitor to protect the children and ensure that sanitary procedures (e.g., handwashing) are carried out. For diapering, adequate supervision means that staff pay sufficient attention to the child, for example, by keeping one hand on the child who is on the diapering table at all times or by cleaning the child so that the spread of germs is minimized. For toileting/toilet training, staff keep close watch on a child using the toilet to ensure that the child is secure, toilet paper is used, the toilet is flushed, and hands are washed as needed. Staff closely supervise children in the toileting area to prevent children from inappropriate or dangerous activity.

To give credit for this indicator, none of the *supervision* can be unpleasant. However, supervision can be *neutral* in its affect (for example, staff are not unpleasant, but they are not particularly pleasant; warmth is not obvious, but neither is harshness or coldness); it is not required that supervision be pleasant to meet the requirements of this indicator at the minimal level.

5.1 As noted in the "Notes for Clarification" (on page 23 of the ITERS-R), *usually* means 75% of the time. In this case, it is required that sanitary conditions discussed in Indicators 1.1 and 3.1 are maintained in 75% of the instances observed. To score, use the same tracking systems and decision rules discussed earlier for this item.

5.2 Sanitary conditions are *easy to maintain* when the area (e.g., floors and walls) is uncluttered and made of easy-to-clean materials. Equipment (such as toilets, sinks, and diapering surfaces) must also be easy-to-clean. There is warm running water in the area and easily accessible supplies, such as liquid soap, toilet paper, paper towels, bleach-water solution, and gloves and wipes for adults. Replacement supplies are also readily accessible as needed. When these provisions for sanitary conditions are present, staff and children are less likely to contaminate other areas of the classroom during the completion of diapering/toileting routines.

Since potty chairs are a health hazard, they should be avoided for general use. In the rare case when a special need requires the use of a potty chair, it may only be used for the particular child, and it must be cleaned and disinfected after each use (as described in Indicator 1.1). If potty chairs are for general use, score Indicator 5.1 "No."

5.3 The *provisions* considered in this indicator include the equipment and supplies needed by the children and staff to complete toileting or diapering. *Convenient and accessible* means that the provisions are easy to reach and use with minimal difficulty. This convenience and accessibility applies to those who must use the provisions. For example, a staff member diapering a baby needs access to the diaper, the trash can, and so forth, but the baby does not. (See photos in the diapering procedure on pages 111-113 for examples.) The staff member also needs to have access to a sink where the baby's hands can be washed without difficulty. A 2-year-old who is being toilet trained needs easy access to the toilet paper, and so does the adult helping the child. Accessibility requirements for individuals with disabilities is addressed in Item 1, Indoor space, and not in this indicator; adaptive equipment is considered in Item 2, Furnishings for care and learning.

To be credited as convenient, provisions cannot lead to other difficulties for staff and children. For example, if steps to a sink are unsteady and pose a safety hazard when used, they would not be considered convenient. (See photos 9.5.3a-b.) If diaper storage is low enough for toddlers to reach to get their own diapers, but

9 Diapering / toileting

9.5.3a These steps may be a safety hazard for unsteady toddlers, so cannot be considered "convenient."

9.5.3b A low step to the lower sink is safer for this toddler to use.

9.5.3c A wide step helps two-year-olds feel more secure when using toilet

the children pull things out inappropriately, then this would not be considered convenient, although it is accessible to the children. If the changing table causes difficulties, for example, the steps are accessible to children during non-diapering times and become a safety hazard, or children play on a low diapering surface, then the provision would not get credit for being convenient. In addition, any safety hazards would be evaluated in Item 11, Safety practices.

To score, the observer should observe whether:

- The changing table is comfortable for staff to use, as described in the note for this indicator on page 23 of the ITERS-R. Steps for children are not required, but they are preferred when there are older (heavier) toddlers or if staff have difficulty lifting children to the table surface. Lower changing tables that children can access independently and that allow staff to sit while changing children are also acceptable if sanitary procedures are maintained.

- Accommodations make sinks or toilets easy to use (such as steps or a platform near the sink so that children can wash hands independently or with staff help, or steps near the toilet so that children can seat themselves securely). (See photo 9.5.3c.) Child-sized toilets and sinks fulfill this requirement, and if used, should also be credited in Indicator 7.2.

- Handrails or other adaptations are provided for children with disabilities, as needed.

- Diapering and toileting areas are located in the room used by the children.

- A separate sink is used *only* for diapering/toileting so that sanitation issues related to multiple uses of the same sink are not a problem.

- The diapering/toileting sink is within easy reach of diapering surface and is close to the toilet to reduce chances of contamination.

Indicator

9.5.4a

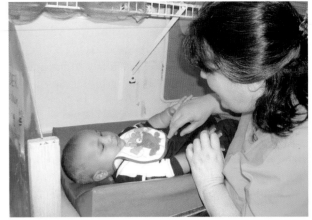

9.5.4b

9.5.4a-b Pleasant interaction between staff and children make the process more enjoyable for everyone.

- Faucets and flushing mechanisms are easy to manage.

- Supplies, such as toilet paper, paper towels, and liquid soap, are easy to reach and use.

- Clean clothes and diapering supplies are within easy reach of staff in the diapering area.

- Children's access to diapering/toileting areas can be controlled, especially access to toilets by mobile babies or toddlers.

To score, observe diapering/toileting carefully, considering both adults' needs and characteristics of the children. When the provisions allow staff or children to complete diapering/toileting reasonably easily, without undue difficulty, give credit (score "Yes") for Indicator 5.3. Whether the provisions encourage appropriate independence for toddlers should also be considered. Perfection is not required, but there should be no problems with provisions that interfere with efficient and sanitary diapering/toileting.

5.4 *Pleasant staff-child interactions* means that interactions during diapering/ toileting are never unpleasant (see Indicator 1.4) and only neutral in unusual cases (see Indicator 3.4). (See photos 9.5.4a-b.) To give credit for Indicator 5.4, any staff member helping with diapering/toileting should be observed paying positive attention to the children during the routine, by showing warmth, patience, encouragement, and support. The observer should watch the children's responses to the interactions of the staff and look for relaxed children who are not anxious and who seem to trust the staff to understand their needs. If the vast majority of interactions are positive, with only a few neutral and no negative interactions, score this indicator "Yes."

7.1 For this indicator, it is required that the sanitary conditions described in Indicators 1.1 and 3.1 be maintained, with no lapses. To score, use the same tracking systems and decision rules discussed earlier for this item.

7.2 *Providing child-sized toilets and low sinks* encourages children to complete their diapering or toileting routines more independently. In addition, there is less physical stress on staff who do not have to lift or support children as they use equipment. It is also easier to maintain the health and safety conditions for children when child-sized equipment is used. For example, if no steps are needed, children will not fall from steps, steps will not present extra cleaning challenges, and on the whole, children will be less likely to have accidents when they can reach the provisions easily.

This indicator may be scored "NA" if all children in the group are non-mobile, never need to use toilets, or are too young to benefit from having access to a child-sized sink. Child-sized toilets would only be considered applicable to older toddlers who are being toilet trained or use the toilet (about 18-30 months of age). Child-sized sinks would only be considered applicable to children who can stand well on their own, usually 12 months of age or older.

9.7.3 This two-year-old manages much of toileting on her own, when supervised by staff.

To score Indicator 7.2 "Yes," toilets and sinks must be smaller than adult-sized equipment and accessible to at least 75% of the children with no extra adult help (such as lifting) or adaptations (such as steps or toilet seats), unless required by the special needs of a child with a disability.

7.3 **Self-help** means that children can manage tasks on their own to the extent possible, with little adult assistance. The extent to which children are able to help themselves in diapering and toileting routines will depend on a variety of factors, such as their ages and abilities, the convenience of the provisions, and the difficulty of managing their clothing. All children within the ITERS-R age group (birth–30 months of age) will require substantial adult help or supervision, but even babies can be encouraged to help themselves to the extent possible. For example, a young baby might be able to hold up his head and stretch out his arms to have his hands washed or lift his legs to help with diaper changes. An older baby will be able to do more, such as helping to pull her legs out of her clothing or standing up to have her clothing pulled up. Toddlers will be able to do even more, such as help to adjust clothing, come to the diapering area when requested, or rub their hands together during handwashing.

To score Indicator 7.3, the observer must determine:

- the extent to which self-help is possible for the children, based on their ages and abilities,

- whether the environment is set up to encourage self-help,

- whether staff teach children the required skills as needed, and

- whether staff follow up on their teaching by supervising adequately and helping when needed (for example, reminding the toddler to flush toilet, wash hands, use paper towels, and guiding and supervising closely to be sure he or she does).

Credit can be given for this indicator (score "Yes") when children appear to manage their toileting routines as independently as they should be able to, considering their ages and abilities. (See photo 9.7.3.) If staff help far too much or too little, or if the basic provisions required to allow children to handle diapering and toileting routines are not present, credit should not be given (score "No").

10 Health practices

General information about this item

This item considers health-related issues other than those required for toileting/diapering, meals/snacks, and nap, which are handled in the respective items. Issues related to these three basic routines are not considered when scoring this item. Instead, all other important health practices used with the group of children to evaluate the quality of the general health practices must be examined.

In scoring this item it is important to listen and watch very carefully for examples of how **staff act to cut down on the spread of germs** throughout the day, in health areas not related to diapering/toileting, meals/snacks or nap. Some examples of the type of health related practices to consider are provided as examples in the item. More extensive examples include:

Keeping spaces, materials, and equipment clean:

- All surfaces that come into contact with potentially infectious bodily fluids (such as blood, saliva, vomit, "spit-up," urine, feces, oozing from wounds or infections, mucus) are cleaned up and disinfected (with a bleach and water solution) immediately, and children's and staff's hands are washed properly without contaminating any other surfaces. (See photo 10A.) The possibility of contamination from bloodborne pathogens, such as the hepatitis B virus, HIV, or hepatitis C must be minimized. Since it is unknown whether any person is a carrier of these diseases, precautions must be taken on the assumption that each person might be infected.

10A The floor is immediately cleaned and sanitized to avoid the spread of germs in "spit-up."

- Special care is given to keeping floors in infant rooms clean, for example, by removing outside shoes or by wearing shoe covers.

- Toys that have been soiled or mouthed are set aside to be washed and sanitized before they are offered again to children. (See photos 10B-D.)

10B Mouthing of toys is typical for babies who are discovering about objects.

10C When the baby's interests turn elsewhere, the mouthed toy is removed.

10D The toy will be washed and sanitized before being used again.

- Pacifiers and teethers are not shared by children, and, if contaminated, they are washed with soap and water (not just rinsed) before being returned to the child.

- Toothbrushes, if used by toddlers, are stored to avoid contamination (brushes not touching and stored in a container to prevent touching other surfaces), and air dried.

- Toothpaste for each toddler is uncontaminated, for example, by using individual tubes or putting pea-sized dots of paste onto an individual piece of clean paper or the back of a small paper cup for each child to use. Toothpaste containers are not contaminated by contact with multiple toothbrushes.

- A hands-free trash container is used, for example, one with a foot pedal, which minimizes contamination of hands. (See photo 10E.) Separate trash containers are used for disposing of diapers and for other purposes by children as well as adults.

- Individual paper towels, disposable tissues, and liquid soap are accessible. No towels, tissues, or wash cloths are used by more than one child or staff member.

- Dirty floors and play surfaces are cleaned up immediately.

- Indoor and outdoor areas used for children are free of animal contamination.

- Dress-up clothes are cleaned on a regular basis and whenever soiled.

10E Children's hands are contaminated when they use this trash can.

Ensuring proper handwashing:

Proper handwashing procedures are followed when needed (do not consider handwashing for diapering/toileting and meals/snacks in this item). Handwashing is required of all staff and children and of visitors who spend a substantial amount of time in the classroom, either working with children or coming into contact with many objects and surfaces. Using gloves, wipes, or antiseptic waterless washes does not count as a substitute for handwashing. If handwashing is required on the playground (after wiping noses, for example), use of a wipe is advised until the hands can be properly washed. Although this cannot be given credit as handwashing when needed, if handwashing were carried out properly at all other times, it would not affect the score.

The hands of babies should be washed under running water unless the babies do not have the head and body control required for safety at the sink. For these babies, wipes are an acceptable substitute for handwashing.

Proper handwashing for children and staff requires that both hands be washed with liquid soap and rinsed thoroughly under warm running water for about 10 seconds (sing one verse of "Row, Row, Row Your Boat"). If staff have long fingernails, a nail brush should be used. Hands should be dried with individual paper towels that are not shared or air-dried with a blower.

Examples of when proper handwashing is needed include:

Upon arrival in the classroom:

- upon arrival in the classroom (for both children and staff, and parents if they stay),

- when returning to the classroom from outdoor play, or

- after staff have been working with another group of children in another classroom.

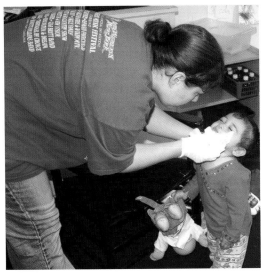

10F

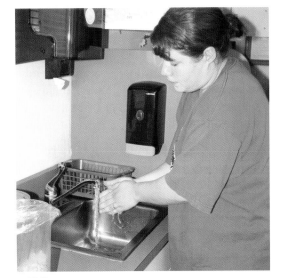

10G

10F-G [above]   After wiping noses, handwashing is needed.

10H-I [right]   After cleaning saliva from play equipment, handwashing is needed.

After messy or sand or water play:

- before and after water play (not needed if water containers are not shared, and if individual water containers are emptied and sanitized after use by one child),

- after using sand, indoors or outdoors,

- after outdoor play,

- after messy play, such as painting or gluing, or

- after messy sensory activities.

To avoid spreading diseases through bodily fluids or skin contact:

- after sneezing or coughing when hands are contaminated,

- after wiping noses (See photos 10F-G.),

- before and after applying sunscreen or lotion to a child if the child has open sores or a skin condition that might be contagious,

- before and after dealing with cuts, scrapes, or other health needs,

- after cleaning up or touching spilled bodily fluid such as drool, "spit-up," blood, etc. (See photos 10H-I.),

- after handling pacifiers or teethers,

- after handling mouthed toys, or

- after changing soiled sheets or covers on furnishings.

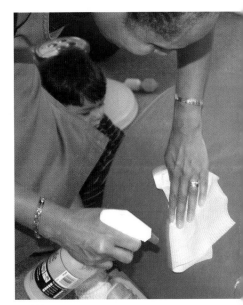

10H

After touching contaminated objects or pets

- after touching pets, insects, or other animals,

- after emptying the trash or touching contaminated trashcan lids,

- after wiping up spills on the floor, or

- after using anything poisonous, such as insecticides or cleaning products.

10I

10 Health practices

To score, observers should be aware of times that cleaning, sanitizing, and hand-washing are carried out when needed. This means that the observer should watch and listen. For example, observers should listen for coughing or sneezing by the children and staff, or watch for noses that need wiping to see that the proper procedures are carried out. Notes should be taken on the score sheet to indicate when needed cleaning or sanitizing has been ignored. It is equally important, however, to recognize when it has been carried out properly.

To collect the necessary information on handwashing, it helps to keep track of whether it was or was not completed as needed. A small chart, such as Chart 1 below, should be made to record when handwashing was needed, and whether or not it was carried out properly.

Chart 1:
Keeping track of handwashing

Times when needed:	Adult		Child	
	YES	No	YES	NO
• Upon arrival in the classroom/ When re-entering classroom after outdoor play	✓✓✓✓	X X X	✓✓ ✓✓✓	X X X X X X
• After messy or sand/ water play	✓✓		✓✓✓✓ ✓✓✓✓	X X X X X X
• After dealing with bodily fluids (e.g., running noses, sneezes) or making significant skin contact (e.g., applying lotions, medications)	✓✓✓✓ ✓✓✓✓		✓✓✓✓	X X X X X X
• After touching contaminated objects (trashcan lids, the floor) or pets	✓✓✓✓ ✓✓	X X X X X	✓✓	X X X X X X X X X X

A closer look at each indicator

1.1 ***Staff do not act to cut down on the spread of germs*** means that staff rarely do any of the procedures listed in the "General Information" section for this item. Do not score indicator 1.1 "Yes" unless serious health problems are observed and staff give very little attention to health requirements, such as those listed.

1.2 Since inhaling second-hand cigarette smoke has been shown to be harmful, children and non-smoking adults should not be exposed to smoking. In addition, no tobacco or waste from smoking should be accessible to children.

Smoking is allowed in child care areas means that either smoking (in any form, such as cigarettes, pipes, or cigars) is permitted in spaces used by children, indoors or outdoors, or that there are signs that smoking occurs in these spaces. Observe to see if there are signs that smoking occurs in areas used by children. For example, look for ashtrays or cigarette butts in spaces used by children. No cigarette

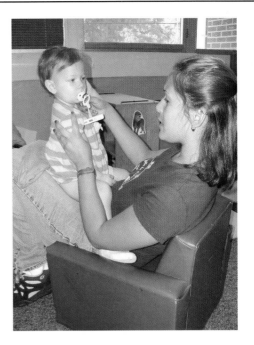

10.1.2 [above]   There should be no signs of smoking or smoking waste found in areas used by children.

10.1.3 [right]   Staff check the temperature of a sick child and keep her separate from others until parents pick her up.

butts should be found on playgrounds used by children or spaces they use at any time while supervised on-site by program staff. (See photo 10.1.2.)

If any signs of smoking or tobacco use are observed in areas used by children, score this indicator "Yes."

If no signs are observed, ask staff whether smoking is allowed in any of the areas used by children, indoors or out. If the answer is "Yes," score this indicator "Yes."

1.3   ***Contagious illness*** means those illnesses that can be passed from one person to another. Examples include respiratory infections, such as coughs, colds, influenza; gastrointestinal illnesses that can cause diarrhea, stomach aches, vomiting; and other communicable diseases, such as chicken pox, mumps, measles, skin diseases, and polio. Also included in this category are nuisance infestations, such as lice and scabies. Although these are not diseases, they are treated similarly to avoid their spread. Some diseases have certain periods during which they are ***contagious,*** meaning the time when they can be transferred to another person. Once this period is over, symptoms may persist but the disease will no longer be "catching." In other cases, a disease is communicable throughout the time the person is ill. Some diseases are contagious before symptoms actually appear, and so staff may not realize that the disease is being transmitted within the group.

Although it is sometimes difficult to decide whether a child should be excluded from the program because of illness, staff can reduce the illness rate among children (and among themselves) by ***removing sick children from contact with other children***, and checking with a health care provider for guidance as needed. (See photo 10.1.3.) The "Note for Clarification" for Indicator 1.3 (page 25 of the ITERS-R), provides the primary reasons for excluding a child from the group. If children become ill while attending the program, they should be removed from contact with others until a health care provider indicates the child is free of a contagious illness.

10 Health practices

To score this indicator, the observer should *first* look for evidence to see whether or not the requirement has been met. For example, if a child who is obviously sick (such as with high temperature, diarrhea, vomiting, or unidentified rash) is present in the group, and staff take <u>no</u> action to isolate the child, score this indicator "Yes." Staff must remove the child from contact with other children until the parents are able to pick the child up. If staff contact the parents to pick the child up but do not remove the sick child, then score the indicator "Yes."

If no obvious evidence can be observed to score the indicator, staff should be asked general questions such as, "How do you handle children who are sick?" These questions usually elicit the information needed to score.

Score Indicator 1.3 "Yes" if it is observed that children are allowed to remain in contact with other children when showing symptoms of a contagious illness. Note that the symptoms of common colds (runny nose, slight fever, sneezing, or coughing) do not usually require exclusion. The presence of diarrhea, on the other hand, does require exclusion. Score "No" if staff are observed carrying out the necessary practices or if it is reported that they do so when needed.

3.1   Requirements for ***staff act to cut down on the spread of germs*** are discussed in the "General Information" section and in the examples for this indicator in the ITERS-R for this item. (See photos 10.3.1a-b.) Handwashing issues are addressed in Indicator 3.2 and not in this indicator.

Usually means that staff cut down on the spread of germs far more often than not. If staff take action to cut down on the spread of germs without many lapses (completed at least 75% of the times needed) during the observation, then score Indicator 3.1 "Yes."

If many lapses occur (more than 25% of the times when needed), or if there are any major problems, such as spilled bodily fluid not being cleaned up immediately or signs of animal contamination in children's play spaces, score 3.1 "No."

10.3.1a [above]   Wiping noses is part of cutting down on the spread of germs.

10.3.1b [right]   Proper disposal of the tissue is another requirement. Note the hands-free covered trash can that reduces spread of germs.

3.2 Because ***handwashing*** at meals/snacks and after diapering/toileting is handled in other items, score Indicator 3.2 based on all other handwashing required, as described in the General Information section of this item on page 125.

Give credit for 3.2 only if it is observed that ***hands of children and staff are washed 75% of the time when needed***. Look across all categories listed in the General Information section for this item to determine if staff and children are properly washing their hands when needed. (See photo 10.3.2a.) Make sure to notice when attempts are made to reduce contamination and as well as times when no action is taken. If either children's or staff members' hands are washed less than 75% of the time when needed, do not give credit for 3.2 (score "No").

10.3.2 Handwashing is needed after wiping the child's nose.

The observer should keep track of handwashing for children and staff separately, documenting when handwashing is properly carried out and when it is not. Do not credit incomplete examples of handwashing, such as when hands are only rinsed with water, when only one hand is washed, or when staff consider their hands washed when they help children wash their hands. Use of a tracking system, such as that shown in Chart 1, is helpful in determining the score. The 75% requirement applies separately for adults and for children. If hands are not washed 75% of the time when needed in either group, score "No."

3.3 ***Extra clothes for children*** should be provided, ***and children changed*** when they become wet or soiled in any way that causes health concerns. (See photos 10.3.3a-c.) Clothes should also be changed if the child's clothes are inappropriate for any reason, for example, they are too warm for outdoor play on a surprisingly hot day or too tight for comfort. Usually programs ask that parents supply extra clothes for their child and that they replenish the supply as needed. However, if no clothes have been provided by parents, it is up to the program to keep a supply that can be used in an emergency. To give credit for this indicator, children must be changed when needed for their health, whether parents have supplied clothing or not. This does not mean that a child with a little paint on her shirt must have her shirt changed, because the paint is not a serious health hazard. But children with very wet bibs, shirts, or pants, or whose clothes have been contaminated in any way, must be changed. Obviously the temperature of the setting, the extent

10.3.3a This child's clothing needs to be changed after lunch.

10.3.3b Staff help parents remember to provide plenty of extra clothes for their toddlers.

10.3.3c Toddlers can do a lot to help with clothing changes.

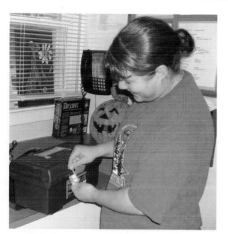

10.3.4a Medications are kept in a locked box, and refrigerated if necessary.

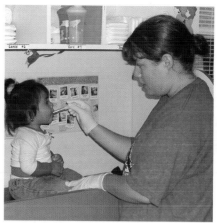

10.3.4b Staff are careful to follow the healthcare provider's instructions.

10.3.4c The dose, when administered, and by whom are recorded before locking medication away.

of wetness, or the nature of the soil will determine whether a child should be changed.

Score 3.3 "No" if no extra clothes are available for any child, either supplied by parents or the program, or if a child is not changed when needed. If in doubt about whether clothing is available, the question provided for this indicator on page 25 of the ITERS-R should be asked during the staff interview.

3.4 ***Medications*** include both prescription and non-prescription drugs. To help in scoring, a "Note for Clarification" is provided for this indicator on page 25 of the ITERS-R. As the Note indicates, *all* medications must be given only when prescribed for a particular child by a physician. This means that even non-prescription medications that are routinely given by parents, or by program staff with the parent's permission, must be prescribed for a particular child by the child's health care provider. (See photos 10.3.4a-d.)

To score, first determine during the staff interview whether any children in care ever require medications that must be administered by the staff. ("Do you or any other staff member ever give medicine to a child?") If staff do not ever give medication to any child, or if there is no child in care requiring medication, score "NA."

If staff administer medication to the children, ask questions during the staff interview to determine how this is handled. ("Who gives the medication? Are there any requirements or rules that must be followed? What is the procedure for giving medicine to a child?") (See photo 10.3.4e.)

If answers indicate that medicines are prescribed by the physician, given according to the physician's instructions from the original container, and recorded when given, score "Yes."

5.1 ***Children are properly cared for*** means that they are dressed to protect their health and safety, kept reasonably neat and clean, and the "little extras" are done as needed, such as putting lotion on chapped cheeks if approved by parents. The examples provided in the item show the range of care considered

10.3.4d Handwashing is required before and after administering medication.

10.3.4e [right] Staff must be fully informed about how to administer different types of medications.

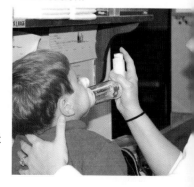

10.5.1a Bibs protect babies who drool.

10.5.1b When weather requires special clothing it should be provided so children can play outdoors.

10.5.1c Staff make sure children are protected while outdoors.

in the indicator. More specific information to consider when scoring includes the following:

To be *dressed properly*, children should wear clothing that allows freedom of movement while protecting health and safety. Outside, children should be dressed appropriately for all weather conditions. During the summer, children should have clothing that will keep them as cool as possible, and use hats and sunscreen when they go outdoors. If children go outside on a rainy day, they should be dressed in boots or raincoats. If the children do get wet outside, and it is cold or chilly, they should be changed into dry, warm clothes when they get inside (considered in scoring Indicator 3.3). When it is cold outside, children should be dressed in coats, mittens, scarves, and winter hats or caps as necessary. If the weather is snowy, boots should be worn to keep the children's feet warm and dry. (See photos 10.5.1a-c.)

Indoors, children should be neither too warm nor too cold. When clothes become wet, they should be changed (considered in scoring Indicator 3.3).

If shoes are *not* worn, surfaces must be safe for bare feet. The indoor floor covering or outdoor areas should be clear of sharp objects, extremely hot surfaces should be avoided, and there should be no other risks, such as a risk of contracting hookworm, getting bitten by insects.

Observers cannot judge whether children are dressed properly based solely on the their own comfort indoors or out. Observers generally move around much less than the children, so children tend to remain warmer. In addition, children can often adjust better to warmer temperatures than some adults can. To score this indicator, observers should look to see whether the children appear to be comfortable and are protected to ensure their health and safety. Observers should listen to hear if children are complaining of being too cold or hot and see if providers are taking action to make them more comfortable, such as putting on warmer clothes or adjusting the room temperature.

If any child lacks needed clothing, staff must be able to supply the child with the required clothing. If it is *observed* that *any* child is not dressed properly, and supplemental clothing is not provided, score 5.1 "No."

Other issues to consider are included in the "Notes for Clarification" for this indicator on page 25 of the ITERS-R. The observer should look to see whether staff

10.5.2a After art, toddlers will need some cleaning-up.

10.5.2b Hands and faces require washing.

generally notice when children need help with their personal grooming and follow through as needed. The amount of help required from staff will vary depending on the ages and abilities of the children and the complexity of what is needed, both indoors and outdoors.

To score "Yes" for this indicator, staff must *usually* take action when needed during the observation period. Watch to see, for example, if staff help a child put on a smock before a messy art activity, put a bib on a drooling infant, replace hair clips that fall out, tie shoes, button or snap clothing, or comb or brush hair as needed. In addition, observe whether hats and sunscreen are used as required in the "Note for Clarification."

If *all* children are observed to be well cared for to meet their comfort, health, and safety needs throughout the observation, with few exceptions, score Indicator 5.1 "Yes."

5.2 Information about observing required handwashing is provided in the General Information section for this item. **Consistently washed** means that the handwashing procedure is done correctly for both children and adults at all times required, with very few lapses. (See photos 10.5.2a-e.)

5.3 Staff who clearly care for their own health needs while in the presence of children are *good models of health practices*. Children learn much about how to care for their health when they watch how staff take care of their needs.

Score this indicator "Yes" if it is observed that staff generally show children that they care for their own health by doing the following:

- washing hands as needed,
- dressing comfortably for the tasks needed as part of the job,
- keeping fingernails short and clean,
- eating only healthful foods in front of children,
- drinking healthful beverages when children can see,
- being active and getting exercise,
- brushing teeth after meals,
- not smoking,
- checking and flushing toilets in the children's bathroom,

10.5.2c After nose wiping both adult and child will require handwashing.

10.5.2d The adult first helps the child.

• protecting clothing when needed, such as by wearing smocks, using "burping cloths," and

• appearing to be reasonably well-rested.

If staff obviously give children the message that they do not try to care for their own health, score Indicator 5.3 "No."

10.5.2e She follows by washing her own hands.

5.4 **_Sand used for outdoor play_** includes any outdoor material that that has been provided for children to dig in, scoop, or pour. Usually sand is provided, but other materials (such as finely ground, non-splintery wood chips), should be considered if children are encouraged to play with them, either by using toys provided with the material or by the staff's verbal encouragement. **_Clean_** means that there is no obvious contamination of the material, such as animal droppings, mold, stagnant water, or trash of any kind. **_Covered when not in use_** requires that the sand (or other material) is covered to protect it, especially from animals, when the program is not in operation. This can be done by covering the sand after the last use of the day, or after every use by a group of children.

To score, the observer should look at any sand used outdoors by the children in the group being observed. This includes sand or sand substitutes in sensory tables, containers, fall zones in which children are allowed to dig, as well as in traditional sand boxes. If necessary, ask staff whether sand is used with the children outdoors, where the sand can be found, and whether and how it is covered when not in use. Score "NA" if no sand is used for play outdoors. Score "No" if the sand (or alternate material) is uncovered when not in use. Score "Yes" if sand is clean and covered when not in use.

7.1 **_Health practices_** considered in this indicator include all children's personal care, such as handwashing, putting on or removing clothes, keeping clean, brushing teeth, caring for hair, or wiping noses.

Manage independently means that children are encouraged to do as much as they can to carry out health practices by themselves. For the youngest children, staff can call their attention to what is being done and encourage them to do whatever possible. It is important to note, however, that infants and toddlers should be encouraged, but not pushed or hurried, in developing self-help skills.

10.7.1a [above] Toddlers are closely supervised to ensure they learn to carry out handwashing.

10.7.1b [right] Washing hands side-by-side allows staff to model how it's done correctly.

Infants and toddlers can be ***encouraged to manage health practices independently,*** either by having staff show them how to complete the actual health practices properly, or by using educational materials about the health practices with the children.

Staff can guide children to complete health-related tasks, follow up to be sure the tasks are completed, and provide help as needed. (See photos 10.7.1a-b.) Examples include:

- Staff teach children to wash their hands by doing the procedure for them initially and then helping them, reminding them to "make bubbles" and sing "Row, Row, Row Your Boat" or count to 10 while they wash. It is unlikely that infants and toddlers will be able to wash hands independently without close staff supervision.

- Staff talk about nose wiping as they do it for infants, help toddlers go to get their own tissues and use them, follow up to complete the job, and then ensure proper handwashing.

- Staff put smocks near the art and messy play areas for toddlers, and remind or help children to use them.

- Staff encourage children to help in dressing ("Push your arm through the sleeve." "Help pull up your pants.") and show children how to fasten clothes or put on or take off clothing.

Examples of teaching materials used with children to encourage independence in health practices include:

Displayed posters or pictures where children can see them:

- a handwashing poster next to the sink that shows pictures of the handwashing steps (with or without printed words),

- posters or pictures of familiar healthful foods or children eating healthful foods, or

- pictures showing children putting on their shoes and socks.

Books used with or by the children on topics such as:

- eating or cooking healthful foods,
- familiar objects used in personal care, such as a brush and comb, bib, apron, or appropriate clothing for various weather conditions,
- toilet training, or
- familiar personal care routine sequences, such as bathing, going to bed, eating, handwashing.

Play materials and activities:

- nutritious play fruits and vegetables in the pretend play area,
- bathing baby dolls or washing doll clothes in soapy water,
- simple puzzles and picture matching games that show healthful personal care routines or healthful foods, or
- singing about handwashing or toothbrushing ("This is the way we wash our hands," etc.)

To score Indicator 7.1 "Yes," there must be evidence of teacher help and follow-through. In addition, evidence of some teaching through activities or materials must be observed or reported by the staff.

7.2 A score of "NA" is permitted for programs open 6 hours or less per day that enroll toddlers or if no toddlers are enrolled in a full-day program.

If an older child with a disability is enrolled, and all the other children are infants, the appropriateness of this indicator will depend on the child's abilities, not necessarily on the child's age. The definition and age requirement for **toddlers** is provided in the "Explanation of Terms Used Throughout the Scale" (page 7 of the ITERS-R).

Individual toothbrushes means that a toothbrush is used only by one child and is stored to avoid contamination by other toothbrushes. Toothbrushes must be properly labeled with a name to show that each child has his or her own toothbrush. Labels ensure that staff can tell which toothbrush belongs to each child, and sharing of toothbrushes does not occur.

Toothbrushes should be stored in a clean storing device (such as a commercial or homemade rack for storing many toothbrushes, or in individual cups), with the bristles up so that they can air dry. Toothbrush bristles should not be touching another toothbrush or any contaminated surface. (See photo 10.7.2.)

Used at least once daily requires that adults help the toddlers brush their teeth at least once a day, preferably after eating. Toothpaste is not necessary for children to use since food and plaque can be removed from the teeth with a dry brush or by using water only.

See the "Note for Clarification" provided in the ITERS-R for this indicator on handling of toothpaste, if used. Toddlers should be allowed to handle small dabs of toothpaste by themselves.

Score Indicator 7.2 "Yes" if most toddlers brush their teeth at least once daily with individual toothbrushes.

10.7.2 Toothbrushes are stored with bristles covered, and labeled for each child.

10 Health practices

7.3 *Health information* includes topics of interest to parents mainly about young children. It can also be supplemented with other topics as long as information on children is included. All materials must be from reputable health care related agencies. Examples of topics are provided in the indicator. Additional topics include the following:

- emergency medical care for infants and toddlers, including CPR and First Aid,
- prevention of Sudden Infant Death Syndrome by putting children on their back to sleep,
- advice on child-proofing the home,
- handling children's illnesses,
- weaning a baby,
- toilet training with older toddlers,
- infants' sleep patterns,
- immunizations—what and when needed, and
- toddler eating concerns.

Available for parents means that the materials are in the facility and parents may have access if requested or needed. The materials may be:

- displayed on parent bulletin boards or other places parents will notice,
- accessible in a parent library on site, or
- available in the facility to be given or lent to parents by staff.

To score, the observer should look around the classroom and facility for displayed health-related materials for parents to use. If any are found, score Indicator 7.3 "Yes." If no materials are observed, ask staff the question provided for this indicator in the ITERS-R and score based on what is reported.

11 Safety practices

General information about this item

When serious injuries happen to infants and toddlers, adults wonder what might have been done to prevent the accident. Everyone knows that very young children must be carefully protected by adults because they do not have the understanding or experience that is needed to know what might be dangerous. No one wants an infant or toddler to be seriously injured or killed, especially while they are responsible for the child.

Safety practices consist of a combination of minimizing hazards in the spaces used by the children and diligent supervision by the adults who care for them.

In this item, the term hazards that could result in serious injury is used. These are dangers in the physical environment that might cause injuries for infants and toddlers resulting in enough harm to require a hospital or doctor visit for treatment. Often serious hazards do not appear to be very dangerous to adults because they do not cause accidents very often, and adults have the practical experience with the world to know how to avoid injury. But many dangers are not clear to infants and toddlers because they are too young to understand how things work. For example, they will not know that an electrical outlet poses a serious threat if they push something into the holes, because it does not look frightening to the child. If serious hazards are present in the spaces used by very young children, an accident may not happen today or even tomorrow, but chances are that it will happen eventually.

Young children learn about the world by exploring and trying things out. If they have been told that something is dangerous, they might not understand, and even if they do, they can easily forget. It is up to responsible adults to protect the infants and toddlers in their care by minimizing hazards in a child's space, and also by supervising carefully. Supervision alone cannot take the place of minimizing hazards. Accidents will happen despite common rationalizations such as, "I know it is dangerous, but the children know not to go near it," or, "We have never had a child fall from that place," or, "We are always watching."

The "Notes for Clarification" (ITERS-R, page 27) for this item list indoor and outdoor hazards that could result in serious injury, such as lack of safety caps on electrical outlets or poisonous substances that are not locked away. However, the list does not include all possible safety hazards. It is up to the observer to consider all aspects of the indoor and outdoor settings used by children, and to document all hazards observed.

11 Safety practices

A closer look at each indicator

1.1 This indicator requires that all hazards found in the **_indoor_** spaces used by children be evaluated. (See photos 11.1.1a-f.) **_Indoors_** includes the classroom(s) that are used by children at any time and any other spaces children have access to, such as multi-purpose rooms, gymnasiums, rest rooms, storage areas, hallways, or stairwells. To score this indicator, the observer should look for hazards in all the indoor areas used by, or accessible to, children. The "Notes for Clarification" list does not include all possible indoor hazards—there are many others that could cause serious injury, and if observed, they should be listed on the score sheet and considered in scoring. Examples include:

- There is an insufficient fall zone with appropriate cushioning surface around indoor climbing equipment or slides. Climbers should be checked to determine the highest point from which a child might fall, the likely velocity of the fall (how hard will the child land), and the surface in the fall zone.

- Crib/playpen slats or mesh sides permit entrapment because they are more than 2 3/8 inches apart.

- Rocking chairs are used in areas where mobile children play.

- Umbrellas with sharp points are left to dry within reach of children.

- Inappropriate materials are used in the sensory table, such as kidney beans (toxic), packing materials that might cause choking, flour, sawdust, or finely milled corn meal or corn starch that might cause asphyxiation if inhaled by children.

- Dangerous or toxic materials, such as shaving cream or glitter, are used in art projects.

- Objects and toys small enough to cause choking, such as pegs, bottle tops, or art materials, are left within children's reach.

- Medications that should be stored in a locked cabinet are removed and left out.

- Doors of classroom are left open so children might leave unnoticed and unsupervised.

- Microwave ovens are used to heat bottles or baby foods.

- Electric fan blades are within reach of children.

- Highchairs, infant seats, or strollers that do not have safety straps (or whose safety straps are not used) are used with children.

- Children play near doors that open inward into infant/toddler play spaces (if opened, children could be hit).

- Space is so crowded that evacuation of children in an emergency would be difficult.

- Electrical outlets that do not have covers and unsecured wires and cords are present where children are allowed to play.

Indicator 1.1 is true (score "Yes") when the observer sees **_four or more hazards that could result in serious injury_**, in indoor spaces used by the children. _Hazards that could result in serious injury_ is defined in the General Information section for this item.

When special safety outlets are used in a program, ask the teacher or director how they are operated to ensure child safety, and check to be sure operation rules are followed correctly. Flip-covers on outdoor outlets are acceptable as safety caps as

Examples of Indoor Safety Hazards

11.1.1a This wheelchair is stored in the fall zone of the climbing equipment, causing danger to children who run or fall down the steep ramp. In addition, a thin carpet does not provide the cushioning surface needed around the equipment.

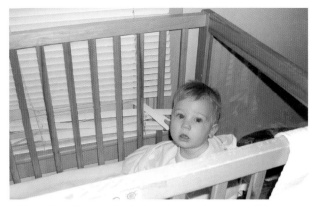

11.1.1b These blinds should not be accessible to a child in the crib.

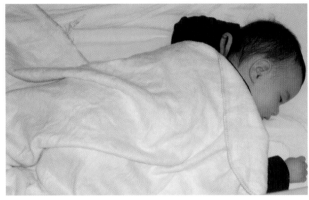

11.1.1c Placing a baby to sleep on his stomach is counted as a major safety hazard. Placement of the blanket near the baby's face would also be considered.

11.1.1d Children can inhale bleach solution when they are at the table during the sanitizing.

11.1.1e [above] Swings and toddlers do not mix well, when safety is being considered.

11.1.1f [right] Heavy toys on top shelves can become dangerous falling objects to children playing on the floor.

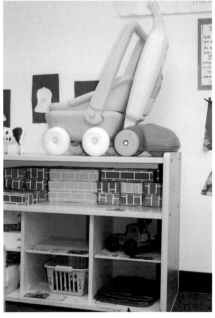

11.1.1f

11 Safety practices

11.1.2a

11.1.2b

11.1.2a-b   Safety hazards, such as the rocks on this playground, can be interesting to children but put an extra burden on supervising staff who must protect them.

long as they are kept closed when not in use. Computer wires should not be within view or easy reach of children.

Minor hazards, which provide low risk of causing *serious* injury that would require hospitalization or a visit to the doctor, are not considered in scoring this indicator, unless there are six or more observed. Examples of such hazards might include an uncovered outlet located high up on the wall in a room with only non-mobile children; or a slight tripping hazard in space with low traffic. If six or more minor hazards are observed during the observation, score Indicator 1.1 "Yes."

1.2   *Hazards that could result in serious injury* is defined in the General Information section for this item. In this indicator, all hazards present in the ***outdoor*** area(s) used by children must be evaluated. ***Outdoors*** includes all playgrounds that are used by children at any time, and any other outdoor spaces children have access to, such as patios, semi-shelters, storage areas, porches, decks, and even public areas if they are ever used for activities. (See photos 11.1.2a-e.)

11.1.2c   Small objects that children can choke on should be minimized on playgrounds for infants.

11.1.2d   Inadequate fall zones and equipment that is too challenging for toddlers create many major hazards on this playground.

11.1.2e   Large, exposed tree roots are considered minor safety hazards.

The "Notes for Clarification" for this item (on page 27 of the ITERS-R) list **outdoor** hazards that could result in serious injury, such as dangers in the playground space and equipment or accessible tools not meant for children's use.

To score this indicator, the observer should look through all the outdoor areas used by, or accessible to, children for such hazards. The "Notes for Clarification" list does not include all hazards—there are many others that could cause serious injury, and, if observed, they should be listed on the score sheet and considered in scoring. Examples include:

- A fence that has sharp prongs or long exposed bolts is within easy reach of children, on which children could become caught or injured.
- Unprotected water, such as pools, deep puddles, bogs, creeks, or rivers, is accessible to children.
- Children are allowed to climb on rocks or in trees without adequate safety precautions, such as resilient ground covers in fall zones.
- Motor vehicles are present in children's play area when children are present.
- Parking lot with cars parked is adjacent to playground, without extra protection (such as cement barriers or bollards) in addition to fence.
- Poisonous plants grow in children's play area.
- Ground cover consists of materials children can choke on, such as pea gravel or small stones.
- Swings are used where infants/toddlers play and could be hit.
- There is no safety accommodation on swings used with infants/toddlers, such as child-safe seat or safety strap, if needed.

Indicator 1.2 is true (score "Yes") when the observer can list **four or more** very serious hazards seen in the outdoor space(s) used by the children.

Minor outdoor hazards (such as tree roots that might cause tripping, very shallow puddles, or a little sand on a sidewalk), which are unlikely to cause serious injury and require hospitalization or a visit to the doctor, are not considered in scoring this indicator, unless there are six or more. If six or more are listed during the observation, score Indicator 1.2 "Yes."

1.3 The requirements of this indicator are based on **supervision** (watching and protecting children from danger) provided by staff both indoors and outdoors.

To score this indicator, consider the actions provided by *all* observed staff supervising indoors or outdoors to protect children. Concentrate primarily on the staff and children in the group being observed, but if groups mix at any time (for example, several classes are sharing the same outdoor space), consider *all* observed children of similar ages and abilities as those in the class being observed and *all* staff supervising in that area. Notice whether there are enough staff to watch all areas used and whether adults are supervising the most hazardous areas and activities adequately.

Meeting or not meeting certain recommended staff-child ratio requirements does not automatically mean that 1.3 is true or false. Ratio requirements vary substantially (for example, by state or agency). It is the *combination* of factors (number of staff to children, stringency of the supervision, the needs of the children, and the nature of the environment) that will determine the score for 1.3.

11 Safety practices

11.1.3a If no staff intervene quickly, supervision of outdoor play will not meet children's safety needs.

11.1.3b This staff member answers the phone, and then turns to keep an eye on the children while talking. Her lapse in supervision was momentary.

11.1.3c

11.1.3c-e If staff are observed to frequently ignore these natural toddler behaviors, supervision would be considered inadequate.

11.1.3d

Inadequate supervision means that staff severely compromise children's safety needs by not watching, guiding, or intervening as required by the children's abilities or the nature of the hazards present. Diligent supervision is required for all infants and toddlers, with closer attention required in more dangerous circumstances. (See photos 11.1.3a-e.)

The observer should be aware that when working with infants and toddlers, substantial staff time must be spent in handling the needs of one child at a time. This has an effect on the ability of staff to supervise the rest of the children adequately. For example, in a class where there is one staff member with a group of four infants, that one staff member will significantly reduce her supervision of three of the children while appropriately diapering or feeding one child. In a class with two staff and 12 toddlers, one staff member must supervise

11.1.3e

11 of the children when the other is diapering one child. If each of the two staff members are involved with one child, 10 receive less supervision. Problems often occur with supervision when all staff are focusing on meeting the needs of one or two children and the others are relatively unsupervised. (See photo 11.1.3f.)

Whether this decreased supervision can be considered **inadequate** will depend on the amount of time most children receive less supervision, the number of children in the group, any safety hazards present, staff awareness of the total group, and the visibility of all children within the space used.

The score for this item must be based on what is seen throughout the observation. The observation must be long enough to provide a range of circumstances, including relatively quiet and more active times, group times and free play, routine and play times, and more and less stressful periods of the day. For example, to score accurately, the observer should observe supervision early in the morning, when children and staff are fresh, and continue to observe to see the more stressful times of the day, such as before lunch or nap when children are hungry or tired.

11.1.3f Although the staff member is closely supervising one activity that requires his attention, he cannot supervise the slide adequately at the same time.

Note that to score this indicator "Yes," supervision must be inadequate both **indoors and outdoors**. Indicator 1.3 should be scored "Yes" if staff leave any child *without* an adult present to supervise him or her, even for short periods of time. Inadequate supervision may also be true (score "Yes") when there are too few staff for the number of children or hazards present, or inattentive staff who ignore children or attend to other interests. When children are not in an area supervised by staff, and they are completely unsupervised for any amount of time (for example, a child leaves the classroom and no adult realizes that the child is absent, or children are put down for a nap in an unsupervised room), score this indicator "Yes."

If 1.3 is scored "Yes," then it is likely that Item 25, Supervision of play and learning, will also receive a score of 1.

3.1   See Indicators 1.1 and 1.2 for definition of safety hazards that could result in serious injury indoors and outdoors. Also see the lists of safety hazards in the "Notes for Clarification" in the ITERS-R on page 27.

To score 3.1 "Yes" there can be **no more than three** safety hazards present, indoors and outdoors combined, which could cause serious injury that would require treatment by a hospital or doctor. There must also be less than six minor hazards observed, outdoors and indoors combined.

3.2   *Adequate supervision to protect children's safety* requires that there are enough staff present to watch children during both routines and play. The staff are positioned to see all areas where children may be playing, move around as needed to keep a close eye on children, are attentive, and respond to children's basic safety needs. There is always an adult present who is supervising, and children are never left unsupervised for any amount of time. (See photos 11.3.2a-c.) Brief periods of decreased supervision of the majority of children, due to a staff member working intensively with one child, may cause minor problems with supervision, but supervision may be considered minimally adequate as long as no serious problems occur.

To give credit for this indicator, staff must intervene when problems occur that could seriously compromise a child's safety (e.g., to stop children from hurting

11 Safety practices

11.3.2a Staff know that this area requires close supervision, so they coordinate their tasks and the children's activities to ensure children are always protected.

11.3.2b This staff member plays ball with one toddler while keeping an eye on the "furniture mover" to be sure no one gets hurt.

themselves or others or to ensure that all children remain within view of adults). They must pay extra attention in more hazardous situations, such as when a child is eating, when an active child is playing near a non-mobile baby, or when children are playing around water or on climbing equipment.

Strategies used to help ensure adequate supervision by staff include:

11.3.2c Staff make sure toddlers use this small slide safely.

- arranging the schedule so that activities and routines that require attention to only one child are not done by all staff at the same time;

- coordinating staff tasks so that the supervision needs of all children can be met;

- if needed, having extra staff to help during the most demanding times in the classroom, such as during feeding and diaper changes, when getting children ready to go outdoors, during a neighborhood walk, or while doing a special activity that requires close staff supervision;

- adjusting supervision for abilities of children and the hazards present;

- standing where all of the children are within easy view, and moving closer to areas where they are playing;

- when helping one child, keeping an eye on the others and being available to step in when needed;

- knowing where the potentially dangerous areas are indoors and outdoors, and supervising these areas more closely when used by children; and

- using a "zone" approach to supervising for safety, where each staff member has primary responsibility for certain areas. If there are no children in an area, staff move to help supervise another area, until children return to their supervision zone.

If there are any serious lapses in supervision, or many minor lapses, score Indicator 3.2 "No."

Essentials needed to handle emergencies are the provisions needed to deal with accidents, fire, or other dangers that require immediate action. (See photos 11.3.3a-c.) The examples listed in this indicator do not include every essential required for every classroom. They only list some of the things the observer should consider in scoring the indicator. For example, a fire alarm, working fire extinguisher, and evacuation plans are not listed, but the observer should consider these as essentials also.

Often the requirement for essentials needed to handle emergencies will depend on local conditions. For example, in an area where earthquakes are possible, procedures to follow in case of earthquakes would be required. Or if an enrolled child tends to have special medical needs, such as seizures or severe allergies, the essentials needed to handle such a case would be required.

Following is additional information to consider about the essentials to handle emergencies in this Indicator:

- *A telephone* must be on site and easily accessible, but not necessarily in the room. If a portable phone is used, staff must know its location. If the phone is in another room, the room must be unlocked so staff can use the phone when needed.

- Emergency numbers must be posted, so they are easily found and used by staff, parents, substitutes, or sometimes even by older children. To get credit, the numbers cannot be hidden (such as in drawers or cabinets).

- A substitute for staff must be immediately available when called upon in an emergency. The substitute must be on site. Arranging for staff from other rooms to share supervision responsibilities in emergencies is acceptable, but the remaining staff must be able to supervise all children adequately.

- The first aid kit must be well stocked with items required for emergencies (such as disposable non-porous gloves, scissors, tweezers, thermometer, bandages and tape, sterile gauze pads, rolls of gauze, various band-aids, safety pins, eye dressings, cold pack, and a current first aid instruction chart). If all such items are not stored together in one kit, staff should have easy access to all of them and know where they are stored. For example, cold packs might be stored in the kitchen freezer rather than in the first aid kit.

- Transportation must be readily available to transport an injured child for medical treatment. Transportation can be called (for example, by dialing 911 for an ambulance) or provided by staff.

- Written emergency procedures must be posted and clear, indicating, for example, the sequence for how emergencies will be handled, who will take responsibility, and who will be called.

- The on-site staff member who is trained in pediatric first aid must have a current certificate to indicate completion of training, with updates as needed. The person must be available in emergencies without compromising the supervision of any other group.

11.3.3a Emergency numbers are posted near this telephone. When phones are portable, the numbers must be posted in an obvious, clearly visible location.

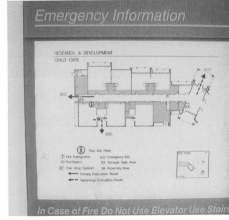

11.3.3b All staff must be familiar with the evacuation plan.

11.3.3c Emergency information for each child is kept in clear view on the teacher's bulletin board.

11 Safety practices

11.5.2a Tying toddlers' shoes to prevent falls is an ongoing practice that helps prevent accidents.

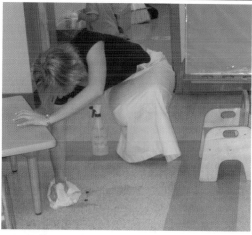

11.5.2b Staff quickly clean up slippery spills to prevent falls.

11.5.2c

11.5.2d

11.5.2c-d When competition begins over this twig, staff quickly intervene to ensure safety of both children.

To give credit for Indicator 3.3, observe to see that essentials are present, and ask staff for information not observed by using the questions provided for this indicator on page 27 of the ITERS-R.

5.1 See Indicators 1.1 and 1.2 for definition of safety hazards that could result in serious injury indoors and outdoors.

To score 5.1 "Yes," there can be *no* safety hazards present, indoors and outdoors, which could cause serious injury that would require hospitalization or treatment by a doctor. There must also be no more than one minor hazard observed.

5.2 ***Staff anticipate and take action to prevent safety problems*** means that staff recognize possible hazards in the areas used by children, and correct the problems before accidents happen. (See photos 11.5.2a-d.) Some examples of such precautions are provided in Indicator 5.2. Other examples include:

- moving active play away from non-mobile children or quiet play,
- placing objects that might cause problems out of the reach of children,

- periodically removing clutter, such as toys scattered in walking areas, to prevent falls,
- ensuring that safety restraints on highchairs, strollers, and infant seats, are intact and fastened,
- removing broken toys and equipment that might cause injury,
- picking up small items children could choke on that are left within children's reach,
- securing loose cords or wires that could strangle children,
- ensuring that purses, backpacks, or tote bags of adults are out of children's reach,
- putting heavy objects that could be pulled or pushed onto children out of the reach of children or down low (e.g., on the floor),
- anchoring wobbly furniture or placing it in a safe position so it will not fall,
- tying children's shoes so that falls are less likely to occur,
- sweeping sand off walking and running surfaces and stairs,
- limiting the number of children on certain climbing equipment if too many children increases the risk of pushing and falling,
- staying close and giving extra supervision to a toddler who is going through a stage of biting or hitting,
- placing possibly dangerous tools used by children or staff (knives, scissors, hammers, saws) out of reach when not being supervised in use,
- preventing children from running in front of swings, and
- ensuring gates or doors are closed.

Such action can occur indoors and/or outdoors.

Score Indicator 5.2 "Yes" if these types of practices are **usually** carried out. The term **usually** is defined on page 8 of the ITERS-R to indicate "the common or prevalent practice observed that is carried out with only a few lapses." This means that staff rarely ignore dangers or fail to notice them. Instead they notice and take action to minimize hazards and avoid problems. The observer should see at least one obvious attempt by staff to prevent safety problems during the observation. If safety problems generally go unnoticed, score 5.2 "No." If all areas are completely safe, and no possible problems arise, give credit for this indicator.

7.1 **Safety rules** for infants and toddlers must be very simple and obvious in their meaning to the children, and adults should not depend on the children's remembering or following the rules that are told to them. (See photo 11.7.1.) In addition, children should never be punished for not following the rules. With very young children, it is up to the staff to **help children to follow safety rules**, to ensure that children do not do things that are not safe. Just telling an infant or toddler a safety rule without taking action (helping) to minimize the hazards or problems will not prevent harm.

Helping children to follow safety rules before they have the ability to do so themselves is an important part of the long-term process of teaching safety. This is similar to helping children learn to understand and use language. In teaching children to communicate with words, the adult provides lots of

11.7.1 Staff remind children of the "one at a time" safety rule for the slide and stay close to help children follow the rule.

input before the child understands and even more input is needed before the child actually talks. But everyone knows that children will not learn to speak well if the adult does not put in a substantial amount of effort "up front." Teaching safety works the same way. It should begin long before a child can show that she or he understands or follows the rules. This is why staff should state rules as they stop dangerous behavior.

At this excellent level of quality *the expectation is that rules used with the children are reasonable,* with the primary intention of protecting children and their environment without being overly restrictive. Therefore, helping children to follow inappropriate rules, i.e., rules that are overly restrictive, would not be counted to give credit for this indicator. Rules, such as the following, are inappropriate:

- "Share the toy" (as child tries to defend toy she is playing with).

- "Don't touch" (as child reaches for something that is within easy reach and looks like a toy but is for decoration only).

- "Stay in your place and don't touch anybody" (as children walk down the hallway in a line).

- "No running allowed" (as child tries to run in the classroom when no other accommodation is made for the child's need for active physical play).

To be an effective teaching tool, the rules children are being helped to follow should relate directly to the danger that poses a threat to the child and should not be overly restrictive. Examples of appropriate rules the observer might hear and see staff helping children to follow are:

- "Be gentle; soft touch" (as child reaches out to touch hair of another child).

- "Don't touch, it's hot" (as child reaches for something that must cool off before use).

- "Stay with me" (as child starts to rush ahead when moving from one space to another, e.g., from indoors to outdoors).

- "No hitting" (as child tries to solve a social problem with force).

- "Feet on the floor" (as child begins to climb up onto furniture).

- "We don't take toys from our friends. Let's find another one" (as child tries to take another child's toy).

To score "Yes," the observer must see at least one example of staff helping children to follow a safety rule. As shown in the appropriate examples, the rules can be stated quite informally, as directions or suggestions to the children. The rule must be stated verbally, and staff must take action to help the child follow the rule.

7.2 Information on appropriate *safety rules* for scoring this indicator is provided in Indicator 7.1. When staff only tell children what they cannot do, with no explanation, children may feel overly controlled by adults and may try to rebel against the rules. Reminding children about how important their safety is to themselves, their parents, and the staff helps them feel that rules are not so limiting, or if there are limits, they are worth following. Reasons for safety precautions are needed to help children understand the importance of what they view as restrictions to their desire to explore and try things out. Even with infants and toddlers, adding reasons to the rules promotes acceptance and lays the foundation for future self-direction.

Providing ***reasons for safety rules*** does not mean that staff have to give long lectures. The reasons should be provided quickly and informally, just as the rule is. When reasons are explained informally, during a time when a possible accident is being prevented, the dangers associated with a hazard must be quickly and clearly stated to the child.

Here are some examples of explaining safety rules informally to children:

- "Be gentle; soft touch. Pulling hair will hurt her."

- "Stay with me. I am afraid I will lose you."

- "No hitting. Hitting hurts. You can ask with words."

- "Feet on the floor. I am afraid you will fall and get hurt."

- "We don't take toys from our friends. Your friends don't like it when you take their toys. You do not like it either. Let's find another toy."

The observer should watch and listen carefully during the observation to hear whether only the rules are stated or whether reasons are also given. It is not required that every limitation or rule used by staff is associated with a reason, as long as some reasons are observed being given to the children. It helps to note examples on the score sheet.

Score Indicator 7.2 "Yes" if at least one example of staff explaining rules to children is observed.

Listening and Talking

12 Helping children understand language

General information about this item

Learning the meaning of the spoken language that surrounds us is among the more important developmental tasks of infancy and toddlerhood, and one that very young children are well prepared to undertake with our help. Even before birth, in the last few months of their pre-natal life, babies listen to their mothers' voice. This results in the newborn's preference for female voices and for speech in their mother's language, because babies have become used to hearing their own mother's voice. During the infant/toddler years, the ability to understand language, and eventually to use language, is developed in the context of meaningful social relationships with the significant adults in children's lives, their parents and caregivers. Since so many very young children attend child care settings for the major part of their waking hours, staff members share this important adult responsibility for helping infants and toddlers learn to understand language.

This item assesses the major aspects of staff-child communication needed by children from birth through 30 months of age as they learn to understand verbal communication and develop their receptive language skills. These include assuring that staff members:

- talk frequently and personally to children;
- maintain a warm, attentive manner as they communicate with children;
- are generally encouraging and positive in what they say to children;
- provide a reasonably quiet environment so that children can hear what is being said;
- use simple, exact words children can understand;
- talk to children during both routines and play about the things that are happening at that time so that the words become meaningful to the children;
- engage in verbal play and enjoy verbal interaction with the children; and
- talk about many topics and different aspects of experiences, including feelings and intentions and the names of objects and actions.

Since language content and tone may change throughout the day, it is best to score this item late in the observation based on notes kept throughout the day in naturally occurring situations. Because observers are often absorbed in evaluating many other aspects of the classroom and can easily miss the important talk, it is helpful to concentrate solely on staff-child communication at least once every half-hour during the observation. During these times the observer should listen carefully, moving close enough to hear what staff are saying to children. The content of the communication, topics covered, range of words used, and tone of voice should be noted. If there is mainly silence, this is important to note also. Sometimes it helps if observers close their eyes to avoid being distracted during the period of listening.

Although there may be some differences among staff members in both the amount and tone of their verbal communication with the children, the observer must judge the quality of what all staff, collectively, are doing to help the children understand language. As in all items in the scale, *staff* means those adults who are directly involved with the children, the teaching staff. "Staff" is used in the plural in all indicators because there is usually more than one staff member with each group. When individual staff members handle things differently, the score for each indicator must convey the overall impact of all the staff members collectively on the children. For example, in a room where one staff member is very verbal and the other is relatively non-verbal, the score is determined by how well the children's need for verbal input is met.

The staff includes all those adults who are in the classroom and who work directly with the children daily or almost daily, for much of the day. This may include volunteers, if they are in the classroom for the required amount of time. Other adults who are in the classroom for short periods, or who are not a regular daily part of the classroom, do not count in evaluating whether the requirements of the item are met. For example, if a parent, therapist, director, or owner of the program comes into the classroom and interacts verbally with the children for short or irregular periods, these interactions do not count in scoring the item, *unless they have a substantial negative impact on the operation of the classroom or on one or more specific children.* If additional staff, such as floaters or part-time assistants, are regularly assigned to work in a classroom for specific periods of the day and are present on a daily basis, their interactions should be considered in scoring. Also in programs such as parent cooperatives or lab schools, whose usual staffing pattern includes different people daily as teaching assistants, these assistants are considered members of the staff when scoring.

As with all three items in the Listening and Talking subscale, it is imperative that the observer understand the language spoken by the staff or have an ongoing simultaneous translation provided so that they can understand what is being said.

A closer look at each indicator

1.1 This indicator considers the amount of **talking to infants and toddlers** done by the staff throughout the observation. **Little or no** means that staff either do not talk to the children at all or do so very rarely during the observation. Staff may not talk at all, or talk to others, but not to the children in the group being observed. If staff talk to one another and to other adults in the room or talk on the telephone, this does not count, even if they are discussing the children. (See photo 12.1.1.) Staff may do some talking to the children, but this occurs only very rarely, and there are many extended periods in which no child is talked to.

Score this indicator "Yes" if there is very little or no talking to the children observed throughout the observation period.

12.1.1 If staff conversations take precedence over talking to the children, children's understanding and use of language suffer.

1.2 **Constant noise** includes any persistent loud sound that comes from within or outside the room during much of the observation. This can include loud music from a CD player, children crying throughout the day in the group being observed or in another classroom, noise produced by the use of toys on hard reverberating surfaces due to insufficient sound absorbing materials in the room or in adjacent rooms or lack of or insufficient sound barriers between rooms. Ongoing noise *interferes* with children's ability to hear language by making it difficult to separate what staff members are saying to them from the general sound overload. This is especially true for infants and toddlers, since they are working to recognize and make the many sounds used in the language they will speak later. Realizing that sensitivity to noise levels differs among people, and noise level may differ in different areas of the room, the observer should move around the room and watch the effect on the staff and children in order to judge whether the noise level interferes with the children's ability to hear language.

12.1.3 Frequent use of a harsh tone of voice or negative comments can interfere with language learning.

Score this indicator "Yes" if staff generally need to raise their voices to be heard or if children seem to be unable to hear staff or be heard by them.

1.3 An *unpleasant manner* means that staff use a harsh tone of voice or say things to children that may make them feel that they are unloved, unworthy of respect or are constantly doing something wrong. *Often* means that an unpleasant tone of voice is used or negative things are said three or more times during the observation and seem to be a usual occurrence. (See photo 12.1.3.)

If staff often talk to children in an unpleasant manner, children tend to avoid listening or may respond out of fear, causing a breakdown in communication and loss of willingness on the part of children to follow staff as language models.

Examples of talking to children in an unpleasant manner include:

- shouting "No," "Stop it" or "How often do I have to tell you that?";
- threatening a child with calling his parents or making her sit in "time out";
- telling children they have done something bad or naughty;
- calling a child a "bad boy" or a "bad girl";
- talking in a harsh or threatening voice with the adult's face close to the child's; or
- looking at the child with a negative, disapproving, or threatening expression, even if the words or tone are not harsh.

Score this indicator "Yes" if three or more instances are observed, even if some, or even many, positive verbal interactions are also observed.

Since negative verbal statements and a harsh tone of voice have a negative impact on staff-child relationships, they are also considered in scoring Item 27, Staff-child interaction and Item 28, Discipline.

3.1 A *moderate amount* of talking means that staff talk to children regularly to some degree. Although there may not be constant talk or extended verbal interactions, talking to children is not an unusual practice. *Throughout the day* means that during the observation staff talk to children during both care routines and play. (See photos 12.3.1a-b, next page.) The instances of staff talking to children can be given credit only if they occur at different times throughout the entire length of the observation and not all at one time. Children need staff to provide verbal communication throughout the day in a variety of situations in order to help them understand language.

12.3.1a Talk with toddlers about the snack they are eating.

12.3.1b Point out and describe features of the musical toys children play with.

Examples of what staff could talk about with children are:

- At arrival, staff greet each child using his or her name and express a warm welcome, and they talk about an activity the child can begin; at departure staff talk about getting dressed for leaving and getting personal things together, and they say a personal goodbye to each child.

- During diapering/toileting staff talk about how good it feels to get rid of the wet or soiled diaper; they provide a running commentary describing the various steps of the diaper change or toileting being experienced by the child; and they amuse a restless child by making the mobile over the diapering table move and talking about what is on the mobile.

- During preparation for feeding, serving food, and while children are eating, staff talk or sing about the steps of washing hands with soap and water before meals; they talk to a baby being held for bottle feeding; or they identify the various foods the children are eating. They explain that "We only eat what's on our own plate, not on anyone else's"; they model asking for more milk or for another serving; and after the meal they talk or sing about washing hands and face after eating.

- At naptime staff talk about each step in getting ready for nap, greet each child as he or she gets up from nap, and comment on each familiar step in the waking-up process (e.g., "Now we're putting on your shoes so you can go and have snack").

Examples of what staff could talk about during play include:

- Staff give a descriptive commentary about the children's movements (pushing, pulling, riding, crawling, jumping, throwing a ball), as children use gross motor materials in active physical play.

- Staff talk about what the gross motor toy is doing while the children use it. ("The wheels of the truck are rolling." "Balls are bouncing high up." Or, "Balls are rolling on the floor.")

- Staff talk about what the children can see when they are outdoors or look-ing outside through a window (trees blowing, birds singing or flying, flowers blooming, butterflies on bushes).

- Staff describe what is happening while children play with various materials, focusing on what is happening with the material as well as what the child is doing. For example, while a child is scribbling the staff can call attention to the marks the crayon is making as well as how the child's arm is moving by saying, "Look at the circle the crayon is making—going round and round. It's a red circle on the paper. Your hand is moving round and round with the crayon. Big round circles and little round circles."

- Staff describe the process and results produced when the child is playing with fine motor materials, art materials, music materials, blocks, dramatic play items, sand and water materials, or nature and science items. For example, a staff member talks about the texture of the sand and what the children are doing with it (digging, pouring), about the different clothing in the dramatic play area and who wears such clothing, or what the dolls are doing (eating, sleeping, crying because they are hungry).

Score Indicator 3.1 "Yes" if some instances of staff talking to children are observed regularly, at various times throughout the observation. Do not score "Yes" if there are many long periods during the observation in which no talking to children occurs.

3.2   ***Reasonably quiet*** means that the sound level in the room allows children to hear what the staff and other children are saying. It is expected that some noise from human voices and from necessary movement by people and things will be apparent, but that the noise level will be low enough so that communications in a normal tone of voice can be heard almost all of the time.

Score this indicator "Yes" if the room is quiet enough for verbal communication to be heard by the children almost all of the time.

3.3   ***Tone*** of voice means the feeling expressed in the voice itself when someone is speaking, apart from what is being said. The tone of the voice can range from positive or ***pleasant*** to negative or harsh. A ***neutral*** tone is neither positive nor negative. A positive tone of voice conveys feelings of acceptance, warmth, pleasure, enthusiasm. A negative tone of voice conveys feelings of annoyance, disapproval, anger, threat. Young children respond to the tone of voice as much as they do to the content or subject of the talk. Instead of judging whether the tone of voice is pleasant solely from the observer's point of view, gather evidence needed to score from the child's response to the adult's tone. The observer must see whether chil-dren react with interest and happiness and are relaxed, rather than responding with fear, anger, or sadness.

According to the "Explanation of Terms Used Throughout the Scale," on page 7 of the ITERS-R, ***usually*** means "the common or prevalent practice observed, that is carried out with only a few lapses." Therefore, in order to score Indicator 3.3 "Yes," in all staff interactions with the children, no more than two lapses are allowed to give credit, and only mildly negative tones can be used to give credit. Credit cannot be given if staff ever use extremely unpleasant or harsh tones with the children.

3.4   The ***content*** of what is said to children refers to the meaning that is conveyed in the communication or the subject matter covered. ***Positive and encouraging*** means that the child is accepted in what he or she wants to do, to say, or feels.

Examples of **positive or encouraging** content include:

- Praise for accomplishment: "You're standing up all by yourself!" " Yes, I see your nice scribble picture. Let's put it up on the wall." "All gone! You ate all the cereal." "Good try!"

- Encouragement: "You can do it; just a little more crawling to reach the ball." "You're pointing to the books. Want me to read a book? This one? Okay!" "Do you want to try to drink a little more of the bottle? Need to sit up to have a burp first? Good." "Sleepy, sleepy nap time." "Good talking. You told me, 'No more,' so I'm taking the cereal away." "Here's a ball for you. That one is Jimmy's ball."

- Acceptance: "You are really tired, aren't you? Do you want to rest on my lap for a little while?" "Are you bored with that rattle? Here's a music toy you can play with. You don't want that? Oh, you want the book about the kitten." "You do not like carrots, do you? You like the broccoli, though." "You are so full of energy. Let's get our coats and go outside to use up our wiggles."

Negative and discouraging content of talk gives the child the message that he or she is wrong, unaccepted in what he or she wants to do, say, or feel. Examples of negative or discouraging content include:

- "Stop that crying! You hit him first."
- "Don't touch that book. You'll get it dirty."
- "Stop wiggling. You must sit quietly and listen."
- "Bad girl! You can't take that doll away from Mary."
- "Leave that alone; it's not yours."
- "No, that's Jimmy's ball," said while taking the ball away.
- "You're playing with your food! You're finished now," said while taking food away as child protests.

This requirement does not mean that staff cannot keep children from hurting themselves or others, or from being destructive. However, it is required that when placing necessary limits on children, the limits are minimized, for example by setting up child safe environments and having appropriate expectations of children based on their age and abilities. When limits must be enforced, this is done through positive redirection, or with explanations and comfort that help children accept the restriction.

Score Indicator 3.4 "Yes" if the content of staff talk is encouraging and positive about 75% of the time, and neutral the rest of the time. It is rarely negative or discouraging, even if this is observed with just one child. It is not necessary to calculate this percentage. Instead, determine whether typical talk is most often encouraging and positive with only one or two mildly negative exceptions.

5.1 **Staff talk to the children frequently** means that staff talking is part of almost every interaction with the children. A verbal comment accompanies almost all interactions between children and staff, whether the interaction is initiated by a child or a staff member. Staff talking to children must be **throughout the day** as staff care for the children during routines (greeting/departing, feeding, diapering/toileting, and nap) and play (outdoors and indoors with all materials and activities offered to the children to use and enjoy). (See photos 12.5.1a-f.)

12.5.1a-f Talking to children frequently throughout the day during routines and play helps them understand language.

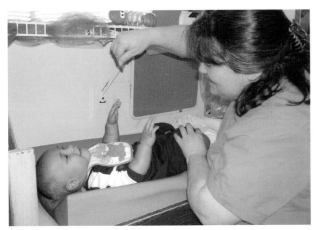

12.5.1a Talk about steps in the diapering process and engage in verbal play.

12.5.1b Talk playfully as the child is being bottle fed.

12.5.1c Talk about the foods at lunch and the events of the morning.

12.5.1d Talk about toys as they are offered to non-mobile babies.

12.5.1e Talk about and express interest in the art-work children do.

12.5.1f Lift a child up to see the hanging display and talk about how it moves and what it is about.

12 Helping children understand language

In addition to the frequency of staff talk, this indicator as stated in the "Note for Clarification" on page 28 of the ITERS-R requires that all staff must use either a neutral or pleasant tone of voice in order to get credit for this indicator. Variation in the amount of talking done by different staff members is acceptable, and each staff member does not have to contribute equally to the collective amount of language modeling to meet the requirements of this indicator. The word "staff" is used as a plural in the scale, therefore this indicator assesses the amount of talking with the children produced by all classroom staff together during the observation.

See the "General Information" section for information on judging how much and what kind of talk takes place during the observation.

Score this indicator "Yes" if staff talk to children in a neutral or pleasant voice throughout the observation during both routine care and play. There should be no long periods in which staff do not talk to children. For examples of things to talk about see the "General Information" section for this item and Indicator 3.1 of this item.

5.2 Talk that is ***meaningful*** to children helps children link words to their experiences. When staff add words to the immediate experience of a young child, the connection becomes clear between the specific word and the specific experience. The words associated with commonly recurring experiences are understood long before the child can say them.

Staff can make their talk meaningful to infants and toddlers by:

- talking about what the child is experiencing through his senses at that moment (how things taste or feel or what he sees or hears);
- using simple sentences with few words;
- using gestures to enhance the meaning of words;
- pointing to objects, if needed to establish a common focus for staff and child; or
- recalling experiences that happened a little earlier or that happen every day.

Score "Yes" if staff talk is almost always simple in construction and obviously connected to the child's experiences. Score "No" if staff frequently talk about things the children would not understand, e.g., far away or unfamiliar topics or abstract ideas.

5.3 ***Verbal communication*** means talking to children or using any other alternative communication mode needed by children, including signing or a communication board. When verbal communication is personalized, it is made clear to the child that the communication is directed to him or her. Staff can personalize communication by:

- addressing one child, not a group of children;
- using the child's name to establish the connection to a specific child;
- talking about something the child is doing or experiencing directly;
- making eye contact with the child to whom the staff member is talking;
- using language at the level of complexity suited to the child's level of understanding (e.g., single words or two-word sentences for infants, simple sentences for young toddlers, longer sentences for older toddlers and twos);
- using the child's primary language, adding words in the school language as children gain experience with it;

12.5.3a

12.5.3b

12.5.3a-b Communication is personalized, relates to the immediate situation, and is at the right level to be understood by the child.

- using alternative modes of communication if needed by individual children (e.g., signing, communication board); or

- using a pleasant, enthusiastic tone of voice that makes the child want to listen.

Score "Yes" if communication is personalized the vast majority of the time, with only occasional lapses. (See photos 12.5.3a-b.)

5.4 **Descriptive words** name specific attributes or exact properties of objects or actions. (See photo 12.5.4.) For example, attributes of objects that make them unique or recognizable include:

12.5.4 Staff use simple, descriptive words when playing with children. "A hat. You put on the hat. I am wearing a hat, too."

- specific name of the object ("Please give me the doll," not non-specific words such as "thing," "it," "that");

- size ("a big block," "a small doll");

- shape (the "round hole" or "square hole" in the shape sorter);

- color ("the red ball," "the black crayon");

- texture ("soft," "smooth"); or

- sound ("loud," "soft"; high or low pitched).

Actions can be described by saying:

- what is happening ("We're washing hands. First we use soap.");

- who is doing it ("I'm helping you. Brian will wash next.");

- where it is happening ("We wash hands in this sink before lunch.");

- when the action occurs ("Now our hands are clean. It's time for lunch.");

- how the child feels about the action ("You like making bubbles, don't you?"); or

- how other people feel about the action ("I'm so happy your hands are clean. Now Jimmy wants to wash his hands.").

12 Helping children understand language

12.7.1a

12.7.1b

12.7.1a-c Staff use a wide range of simple, exact words to describe children's experiences as they engage in play and observe the world around them.

When staff use many simple, descriptive words in talking about daily activities and common objects in the environment, children expand their understanding of spoken language and also increase their information about the world around them.

A "Note for Clarification" on page 28 of the ITERS-R gives a strategy to use when gathering information for this indicator.

12.7.1c

Score "Yes" if staff use simple descriptive words the vast majority of the time when talking to children. The use of simple descriptive words should far outweigh the use of complex or non-specific words, with complex, abstract, or non-specific words used very infrequently.

7.1   This indicator assesses the *range* (or number) of different simple words used by staff in talking with children. A *wide range of exact words* means that many different words are used to describe particular properties of numerous objects and actions children experience during the observation. Attributes such as color, size, and shape are often pointed out, and actions are described in great detail, although the words used remain simple and meaningful to the children. (See photos 12.7.1a-c.) The staff communicate with the children throughout the day as they conduct routines, supervise, and participate in play activities.

It is less likely for staff to use a wide range of words when there is not much to talk about in the classroom (for example, only a few toys), or when staff do not take full advantage of talking about what is present and happening. It is unlikely that a wide range of words will be used if staff frequently repeat the same statements over and over, saying, for example, "You like your bottle?" when feeding, "Doesn't that feel better?", after changing each diaper, or "What does the duck say? Quack, quack, quack!" when playing. Using a wide range of words would require more. For example: "You're drinking lots of milk today. The bottle is almost empty. There are just a few bubbles left in the bottle. You were very hungry," or "Now your diaper is changed. Let's put your clothes back on. First your brown corduroy pants. I have on a brown shirt, see. One leg, two legs. Now your tan shoes. One shoe, two shoes. You're all dressed."

To keep track of the many specific words staff use in different situations during the observation, the observer can create a simple chart such as the one below.

	Exact words used by staff
Greeting/departing	
Meals/snacks	
Diapering/toileting	
Nap	
Size	
Shape	
Color	
Texture	
Sound	
Play materials	
Actions	
Feelings	
Other	

Score "Yes" if staff use many exact words throughout the day to describe objects and actions.

7.2 *Verbal play* means that staff and children engage in activities using sounds and words in a playful way, solely for enjoyment. Such activity differs from the purely functional use of language, where words are used to communicate specific meanings for the purposes of influencing action or enhancing understanding. In verbal play, the sounds and meanings of words are used mainly for the joy of saying and hearing them. Therefore, nonsense words and meaningless sounds can be used in verbal play along with real words and names.

Many conversations that staff carry on with infants consist of the staff member repeating sounds the baby has made, then waiting for the baby to respond to the sounds the staff member has made, which starts another round of back-and-forth conversation using sounds, often interspersed with encouraging comments by the staff (e.g., "Good talking!" "Yes." "That's right!"). This type of verbal interchange with infants encourages children to produce sounds and to listen to those produced by others, and also to enjoy the give and take of conversation.

When older infants and toddlers learn words, they enjoy hearing nursery rhymes, sequences of rhyming words, simple songs, and made-up chants or songs with their names in them or about recurring daily experiences, such as washing their hands, building a tower with blocks, climbing up on the climber, or swinging back and forth on a swing outside. (See photos 12.7.2a-e, next page.)

To score "Yes" at least two instances of verbal play should be observed during the 3-hour observation.

7.3 During the course of the day, infants and toddlers experience a wide variety of care routines and play activities, social interactions with adults and peers, and various physical and emotional states. This variety of experience brings up many *topics*

12 Helping children understand language

12.7.2 a-e Staff and children enjoy verbal play such as imitating sounds, singing songs, rhyming words, and repeating nursery rhymes.

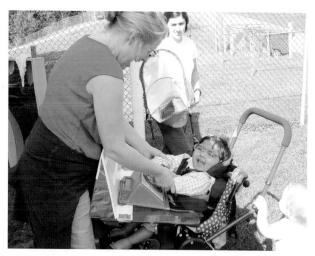

12.7.2 a

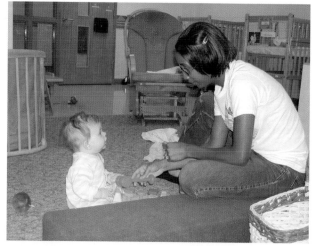

12.7.2 b

12.7.2 c

12.7.2 d

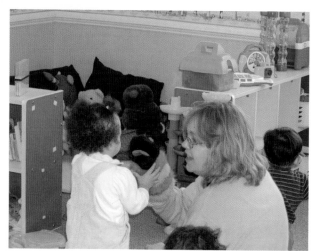

12.7.2 e

or subjects to talk about, some dealing with aspects of the immediate environment or activity and others with the feelings of the various people involved or their intentions and reactions. The wider the range of topics staff talk about, the greater the opportunity for children to learn more words and concepts. ***Many different topics*** is differentiated from the wide range of simple and exact words required in Indicator 7.1 in that a wide range of words is possible within a limited number of topics. In this indicator, the observer must attend to the various topics staff talk to children about.

In addition to naming objects and describing activities as they are happening, other topics that might be discussed when the occasion arises that makes them immediately relevant include:

Feelings:

- feeling sad when Mommy leaves and happy with she returns;
- feeling angry when someone takes the toys you are playing with;
- feeling happy when a friend gives you something you want; or
- feeling hungry or tired and then full and rested.

Intentions:

- knocking down someone "by accident," so you must watch carefully where you are going;
- helping one child tell another child he intends to come back to play with his trike, so the newcomer has to get another one for himself; or
- being helpful and kind to friends by explaining pro-social intentions to the child;

Events past, present, future:

- helping a toddler remember that Mommy comes back every day;
- describing a familiar pattern of events;
- commenting on new things that are added to the classroom, such as natural objects or pets;
- discussing the changing seasons or the weather;
- describing the baby that visited yesterday;
- talking about new toys to play with in the room; or
- reading a book about babies and talking about their own experiences.

Staff should point out and talk about positive or pro-social feelings and intentions, such as helping, being kind, or giving someone something, as well as anti-social feelings, which often cause the more dramatic responses.

Score this indicator "Yes" if many different topics are discussed, such as feelings, intentions, things in the past or the future, or new topics arising from something introduced into the classroom.

13 Helping children use language

General information about this item

During the infant-toddler years, children learn to use language to communicate their needs, desires and interests to those around them. In the brief span of the first few years, children learn to transform crying into differentiated sounds and gestures and then into recognizable words that express exact meanings. No child can successfully accomplish this amazing transformation without the help of adult language models. In this item, the role of the staff in helping very young children learn to use language is evaluated.

Since many infants and toddlers spend the majority of their waking hours in group settings, the language stimulation skills of the staff exert a considerable influence on the expressive language abilities (the ability to talk) of the children they care for.

In this language item, as in all items involving any type of interaction, *staff* generally refers to those adults who are directly involved in the classroom with the children daily or almost daily for much of the day. This can include volunteers, if they are in the classroom the required amount of time. Adults who are in the classroom for shorter periods of the day or who are not a regular part of the classroom do not count in evaluating whether the requirements for this item are met. For example, if a therapist or the director of a program comes into the classroom and interacts with the children for short or irregular periods, these interactions do not count in scoring language items, *unless the interactions are extremely negative.* As an exception, in a parent cooperative or a lab school, in which the usual staffing patterns include different people each day as teaching assistants, these assistants are counted as staff.

In the scale, "staff" is used as a plural because there are usually more than one staff member working with a group. When individual staff members handle communication with the children differently, it is necessary to arrive at a score that characterizes the overall impact of all the staff members on the children. Thus, in a room where one staff member is very responsive verbally and the other is relatively non-verbal, the score is not based on what each staff member produces but rather the total amount of encouragement to communicate that the children get from the whole staff. An analogy that might help is to think of something physical the children experience in the classroom, for example, the temperature of the room. Suppose it is warm enough in the room even though only one air vent is producing all the heat and the other is partially blocked or not functioning at all. It is still warm enough for the children despite the poorly functioning vent. We are concerned with the overall temperature, not with which of the vents is pumping out the air. Similarly, in this item we are scoring the overall encouragement to communicate produced jointly by staff. If the one communicative teacher is supplying enough encouragement for children's communication, then the classroom will meet

13 Helping children use language

certain requirements in the item. In a room with too few staff to meet the needs of all children at a good level of quality, staff may not be able to meet the requirements of this item, although they work very hard. If communication with children by staff (through efforts of either one staff member or several staff) fails to meet the children's needs, the requirement will not be met.

The score for this item must be based on what is observed throughout the observation, not on anything reported by staff. It is best to decide on a score after a considerable length of time, towards the end of the observation, because communication during various situations with all the children in the group should be included. Jotting down instances that show how staff help children use language during the observation will provide the information needed for accurate scoring. The score sheet or another piece of paper can be used for these notes.

Key aspects of staff behavior that affect the development of children's use of language include whether staff:

- generally respond in a positive, timely manner to children's attempts to communicate so children see that their communication brings results;
- are skillful in correctly interpreting what children are trying to communicate when they cry, point, or approximate words;
- add words to the actions they take in responding to children;
- engage in many turn-taking conversations with both infants and toddlers;
- expand on and add more words to children's attempts to communicate;
- ask simple questions and wait for an answer, then give answers themselves if children do not answer but seem interested; and
- maintain a good balance between listening and talking to them.

A closer look at each indicator

1.1   *Children's attempts to communicate* (both verbal and non-verbal) include:

- infants and toddlers crying to communicate that they are uncomfortable because they are hungry, wet, bored or unhappy;
- older infants and toddlers using gestures such as pointing to what they want, or reaching with outstretched arms to be picked up, often accompanied by vocalization;
- toddlers nodding "yes" or "no" or using facial expressions and gestures to express emotions; and
- children trying to use words to explain how they feel or what they want or do not want to happen.

Positive response by staff includes behaviors such as:

- acting to meet the child's needs, such as picking up a crying baby, patting a fussy infant who is trying to get to sleep, or responding with some other satisfying actions to show that the child's communication has been understood;
- adding words or other vocalization to soothing gestures and actions;
- making eye contact with the child who is communicating;
- looking at or focusing on the same thing the child is pointing to or looking at, and talking about it; and

- using simple words that are meaningful to the child to signify that the child's communication is understood ("Yes, you want your sippy cup. I'm getting it for you." "Becky has a doll just like yours.").

Little or no positive response means that staff generally seem disinterested when children try to communicate, and may react only when they want to or when they find it convenient, but not necessarily when the children want them to. Sometimes, staff may respond but not in a way that satisfies the child, because they have misunderstood the child's communication and make no attempt to accurately understand what the child needs. For example a child might cry and the staff members assume she is tired, so they put her in her crib. But the child continues to cry, for some other reason, which no one tries to determine.

Score this indicator "Yes" if staff rarely respond positively to children's attempts to communicate because they very frequently miss or ignore the attempts made by children, children have to wait very long for responses, or the responses do not match what the children want. If staff respond positively more than half of the time, then score Indicator 1.1 "No." To score, it is not necessary to calculate a percentage, but rather note if staff tend to positively respond to children's attempts to communicate significantly less than half of the time.

1.2 *Respond negatively* means that staff react to children's attempts to communicate their needs with annoyance, displeasure, or even anger, either verbally or non-verbally through body language or facial expression.

Ignore means that staff pay no attention to children when they cry or try with gestures or words to communicate. Staff may continue with the task they are completing or talk to one another, but they do not make eye contact with the child or in any way acknowledge that they are aware of the child's attempt to communicate.

Often means frequently or generally throughout the observation. Ignoring or responding negatively may be directed towards one child, several children, or generally towards all the children, and may be evidenced by one staff member or all staff members.

Score "Yes" if children's attempts to communicate are frequently ignored or met with negative responses during the observation.

3.1 *Positive verbal response* includes:

- using a pleasant tone of voice that is soothing, interested or enthusiastic;
- making reassuring sounds when calming a fussy or crying child;
- repeating babies' and toddlers' nonsense words and sounds in a playful conversation;
- repeating toddlers words; and
- adding more words to what children are saying.

Positive non-verbal response includes:

- taking action to satisfy the child's needs without a long wait;
- making eye contact or nodding to let the child know his communication has been seen or heard;
- using a pleasant facial expression or smiling; and
- moving towards the child or picking the child up in a relaxed, reassuring way.

13 Helping children use language

13.3.1a

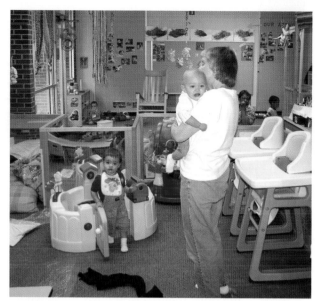

13.3.1b

13.3.1a-b Timely, positive response by staff to meet the needs expressed by children encourages children to use language because it gets results.

A **moderate amount** of such responses means that **throughout** the observation, some positive verbal or non-verbal responses are observed, and very few, if any, instances of staff ignoring or responding negatively to children's communication are observed.

Score this indicator "Yes" if staff respond regularly, although not necessarily frequently or consistently (as would be required in Indicator 5.1) to all children in the group. A positive response must be given to at least half of the communication attempts by the children. There can be no negative responses and little obvious ignoring observed in response to any child's attempt to communicate throughout the day. However, staff might miss some of the children's more subtle attempts, such as if a child pointing to something, and staff do not see this and therefore do not respond, but can still receive credit. (See photos 13.3.1a-b.)

3.2 In order to give credit for **an attempt to correctly interpret,** staff must successfully answer the children's attempts to communicate, doing what is required to answer them in a satisfying way. Usually, competent staff will be able to do this with their first response ("Oh, you are hungry. Here's your bottle. That's better, isn't it?"). However, if the first attempt does not work, staff must persist in trying to understand what the children want when they use crying, gestures, sounds or approximate words to express themselves. (See photos 13.3.2a-c.) The staff members' attempts to respond correctly may be non-verbal, verbal, or a combination of the two. For example, a staff member may immediately realize that a cranky, crying toddler wants his "sippy" cup because he is thirsty, and may fill it and give it to him, successfully meeting the child's needs without a word. On the other hand, the staff member may not get the right solution on the first try with the "sippy" cup. ("Oh, you don't want a drink. Maybe you want me to rock you in the rocking chair, or read you a story.")

When children start to use approximations of words that are somewhat difficult to understand, it can be frustrating for both the child and the staff. If a staff member

13.3.2a Crying can communicate a physical need, such as hunger.

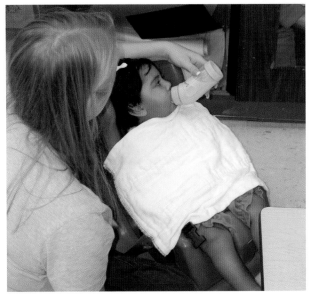

13.3.2b To respond correctly staff must be able to understand what the child is trying to say.

cannot understand what a child is saying, she may ask, "Tell me again, please," and progress to "Can you show me what you want?" Every attempt to understand what the toddler means should be made, including asking another staff member to interpret, if needed. ("Now, I see. You want the drum from the high shelf.") Repeating the word clearly in a simple sentence as the object is given to the child ("Here is the drum you want.") helps the child to refine his pronunciation and completes the communication-response cycle for him.

In order to score this indicator "Yes," attempts by staff to correctly interpret what the children are trying to communicate must be observed, regularly (half or more of the time) throughout the observation. When scoring, it is not necessary to calculate an exact percentage. Instead, base the score on the prevalent practice used.

13.3.2c Crying can also mean boredom—needing a new toy to be brought, wanting stimulating company, or a change of scene.

5.1 Responding to a child's attempt to communicate in a *timely and positive manner* means that staff give a positive response immediately at least 75% of the time, and that no negative responses or lengthy waits for children who are obviously much in need are observed. (See photo 13.5.1.) Since the staff in an infant/toddler room are usually very busy, some short delays in responding may be observed, but there

13.5.1 This child learns that her attempts to communicate get results. This is an important part of learning to talk.

13.5.1

13.5.2a   13.5.2b

13.5.2a-b When the child hands a piece of dress-up clothes to the staff member, she provides a commentary as she helps him dress-up: "Want to wear this shirt? Let me help you put it on. First over your head; now hands in the sleeves."

should be no ignoring of children's communication or negative responses. If a long delay is unavoidable, the staff should at least acknowledge the child's communication and let the child know he has been heard. For examples of positive verbal and non-verbal responses, see Indicator 3.1.

Give a score of "Yes" if at least 75% of staff responses to children's communication is immediate and positive, and no negative responses or ignoring is observed. When scoring, it is not necessary to calculate an exact percentage. Instead, base the score on the prevalent practice used.

5.2   ***Adding words to actions*** means that staff use a verbal commentary that describes the actions they are taking as they care for the children. (See photos 13.5.2a-b.) ***Throughout the day,*** during both routines and play activities, staff should be observed describing what they and the children are doing.

During routines, the staff commentary might include:

- naming the beverages and foods the child is eating; describing the properties of the beverage or food—it's color, texture, how it tastes;

- describing the steps of a diaper change or toileting ("I'm taking off the wet diaper. Now I'm wiping your bottom. The wipe is a little cool, isn't it? Doesn't the dry diaper feel good? I'm pulling it tight across your tummy and sticking the flaps down so the diaper will not fall down when you run. All finished. Now let's wash your hands.");

- easing the transition to nap by singing or talking; holding and rocking the child in a rocking chair; rubbing the child's back ("You're getting tired, it's nap time."); or

- easing the transition from napping to waking, by talking about open eyes, about seeing various features of the room, about being lifted from the crib and being fed a snack, or putting shoes and socks on.

During play activities, staff comments might include:

- reading a book and talking about how the pictures relate to the particular child ("This baby has a daddy just like you. See the daddy in the picture?" "What is the boy playing with now? Yes, a ball. Sometimes you play with a ball too.");

13.5.3a-d   Correctly interpreting what a very young child is trying to communicate takes both skill and perseverance. It is important to keep trying and follow through appropriately.

13.5.3a Child: "I want that."

13.5.3b Staff: "The sound shakers?"

13.5.3c Child: "No! That."

13.5.3d Staff: "The container with the connecting fish? They were up high, weren't they?"

- talking about the hanging objects displayed in the room that the child can see when he looks up, such as their size, shapes, and colors, or what they are and how high up they are;

- describing what the child is doing with the dolls in the dramatic play area (putting the baby to bed, feeding the baby, rocking the baby, giving her a ride in the carriage, covering her up because she's cold);

- describing the process of drawing and what he is creating as the child makes marks, circles, and lines of different colors on the paper; and

- describing weather conditions outdoors, such as sunny, windy, raining, snowing ("See the leaves on the trees moving? It's the wind blowing the leaves." "It's raining outside. See the water puddles in the grass. Listen, the rain on the window goes ping, ping, ping.")

In order to score this item "Yes," many examples of staff providing a verbal commentary must be observed while they are caring for children during both routines and play activities.

13 Helping children use language

5.3 Staff need to be able to interpret correctly what children are trying to communicate either verbally or non-verbally, in order to meet the children's needs appropriately. A child's ability to communicate her needs develops rapidly during the infant and toddler years, and includes combinations of crying, gestures, vocalizations, and approximating words before the words become easily recognizable. ***Skillful at interpreting*** means that staff usually understand what children mean, with few exceptions. ***Follow through appropriately*** means that staff indicate verbally that they understand what the child is trying to communicate and then take action in a timely way to meet the children's needs. (See photos 13.5.3a-d, preceding page.) For examples of trying to interpret correctly, see Indicator 3.2.

Score this indicator "Yes" if staff succeed in correctly interpreting what children mean at least 75% of the time, and successfully act to meet the children with few exceptions.

7.1 In order to be given credit for a ***conversation*** there must be at least two participants who alternately take turns being the listener or the communicator. Engaging infants and toddlers in conversations gives them the experience of taking turns to vocalize and to listen to someone else's vocalization. Having a conversation requires that the two participants maintain a common focus of interest as well as pay close attention to one another so that each one can take turns appropriately in the role of listener and communicator. (See photos 13.7.1a-d.) Here are examples of turn-taking conversations.

- A staff member makes eye contact and becomes the "listener" for a vocalizing infant, then imitates the infant's sounds as the "communicator" in the conversation, followed by several changes of "listener" and "communicator" roles with the infant.

- A baby lifts her arms to the staff member, who says, "You want to get up?" The baby lifts her arms again and says, "Uh, uh." The staff member picks her up and asks, "Want to go see the books?" The baby says, "Uh, uh" and looks towards the books.

- While playing in the housekeeping area with a toddler, the staff member comments on the child's actions, "Are you putting the baby to bed?" The toddler nods in agreement and says, "Bed," giving the staff member a chance to continue the conversation with further comments and pausing to let the toddler add words and gestures.

- An older toddler says, "Look!" to call the staff member's attention to the drawing he is making. The staff member talks about the circle the toddler is making going round and round and the child nods. The staff member asks if he will take the picture home and child says "For mommy."

- A toddler uses the sign-language hand movements to say "more" at snack. The staff member says as she signs the words, "Do you want more juice or bagel?" The child lifts her cup and the teacher says, "Oh, you want more juice." They both smile as the toddler nods.

- While having her diaper changed, the toddler looks up at the mobile hanging above the changing table and says, "Bird." The staff member says, "Yes, a blue bird. Is it flying?" The child says, "Bird flying."

- A toddler points to a picture of his family on a low bulletin board and says "Mama." The staff member says, "And daddy and you, Peter" (pointing to the people in the picture). The toddler moves to another picture, points to the

13.7.1a-d Conversations involving staff and children taking turns at listening and talking help children develop expressive language skills.

13.7.1a Teacher comments.

13.7.1b Child answers.

13.7.1c

13.7.1d

13.7.1c-d Turn taking occurs back and forth, alternating listening and talking.

child and says, "Jenny." The staff member says, "That's Jenny with her Mama and Grandma and her big sister Beth." The child nods.

Score Indicator 7.1 "Yes" if throughout the observation staff are observed having frequent turn-taking conversations with children. The level of communication should be appropriate for the child, such as baby conversations with infants using body movements and sounds or conversations with toddlers using gestures, sounds and words. Conversations should be observed during both routine and play activities. Such conversations should be part of the regularly observed practice, not an isolated or unusual event.

7.2 This indicator may be scored "NA" only if there are no children in the group who are able to say words. However, as soon as even one child can use single words to communicate his or her needs and interests, staff must help develop the ability to use language by adding ***more words and ideas*** to expand on what the child has said. Toddlers usually start to use single recognizable words related to their daily experiences, including names for family members, staff, a classmate, foods they eat, objects they use, or toys they play with. If staff only repeat the word the toddler said, this repetition does assure the child that he has been heard and understood,

13 Helping children use language

13.7.3a-g Simple questions focus children's attention, even though they might not yet be able to answer them. If no answer comes from the children after a short wait, staff can give the answer in simple sentences.

13.7.3a "Where's Mia? Peek-a-Boo! There's Mia."

13.7.3b "What did we eat for snack? Do you want more cereal?"

13.7.3c "What's in this picture?"

13.7.3d "What's eating seeds from the bird feeder?"

but it does not add other words and ideas to expand the child's vocabulary and add concepts related to the word he already knows. Only staff communication that adds more words and ideas can be given credit in this indicator. For example, contrast how two teachers might deal with the same situation: Suppose a child with limited verbal ability points to a ball another child is playing with and says, "Ball."

Staff member 1 might say, "Yes, that's a ball. Good talking!"

Staff member 2 might say, "That's a big, round red ball. Would you like to play with a ball like the one Peter has? Look, he made it roll. Let's go find a ball for you to play with."

We would not give credit to staff member 1 because she used very few words, and in essence only repeated what the child said. Staff member 2 would get credit for this indicator because she used several descriptive words about the ball ("big, round,

13.7.3e

13.7.3f

13.7.3e-f "Where does this big triangle go? Yes, it goes there!"

13.7.3g "Which triangle will fit here?"

red"). She also verbalized the child's intention ("play with a ball like the one Peter has") and suggested a solution ("find one for you to play with").

In order to give credit for this indicator, at least two instances must be observed.

7.3 Questions help focus children's attention on a particular topic and increase the possibility that they will listen to the answer, even if they cannot yet answer the question themselves. This indicator requires that staff ask **simple** questions as a way of focusing a young child's attention on a verbal interaction. (See photos 13.7.3a-g.) The following are examples of using simple questions with children who have varying levels of verbal skill levels.

- Staff play a game with babies, asking and answering where various parts of their bodies are: "Where are your toes? Oh, here are Jordan's toes." (touching baby's toes) "Where are your hands [nose, tummy, etc.]?"

- A staff member says, "What's for lunch? What are you eating? Oh, I see the peas and chicken. Do you see the bread? Here it is. Brown bread."

- A staff member plays peek-a-boo, hiding her face behind a book and asking, "Where's Miss Mary?" Then she peeks out and says, "Here's Miss Mary."

- As a child is climbing down steps and stops, uncertain about how to proceed, a staff member says, "Are you stuck? Yes, you're stuck. Here, let me help you."

- When reading a book to an infant, the staff member asks specific questions about what is happening in the picture on the page she is reading. She asks very simple questions ("What is this?" "What is the dog doing?") and answers them herself, often pointing directly to the pertinent object ("That's a ball, isn't it?" "The dog is sleeping.")

- When reading a book to several toddlers, the staff member asks simple questions and waits for the toddlers to answer with gestures or words before she gives the answer herself.

13 Helping children use language

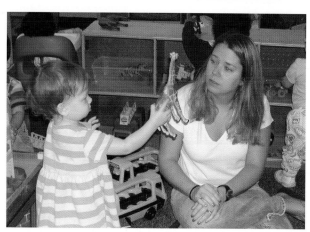

13.7.4a

13.7.4b

13.7.4a-b It is important to maintain a good balance between listening and talking. As toddlers can say more, staff need to give them more time to express themselves. Adding words and asking simple questions should help, not substitute for, the child's communication.

- When a toddler is looking at the photos of the children's families posted on the bulletin board at his eye level, a staff member asks, "Who is that in the picture?" After a little wait, the child looks at the staff member and smiles, so she says, "Kyle. That's you, Kyle, isn't it?"

To score this indicator "Yes," at least two instances of staff asking simple questions, waiting for an answer, and answering for children if they cannot answer by themselves must be observed.

7.4 Children learn to use language both by listening to others speak, and by having others listen as they speak. Staff are good language models if they adjust the ***balance*** or the relative amount of listening and talking they do to match the abilities of the particular child with whom they are conversing. In general, communicating with young infants requires staff to do most of the talking, because babies still have a limited range of vocal responses (e.g., crying, cooing, and experimenting with sounds). Older infants and toddlers who can say some words need considerable time to think of what to say in a conversation. Therefore, it is very important for staff to maintain eye contact and listen attentively for some seconds to see if an answer is forthcoming, before answering the question themselves. (See photos 13.7.4a-b.)

To give credit for this indicator, consider all the verbal and non-verbal interactions observed throughout the observation to decide whether staff have maintained an appropriate balance between listening and talking, suited to the various ages and individual abilities of the children in the group. Remember that a lot of adult talking that makes sense to infants and toddlers is required for successful language development. However, listening and attending to children's communication attempts are also important to encourage them to use language.

14 Using books

General information about this item

Giving infants and toddlers many opportunities to develop a close and enjoyable relationship with books is a vital first step towards preparing for literacy in an appropriate way. Very young children who regularly have books read to them in a warm and personal context progress from studying the pictures intently and learning to turn the pages to requesting favorite stories and anticipating the next action in a familiar book. Infant/toddler program staff have an important role to play in preparing children for lifelong literacy by making many appropriate books accessible to them for independent use and by sharing the joy of reading with them.

In this language item, as in all items involving any type of interactions, *staff* refers to those adults who are directly involved in the classroom with the children, daily or almost daily, for much of the day. This can include volunteers, if they are in the classroom the required amount of time. Adults who are in the classroom for shorter periods of the day, or who are not a regular part of the classroom, do not count in evaluating whether the requirements for this item are met. For example, if a therapist, parent, or the director of a program comes into the classroom and interacts with the children for short or irregular periods, these interactions do not count in scoring language items, *unless the interactions are extremely negative.* As an exception, in a parent cooperative or a lab school, where the usual staffing pattern includes different people as teaching assistants daily, these assistants are counted as staff.

In scoring this item, the observer should consider only those books that are accessible in the classroom for the children to use. In order to be counted as a **book**, the cover and pages must be intact, and the pages not so torn or defaced that they cannot be read. Cloth books should have clear pictures (not washed too many times). In addition to commercially produced books, books made by staff for the children can be counted. For example, staff might make a picture book using photos of the children and their families or pictures of real objects used in daily life cut out from a magazine, or a touching book with different materials of varying textures (rough, smooth, soft, hard) to feel and talk about.

In a high quality classroom, staff read books to infants and toddlers spontaneously throughout the day, as the occasion arises. In addition, for older toddlers, a short story time for a few children may also be planned daily, but children should never be forced to participate. Even if children choose to join the story group, they should be allowed to leave if they lose interest. The important thing to remember is that each time a staff member reads to children or talks about the pictures in a book, it should be an interesting and rewarding experience, so that the children form pleasant associations with literature from these early experiences, rather than negative associations.

14 Using books

A closer look at each indicator

1.1   *Appropriate books* for infants/toddlers include books that are sturdy and have pages that do not tear easily, such as books made of vinyl or cloth or those with thick cardboard pages. The pictures should be simple and clear, the content of the story of a suitable level of difficulty for the children, and no violent or frightening pictures or story content. Give credit only for appropriate books, either commercially or teacher-made, suitable to be read to the children or used independently by them. Do not count books or magazines meant for use by older children or adults, or for other activities, such as magazines or equipment catalogs being saved to be cut up for an art project. Accessible means that the books are placed where the children can easily reach them by themselves, and that the children are allowed to use them. ***Much of the day*** means most of the time that any of the children may be awake and able to play. Be sure to read the definitions of ***accessible*** and ***much of the day*** in the "Explanation of Terms Used Throughout the Scale," on page 7 of the ITERS-R.

14.1.1   Having too few books (less than six) for children to access by themselves, results in little interest in the book area.

Since infants and young toddlers are often on individual schedules, access must be provided throughout the day in such programs. For non-mobile infants, books need to be brought to them or the children need to be moved where they can access the books to be considered accessible to them. Staff may have to hold the book for a very young baby to see. The required number of books do not all have to be made accessible at the same time for non-mobile children, but it must be observed that different books are made accessible to them. If the children in the group are kept from having access to books for long periods, for example, by being confined in highchairs, swings, or playpens when awake, or by being prevented from using books by lengthy routines, credit should not be given for accessibility for much of the day. (See photo 14.1.1.)

Score Indicator 1.1 "Yes" if fewer than six appropriate books are located where children can easily reach them, or if children are not given the opportunity to use books for much of the day.

1.2   A book is in ***poor repair*** if it can no longer function as a book. The book may have lost its cover or be incomplete due to missing, torn, or scribbled-on pages. Cloth books that have lost their color from repeated washing or are wrinkled or threadbare are also in poor repair.

Generally in poor repair means that the majority of the accessible books, more than 50% of them, are in poor repair. In some cases there may be many books accessible for the children to use, but more than 50% of them may be in poor repair. Allowing children to use books that are torn or scribbled on gives them the incorrect message that it is acceptable to treat books this way. In addition, books that are in poor repair cannot be used by children or read to them by staff in a meaningful way, because the content and pictures have been distorted. (See photo 14.1.2.)

Score Indicator 1.2 "Yes" if more than 50% of the accessible books are incomplete, torn, scribbled on, or otherwise in poor repair.

14.1.2   Torn, defaced or incomplete books are not counted because they give the wrong message about how books should be treated.

1.3

When a staff member looks at a book and comments on the pictures or reads a book to an individual child or small groups of infants and toddlers, this is considered *using books* with children. Simply handing a book to a child or moving a non-mobile baby near books should not be given credit. (See photo 14.1.3.) The staff member has to conduct an appropriate activity with books to be given credit for using books with children. Just as the staff member might demonstrate by scribbling with a crayon that it is for marking on paper, reading a book to a child is part of helping the child understand how books work. The activity must last long enough to be a meaningful experience for the child, as long as the child remains interested. For example, if a staff member sits down to read with a child, but is interrupted and must leave without fully conducting the activity, then this would not be counted.

If no use of books is observed but a story or book time is listed on the posted schedule, and the rest of the schedule is fairly well carried out, ask the staff member to describe how this is handled, when it occurs, and how often it occurs. If a story or book time is reported to occur regularly several times a week and involves the use of a book by staff with children, then 1.3 must be scored "No."

Score Indicator 1.3 "Yes" only if staff are not observed using books with children and staff report that books are not used at least three times a week with children.

14.1.3 Simply making books accessible by putting them near a non-mobile baby is not considered using books with the baby.

3.1

This indicator describes how to determine the number of *appropriate books* that must be *accessible* to the children for *much of the day* to meet the requirement at this minimal level of quality. For definitions of *appropriate, accessible,* and *much of the day* see Indicator 1.1 and page 7 of the ITERS-R.

In order to score this indicator "Yes," a minimum of six appropriate books must be accessible, but no fewer than one book for each child in groups where more than six children are allowed to attend on any day. Thus, if the

14.3.1 At least six books, but no less than one per child, is required at a minimum. It is necessary to consider the maximum number of children allowed to attend on any day.

maximum number of children allowed to attend on any day is four, there must be a minimum of six books accessible. However, if the maximum daily attendance allowed is eight children, there must be at least eight books accessible at a minimum, at least one book for each child in the group, even on days when only four children are present. The minimum number of books required is based on the maximum number of children allowed to attend daily, not on the number present during the observation. For groups of one to six children, at least six books must be accessible; for groups of seven or more, one additional book must be accessible for each child daily, whether that child is in attendance or not. (See photo 14.3.1.)

As the note for this indicator in the ITERS-R book on page 30 explains, only books that are in *good repair and appropriate* may be counted towards the minimum number required in this indicator. A book is considered to be in good repair if it has a cover, if all of its pages are attached and readable, and if none of the pages is

14 Using books

badly torn, scribbled on, or faded so that it is not readable. An appropriate book is neither too difficult nor too easy, and has no frightening or violent content.

Score Indicator 3.1 "Yes" if a minimum of six appropriate books, in good repair, none of them violent or frightening, are accessible daily for most of the day, for groups of one to six children, with at least one additional book for each child in groups of more than six children.

3.2 In order to be considered in ***good repair*** a book must be complete, with its cover and all pages intact and readable. Books with torn or marked up pages, or pages that are threadbare, faded, or wrinkled, are not considered to be in good repair. If there are no more than three books that are in poor repair accessible to children, then the books may be considered to be ***generally*** in good repair. (See photo 14.3.2.)

Score Indicator 3.2 "Yes" if only three books or fewer of the accessible books are in poor repair, and all the other accessible books are in good repair.

3.3 For a definition of using books with children, see Indicator 1.3. ***Staff-initiated*** experiences with books are started by an action of the staff, whereas ***child-initiated*** experiences are started by the action of the children. Examples of ***staff involved*** in using books with children include:

14.3.2 No matter how many books are accessible, no more than three of the accessible books may be in poor repair to meet this indicator.

- A staff member reads books to a young baby who has enough head control to be seated on the staff member's lap. (staff-initiated)

- The staff member is careful to hold the book at the correct distance so that the child can see the book, knowing that the infant or toddler will show excitement if the pictures are visible. (staff-initiated)

- Books with simple, clear pictures or photographs are selected to be looked at and commented on with infants. (staff-initiated)

- Books about common experiences, such as personal care routines (feeding, sleeping, diapering), family relationships, and play activities are selected for reading and discussing with toddlers. (staff-initiated)

- When a mobile infant picks up a book and starts to explore what can be done with it by banging it on the floor or chewing on it, a staff member gently redirects the exploration by opening the book and starting to comment on the pictures with the child. (child-initiated)

- Staff bring different books over to non-mobile infants or move them close to where the books are, and read to the infants periodically. (staff-initiated)

- When a toddler picks up a book and starts to look at it, a staff member joins the child and reads the book to him. (child-initiated)

- Other toddlers who are interested are welcomed into the activity when a staff member is reading to one toddler. (staff-initiated)

- A short amount of story time is offered daily for older toddlers, using favorite books. (staff-initiated)

- As a staff member is discussing the pictures in a book or reading a book to toddlers, she allows time for the children to point to the pictures, say words, and try to answer her simple questions. (staff- or child-initiated)

- A toddler brings a favorite book from home, and a staff member reads it. (child-initiated)

14.3.3a

14.3.3b

14.3.3a-c Using books requires active involvement by staff in reading or looking at books with the children.

14.3.3c

If no involvement of staff in using books is observed, and a book or story time is listed on the schedule, ask staff what is done at that time and how often it occurs.

Score Indicator 3.3 "Yes" if staff are involved in any way in using books with children during the observation, or if staff report that they use books with children daily at another time that is identified on their schedule. (See photos 14.3.3a-c.) For observed staff involvement to count towards meeting the requirement for this indicator, the activity must be meaningful to the child (see Indicator 1.3).

3.4 *Encouraged* means that staff invite children to join them in using books and try to keep them interested in a book-related activity, but that children may choose to join or may move on to another activity when they wish. (See photo 14.3.4.) *Forced* means that no other choice of activity is allowed, and children must join and remain in the story group for as long as the staff determine. If the only alternative to joining a reading group is punishment of some kind, such as time-out, or having nothing to do, then the child is being forced to participate. However, if a staff member sits near a reluctant child or lets him sit in her lap and the child chooses to stay in the group, then this would not be

14.3.4 Children are allowed to leave the story group when they lose interest. They are not forced to participate.

considered being forced, if the child may leave and choose another activity at any time. If staff strongly insist that a child participates and the child does so, because compliance is required, then this is counted as being forced.

Score Indicator 3.4 "Yes" if children may voluntarily join book-related activities for as long as they are interested, and are allowed to leave and find another activity when they lose interest. The observer must be sure not to confuse compliance with interest.

14 Using books

14.5.1a

14.5.1b

14.5.1a-b Having enough appropriate books accessible makes the book area more attractive and the selection process more interesting. At least 12 books but no less than 2 for each of the maximum number of children allowed to attend daily is required. None of the accessible books can be violent or frightening.

5.1 This indicator at the good level of quality requires a minimum of 12 books that meet the definitions of *appropriate, accessible,* and *much of the day* found in Indicator 1.1 (defined on page 7 of the ITERS-R). For groups of 1-6 children a minimum of 12 books must be accessible. For groups of 7 or more children, a minimum of 2 books for each child is required. The number of books required to be accessible daily is based on the maximum number of children allowed to attend daily, not on the number attending during the observation. For example, if there is a maximum of 5 children allowed to attend daily in the group, there must be 12 books accessible because at least 12 books are required as a minimum to meet this indicator. However, if the maximum group size in the classroom being observed is 12 children and only 5 are present during the observation, the minimum number of books required to meet the indicator would still be 24 books, since at least 2 books are required for each child in this group of 12 children. (See photos 14.5.1a-b.)

To score this indicator "Yes," there must be a minimum of 12 appropriate books that are accessible for much of the day, and at least 2 books per child in groups of 7 children or more. All books counted must be in good repair. None of the accessible books can be violent or frightening.

5.2 A *wide selection* of books, defined in the "Note for Clarification" provided for this indicator (ITERS-R, page 30), includes books about various topics:

- picture books and stories about people of different races, different ages from infancy through old age, and people with disabilities;
- clear, non-frightening pictures of animals, including common pets, farm animals and zoo animals;
- familiar, easily recognizable objects used at home and used in the child care environment, during play or in routines; and
- stories about familiar routines, such as eating, sleeping, toileting, or dressing.

It is necessary to leaf through all the books accessible to the children in order to see what each book is about. (See photos 14.5.2a-c.) Recording examples of each of these categories is helpful for keeping track of the content of the books and to justify the score given (see chart on next page).

14.5.2a Leaf through each book to see whether it is appropriate and what the general subject matter is.

14.5.2b Books made by the staff, such as this album with pictures of the children in the group, are good additions to the book collection.

While looking at the accessible books, also note and record information needed to score other indicators. These include:

- realistic or factual books about nature/science (for credit in Item 22, Nature/science); and
- books showing racial or cultural diversity (for credit in Item 24, Promoting acceptance of diversity).

14.5.2c Look around the classroom to find all the accessible books. The box of books in this photo was found in the housekeeping area and the bookshelf was in the library center.

People
Race ✓✓✓
Age ✓
Ability ✓
Animals ✓✓✓✓✓✓
Familiar Objects ✓✓✓
Familiar Routines ✓✓
Nature/Science ✓✓✓

14 Using books

In order to score "Yes" for this indicator, the selection of accessible books must include at least one example of each of the categories mentioned in the scale. Although information may have been collected about books for other items, do not consider the specific requirements for those items here.

5.3 This indicator requires that staff *read books* to children daily. (See photo 14.5.3.) For examples of different ways that staff can be given credit for reading books with individual children or with very small groups, see Indicator 3.3. Since this indicator requires that the books are read *with individuals or very small groups,* a large-group story time would not count as an appropriate social setting to meet the indicator.

To score this indicator "Yes," at least one instance must be observed of staff reading books with an individual or a small group. The instance may be initiated by either the staff or the children, but it must be observed during the first 3 hours of the observation to be given credit as a daily occurrence in the classroom. As with earlier indicators (1.3, 3.3), the reading experience must be meaningful to count.

14.5.3 At least one instance of staff reading books must be observed. Reading to individuals or groups is acceptable.

5.4 This indicator addresses the emotional tone of the times when staff use books with children and must therefore be based on observation, not on staff report. A warm affect or emotional tone is evidenced by staff actions such as:

- gently holding the child or sitting very close to the child who is being read to;
- using the books only with children who are interested;
- using a pleasant voice;
- making eye contact with the child or children involved;
- smiling or maintaining a pleasant facial expression; and
- enjoying the book with the child or children.

An *interactive* use of a book with children is evidenced by staff actions such as:

- making sure each child can clearly see and hear the story;
- allowing time for the child or children to make comments or point to pictures as the book is read;
- encouraging toddlers to turn pages or help in reading the book by supplying words;
- asking children to select the book to be read;
- asking simple questions about the book, and waiting for an answer, then answering the question for the child if no answer is given; and
- personalizing the story for the child or children by weaving in their own experiences at home or at the center so that the story becomes more meaningful.

If observed book times are warm and interactive, score "Yes." (See photos 14.5.4a-c.) If any book time, for example, a single large-group story time, does not meet the requirements of this indicator, score "No," even if other, less formal times with books are pleasant.

14.5.4a

14.5.4b

14.5.4a-c Book reading times must be observed to be warm and interactive in order to give credit.

14.5.4c

7.1 This indicator is scored "NA" if no toddlers are included in the group. For a complete explanation of ages of infants and toddlers and the rule for when to score "NA," see page 7 of the ITERS-R, "Explanation of Terms Used Throughout the Scale."

If an older child with a disability is enrolled, and all the other children are infants, the appropriateness of this indicator will depend on the child's abilities, not necessarily on the child's age.

A **book area** includes an accessible arrangement for offering books to children with a convenient place nearby and out of traffic to use the books **independently.** (See photos 14.7.1a-d, preceding page.) Some examples of book areas for toddlers are:

- a low, child-sized bookrack that holds the books so that the front covers are visible, with a rug area nearby for children to sit on undisturbed while looking at books;
- a basket of books near a futon or mattress used for reading or quiet play;
- a low table with books on it and child-sized chairs around the table.

Score this item "Yes" if there is an accessible arrangement for offering books to toddlers and a convenient place for them to use the books independently. The area cannot be considered a book area if many toys and materials other than books are included, thus confusing the message about the area's purpose.

7.2 For a definition of being involved in **using books with children,** see Indicator 1.3. For descriptions of a variety of ways for appropriate staff involvement, see

14 Using books

14.7.1a

14.7.1b

14.7.1c

14.7.1a-d A book area for independent use by tod-dlers includes easy-to-reach books and a comfortable, convenient place nearby to read them.

14.7.1d

Indicator 3.3. ***Periodically throughout the day*** means that throughout the observation, staff are repeatedly observed using books with individuals or small groups of children. (See photos 14.7.2a-b.)

Score "Yes" if several instances are observed throughout the observation.

7.3 This indicator requires that different books are added to or exchanged periodically with the accessible materials in the classroom, in order to keep the children interested in looking at books. (See photos 14.7.3a-b.) Young children are attracted to and excited by new things to explore. Since this indicator is difficult to observe, several questions to ask the staff are included in the scale to get this information. The staff may describe the materials or show where some of them are stored. Ask how often books are rotated.

In order to give credit for this indicator, some books must be added or changed in the classroom at least monthly.

14.7.2a

14.7.2b

14.7.2a-b Throughout the observation, staff must be observed to use books with children several times so that it is clearly a regular occurrence.

14.7.3a

14.7.3b

14.7.3a-b Adding new books maintains interest in the book area. Staff answers to the questions in the scale will provide information about the frequency of changes.

Activities

15 Fine motor

General information about this item

Fine motor activities are those that encourage the development of eye-hand coordination—using the fingers and eyes together to manipulate objects. Developing good eye-hand coordination is one of the major tasks that infants and toddlers work on. It takes years to become adept at coordinating the eyes and hands, with each task requiring practice, and some being more difficult to achieve than others.

Infants and toddlers usually know what to practice and will do so, given the right opportunities. To meet the needs of these youngest children, staff should observe each child to become aware of the skills the child is working on and provide toys and activities that allow the practice needed. For example, if staff notice a baby is working on using her thumb and forefinger together to pick up things, toys can be provided where she can grasp small objects (without being able to remove and swallow them), or little pieces of safe foods can be served for the child to feed herself at meals and snacks.

The types of activities and materials children can access will determine the kinds of fine motor skills they can practice. Since there is tremendous developmental progress in this area during just a few months' time, it is necessary that the experiences for children match their rapidly changing skills.

Fine motor materials help children practice the skills required to handle or manipulate small objects with their fingers, especially the fingers and thumb working together. Using fine motor materials usually requires that children will use their sight to guide their finger movements, such as looking to see where the hole is in a box in order to drop a block into it. *Appropriate fine motor materials* for infants and toddlers are those that generally match their developing skill levels and are challenging but not frustrating. In addition, they must be safe for the children. Books are not given credit in this item as a fine motor material, even though eye-hand coordination is used to turn pages. (Consider books in Item 14,Using books.) Examples of appropriate fine motor materials for infants and for toddlers are given in the "Notes for Clarification" on page 31 of the ITERS-R. Other examples include:

For Infants:

- rattles to shake and grasp (of different textures, colors, shapes, with varying noises), (See photo 15A, next page.)
- safe hanging things to bat at or to grasp, (See photo 15B, next page.)
- small soft grasping toys, such as animals, rings, or dolls,
- simple stacking rings,
- clean teething toys,

15A Rattles are age appropriate fine motor materials for infants because they are easy to grasp and shake.

15B Young infants can practice their fine motor skills – batting, grasping and pulling – while using this cradle gym.

15C Simple containers and objects provide older infants and young toddlers with experiences of grasping and dropping.

15D Bead mazes require the coordination of both eyes and hands working together to move beads along the wire.

15E Large stringing beads are appropriate for older toddlers who have the precise control needed to push the string through the small hole and then grab it to pull it through.

- large pop beads, and
- cause-and-effect toys, which respond with sounds or other responses when buttons are pushed

For Toddlers:

- containers to drop objects into, (See photo 15C.)
- bead mazes, (See photo 15D.)
- sets of manipulatives with larger than preschool-sized pieces, such as links, interlocking stars, medium-sized interlocking blocks, or large beads to string, (See photo 15E.)
- simple lacing toys,
- finger paints,
- large watercolor markers, and
- puzzles with knobs and large pieces.

A closer look at each indicator

1.1

No fine motor materials means that there are few items to help children develop fine motor skills in the classroom. Only a few examples of incomplete fine motor materials might be present, and the pieces needed for using them are so scattered that it is impossible for a child to do the task for which the material was designed. For example, if there are pop beads in the classroom, but they are so scattered that a toddler might not easily find two to put together, these beads would not be counted to meet the requirement of fine motor materials. However, if at least two pop beads are routinely stored together, and periodically cleaned up, even if they become scattered during play times, they would be counted as one fine motor material.

Appropriate means that the materials interest and challenge children in terms of their ages and abilities, without being frustrating. In addition, the materials are safe for those who use them. The best way to determine if materials are developmentally appropriate is to observe children using the materials and notice whether the materials are too difficult or easy, are safe, and whether children maintain interest while using them. The observer should be especially careful when evaluating fine motor materials for the older toddlers to ensure that the majority is neither too easy nor too hard to use. Of course, any fine motor materials for infants/toddlers must not have any pieces small enough to swallow.

Accessible means that children can reach and use materials by themselves. This term is defined in the "Explanation of Terms Used Throughout the Scale" on page 7 of the ITERS-R.

Observers should determine whether toys stored on open shelves are actually *accessible* to the children. This is usually discovered by watching whether children are allowed or encouraged to take toys from open shelves. However, when children do not seem to feel free or are not able to take toys from shelves, the observer must find out how and when the materials are used and whether there are rules about special times when children are allowed to access them. For example, toddlers may tend to use a few toys in one area of the room, but stay away from others that are also stored within their reach (such as art materials, puzzles, or

15 Fine motor

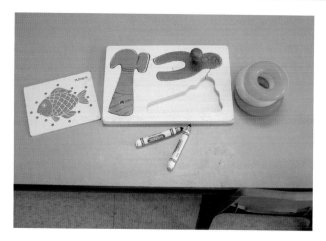

15.1.2 Puzzles with missing pieces, dried out markers, and other incomplete materials are considered in poor repair.

15.3.1a At the minimal level of quality, at least five fine motor toys must be accessible to infants.

sets of manipulatives). The observer must determine how and when those materials are accessible to score this item, preferably by observing, but also through questions asked during the staff interview.

***For daily* use** means that the materials are accessible every day.

To score Indicator 1.1 "No," children must have access to at least three intact, usable fine motor materials for some time during each day. Otherwise, score this indicator "Yes."

1.2   ***In poor repair*** means that fine motor toys and materials cannot be used properly because too many pieces are missing, parts are broken, or other problems exist. For example, most of the watercolor markers are dried out, pegboards do not have pegs, shape sorter toys are missing their shapes, the beads have come off the bead mazes, stacking rings are missing the base to stack on, or puzzles are missing pieces. (See photo 15.1.2.)

Generally in poor repair means that *most* (about 80%) of the materials cannot be used properly because of their poor condition. Score this indicator "Yes" if most of the fine motor materials are in poor repair.

15.3.1b Appropriate fine motor materials provide challenge, without frustration.

3.1.   ***Appropriate fine motor materials is defined in*** the "General Information" section for this item and in the information provided for Indicator 1.1. The term ***some*** is defined in the "Explanation of Terms Used Throughout the Scale" on page 7 of the ITERS-R. ***Some*** for this item means at least *five examples* of fine motor toys listed in the "Notes for Clarification" for this indicator on p. 31 of the ITERS-R, since the term "materials" is in the plural. (See photos 15.3.1a-b.)

To count as one example, the toy must be intact, functional, and have enough pieces to allow the type of activity for which

15.3.1c To be accessible to a non-mobile baby, the child must be placed next to the toys, or the toys brought to the child.

15.3.1d Fine motor toys are made accessible for all children in the group, including children with disabilities.

15.3.1e Children who are mobile can easily reach and use toys when there are no barriers that prevent use.

it was designed. One rattle counts as one example. Markers cannot be dried out and must have drawing paper with them to be counted as an example. A bead maze must have beads that move along the wires. There must be at least two pop beads to snap together to count as one example. Toddler-sized interlocking blocks must consist of a set with enough blocks to make a simple tower of connecting pieces. A puzzle must have all its pieces. A functional set, rather than its individual pieces, is considered as one toy. For example, several crayons count as a single example of fine motor materials, as does a set of big beads with strings.

To give credit for Indicator 3.1 (score "Yes"), the five or more examples must be observed to be ***accessible for daily use*** at some point during an observation of 3 hours. Do not give credit if, during a longer observation, the toys are not accessible during the first 3 hours observed or if there is evidence that the toys are not accessible on a daily basis. When observing in a group with both non-mobile and mobile children, look for accessibility for all children. (See photos 15.3.1c-f.)

15.3.1f Toys on the lowest shelf are accessible to the infant, but those stored on the higher shelves are not.

3.2. The term ***much of the day*** is defined in the "Explanation of Terms Used Throughout the Scale" on page 7 of the ITERS-R. To give credit, children must be free to reach and use fine motor materials for much of the time they are awake and able to play, and not involved in routine care. If babies are held much of the time they are awake, fine motor toys must be used with or offered to them by staff. When awake, children cannot be restricted to groups or kept in spaces where there is no access to the fine motor toys for lengthy periods. (See photo 15.3.2.) If long periods of time are spent outdoors, some fine motor materials must be among the toys they can choose to use. For toddler materials that require very close supervision, such as watercolor markers, paints, or materials with pieces that might be a danger for younger children enrolled in the group, staff should make the materials accessible when they can be supervised. However, they cannot be counted among those materials that are accessible much of the day.

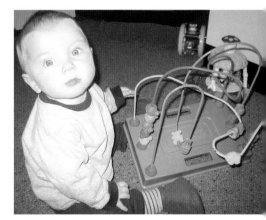

15.3.2 Placing a toy next to a non-mobile baby makes access possible.

15 Fine motor

15.5.1a In a good quality classroom, children can access enough fine motor materials so that there is little or no competition over toys.

15.5.1b Duplicates of toys are accessible so children are less likely to wait or argue over their favorite toys. There are multiple soft, stacking rings, shape sorters and busy boxes in this toddler room.

3.3 Credit can be given for this indicator (score "Yes") as long as fine motor **materials are generally in good repair.** This requires that about 80% of all accessible fine motor materials and toys are in good shape, unbroken, have all their pieces, and can be used by the children in the way for which they were designed. This indicator does not require that all fine motor toys and materials be complete and in good repair, as long as about 80% are. The requirement applies not to just the "some" fine motor materials required in Indicator 3.1, but also to all that are accessible.

Credit can be given for this indicator even if there are some fine motor materials with missing pieces or that are in poor repair. For example, it is observed that a classroom has many rattles, a bead maze, a busy box,

15.5.1c Variety can exist among similar types of materials for example, a soft, textured stacking ring and a hard plastic one.

and a shape sorter, but one ring is missing from a stacking ring toy, and the set of nesting cups is missing a cup. Credit can be given because most of the fine motor materials are in good repair and complete. To determine if 80% of the materials are in good repair, make a list of the fine motor materials. Put an "X" next to the materials that are either in poor repair or missing pieces. Evaluate the list to determine if this indicator is true.

5.1 The terms **many** and **varied** are defined in the "Notes for Clarification" for Indicator 5.1, in the ITERS-R. **Many** will depend on the number of children in the group and their interests. If children are observed to compete over popular fine motor materials, duplicates or interesting alternatives must be accessible to the children to give credit for many. (See photos 15.5.1a-b.) **Many** means numerous accessible materials even for a very small group of children. As the group size increases, so must the number of materials, so that the total is plentiful for the group. Examples of fine motor materials are listed in the "Notes for Clarification" on p. 31 of the ITERS-R. The observer should carefully evaluate the materials to make sure that

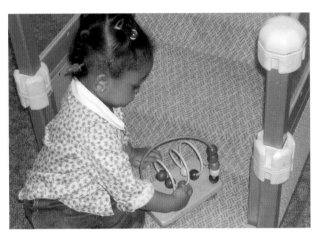

15.5.1d   **15.5.1e**

15.5.1d-e This toddler enjoys different experiences with two types of bead mazes.

15.5.1f [right] Many and varied fine motor materials are placed on low, open shelves and are easily accessible to children who can crawl and walk. In addition, staff take materials off the shelves and place them in front of the non-mobile infants so that these materials are accessible for them as well.

each fine motor toy counted to meet the requirement of "many" meets the developmental needs of children. If a toy does not meet the developmental needs of the age group being observed it does not count as one of the "many" materials." For example, stringing beads would not be considered a fine motor toy for young infants, who have limited use of their hands and fingers. However, rattles or soft grasping toys may be easily used by the infants and can be counted as one of the "many" fine motor materials/toys. Similarly, rattles and grasping toys would not meet the developmental needs of older toddlers, while simple puzzles and sets of large interlocking toys would. There should be no fewer than 10 toys for a group of 5 infants or 15 toys for a group of 5 toddlers, and at least 1 additional toy for each child over that number in each age group. For example, 10 fine motor toys would be considered many fine motor toys for a group of 4 younger infants, but would not be considered many for a group of 12, especially if the children had to compete for use.

15.5.1f

Since *varied* means requiring different skills, as well as having different characteristics, duplicates of the same toy do not count towards meeting the requirement of *varied*, although they do count towards the requirement of *many*. To evaluate whether fine motor materials are varied, note the skills that each toy promotes, as well as differences in color, size, shape texture, sound, and action. (See photos 15.5.1c-e.) If differences are found for most of these characteristics, credit can be given for *varied*.

Accessible much of the day refers to the *many and varied* fine motor toys/ materials (not just to the "some," required in Indicator 3.1). (See photo 15.5.1f.) For toddler materials that require very close supervision, such as watercolor markers, fingerpaints, or materials with many pieces that might be dangerous for younger children enrolled in the group, staff must make the materials accessible when they can be supervised.

15 Fine motor

15.5.2a

15.5.2b

15.5.2c
15.5.2a-c There are many options for organizing fine motor toys, as long as the order is maintained so materials are complete and accessible to children.

15.5.2d These connecting blocks, consisting of many pieces, are organized in the same container making it easy for staff to pick up and easily sort materials several times thoughout the day.

5.2

Well organized means that each of the fine motor materials is stored with all its pieces in an area designated for its use, so that children know where to find the materials they need for an activity and the materials can easily be put away. Mobile children are able to easily see and access these materials with little or no help from the staff. Staff are able to easily access the materials to provide them for use by non-mobile children. Well organized also means that materials for a specific activity are stored together so that a child can easily find all the materials needed to complete the activity. (See photos 15.5.2a-c.) For example, the chalk is stored with the chalk boards, the rattles are stored in a bin that can be taken out and put next to a non-mobile child, and the peg boards are stored with the pegs that fit the board.

Fine motor materials containing many pieces should be stored in individual containers. If pieces of different fine motor materials are all jumbled together, so that it is difficult to find the pieces needed for a certain activity, or if puzzles are stored without their pieces in place, do not give credit for Indicator 5.2 (score "No"). If the vast majority of fine motor materials are stored so it is easy for children to use them and easy for staff and children to clean up, score "Yes." Perfection is not required to score "Yes," and all fine motor materials do not have to be stored together in the same area of the room. However, most should be in one area, and sets with many pieces stored in their own containers. (See photo 15.5.2d.) Check for organization of fine motor materials several times during the 3-hour observation because mobile

15.7.1a

15.7.1b

15.7.1a-b Staff put away old toys and replace with new toys so that children can practice different skills and have exciting new learning opportunities.

children usually scatter them as they play. If staff pick up, sort, and replace materials several times to restore order, give credit.

7.1 *Materials rotated* means that the fine motor toys that are accessible to children are changed so children can practice different skills, find new interests, and use toys that they have used before, but in a new way. Rotating toys keeps children from becoming bored with the choices they can make for play and adds new learning opportunities. (See photos 15.7.1a-b.)

Toy rotation should occur when children become bored with the materials because they no longer find them interesting or challenging. The materials should then be put away and different materials brought out. Toys should also be rotated to provide new types of experiences.

Calling children's attention to a fine motor material that is regularly accessible to children does not count as "rotating materials." For example, when staff take stringing beads off the shelf where accessible toys are stored and place the beads on the table for toddlers to use, credit for "rotation" is not given. Credit is given only when toys are removed from the accessible shelves in the classroom and replaced with toys that were formerly inaccessible.

Inaccessible materials can be made accessible as either special projects or for free play. The rotated fine motor materials can be brought from storage or other classrooms, newly purchased, or borrowed from a toy lending library.

To give credit, some toys should be rotated at least *monthly*.

7.2 *Different levels of difficulty* means that there are some fine motor materials which are more challenging and some that are less challenging to the children in the group. (See photo 15.7.2.) The less challenging materials require less advanced eye-hand coordination, while the more difficult materials require higher

15.7.2 Because children vary in their fine motor skills, puzzles on different levels of difficulty provide them with materials that match their abilities.

15 Fine motor

levels of skill. Since children's fine motor skills will vary within any group, it is important to have a variety of materials so children are not frustrated with difficult-to-use materials or lose interest in materials that are too easy. When children with disabilities are enrolled in the group, special materials to meet their needs for fine motor development should be provided if needed.

Examples of materials of different levels of difficulty include:

Easier	More challenging
Simple rattles to grasp	Complex rattles with small pieces to handle with fingers
Knobbed puzzles	Puzzles without knobs
Puzzles with few, large pieces	Puzzles with many smaller pieces
Open container into which to drop blocks	Shape sorter with lid
3-cup set of nested cups	6-cup set of nested cups
Large watercolor markers	Crayons
Glue sticks	Squeeze bottles of glue
Finger paints	Tempera paint with brush
Bead mazes	Stringing beads

Score Indicator 7.2 "Yes" if there are at least two examples of materials on different levels of difficulty, suitable for the children in the group, and no materials that are too difficult for the child with the most fine motor abilities.

16 Active physical play

General information about this item

During the infant/toddler years, major progress is made in the development of gross motor skills. Control and coordination of the large muscles begins at the center of the body and develops outward to the arms and legs. A very young baby must gain the ability to control neck muscles (to hold up the head) and body (trunk) first. They spend lots of time moving their arms and legs, seemingly in a random way, but they are really developing the skill to control their inexact movements so that they can move for a purpose, such as batting at a toy or reaching out to be picked up. Given the opportunities, babies naturally reach such milestones as sitting, reaching with accuracy, pushing up, crawling, cruising, standing unsupported, and walking. Toddlers continue refining all these skills, learning to coordinate movements more smoothly and get around more quickly. These skills will develop naturally, in their own time according to each child's characteristics, unless a child is prevented from moving. It is unlikely that adults can make gross motor skills develop more rapidly. For example, walking will not necessarily happen sooner if adults hold children up and make them appear to walk before they really can do so. However, adults can encourage the development of gross motor skills by providing many appropriate opportunities for children to practice using their large muscles.

In order to determine the score for this item, the observer must be familiar with basic infant/toddler gross motor development, and recognize what is needed at the vastly differing stages that occur in rapid succession during the first 2 ½ years of life. It will be necessary to observe whether children are passive or active physically to distinguish which activities encourage gross motor development. For example, infants and toddlers who are put in swings or taken for rides in strollers are being passive, rather than active, participants, while a baby lying on a mat, freely able to move arms and legs is active and able to practice gross motor skills. (See photo 16 A-B.) Similarly, toddlers who are cautioned to be quiet for long periods, or to always use "walking feet," are not sufficiently encouraged to participate in active physical play.

16A

16B

16A Even though infants enjoy swinging in outdoor swings, this is not counted as the active physical movement needed for gross motor development.

16B Taking children outside for stroller rides does not count as active physical play.

16C Space for active physical play can be either indoors, in a special gross motor room, ...

16D ...in an open space within the regular classroom, ...

The two major requirements for infants and toddlers to develop gross motor skills are **space** that allows free movement and **materials and equipment** that promote the practice of large muscle coordination. These are the two primary issues evaluated in this item. Since it is stated on page 6 of the ITERS-R, under the section "Scoring System," that "requirements of the scale apply to *all* children in the group being observed, unless an exception is noted in an item," every child must have access to space and materials or equipment for active physical play that meet their developmental needs.

Space for active physical play is space that allows free movement of the large muscles. It includes both indoor and outdoor areas and must be large enough for children to move freely without being restricted by crowding. (See photos 16 C-E.) Of course, the space required for such movement is far less for non-mobile children than for older toddlers, who are usually quite mobile.

16E ... or outdoors.

No minimum square footage is required when evaluating the amount of space for active physical play. Instead, the adequacy of the space should be determined by the number of children using the space at one time, the furnishings, materials, and equipment in the space, and how well the space functions to meet the developmental needs of all the children being observed. Outdoor space adds new experiences to what is available in indoor space by providing fresh air, more room, and surfaces that usually differ from those indoors.

Because the majority of serious accidents in early childhood programs occur during gross motor play, this item considers the safety of the space. Safety should be evaluated in terms of general hazards in the space, including the adequacy of fall zones around and between gross motor equipment.

All spaces regularly used for gross motor activities should be considered in scoring this item. Outdoor space is defined as space that exposes children to fresh air and the natural world during gross motor play. Indoor gross motor space is enclosed, as inside a building, even if windows are present. Obviously, there will be some spaces that are "in between," such as screened porches, semi-shelters, or covered patios. The observer must determine whether these should be considered indoor or outdoor spaces, taking into account the amount of fresh air, exposure to the natural world, and the play surfaces that are provided.

To be considered in this item, the space must actually be used for gross motor play. For example, an outdoor porch that is used for sand and water play, but not for gross motor play, would not be counted. On the other hand, a toddler block area used for dancing every afternoon would be included as an indoor gross motor space.

Even if gross motor areas are not used during the observation (e.g., if the weather is bad, or no one is using the space), the spaces must be examined before the item can be scored. To supplement observed information, questions can be asked of staff to get more information about how the area is used, what types of activities occur in the space, and how the space is arranged. Another option for observing the outdoor space in use is to return to the program on another day, when the weather permits outdoor play.

There are many types of ***materials/equipment*** that can be used with infants and toddlers to assist the development of large muscle skill and coordination. In this item, the two terms "materials" and "equipment" are used interchangeably. The appropriateness of the gross motor equipment for all the children who use it is covered in this item to ensure that each child has safe opportunities to practice the necessary skills. Because individual infants and toddlers have differing needs and interests, requirements for variation in challenge are included at the higher quality levels, in addition to ensuring that plenty of safe equipment is present for children to use.

Gross motor materials/equipment include *anything* provided for or regularly permitted by the staff to be used for stimulating gross motor activity. This includes manufactured, custom-made, and natural objects used for climbing, sliding, balancing, or other gross motor activity. It does not include objects meant to be used for other purposes, such as benches to sit on, shade trees, or shelves children are not supposed to climb on, unless children are allowed to use these for active physical play.

Stationary equipment is equipment that has been installed on a playground or is anchored. Stationary equipment can also include unanchored equipment that can be moved by adults, but that is too heavy for children to move as part of their play.

Portable gross motor materials/equipment that is meant to be moved or rearranged by children as part of their gross motor play (e.g., riding toys, balls) is

also considered. (See photo 16 F.) These materials are not to be confused with other types of play materials, such as dramatic play props, sand/water toys, or blocks, because the primary use of such playthings is not for gross motor activities.

Examples of ***appropriate*** materials and equipment are found in the "Notes for Clarification" on page 32 of the ITERS-R.

In scoring this item, decisions should be based on observation of how both ***indoor and outdoor*** gross motor spaces and materials function for the children who are using them.

16F [right] Push toys are considered appropriate for gross motor development. Notice the child being held is not provided with space or materials for active physical play at the moment.

16F

Especially with unusual, natural, or innovative play opportunities, which may vary greatly, it is essential to observe carefully to see how children use the provisions and whether they encounter problems.

A closer look at each indicator

1.1 Issues to consider when evaluating *space for active physical play* are discussed in the "General Information" section for this item.

For active physical play space to be *appropriate*, it must

- allow freedom of large muscle movement as described in the "General Information" section for this item; and

- be safe for the children who use it.

The safety of all spaces used for gross motor activities must be considered in scoring this indicator. Indoor space should be examined for safety hazards, as well as outdoor space. Space that is used more frequently should be given more weight than space that is rarely used, in determining the appropriateness of the space. However, no space, if used, can be ignored in determining a score.

Characteristics of "safe" gross motor space

The characteristics of "safe" gross motor space must be applied to both indoor and outdoor spaces used for active physical play. Often the indoor space used is in the classroom where children spend much of the day. Examples of safety hazards commonly found in the indoor space are provided in the "Notes for Clarification" for Item 11, Safety practices, on page 27 of the ITERS-R. However, other hazards should be considered as well. For example, if a non-mobile baby is put down on a mat to encourage kicking his legs or pushing up on his arms, the observer must consider whether the baby is safe in that space. Is the space protected or in traffic pathways? Is the baby likely to be stepped on or able to reach dangerous objects?

In addition to the common hazards found indoors, special hazards associated with the use of gross motor equipment should be considered. For example, the indoor space in which a climber is used would require an appropriate fall zone and a cushioning surface that reduces the impact of falls.

The Consumer Product Safety Commission (CPSC) provides guidelines for determining whether *outdoor* spaces for active physical play are safe for children in the publication, Handbook for Public Playground Safety. The complete handbook is available at no cost when downloaded from the Internet website, www.cpsc.gov.

The CPSC Handbook for Public Playground Safety includes guidelines for safe fall zones, with requirements for adequate cushioning surfaces to minimize injury from falls. The guidelines discuss organization of areas on the playground, appropriate surfaces, and general safety suggestions. The major points covered in the Handbook are summarized in the Playground Information Sheet located at the end of this item.

It should be noted that, at the time of this writing, CPSC only gives fall zone guidelines for outdoor anchored equipment for children who are older than infants/ toddlers. Standards are currently being developed for children in the younger age group, and observers should use up-to-date information to assess safety conditions when such guidelines become available. For the present, when using the ITERS-R, standards similar to those currently used for preschool children apply in determining whether gross motor space is safe for the children who use it. For example, a safe fall zone, with adequate cushioning surface, would be required around a climber if an infant could fall from higher than 12 inches.

The criteria for verifying the resilience of fall zone cushioning surfaces not covered in the chart on the Playground Information Sheet (such as poured or installed foam or rubber surfaces) are as follows: the materials must meet the ASTM F1292 requirements for the material used under equipment. This is best verified with a written statement from the manufacturer.

Anything permitted by the staff to be used for stimulating gross motor activity must have an adequate fall zone if there is the potential for children to be injured from a fall. Height and velocity should be considered when determining whether a fall zone with cushioning surface is needed. Although the CPSC guidelines apply only to anchored equipment, for purposes of scoring, similar standards should be applied to all surfaces onto which serious falls can occur.

Although falls from significant heights are often emphasized in determining the safety of a gross motor space, everything in the space used by the children should be considered. Often there are structures or other types of equipment present that can be hazards. For example, long bolts on fences are protrusions; exposed links or wooden points on top of fences can be catch points for clothing; spaces between stairs or between railings of stairs used by children might cause entrapment; or certain types of natural objects, such as plants, insects, water areas, or rocks might be safety hazards. The location and characteristics of the space and the hazards associated with accessing or using it must be evaluated in determining the safety of the gross motor space. For example, having to cross a busy street or being near traffic with inadequate barriers might be safety issues.

Major safety hazards are those that are likely to cause serious injury requiring hospitalization or medical care, such as broken bones, major bleeding, drowning, or strangulation. *Minor hazards* are those that are only likely to cause mild injury, such as small cuts, bumps and bruises, pinched fingers, and splinters. To score Indicator 1.1, the observer must determine whether the spaces used for gross motor play, both indoors and outdoors, are safe.

Within the classroom, only the space actually used for active physical play should be considered in determining safety for this item. In some cases, when children are allowed to access all space freely, all the space in the classroom will count. But in other cases, where children are restricted to certain areas for play, only those areas where gross motor activity takes place should be considered, for example, a climbing structure located in the corner of a classroom where climbing and sliding is encouraged. Other indoor spaces used for active physical play, such as gross motor rooms, hallways, other classrooms, or multi-purpose rooms, should also be considered.

All spaces used must be inspected. The depth of cushioning surfaces and size of fall zones must be measured to determine adequacy. (See photos 16.1.1a-b, next page.) The observer should bring a tape measure and something to dig or probe with, and the whole space accessible to children must be carefully examined for hazards. Anything other than gross motor equipment that children have access to in the space, such as fences, storage sheds, air conditioning units, dramatic play structures, benches, picnic tables, or water areas, must also be assessed for safety in this item.

Score Indicator 1.1 "Yes" if there is *no* gross motor space used by the children daily.

16 Active physical play

16.1.1a　　　　　　　　　　　　　　　　　**16.1.1b**

16.1.1a-b　All spaces used for active play, both indoors and outdoors should be evaluated for safety hazards, such as inadequate fall zones or a lack of cushioning surfaces for climbing equipment.

If space is available, but used less than daily for each child, score "Yes." Different spaces may be used for the various children, but each must have the use of gross motor space at least once a day. If *any* infant spends the vast majority of time in an infant seat, crib, swing, or other equipment that restricts movement, or is held, restricting movement, and never has access to any space for active physical play, then this indicator is scored "Yes."

All major and minor safety hazards should be noted in each of the spaces used for gross motor play, in order to judge the general safety of all the gross motor spaces used. In judging the general appropriateness of all the active play space, the observer will need to weigh various factors, including the severity of the hazards in the particular spaces, the likelihood of the hazards causing an accident, and the amount of time children use particular spaces. This information is needed later in Indicator 5.5, and also in Item 11, Safety practices.

All that is required to score this indicator "No" is that there is at least one appropriately safe space, used daily indoors or outdoors and large enough to allow free movement, that has no hazards that are likely to cause serious accidents.

1.2　　*Equipment/materials* for active physical play is defined in the "General Information" section for this item. ***Appropriate*** equipment/materials challenge children to develop and practice large muscle skills safely. (See photos 16.1.2a-b.) Equipment that is too easy for children to use, too difficult, or not safe is ***not*** appropriate. Both indoor and outdoor gross motor equipment should be considered when determining how to score this indicator. Both stationary and portable equipment, if present, should be considered. (See photo 16.1.2c.)

Too easy or too difficult

Equipment that is "too easy" for children to use does not challenge them. Children tend to become bored with too-easy equipment, ignore it or misuse it. For example, a cradle gym that would challenge a baby who cannot yet sit up would not be of much interest to a toddler if used as intended. Instead, the toddler might try to pick it up and drag it around. Similarly, a bar to pull up on would interest an older baby, but usually be ignored by a 2-year old. Using equipment that is too easy for toddlers is asking for trouble, because they will look for the challenges they need in activities that are not safe, such as climbing on toy shelves and chairs.

16.1.2a Equipment and materials for infants may include blankets and cradle gyms with hanging toys.

16.1.2b This climber is too challenging to be considered appropriate for the toddlers who use it.

16.1.2c Although infants and toddlers enjoy this climbing arrangement, the inadequate fall zone poses safety hazards.

16.1.2d Toddlers easily fall from swings with open seats.

Equipment that is "too difficult" frustrates children and encourages accidents. A climber that is just two feet high, with a slide, may look very easy to use but would be dangerous for infants or younger toddlers (12-23 months of age). The large vinyl covered foam shapes that can be arranged in many ways can be set up to match children's abilities, but they are often arranged so that they pose safety hazards for babies who use them. (See photo 16.1.2c.) Swings with open seats are too difficult for toddlers, allowing them to fall. (Remember that passive sitting in swings is not counted as active physical play.) (See photo 16.1.2d.) Portable equipment meant for older children, such as wheel toys with pedals or large rocking horses, are too difficult or dangerous for most infants and toddlers.

Characteristics of "safe" gross motor equipment

The Consumer Product Safety Commission (CPSC) gives guidelines for determining whether outdoor anchored equipment is safe for children in the publication, Handbook for Public Playground Safety. The complete handbook is available at no cost when downloaded from the Internet website: www.cpsc.gov.

The major points covered in the Handbook are summarized in the "Playground Information Sheet" (see pages 212–213).

It should be noted that CPSC gives guidelines only for outdoor anchored equipment for preschool and older children. However, similar standards should be applied

Playground Information to Use with the Environment Rating Scales

Based on information from the U.S. Consumer Product Safety Commission, **Handbook for Public Playground Safety,** *Pub. No. 325. These guidelines are a basic overview of areas to review when scoring playground and safety items in the ECERS-R, ITERS-R, FDCRS, or SACERS. This list is not to be used as a comprehensive guide for playground assessment.*

Catch Points and Protruding Hardware – There should be no dangerous pieces of hardware, such as protruding bolt ends and narrow gaps in metal connections or open "S" hooks at the top and bottom of swings. Exposed hardware can cut children, puncture skin, or catch clothing drawstrings, which could strangle a child. The top of fences less than 4 feet in height also should be checked for protrusions.

Entrapment – Children can get trapped and strangle in openings where they can fit their bodies but not their heads through the space. Therefore openings in guardrails, spaces between platforms, between ladder rungs, and uprights in protective barriers, should measure less than 3.5 inches or more than 9 inches. However, if the ground is the bottom edge of a space between 3.5 inches and 9 inches, it is not considered an entrapment hazard because the child will not be in danger of choking.

Pinch, Crush, Shearing, and Sharp Hazards – Equipment should not have sharp points or edges that could cut skin. Moving pieces of equipment, such as suspension bridges, track rides, merry-go-rounds, or seesaws, should not have accessible moving parts that might crush or pinch a child's finger or other body part.

Protective Barriers – A protective barrier is an enclosing device around an elevated platform that is intended to prevent both inadvertent falls from the platform and deliberate attempts to pass through the barrier. In other words, children should not be able to jump over it or move through it.

For preschoolers, full protective barriers are preferred because they provide more protection from falls. Protective barriers are required for platforms that are over 30 inches above the ground. The top surface of the barrier should be at least 29 inches above the platform. No child should be able to climb over, under or through the barrier. For equipment used *only* by school-aged children, including 5-year-olds, any platform more than 48 inches above the ground requires protective barriers. The top surface of the protective barrier must be at least 38 inches high.

Guardrails – A guardrail is an enclosing device around an elevated platform that is intended to prevent inadvertent falls from the platform. A child might be able to climb over, under or through the guardrail.

For preschoolers through 4 years of age, guardrails prevent falls from elevated platforms that are higher than 20 inches, and up to 30 inches, above the ground. For preschoolers through 4 years of age, the top surface of the guardrails should be at least 29 inches above the platform, and the lower edge should be no more than 23 inches above the platform. For equipment used *only* by school-aged children, including 5-year-olds, any platform more than 30 inches above the ground (but not over 48 inches above the ground) will need guardrails at least 38 inches above the platform, with the lower edge no more than 28 inches above the platform.

When mixed age groups of preschool- and school-aged children use the same equipment (e.g., 4- and 5-year-olds) the most stringent requirements are applied to ensure safety for all. For example, platforms used by the group will require protective barriers, rather than guardrails if they reach the height listed for preschoolers. Guardrails and barriers must be of the height required for school-aged children, which is higher than required for preschoolers.

Platforms that are layered on equipment, (e.g., one platform leading up to another in a step-like manner), so that it would be impossible for preschoolers to fall more than 20 inches from one level to another (or school-aged children to fall 30 inches to another platform) do not require barriers or guardrails if they would interfere with the intended use of the equipment (e.g., stepping up to the next level).

Tripping Hazards – There should be no exposed concrete footings, abrupt changes in surface elevations, tree roots, tree stumps, and rocks, which can trip children or adults.

Protective Surfacing – The surfaces under and around play equipment should be soft enough to cushion falls, which are the most frequent causes of injuries on playgrounds. For specifics on depth of material, see the chart below. When the surfacing in much used areas becomes displaced (e.g., under swings, slides) it should be raked back or replaced to maintain correct depth.

Fall Zones – Resilient surfacing shall extend beyond the external limits of stationary equipment for a minimum of 6 feet. Swings shall have resilient surfacing that extends 2 times the length of the pivot point to the surface below. The surfacing shall be to the front and rear of the swing. Tot swings shall have resilient surfacing that extends 2 times the length of the pivot point to the bottom of the swing seat, both in the front and rear of the swing. Tot swings are defined as swings with enclosed seats. Tire swings shall have resilient surfacing that extends a distance of 6 feet plus the measurement from the pivot point to the swing seat and 6 feet to the side of the support structure.

Equipment Spacing – Play structures should be spaced at least 12 feet apart to allow children space to circulate around or fall without striking another structure. Moving pieces of equipment should be located in an area away from other play structures so children have adequate room to pass from one play area to another without being struck by a moving swing or by another child exiting from a slide.

Critical Heights of Playground Equipment for Various Types and Depths of Resilient Surfaces

Based on Information from the U.S. CONSUMER PRODUCT SAFETY COMMISSION (CPSC Publication No. 325), Handbook for Public Playground Safety. When no requirement is provided for a specific height of equipment, we have used the requirement for the next higher height, so requirements are conservative, erring on the side of safety.

	Wood Chips	Double Shredded Bark	Uniform Wood Chips	Fine Sand	Coarse Sand	Fine Gravel
Equipment Height	**Uncompressed Depths of Materials In Fall Zone					
Five feet or less	6 inches	6 inches	6 inches	6 inches	6 inches	6 inches
Six feet	6 inches	6 inches	6 inches	12 inches	12 inches	6 inches
Seven feet	6 inches	9 inches	9 inches	12 inches	12 inches	9 inches
Eight feet	9 inches	9 inches	12 inches	12 inches	12 inches	12 inches
Nine Feet	9 inches	9 inches	12 inches	12 inches	N/A	12 inches
Ten Feet	9 inches	9 inches	12 inches	N/A	N/A	12 inches

For poured or installed foam or rubber surfaces, the materials must meet the ASTM F1292 requirements. Verify through a written statement from the manufacturer.

16.1.2e Toddlers can use these low rocking horses without much risk. However, they would be safer if moved away from the fence.

16.1.2f A trampoline challenges this toddler, but risk of injury is very high.

16.1.2g Balls are safe, portable gross motor equipment for infant and toddlers.

in determining whether other gross motor equipment with similar characteristics is safe for the infants and toddlers who use it. Anchored equipment means stationary equipment that is fixed in the ground so that it cannot be moved. An outdoor or indoor climber used by infants and toddlers might not be anchored, but it would still require protective barriers or guardrails to prevent falls, just as an outdoor anchored structure would.

Portable materials and equipment should also be evaluated for safety hazards. (See photos 16.1.2e–h.) The materials should not present serious threats to infants and toddlers. For example, jump ropes should not be used because they could cause strangulation. Things that toddlers might swing and inadvertently hit others with, such as plastic baseball bats or golf clubs, might also be hazardous.

Non-traditional materials and equipment that children are encouraged to use for active physical play must be considered in scoring. For example if children *are encouraged or allowed* by staff to climb on benches or rocks and jump from them, consider the appropriateness of that type of provision.

Examples of appropriate gross motor materials/equipment are given in a note for this item in the ITERS-R, page 32.

Score Indicator 1.2 "Yes" if there are **no appropriate** materials and equipment used for active physical play for *any* child in the group. Children must have access to the materials/equipment to be considered. If there is at least one appropriate piece of equipment or material that each child can use, score 1.2 "No."

16.1.2h Balls are used in many ways in this classroom: to hit at, to roll, to use with the toddler-sized basketball goal.

1.3 ***Poor repair*** means that the condition of the materials and equipment used for active physical play is likely to cause accidents or injuries by being broken or having missing parts. For example, if the barrier on a climber, meant to prevent falls, is broken or missing, the climber would be assessed as being in poor repair. However, a little rust on the climber, with all parts present and unbroken, would not indicate poor repair. (See photo 16.1.3.) ***Poor repair*** also means that the equipment cannot be used as it was originally designed. For example, a riding toy with a missing wheel or a deflated ball would be in poor repair, even though these might not be particularly dangerous.

Generally in poor repair means that the *majority* of materials and equipment for active physical play (either portable or stationary) is broken or has missing parts. There may be some equipment that is not broken or does not have missing parts, but for the most part, few pieces of equipment are in good shape.

To score the indicator, *all* materials/equipment that is used by children for active physical play, including both indoor and outdoor, portable and stationary equipment must be evaluated for condition.

If the majority of gross motor equipment is in such poor repair that accidents could occur or the materials/equipment cannot be used as intended, score Indicator 1.3 "Yes." If there are some materials/equipment in poor repair, but most for use by children are in good repair, score 1.3 "No."

16.1.3 If this cracked wheel were the only problem found, Indicator 1.3 would be scored "No."

3.1 Space for active physical play is defined in the "General Information" section for this item and discussed in Indicator 1.1. To give credit for this indicator, the space must be

- indoors (see "General Information"), and
- allow freedom of movement.

The term ***open*** means uncluttered by routine care furniture, play furniture, or toys so children can move freely. Their large muscle movements must not be limited by clutter, crowding, or furnishings and equipment that can restrict movement. In addition, the space must be large enough so that it accommodates all people (adults and children) who use it. Examples of such space are provided in the indicator and "Notes for Clarification" in the ITERS-R, page 32. Often this space is an uncrowded play area in the classroom, rather than a special space outside of the room. In some cases, a group may have space in the room, plus space outside the room. All indoor spaces used for active physical play must be considered to score this indicator.

The amount of space required will differ based on the abilities and needs of the children using the space. For non-mobile infants, a relatively small mat upon which a baby can lie and move her arms and legs or push up on her arms would suffice. (See photo 16.3.1a.) For crawlers and toddlers, however, a larger open space would be required so that children could crawl, walk, or run a short distance. There can be toys and materials in the space, but if crowded conditions *severely* inhibit the children's movement,

16.3.1a Active physical play for infants requires space and time to move freely, kick their legs, reach out with their arms, and develop trunk control.

16 Active physical play

16.3.1b Children who are placed in swings for most of the day are not provided with an open play space. Safety issues related to swings are addressed in item 11. Safety practices.

credit cannot be given. For example, a child would need enough clear space to push a wheel toy without being stopped after just a few steps by things in his way, with no option for moving in another direction. *Note that a large space (see Indicator 5.2) is not required at this minimal level of quality.* However, the space must accommodate the basic needs for active physical play of the children in the group being observed.

The open space must be accessible to the children in the group for **much of the day**. This term is defined on page 7 of the ITERS-R, in the "Explanation of Terms Used Throughout the Scale." **Much of the day** is required every day. If any child is confined to a space that severely restricts active physical movement for long periods (e.g., 30 minutes or more), credit cannot be given. For example, if a child is kept in a highchair, an infant seat, sitting at a table, or in a passive group activity without the option of being able to use the open space for active physical play, credit would not be given. (See photo 16.3.1b.) In addition, if the space used for active physical play is so small that only a few children can use the space at one time, credit would not be given because the space would not be accessible to all children for much of the day. All children must have access if they wish when they are awake and not involved in necessary routine care activities.

If an indoor space outside of the classroom is sometimes used for active physical play, the space within the classroom, where children spend much of their time, must still be considered to determine whether **much of the day** is true.

Since the space must be accessible to children for much of the day, the observer should be able to see the space being used during the 3-hour visit in the classroom. If there is no indoor space that meets the requirements stated above for the children to use during much of the day, every day, score Indicator 3.1 "No."

3.2 **Space for (active) physical play** is defined in the "General Information" section for this item, and discussed in Indicator 1.1. To be given credit for this indicator, the space must be

- outdoors (see "General Information"), and
- large enough to allow freedom of movement.

Some space means enough space so children can move freely, according to their abilities and needs. Practice of their large muscle movements must not be limited by clutter, crowding, or equipment that restricts movement. The most typical space used for outdoor active physical play is a playground. However, other outdoor spaces might fulfill the requirements of this indicator. For example, a porch, deck, patio, rooftop area, or semi-shelter might provide the space needed by the children in the group to participate in large muscle activity. Any space used by the children outdoors for active play should be observed and evaluated.

As with an indoor area, the required amount of space will differ according to the abilities and needs of the children using the space. For non-mobile infants, a relatively small porch where a mat can be placed for a baby to move freely would suffice. For older babies and toddlers, however, a larger outdoor space would be required to give credit, such as a larger deck area where children have space to crawl, walk, or run a short distance. The area should not be so small or crowded that free movement is very restricted. The space must accommodate the basic needs for active physical play of the children in the group being observed. When evaluating the space, judgment should be based on the highest number of children allowed to attend on any day, which may differ from the number of children present during the observation

The open outdoor space must be used by the children in the group at least once a day, **three days a week**. This means that *all* children (both infants and toddlers) are taken outdoors at some point during each of the three days the space is used. This is to provide the fresh air and outdoor physical experiences that all children require for good health. It is frequently difficult to get infants outdoors due to their varied schedules for routine care. In addition, programs are often not organized, in terms of staffing or access, to take babies outdoors. An extra staff member (or floater) may be necessary to achieve this goal. Taking infants outside is usually best done with a very small group or an individual child. Infants do need to get outdoors, especially in a full-day program, and if this cannot be arranged for any reason (except weather), credit for this indicator is not given for groups with infants.

There is no specified *time requirement* for being outdoors for active physical play. However, children must be outdoors long enough to reasonably benefit from the experience. Only 5 to 10 minutes would not usually be long enough for toddlers. In a full day program, in acceptable weather, at least ½-hour would be expected for toddlers, shortened proportionally for programs of less than 8 hours. For example in a 4-hour program, only ¼-hour would be expected. The length of time outdoors for infants might be shorter, depending on the children's response.

Except in very bad weather means that the outdoor time must be carried out if the weather allows children to play outdoors. There will be relatively few days in most areas where children will not be able to be outdoors at all. Even in climates with more severe weather, children should be dressed properly and taken outdoors (as stated in the "Note for Clarification" for this indicator) unless there is a danger associated with outdoor exposure. (See photo 16.3.2.) To an extent, whether children should be allowed to play outdoors is a location-related consideration. For example, people who live in very rainy climates will be more likely to take children outdoors on wet days than people who live in drier climates. Similarly, people who live in cold climates are more likely to take children outside on snowy days than people for whom snow is less usual. In some areas, pollution levels can become dan-

16.3.2 Toddlers enjoy playing in the snow in this outdoor play area that is used daily.

gerous to the health of children on certain days. On those unusual days, children should not play outdoors.

In most cases, however, children can (and should) be taken outdoors every day to get fresh air, and to be more active and noisy than they can be when indoors. On days of truly poor weather (active precipitation, days of public warnings for people to remain indoors due to cold, heat, or pollution), the ½-hour requirement for toddlers in full-day programs of 8 hours or more can be relaxed with less, or even no, time being spent outdoors. More often, however, although children may not be able to go out at the usual time, this can be rescheduled for earlier or later in the day. When the weather is bad at the regularly scheduled outdoor time, staff should try to schedule another time during the day to go outside. If the weather is bad on one of the three required days when children would usually be taken outdoors, another day in the week should be used as a make-up day, if possible. Options for taking the children outdoors should be explored, rather than simply not going out at all. For example, if the playground is too wet, using an outdoor covered area or taking a walk (not a stroller ride) around the neighborhood should be considered in place of playground time.

To score, it is not required that the observer see the children use the outdoor space. If outdoor active physical play is not observed, the observer should ask staff the questions listed for this indicator. The observer must then inspect any outdoor spaces used, and consider both the information provided by staff and what was observed to score.

3.3 ***Materials/equipment*** for active physical play is defined in the "General Information" section for this item. The requirements for ***appropriate*** are given in Indicator 1.3. To give credit for this indicator, the equipment can be either indoors or outdoors. However, use of materials/equipment is required even if the weather does not permit outdoor play. If there is inclement weather and children are unable to go outside, then some gross motor materials/equipment must be available indoors.

Some means that children can use the equipment without having to wait with *no other* appropriate gross motor material or equipment option. Many materials/equipment are not required (as in Indicator 5.3), and no specific number of materials/equipment is given to determine whether to give credit. Instead, the observer should watch children to see if there is something for each child to use while engaged in active physical play. For example, if the child wants to use a ball being used by another child, staff should redirect the child to something else for gross motor play, such as a pull toy or a climber. If several children have no other options for materials/equipment to use for active physical play, score Indicator 3.3 "No."

Good repair means that the condition of the materials/equipment for active physical play is not likely to cause serious accidents or injuries because of broken or missing parts. In addition, the children can use the equipment as it was originally intended to be used. (See photos 16.3.3a-b.)

Generally means that the vast majority of equipment (indoors and outdoors, stationary and portable) that is counted to give credit for this indicator is in reasonable condition so it is safe and usable. To evaluate whether ***generally*** is true, consider the number of children who use it and the frequency of use. For example, if a major piece of equipment that is often used by children is not in good repair, but several other smaller or less popular pieces are in good repair, credit for ***generally*** would not be given. However, if problems are minor and do not create a serious safety

Indicator

16.3.3b This tractor wheel toy is safe and fun for this toddler to use.

16.3.3a Toddlers may have difficulty using equipment which needs repair, like this trike without pedal pads.

hazard, then give credit for this indicator. For example, if a ball is deflated or there is a little rust on a climber, but no other problems are observed with the rest of the equipment, do not count off for these small things.

To give credit for this indicator (score "Yes"), some materials/equipment for active physical play must be appropriate with options for each child, used daily, and generally be in good repair.

5.1   For the ***outdoor area*** to be ***easily accessible***, staff must be able to take the children to the outdoor play space without undue effort or complications. The space must be reasonably close to the classroom used by the children and have few, if any, barriers, so that the time and challenges required to access the space are minimal. (See photos 16.5.1a-b.) If it is difficult to access the space in any way, score Indicator 5.1 "No."

16.5.1a When the outdoor area is located just outside the classroom it reduces the time and challenges that are sometimes required to access the space.

16.5.1b This group must walk a long distance from the classroom to reach their outdoor play space.

16 Active physical play

This indicator applies to accessing the gross motor area, but not to specific spaces within the gross motor area. Be sure to read the "Note for Clarification" for this indicator on page 32 of the ITERS-R for information on who is required to have easy access.

Examples of conditions that make space for active physical play difficult to access include:

- using a steep or long staircase or an elevator with the children;
- leaving any children unattended while taking others indoors or outdoors;
- going long distances, either indoors or outdoors;
- going through other classrooms or rooms that are currently in use; or
- using doors or gates that are hard to manage while adequately supervising the children or while pushing baby buggies or strollers

If the gross motor space has been made easily accessible, for example, with the help of additional staff, a stroller to carry the children, or automatic door openers, but the necessary provision is not used, credit cannot be given for easy access.

Separated from older children means that infants and toddlers are not mixed with preschoolers and older children in the outdoor area. (See photo 16.5.1c.) The separation can occur either through having separate play areas, or by using the same play area but on different schedules. It is not necessary for 2-year-olds to be separated from preschoolers to give credit. However, if the 2-year-olds are at a distinct disadvantage, in terms of safety or access to appropriate active physical experiences, due to the presence of the older children, credit cannot be given.

16.5.1c Infants and toddlers use an outdoor space that is separated by a fence from the playground for older children.

To give credit, the space must be ***used*** for ***1 hour daily*** in full-day programs of 8 hours or more, except in very bad weather. ***Except in very bad weather*** is defined in Indicator 3.2.

The 1 hour may take place at one time, or be a combination of times throughout the day. All children do not have to use the space for the full hour, but most children should do so, and all children should use the space for some time during each day. Children who do not have a full hour's use should be the rare exception. For example, a very young baby, who spends long periods sleeping and who requires a long time for feeding, might not have access to the space for the full hour per day. Similarly, a toddler who is unhappy outdoors and is thus taken inside, while others stay outdoors to play, would not require the full hour on that day. Also, time outdoors might be shortened slightly when the weather is not very bad, but also not particularly pleasant, and the children show obvious signs that they are not enjoying their time outdoors. The observer should watch the children to determine if they are uncomfortable and not benefiting from the outdoor time, or whether they are unhappy about being brought indoors after only a short period outside.

Less time outdoors is required for programs operating less than 8 hours a day, with the amount of time calculated proportionally, based on the ratio of 1 hour for programs of 8 hours or more. For example, if a program operates for 6 hours a day, this would be ¾ of a full-day program, so the time required would be ¾ of the 1 hour. If the program operates 4 hours a day, the requirement would be ½-hour.

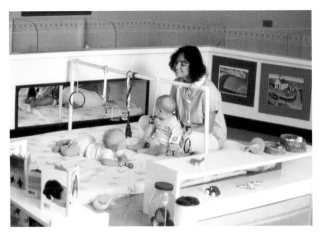

16.5.2a These young infants have a large, open active play area that is not crowded or cluttered with toys. However, this space would be inadequate for mobile children.

16.5.2b Because this indoor space is so large, toddlers have many opportunities to practice their gross motor skills without restrictions or interruptions.

If any one of the requirements of this indicator is not met, including ***easily accessible***, ***separated from older children***, and ***used one hour daily***, score Indicator 5.1 "No."

5.2 A ***large*** active play area has enough space to allow gross motor activity with few restrictions. (See photos 16.5.2a-b.) This play area cannot be ***cluttered*** with materials/equipment or ***crowded*** with people. Children should be able to take advantage of the area to practice their gross motor skills to a great extent, for example, by crawling, walking, or running for a distance without being stopped by a shortage of space or crowding. The space should be large enough to accommodate a lot of materials and equipment and all the adults and children using the space at any one time. If many children use the space at one time, for example several groups, this cannot cause problems with the ability of the children to move freely. Of course, young toddlers will tend to bump into one another, but there should be space available for them to get away from others. No specific square footage is required, and the amount of space needed to meet the requirement of ***large*** will differ based on the ages, abilities, and number of the children using the space.

The space can be located either indoors or outdoors. A space that meets the requirements of Indicator 5.1 might meet the requirements of this indicator as well, if it is large enough and not crowded or cluttered. Be sure to read the "Note for Clarification" for the indicator to determine how to score the use of two or more spaces for active physical play.

At this "good" level of quality, the space must be used daily with all the children. If no large active play area is used daily, score this indicator "No."

5.3 ***Ample*** in this indicator is used to mean "many," in contrast to "some" in Indicator 3.3. In 3.3 "some" means that each child can use equipment without having to wait with *no other* gross motor option. ***Ample***, however, means enough materials and equipment so children do not have to wait long periods of time to use the equipment they *choose* to use. In other words, there are enough pieces of popular equipment so children do not have to compete or wait, and there are enough interesting options so that no one thing is overwhelmingly popular. For example, there are enough riding wheel toys so children do not feel competitive pressure when they want to ride. There are enough balls so children who want to play alone do not have to share. Push and pull toys have duplicates. A climbing structure is large enough to accommodate the number of children wanting to use it or there are several climbing structures.

There is no specific number of materials/equipment required to judge whether *ample* is true. Instead the observer should note the number of children present, their abilities, and how the materials/equipment provide for challenging and satisfying active physical play for each child. Consider both portable and stationary equipment when determining whether there is ample equipment.

A long period of time, for an infant or toddler, is not long at all. Infants and toddlers do not understand time well and tend to want what they want immediately. Therefore, no specific time period is given to judge what is a long period. *Long* will depend on how upset the child might be and how easily the child's attention can be transferred to another physical play option. The more options, the better the likelihood that waiting time will be minimized.

When observing to see if this indicator is true, determine whether competition over equipment is caused by a lack of popular materials/equipment for active physical play or whether competition is really being caused by social issues between children. For example, if two toddlers are fighting over a ball and there are several other balls of the same type accessible for use, this would not be due to lack of *ample* balls. In addition, consider the total number of gross motor play options that children have in the area. Remember, playing in the sandbox or being pushed in a swing is not considered gross motor or active physical play. Often, children might settle for sedentary play rather than wait for a turn on gross motor equipment. Score this indicator "Yes" if there are ample gross motor options without much waiting.

5.4 To score this indicator, the observer must watch to ensure that each child in the group being observed has at least one appropriately challenging gross motor materials/equipment option to use.

If there is a child with special needs that requires *adaptations or special equipment,* then these must be provided. Even in cases where an infant or toddler has very limited gross motor skills, active physical play should not be ignored.

For example, the child should not be kept inside while others go out, or be left with nothing to do in a swing, stroller, or wheel chair while others participate in active physical play.

Score Indicator 5.4 "Yes" when all children, including those with special needs, can participate in active physical play to the extent possible. Extra equipment, adaptations, or help from staff should be provided to allow a child to participate as fully as possible, even though some children will not be able to participate in the same way as their typically developing or older peers.

5.5 *All space and equipment* means any space children use for active physical play and any gross motor materials/equipment used by the children in the group being observed. *Appropriate,* as discussed in Indicators 1.1, 1.2, 3.3, and in the "Notes for Clarification" for this item, means safe and challenging without being frustrating. (See photos 16.5.5a-b.) If any space used for active physical play has even one major hazard or several minor hazards, this indicator is scored "No." For example, if the area of the classroom used for active play has no hazards, but the playground has a gate that does not shut securely, then Indicator 5.5 would be scored "No." If

16.5.5a

16.5.5a-b Appropriate climbing and sliding equipment for infants and toddlers is smaller than equipment used for preschoolers. It should be challenging but not dangerous or frustrating for young children to use.

16.5.5b

the playground and play area of the classroom have no hazards, but toddlers tend to run and play in the crib area that contains several uncovered electrical outlets and dangling electrical cords, 5.5 would be scored "No."

Similarly, if most materials/equipment used for active physical play are appropriate, except a climber used by the toddlers in the gross motor room which is used only on rainy days, Indicator 5.5 would be scored "No," because the requirement is for all space and equipment.

7.1 The term *surface* generally means the covering on the ground outdoors where children can carry out their active physical play. Examples of surfaces are provided in the indicator, but others might include soil, sand, black-top, or cement.

In order to give credit for *2 or more types of surfaces,* determine whether the surfaces in the outdoor spaces enable children to participate successfully in different types of active play. For example, non-mobile babies may need a soft but firm mat to lie on while playing with toys they can bat with their arms and legs. Babies who are crawling need a smooth firm surface. Toddlers learning to walk, push or pull wheel toys, and throw balls require a harder firm surface. All children gain information about how their world works as they try out various activities on different surfaces. They also have better chances for successful practice of gross motor skills when the surface matches the skill they are practicing.

Surfaces within the fall zones of equipment are not counted to meet the requirements of this indicator, because no activity is supposed to occur in a fall zone, whose only purpose is to protect children in case of falls. However, if a soft surface extends beyond the fall zone of equipment and is large enough to permit another type of active physical play, then that area can be counted as one of the multiple surfaces required in this indicator.

To give credit each different surface must be large enough to permit a type of play without much interruption from other activities. At least one firm and one soft play surface must be accessible daily outdoors. They do not have to be accessible at the same time, but each must be experienced daily for active physical play. All children do not have to use both surfaces each day, but both must be accessible daily. For example, a tiny baby may only use a soft vinyl covered foam mat, while others in the group may crawl on the grass.

7.2   The *elements* are the natural conditions associated with the outdoors and the weather. The elements often provide pleasant experiences, such as a warming sun or a gentle breeze. However, they can also cause discomfort or problems in the outdoor space. Examples of elements that cause discomfort are:

- the sun in hot weather;
- the wind in cold, dusty, or sandy areas;
- rain, snow, or other precipitation; and
- standing water, causing puddles, muddy areas, or erosion.

16.7.2 This large awning provides protection from the hot summer sun.

Protection from the elements for outdoor areas relieves discomfort or problems. Protection from the sun comes from things that provide shade, such as trees, buildings, partial roofs, or awnings. Solid fences, buildings, or rows of trees provide windbreaks. Open areas allow sun to warm spaces on cold days. Covered areas serve as protection from precipitation. Drainage helps to prevent large puddles or standing water. (See photo 16.7.2.)

To give credit for Indicator 7.2, the most necessary protection for the location and season must be provided. For example, on very hot summer days in a warm climate, shade must be available. If the gross motor space is located in a place with frequent rain, it must be properly drained, so children will be able to use the play area during non-rainy days.

To give credit for *some* protection, only one example must be observed. But the protection observed must match the most prevalent adverse condition caused by the elements in the local area. For example, shade would not be acceptable as a protection from the elements in a place where it was rarely sunny, or drainage would not be credited in a place where rain was very unusual.

7.3   *Materials stimulate skills* means that the gross motor materials/equipment encourage children to use their large muscles in certain ways. The nature of the equipment gives children the opportunity to use their large muscles in particular ways. For example, steps on a climber invite a child to practice climbing. A riding toy encourages a child to balance, push with the feet and legs, steer, and to coordinate these various skills.

The intent of this indicator is for the equipment to stimulate a *variety* of skills, rather than a limited set. A limited set of skills is encouraged when there are only a few types of materials or equipment for children to use. For example, if a slide and some balls are the only gross motor equipment for toddlers to use, the primary skills being stimulated would be climbing and sliding, throwing, and kicking. However, if there is a more complex climber, with a slide and several ways to climb up, plus balls of various sizes, with a low basketball hoop, then more variety of stimulation is provided. Generally one piece of equipment will not provide the required variety, but in the case of a very complex climber, with many skill options, the indicator might be met.

Note that there is the expectation that the skills being encouraged would be developmentally challenging for the children in the group being observed. For example, if toddlers use only equipment that is designed for infants, it is unlikely that credit would be given for this indicator.

To meet the requirement for a ***variety of skills***, there should be seven to nine different developmentally appropriate skills that are obviously encouraged *by the materials/equipment children can use.*

Gross motor skills for infants may are included in the ITERS-R. Other skills for infants might include:

- extending arms and legs,
- raising and lifting head,
- sitting up,
- reaching movements,
- rolling over,
- moving from sitting to crawling,
- balancing in a standing position,
- grasping toes,
- cruising (walking by holding onto supports, such as furniture, a bar mounted on the wall, play equipment), and
- squatting from a standing position.

Gross motor skills for toddlers are included in the ITERS-R. Examples of others for toddlers include:

- throwing,
- kicking,
- sliding,
- tossing a ball,
- pushing and pulling,
- jumping,
- hopping,
- riding on a tricycle without pedals, and
- riding on a tricycle with pedals.

To score, observe to see how many skills the materials/equipment encourage and list them. Consider both portable and stationary materials/equipment.

17 Art

General information about this item

Since there are many learning experiences that are far more appropriate for infants than using art materials, this item is not required for groups that only have children under 12 months of age. This is because art materials require more advanced eye-hand coordination and the self-control to keep from eating them, which infants have not yet developed. However, if art materials are ever used with infants under 12 months of age, the item must be scored, and Indicators 3.1 and 5.1 should be scored "NA." (See photos 17A-B.)

Young toddlers are more interested in exploring and manipulating art materials than in creating works of art. (See photo 17C.) It is not surprising that the children, when first introduced to crayons and paper, may be most interested in touching, looking at, and even tasting the crayons. Once children find the marks crayons make on the paper more interesting than how they taste, then they are ready for art experiences. At this point, staff need to provide close supervision and decide how to slowly introduce art materials as children become ready.

Appropriate early experiences with art materials can provide toddlers with opportunities to practice their eye-hand coordination. Simple art materials, such as crayons and paper, give toddlers opportunities to use their arms and hands in new ways. As toddlers refine their fine motor skills they are able to handle art materials and tools that require the use of hands and fingers, such as playdough with rollers and plastic utensils (but not cookie cutters which do not encourage creativity).

17A Art is not necessary for infants who can learn from many other more appropriate experiences.

17B When art materials are used with infants, proper supervision and use must be considered.

17C Young toddlers are more interested in touching and feeling paint than creating a finished product.

For the various indicators in this item, the term "art materials" is used. "Art materials" refers to the basic substances or ingredients the children use as they experiment with visual representation (e.g., crayons, paper, paint, play dough). One major difference among art materials is whether they result in 2-dimensional, flat work (drawing, painting, collage) or 3-dimensional work that has height, width and depth (play dough). The types of art materials are drawing, painting, and collage (two-dimensional) and play dough (three-dimensional). A variety of different art materials may be used for drawing, but essentially the same process is used by the child (material held in hand or with fingers). Drawing materials usually include thick and thin crayons, watercolor markers, and chalks. Painting can be done on paper using different kinds of paint (tempera, watercolors), but the process is essentially the same. Collage is gluing smaller pieces to a larger flat piece, using a variety of materials including small paper shapes, self-stick stickers, and pictures cut out of catalogues or magazines. Play dough is a three-dimensional material and is different from "silly putty" or "goop" because it holds its shape and can be molded by the hands into forms that have height, width and depth. "Tools" are the aids used in manipulating and controlling art materials, with the primary tools being the child's hands. Other tools are brushes to spread paint, blunt scissors to cut paper, and glue sticks or other ways of applying glue to hold things together.

Toddlers are interested in the characteristics of the art materials they are using, such as the colors, shapes, and textures. They learn by exploring and experimenting with art materials. Staff can extend these learning opportunities by talking to the children about what they are doing, seeing, and creating.

Art for toddlers also has benefits for emergent literacy. As with other areas of development, there are preparatory stages for emergent writing. Initially with arm movements, instead of fine finger movements, toddlers begin to make marks on paper using crayons or markers. At this stage, children's artwork will typically consist of scribbles, mostly with one color. At the next stage, the scribbles begin to take shape and might look like circles. Children are still not able to plan their artwork and the product still shows random abstract designs. However, these experiences will later lead to the ability of preschoolers to draw things that they see and know from their environment, such as people and familiar places, animals, or objects. This sets the stage for representation in words and for later writing, which begins for some at the end of the preschool years.

Adult expectations and their approaches to providing art activities for children will determine the benefits children obtain from art experiences. Staff should slowly introduce the simplest, easiest-to-control art materials to toddlers, beginning with paper and crayons or watercolor markers. Staff should encourage children, allowing them to use and handle the materials freely. They should intervene to help when children become frustrated or to redirect the children when they use materials improperly, such as chewing on them or drawing on walls. For example, a staff member notices that the toddler cannot hold his paper down while scribbling, and she intervenes to help by taping the paper to the table. Or a staff member sees a child coloring on the table surface around her small piece of paper, and gives her a larger piece of paper to use instead.

Expecting young children to participate in a large-group art activity or to follow adult-created examples is not appropriate. Young children are more interested in the process of creating rather than in the end product. Requiring 2-year-olds to participate in a group to do art when they are not interested is inappropriate because these children are developmentally focused on learning to make their own choices.

As stated earlier, this item can be scored "NA" if *all* children in the group are younger than 12 months of age and staff do not use art activities with infants. However, if there are children 12 months or older or art activities are used with infants, this item must be scored. Exact details for applying this general age requirement are included in the "Explanation of Terms Used Throughout the Scale," on page 7 of the ITERS-R. If an older child with a disability is enrolled, and all the other children are infants, the appropriateness of this item will depend on the child's abilities, not necessarily on the child's age.

If art activities are used with infants, when scoring the item, specific indicators which apply only to toddlers should be scored "NA." If art activities are not observed during a 3-hour observation, the observer should ask the questions on page 33 of the ITERS-R and score each indicator based on answers received from staff.

A closer look at each indicator

1.1   ***Art materials*** are used by children to scribble, draw, paint, manipulate play dough, and glue materials to create visual presentations. ***Appropriate*** art materials are those that interest the children and ones they can handle well, matching their ages and abilities. For example, large crayons that can be easily grasped are age-appropriate for toddlers instead of thin, colored pencils, which may be appropriate for preschoolers. Blunt scissors are inappropriate for young toddlers (12–23 months of age) with limited fine motor skills but easily used by older preschoolers. Foods are not counted as art materials for young children (indeed for all children) because of health and safety issues. Children usually eat food when it is used for art which is undesirable because the necessary sanitary measures used with food have been ignored. (See photo 17.1.1.) Moreover, it is confusing for children who are learning about the proper uses of food (to eat neatly, without smearing) to use food as an art material (to smear on the paper but not to eat).

17.1.1 Foods are not considered art materials, but if used as a sensory activity, the health concerns must be considered in scoring Item 10, Health practices.

Furthermore, using food as a play material in art activities would be considered wasteful, and some families might find this offensive or ill-advised.

For further explanations of the term "appropriate," refer to the "Explanation of Terms Used Throughout the Scale," on page 7 of the ITERS-R.

Examples of a**rt materials** are provided in the "Notes for Clarification" on page 33 of the ITERS-R. Other materials may include:

For young toddlers (12-23 months of age):

- Large, non-toxic crayons,
- Large paper (white and different colors) taped to a surface (table, easel, wall),
- Non-toxic finger paint, and
- Large, non-toxic chalk on a chalk board.

For older toddlers (24-30 months of age), the items listed above for younger toddlers, plus the following non-toxic, safe materials and tools:

- Watercolor markers,
- Tempera paints,
- Painting tools, such as paint brushes of various widths with short handles,
- Paper of different sizes and colors,
- Easy-to-use blunt scissors,
- Unbreakable chalk board with chalk and erasers,
- Play dough to manipulate with fingers and with simple tools (rollers, plastic or wooden utensils that are safe and free of sharp or pointed ends, but not cookie cutters),
- Large self-stick stamps, stickers, and tape (no licking required), and
- Scrap paper and cut-out pictures for collage with glue sticks.

Provided for use means that the children in the group can reach and use the materials when made accessible by staff.

This indicator is scored "Yes" when ***no appropriate art materials*** are made accessible for use by the children. For example, the center may have art materials in storage but they are never used by the children in the class. Or materials may even be present in the room or on low shelves, but children are not allowed to use them. If only inappropriate materials are used with the children, even though they are art materials, this indicator must be scored "Yes." If any appropriate art materials are used, but so infrequently so that they have little impact on children's learning (such as less than once every 2 weeks), score this indicator "Yes."

If appropriate art materials are used by the children, frequently enough to impact children's development, score this indicator "No," even if the materials are used in a way that does not satisfy requirements at a higher level of quality. For example, if crayons and coloring book pages are used by older toddlers, and the children are allowed to scribble freely on the pages and are not urged to "stay within the lines," score this indicator "No."

1.2   ***Toxic materials*** may cause children harm when used. ***Toxic*** means that the materials, if used or swallowed, may be poisonous to young children or make them sick. Examples of toxic materials are included in the item on page 33 of the ITERS-R. Others may include uncooked red kidney beans, and even some foam paints that are marketed for children's use. Staff should read the labels and directions for use for all materials used in art projects with children. For example, if the label states, "Keep out of the reach of children," it should never be used with children.

Unsafe means that the art material may be a safety hazard and cause injury when used. Examples are included in the item; others may include sharp pointed scissors (even ones meant for older children), play dough molds with sharp edges, staplers, or sharp tools. Small pieces of broken crayons, the tips of watercolor markers or plastic packing "peanuts" may also pose a choking hazard for young children, who frequently mouth or chew on objects. Thin pencils with sharp lead points may be unsafe for toddlers to use. If there are problems with the safety of materials, consider this also in Item 11, Safety practices, on page 26 of the ITERS-R. (See photo 17.1.2.)

The observer must base the score for this indicator on what is learned from several sources of information, including: what is observed when children use art materials, displayed materials, activity plans (also called "lesson plans" or "curriculum plans"), and staff responses to questions provided for the indicator. All art materials should be examined. In a preschool classroom, art materials are usually stored on low, open shelves, so that children can easily reach and use them. However, in a toddler program closer supervision is required, and therefore staff may store art materials in closed cabinets and containers, bringing them out only at times when they can closely supervise children. Observers may not see children actively using art materials or notice the art materials in closed storage, and thus may need to ask staff the questions provided in the ITERS-R on page 33 for Indicators 1.2 and 3.2.

If any toxic or unsafe art materials are used by children, score this indicator "Yes," even if most are non-toxic and safe.

17.1.2 Glitter is considered an inappropriate art material because the sharp particles may cause eye injury if children rub their eyes.

3.1 **Some art materials** means that there is at least one art material in usable condition that will allow children to complete an art activity (e.g., crayons with paper; paste, paper, and scraps for collage work; or paints with paper, and brushes). For example, if there are usable markers and paper, credit can be given. However, if the markers are dry and not usable and this is the only art material available, credit cannot be given. Similarly, if there are usable markers or paints, but no paper is provided to draw or paint on, credit cannot be given.

Used at least once a week means that staff offer children art materials one day a week. Staff must place materials within reach of the children and allow children to use the materials without impediment. For example, staff remove lids on plastic containers of crayons and put paper on table or easel within children's reach. This indicator addresses the frequency and opportunity for use of art materials. It does not look at the appropriateness of materials used and the setting; these issues are addressed in Indicators 3.2 and 3.3.

This indicator should be scored "NA" if the item is being completed for a group in which all children are under 12 months of age. If toddlers are present, the indicator must be scored "Yes" or "No," but not "NA." Ask staff the question in the ITERS-R on page 33 to find out how often art materials are offered, and score based on both the condition of materials and frequency of use.

3.2 All means that every art material used with children is safe, non-toxic and appropriate. See Indicators 1.1 and 1.2 for the meanings of these terms. Art materials are defined in the "General Information" section for this item and in the "Notes for Clarification" on page 33 of the ITERS-R. This indicator has the same requirements for safe and non-toxic art materials as stated in Indicator 1.2; however, this indicator requires that all materials be appropriate.

3.3 Toddlers enjoy doing many different things, but they usually spend a very short time on each activity. They are likely to play with things for only a few minutes, then drop them and quickly move on to the next interesting thing. They tend to flock to an interesting activity, but often there will be a child who does not go with the group. Even those who flock together will not necessarily want to remain with the group for long. Staff who work with very young children must understand that toddlers have short attention spans and that they enjoy selecting activities that are of interest to them. Children learn more naturally and spontaneously when they are able to select the things that interest them the most. Therefore, children not required to participate means that children can join or leave an art activity as they wish, and staff respect their choices.

The art activity can be child-initiated or teacher-initiated, but children should be free to join and leave the activity at any time. The art activity must be one of several alternative activities that are offered to children at the same time. (See photo 17.3.3.) There must be at least two other interesting activities available that children can choose to do without a negative response from staff. The alternative activities must be offered without any barriers, such as being out of view or not within reach or fear of teacher's negative response. Score this indicator "No" if any of the following is observed:

- Children leave the art activity to play with other toys and are made to come back to the art table.
- Staff expect that children, whether in a large group, in a small group, or individually, must participate in the art activity.
- Children must sit and wait for their turn.
- Staff expect the children to finish the art product.

17.3.3 Some toddlers want to enjoy this art activity with glue and paper while others are free to play elsewhere.

5.1 Younger toddlers include children 12–23 months of age; older toddlers are children 24–30 months of age. The requirements for how often and when art activities and materials are offered to toddlers vary depending on the children's ages. Since younger toddlers have less skill in controlling art materials, and often prefer to eat them, which can result in conflict with staff, this indicator requires that some art is only offered to them at least three times a week. The time it is offered during the day can vary from one day to the next throughout the week, but credit cannot be given if it is offered three different times during only one day of the week. Toddlers, who use materials with more skill and self-control, require more frequent art experiences. To give credit for this indicator (score "Yes"), the art activities must be available daily. (See photos 17.5.1a-b.) The art media offered do not have to differ during the week. For example, credit may be given if crayons and paper are the only activity offered each day. Nor does the activity need to meet the other requirements in the indicators at the good or excellent levels of quality. However when offered, the art activity must be accessible to children for a reasonable amount of time, evidenced by whether children are rushed or allowed to work long enough to be satisfied with the experience. If most children are rushed, cry, or complain that they do not want to stop, then score this indictor "No." Ask staff the question for this indicator on page 33 of the ITERS-R, and score accordingly.

17.5.1a Younger toddlers should be offered simple art materials at least three times a week.

17.5.1b Older toddlers can use simple art materials every day. They must be closely supervised during art times.

17.5.1b

Individual expression means that children are allowed to use art materials in their own creative way. They are free to express their own ideas, using the skills that they currently possess. However, there may need to be some limits on individual expression. For example, staff may limit children who wish to use materials inappropriately, such as drawing on another child's clothing or artwork. Staff may also limit the number of materials made accessible to children. For example, the number of paint colors may be limited to encourage children's control of the medium. Thus for the purpose of this item, ***individual expression*** means that children are given the opportunity to select the subject matter or the medium in an art activity or use their own ideas in creating the art. (See photos 17.5.2a-d.) General topics for art work or the art materials used can be selected by the adult, but the child should be able to decide the way in which they are used, within the rules of acceptable use.

17.5.2a Individual expression means that children can select the subject and/or the medium to use in an art activity.

17.5.2b Ditto sheets do not encourage toddlers to express their own ideas, and if staff expect children to color within the lines, then this type of activity can be very frustrating.

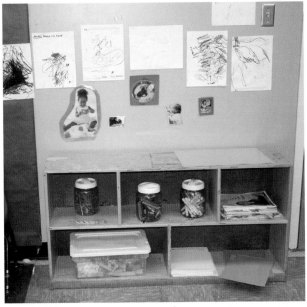

17.5.2c In this classroom, the art work created by the children is varied and individual because they are encouraged to use creative expression.

17.5.2d Although children used the same materials, each did the work in his or her own way.

To score, the observer must get a sense of what the children are able to create on their own, using their own ideas and abilities. This can easily be seen while children are participating in an art activity. However, if this opportunity does not present itself, the observer may also consider the child-created artwork that is displayed. If children are encouraged to use individual expression, the displayed work will probably consist of scribbles, marks, and circles on paper, i.e., abstract work. However, if children are only provided with ditto sheets or coloring books to use, or if all children's work looks completely alike because they have been given an example to follow, then individual expression is not encouraged.

To give credit for this indicator, *all* of the art activities used by children should encourage individual expression. If coloring books or ditto sheets are used with toddlers or if they are expected to follow an example (e.g., to create a snowman like the one shown in a book about winter), then score this indicator "No." However, the observer must look for individual expression in art work that may, at first glance, all look similar. For example, finger paintings, where the same color was used by all, may all look alike but actually be quite individualized because each child used the paint in his or her own way.

5.3 Staff guidance is important in helping toddlers successfully and properly use art materials. Young toddlers (12–23 months of age) may be more interested in finding out what the play dough tastes like rather than squeezing and rolling it around on the table. Therefore, staff supervision and guidance is needed to show children how to use these new and interesting materials. This is not to be confused with limiting individual expression (see Indicator 5.2). Staff assistance for the purpose of preventing frustration and disappointment when children use art materials is what is meant by ***staff facilitate***.

There are many ways that staff can ***facilitate the appropriate use of art materials***, such as introducing materials that the children can easily handle, closely supervising them, and adding language and encouragement when needed. (See photo 17.5.3a.) Some examples of staff facilitation are listed in the indicator on page 33 of the ITERS-R; others may include:

- limiting art activities to what children can do on their own;
- taping the paper to a table or securing it to an easel so that it doesn't slide around, making it difficult for the toddlers to use; (See photo 17.5.3b.)

17.5.3a Staff talk to children about their art work, naming materials and talking about their experiences.

17.5.3b Taping sheets of paper to the table so that they do not slide can help make art activities easier for toddlers.

- providing messy materials (paints, fingerpaints, glue) in small amounts, so large spills will be minimized;

- talking to children as they do their artwork, naming the art materials and what the child is experiencing, for example, "You're using play dough. It feels cold and squishy";

- limiting the number of materials children must coordinate to do the activity, for example, providing only one or two colors of paint at a time or limiting collage materials to paper shapes, a glue stick, and a sheet of paper;

- adding simple tools that are easy for children to use and control, such as tongue depressors for poking holes in play dough, thick paint brushes or sponge brushes with short handles;

- showing children how to use materials properly (for example, how to put paint brushes into the paint containers, especially those with lids preventing large spills) but not dictating what they produce;

- ensuring that children do not have to share art materials by providing enough for each to have his or her own supply; or

- setting up activities so clean-up will be easy (for example covering the art table with newspaper).

When scoring this indicator, consider the facilitation done beforehand in the set-up as well as during the use of materials.

7.1 Staff plan and choose art materials to match the skills of the children in the group. Children will vary in their abilities, but all should first be introduced to simple art materials, with complexity added as children become ready. In Indicator 5.1, staff are given credit even if they provide the same art materials repeatedly. In Indicator 7.1, different kinds of art materials that offer different kinds of experiences are required.

Introducing a variety of materials means that staff provide children with materials that have different properties, each requiring a different skill or adding to what children can learn from art experiences. (See photo 17.7.1a.) Variety can be provided within materials (for example, several colors of paint at a time instead of just one or thin chalk as opposed to thick chalk). Variety can also be provided by offering different types of materials, such as collage for children who can use glue sticks.

17.7.1a 3-D art materials are introduced to toddlers under close supervision. Play dough provides children with a material that they build up, probe, and squeeze.

As children are ready means that the materials challenge and interest but do not frustrate the young child. (See photo 17.7.1b-d, next page.) For example, young toddlers (12-23 months of age) who have limited control of their wrist movements, mostly using their arms and hands, can easily handle large crayons, large pieces of paper to make marks and scribbles, and soft play dough for rolling and squeezing. As toddlers improve their fine motor skills, they can handle different art materials and tools with greater precision, because they have better control of their fine motor abilities and more restraint and purpose in the way they use the materials. For example, older toddlers (24-30 months of age) may be able to use non-toxic felt pens with thinner tips on smaller pieces of paper or narrow brushes with more colors of paint.

To give credit, younger toddlers (12-23 months of age) must have access to at least three different art materials. (Paper that must be used with materials may not be

17.7.1b Older toddlers can successfully handle art activities using tempera paints, brushes with short handles and child-sized easels.

17.7.1c

17.7.1d

17.7.1c-d Using different tools with paints provides variety, but such activities should never replace the use of brushes or fingers that are more easily controlled.

considered one of the three). All are not required to be accessible at the same time, but at least three different materials must be offered during the week.

Older toddlers (24-30 months of age) must have access to more than three types of materials on a weekly basis, and there must be variation within each type (e.g., color, size of paper used, size of brushes, tools provided with play dough) to give credit. To score, consider which art materials are accessible during the observation, the children's art that is displayed, and staff responses to questions listed for the item.

7.2   ***Access to materials*** means that children can reach and use art materials. How and when these materials are made accessible will depend on the ***children's abilities*** and ages, as well as the type of material. Younger toddlers (12-23 months of age) require closer supervision because they are more likely to eat the materials or carry them around the room, dropping and spilling them along the way. At this stage, staff may need to store materials, such as paints, collage items, and play dough on higher shelves or in closed storage cabinets. Staff can then introduce these art materials at specific times, when close supervi-

17.7.2 Crayons and paper are stored on open shelves so that these older toddlers have easy access to some art materials throughout the day.

sion is possible. For older toddlers (23-30 months of age), who are able to use materials more independently, materials such as crayons and paper can be stored in containers on lower shelves. (See photo 17.7.2.) However, this indicator does not require that all art materials be placed on low, open shelves for easy access by older toddlers. For example, some materials, such as glue or scissors, may require more supervision, even for older toddlers, and staff need to plan and set up these activities for children.

18 Music and movement

General information about this item

From the earliest age, children show us signs that they enjoy *music*—the combination of tones and rhythms that often follow a melodic pattern—either using voices or sound-making instruments. An infant will respond to musical sounds by being soothed or showing interest, becoming alert and turning his head, and moving his arms and legs. A toddler will often ask to hear or sing the same songs over and over. (See photo 18A.) This item considers how musical experiences, such as chanting, singing, listening to and making music with toys and instruments are provided to infants/toddlers. *Music* can encourage children's language, social-emotional, and motor development.

When infants listen to singing, they are learning about rhythms and vocal sounds needed for later language development. Eventually infants will respond to the songs and rhythms they hear and enjoy imitating these sounds. For example, when a staff member sings, the baby may try to imitate the singing by cooing or making sounds. Toddlers also enjoy listening and singing along as they learn new words. For example, singing songs about what toddlers are doing helps them to learn new words to describe what they are experiencing. Singing "If You're Happy and You Know It, Clap Your Hands" exposes toddlers to new words that describe actions.

18A Infants and toddlers enjoy music.

Singing can be used as an opportunity to give individual attention to a child. For example, a staff member singing to an infant, "This is the way we change Jamie's diapers, change Jamie's diapers," gives the staff member an opportunity to add social interaction to the diapering procedure. Singing, smiling, and clapping with a small group of toddlers is a way of showing toddlers that it is enjoyable to do things with others. In addition, singing to infants can be very calming, for example, rocking a child before naptime and singing in a soft, gentle tone, "Hush, little baby." Playing soft music at the beginning of naptime may also help to soothe children and provide a smooth transition from the busy lunch time to nap time.

Music can be used for quiet listening or for more active play. A variety of musical toys and instruments gives children interesting things to use as they learn about cause and effect. (See photo 18B.) When an infant is developing fine motor skills for grasping, he will be interested in shakers and rattles that he can use to produce interesting sounds. Toddlers will become interested

18B Having access to musical instruments helps this baby learn about the effects of her actions.

in using materials that require more finger dexterity and eye-hand control, such as drums, triangles, and rhythm sticks. Dancing and moving to the beat of the music helps young children develop coordination and balance. Therefore, it is important for children to have music and movement opportunities that encourage dancing, bouncing, clapping, and swaying.

Although infants and toddlers enjoy music, they can quickly learn to dislike music activities that are not appropriate. Children should not be forced to sing, play with musical materials, learn the words to a song, or participate in a group music activity if they want to leave, because this can take the enjoyment out of music.

Although music is a "good thing," too much music at the wrong time is not good. Music should be used for musical experiences for young children and not as background sound, because this causes staff and children to talk over the music in order to be heard. When this happens, it increases the noise level in the room. Continuous background music, especially if it is loud, also interferes with a child's ability to listen to spoken language, which is extremely important for the speech development that must take place during the early years.

Examples of adult- or child-initiated music activities include:

Adult-initiated

- tape recording a child or a group singing and playing it back for them to listen to;
- singing to a child during handwashing, "This is the way we wash our hands;"
- playing recorded music for children to listen to;
- humming and rocking a baby to sleep;
- chanting and doing finger plays such as "Open, shut them;"
- singing softly to children before or after naptime;
- singing a "Clean-up" song during transitions;
- encouraging children to clap to music;
- singing while using puppets with a small group of children;
- singing and playing records of different tempos, e.g., very fast, relatively fast and slow;
- singing in different pitches (very high and low) and talking about the differences with children;
- playing a simple musical toy for a child; and
- playing a musical instrument alongside children playing the same instruments.

Child-initiated

- pulling or pushing toys that make musical sounds when rolled;
- playing with noise-making rattles;
- shaking wrist bells;
- banging cymbals or clackers;
- pressing keys or buttons on musical toys;
- grasping and shaking soft objects with bells inside; and
- using beaters on drums, xylophones, or bells.

Indicator

Movement is the action made by children when listening to music. Movement includes swaying, bouncing, dancing, marching, and clapping to music or rhythms, as well as acting out the content of songs, rhymes, or chants with large muscle actions. (See photos 18C-D.)

Movement activities can be adult- or child-initiated. They can be done in a group or individually. Movement activities might require that children do prescribed body actions or create their own individual motions. Examples of some adult-initiated **movement experiences** include:

- dancing while holding a non-mobile infant, so he can feel the movements with the music;
- holding hands with one or two children and swaying to music;
- gently bouncing a child on lap to rhythms or a song;
- encouraging older infants and toddlers to move to recorded music as a free choice activity;
- encouraging 2-year olds to dance or move to the tempo of music;
- encouraging children to clap to different rhythms; and
- encouraging a small group to move and dance with musical instruments or scarves.

Music and movement experiences can be offered during group times, free play, or routines. Since infants spend so much of their time involved in routine care activities, such as diapering, feeding, and sleeping, staff often incorporate musical experiences during these times, such as informally singing while bottle-feeding a baby. On the other hand, toddlers are interested in trying what others are doing, so a staff member playing musical instruments with one child may turn into a short, group activity. Music and movement experiences can be informal or planned, as well as adult- or child-initiated. Children should never be forced to participate in group movement activities or required to do movements perfectly, such as marching in a straight line.

18C Children clap along to the song their teacher is singing. Children also use musical instruments to add their own part.

18D Older toddlers create their own music to dance to.

A closer look at each indicator

1.1 Examples of **music/movement experiences** are provided in the "General Information" section for this item. Experiences can vary depending on the children's ages and abilities. Score this indicator "Yes" if the children in the group do *not have any* **music/movement experiences** *at least once a day.*

1.2 **Loud music** is music played at a level that adds significantly to the general noise level in the classroom. This is especially serious in rooms where infants and toddlers are enrolled, due to their frequent ear infections, which makes hearing clearly more difficult during a stage when hearing language is so important. Such "noise pollution" should therefore be minimized.

18 Music and movement

Loud music *interferes with ongoing activities* when the children and staff have a difficult time hearing one another. Loud music may prevent children from being able to hear the words staff use and participate in conversations with them. For example, in a classroom with loud music, staff might say, "It's time to change your diaper now. Ready?", but the loud music prevents the toddler from hearing. The toddler may be startled and upset when she is picked up abruptly without warning. When the music is loud and interferes with ongoing activities, children will not be able to hear the talking that is going on in the room, which is important to their own language development. Loud music also prevents children from being calm, so they may need to use more effort to engage in challenging tasks.

Loud background music may also be distracting to the staff, so that if they are recording feeding and diapering schedules, it may be difficult to concentrate. If it is observed that people in the classroom are forced to speak loudly to be heard, or if music seems to be adding to a chaotic atmosphere in the room, then the loud music *interferes with ongoing activities.*

Often, the observer might be irritated by music in a classroom, because she is concentrating on gathering information needed to complete an assessment. However, this is not enough evidence to conclude that the music in the room "interferes with ongoing activities." The observer must understand why the music is being used by the staff and judge its effect based on the behavior of the children and staff.

A definition for *much of the day* is given on page 7 of the ITERS-R. For this indicator however, if loud music is on for most of a 3-hour observation, the requirement for *much of the day* would be met.

Score this indicator "No" if loud music is not used, even if quiet music is played for much of the day. The indicator is also scored "No" if loud music is used, but only for a small portion of the day. Score "Yes," only if the loud music is on for most of the observation and interferes with ongoing activities.

18.3.1a Musical toys include rattles and shakers that infants and toddlers can use to create pleasant sounds.

3.1 *Musical materials* include anything that children and staff can use to make or listen to music, defined broadly to include the sounds of many things. Types of musical materials include both toys and instruments.

Musical toys allow children to create noise, music, or musical sounds. Examples include rattles, rain sticks, busy boxes that make noises, homemade shakers such as unbreakable bottles filled with hard objects, musical mobiles, soft toys with bells inside that make pleasant sounds when shaken, push and pull musical toys, and soft dolls or other toys with music boxes inside. (See photo 18.3.1a.)

Musical instruments allow children to make noises and musical sounds, and include drums, keyboards, bells, toy pianos, guitars, triangles, xylophones, and rhythm sticks. (See photo 18.3.1b.) The instruments may be homemade or commercially produced.

18.3.1b This collection of musical instruments allows children to experiment with different musical sounds.

In addition to musical toys and instruments, other musical materials are included here, such as an easy-to-use tape player for 2-year-olds.

To give credit for **musical materials,** they must be intended specifically for children to use for music. Furnishings or non-music objects are not counted for this item, even if children are allowed to use them to create sounds. For example, allowing a child to tap on pots with a spoon while playing with dramatic play materials would not count as making musical materials accessible.

The term **some** musical materials, toys, or instruments requires at least two items to be accessible. (See photo 18.3.1c.) To be counted in scoring, all musical materials, including toys and instruments must be safe for children. They should not contain features like sharp edges, which may injure children, or small removable pieces, which are a choking hazard. For this indicator, do not consider items that are unsafe as musical toys or instruments. Count only those that are safe. Safety issues can be addressed in Item 11, Safety practices. Instruments that require blowing, such as flutes or harmonicas, are not recommended because of the likelihood of contamination. If they are used by different children and not sanitized after each child, score this in Item 10, Health practices, and not in this item.

The terms **accessible** *and* **much of the day** are defined in the "Explanation of Terms Used Throughout the Scale," on page 7 of the ITERS-R. For example, a basket containing rattles is stored on the floor where crawling infants and toddlers can easily reach and use the materials throughout the day. However, if the children use the materials for one hour in the morning but the provider puts the basket on a high shelf for the reminder of the day, credit would not be given because the time requirement for much of the day is not met. In this situation, the number of materials is accessible but not the time requirement for much of the day

For materials to be considered accessible, they must be located within view and easy reach of the children. (See photos 18.3.1d-e.) Very young infants, who have limited mobility in their arms and legs, may be physically unable to hold or grasp musical materials, but credit can be given if the young infant is actively involved or responds to the musical material in some way. For example, if a 3-month-old is placed in an infant carrier containing a bar of hanging musical items that make sounds, and it is observed that the child notices the objects by looking or turning his head, then give credit for accessibility. Music experiences should be available for all young infants enrolled in the program.

Materials that are stored in closed spaces, closed containers, or on high shelves cannot be considered accessible. It must be observed that children can freely access and use the materials. For example, some musical instruments might be stored

18.3.1c This classroom meets the requirements for Indicator 3.1 because two instruments (bells and a drum), which are stored on open shelves, are easily accessible to toddlers.

18.3.1d Staff place this musical instrument within reach of the non-mobile child so that he has easy access.

18.3.1e When placed on top of the shelf, access to this musical instrument is difficult.

in closed plastic containers; however, if the teacher opens the lids and places the materials on a low, open shelf so that toddlers can easily use the materials, they are considered accessible during that time. Non-mobile infants must be moved to an area where they can reach the materials, or staff must bring materials to them.

To evaluate the amount of time that musical materials are accessible to children the observer should consider whether the children are allowed or encouraged to take toys from open shelves. If children do not feel free or are not able to take toys from shelves, or if there are rules that limit times when children are allowed to access them, then do not give credit (score "No") for materials being accessible for free play for much of the day. For example, if the observer notices that toddlers use a few toys in one area of the room but stay away from others that are also stored within their reach (such as musical toys, art materials, puzzles, sets of fine motor toys), she must then determine how and when those materials are accessible to score this item. The information preferably would be based on observing, but might include answers to questions asked during the staff interview.

Children should be allowed to play freely with musical materials. **Free play** is defined in the "Notes for Clarification" for Item 30, Free play on page 46 in the ITERS-R. During free play, children are not expected to participate in a whole-group or small-group activities. Staff may introduce the materials, toys, and instruments by making them accessible, but the activity is not teacher-directed; it is child-directed. For example, a drum is on a low, open shelf near a young toddler who is sitting on the floor. The child begins to tap the drum with her hands and, after a few minutes, moves on to other things. During free play, children are free to choose materials and manipulate them in their own way.

Score "Yes" if children have free access to the required number of music materials throughout the observation, as described above. Score "No" if there are too few materials, they are not accessible for the required amount of time, or if they are not offered as a free play option.

18.3.2a Each day staff sing songs with children.

3.2   **Staff initiate** means that the staff think of and start the music activity. Staff initiation is used to introduce children to music and to encourage and extend children's musical experiences. (See photo 18.3.2a.)

There are many different ways that staff can initiate music activities with infants and toddlers, as long as staff take the initiative to bring music into the environment, either by playing music for children to listen to (professionally recorded or staff-created) or by singing to children. Examples of such activities are provided as a part of this indicator on page 34 of the ITERS-R. Additional examples of **staff-initiated musical experiences** for infants and toddlers include:

- singing softly to child while bottle-feeding;
- encouraging infants to shake rattles or shakers;
- singing songs with small groups or individual children;
- playing soft music at nap time;
- playing music to bounce or dance to; (See photo 18.3.2b.)

18.3.2b Playing recorded songs is an example of a staff initiated music activity.

- singing or chanting finger plays such as "Itsy, Bitsy Spider;"

- giving children drums to play by hand, or for older children, with drumsticks;

- giving children easy-to-play musical instruments, such as wrist bells;

- repeating popular chants or songs, such as "Old MacDonald" and encouraging the children to make animals sounds;

- singing a "Good Morning" song with the children's names;

- singing a "clean-up" song to encourage older toddlers to help;

- playing music of different styles, such as folk, jazz, or classical; and

- placing bells and rattles in a basket near the children and demonstrating the sounds they make by shaking them.

For the definition of **staff,** refer to page 7 of the ITERS-R. However, music provided by a special music teacher can be considered only if these experiences are in addition to the music activities staff regularly initiate on a daily basis. For example, once a week a music teacher comes into the classroom, and on other days when she is not present, the classroom staff initiate a musical activity. In this situation, this special person can substitute for the regular staff when scoring indicators that require staff-initiated music activities daily. However, on days when the music teacher is not present, regular staff must meet such requirements.

To give credit for this indicator (score "Yes") at least one music activity must be initiated by the staff daily. The activity may be done formally or informally, as part of a group time, free play, or routine. Score "Yes" if a music activity is initiated by the staff during the 3-hour observation. If no staff-initiated music activity is observed, then ask the staff the questions for this indicator listed in the ITERS-R on page 34, and base the score on the response. If the response is "Yes," ask how it is handled and how often. Activity plans and daily schedules can also be used to obtain the information needed to score, but only if they reasonably match what is observed during the observation period.

3.3   Since infants and toddlers enjoy doing many different things and have relatively short attention spans, staff should **not require** them to **participate in group music activities**. "Group play activities" is defined on page 47 of the ITERS-R, under Item 31, Group play activities. Group music activities are considered a type of group play activity. Many times staff initiate group activities with the expectation that children will participate. Toddlers may first appear interested in joining in activities that others are doing around them, but may soon lose interest and drift on to other activities. Others just want to "do their own thing" and never join in at all. They are busy elsewhere. Staff should respect these preferences, allowing toddlers to choose what they want to play with during much of the day, including playing alone if they wish. Participation in group activities should never be required. (See photo 18.3.3.)

18.3.3 Singing together is a music activity. However, staff realize that toddlers have short attention spans and never require them to participate in group music activities.

Alternative activities available means that if some children choose not to participate, then there are enough materials and toys available so that there are other interesting options. Alternative activities may consist of free play or other teacher-directed activities. There must be more than one alternative activity for the child to choose. If children are allowed to leave the group music activity and go to other areas in the room where there are a variety of toys, then give credit (score "Yes") for this indicator. If children are taken to another room to participate in a special music activity and there are no other options, then score this indicator "No." If children are forced to stay with the group activity, do not give credit.

5.1 The term *musical materials* is defined in Indicator 3.1. The term *many* is defined in the "Notes for Clarification" on page 34 of the ITERS-R as at least 10 musical toys. (See photo 18.5.1a.) To be counted in scoring, all *musical materials, including toys and instruments, must be safe for children. They should not contain features such as sharp edges, which may injure children, or small removable pieces which are choking hazards. For this indicator, do not consider items that are unsafe as musical toys or instruments. Count only those that are safe. Safety issues can also be counted in Item 11, Safety practices.* The number required is based on a group size of no more than 10 children. If more than 10 children are enrolled, then the minimum number would increase, so that at least one musical toy or instrument is accessible for each child enrolled. Note whether children argue or compete for the use of materials. For example, if there is one drum in the classroom and many noise-making containers, but children constantly argue over the drum, then do not give credit for this indicator. Duplicates of favorite toys must be accessible. *Many* can consist of toys and instruments or other materials, such as an easy-to-play tape recorder. Make sure that the musical toys actually make noises when used and are not missing the batteries or other parts needed to produce sounds.

18.5.1a In this classroom, many accessible music materials include bottles to shake, bells, commercial rhythm instruments, xylophones, and pianos.

Pleasant sounding means that the when musical materials are used, a pleasant sound is produced rather than a loud, startling noise. This requirement is meant to cut down on the "noise pollution" in the room. For example, a rattle which makes a soft sound is pleasant to a young infant as opposed to a loud, startling noise like cymbals crashing. Examples of other toys that may be unpleasant include a loud electronic telephone toy or a toy fire truck with a loud siren. Whether sounds are considered pleasant depends on the reaction of the children being observed, not on the observer's preferences. If music toys produce sounds that are disruptive to the group, do not count them as pleasant.

Refer to Indicator 3.1 for the definitions of *accessible and much of the day. Accessible much of the day* refers to the *many musical* toys/materials, not just to the "some," required in 3.1.

To score this indicator "Yes," the *many* music materials must be *accessible* for much of the day. (See photo 18.5.1b.) The music materials can be accessible indoors or outdoors and either as a small-group activity or individually as an informal, child-initiated activity.

5.2 *Informally* means that the activity is not a regular, planned part of the schedule. The singing or chanting may take place at any time during routines or play, when children are not necessarily involved in a musical activity. Examples of informal singing and chanting include:

18.5.1b Placing musical toys on low, open shelves makes them easily accessible to infants and toddlers.

- During handwashing, staff chant to children, "Washy, washy, making bubbles."

- During clean up, staff sing, "Cleanup, cleanup, everybody, everywhere."

- Staff hum while rocking a child.

- Staff see a child playing with a teddy bear and the teacher chants, "Teddy bear, teddy bear turn around."

- Staff playfully take the hands of a few children and sing, "Ring around the rosy."

- Staff play "Pat-a-Cake" with one child.

- Staff sing to children while they eat snack.

- Staff sing a finger-play song to a child during free play, showing the child how to imitate the finger movements.

For the definition of **staff** see Indicator 3.2. As stated in the "Note for Clarification" for this indicator, such informal singing/chanting must be observed once during the 3-hour observation. To give credit in a longer observation, it must be observed during the first 3 hours.

5.3   To receive credit for this indicator, staff must **sing** to children and provide some **other musical experience daily**. During a 3-hour observation, at least one instance of staff singing **informally** to children must be observed and can count to give credit for Indicators 3.2 and 5.2. However, to give credit for this indicator, the music experience must be in addition to singing and must be staff-initiated, either during group time or free play. (See photos 18.5.3a-b.) Examples are provided in the indicator and in the "General Information" section for this item. The additional experience can be child-initiated or staff-initiated. See examples of musical activities listed in the "General Information About this Item" and examples listed for this indicator in the ITERS-R on page 34. The additional experience must take place daily to be given credit. If an additional music experience is not observed, then ask the question provided in the ITERS-R on page 34, and score based on the answer given by the staff.

5.4   Examples of **recorded music** include tapes, CD's, MP3 players, computer generated music, music on videos or T.V., radios, and records. **Limited times** means

18.5.3a In addition to singing, staff encourage children to listen to the various sounds that musical bells and shakers make.

18.5.3b In addition to singing, staff have put on recorded music and are dancing with the toddlers.

18.7.1a

18.7.1b

18.7.1a-b Staff rotate materials by taking musical toys out of storage and placing them on shelves in the classroom.

that children are listening and the music is being used in some way (e.g., for a movement activity), and is not left on as background music after the intended activity has been completed. ***Positive purpose*** means that the music being played is not used just to add sound or noise to the room, but rather to have a specific impact on the children, such as for dancing, to soothe at nap, to teach a new idea, or to encourage language development. The purpose must have positive educational or developmental value for the children. Score "No" if music is used for long periods (e.g., 20 minutes) as background sound, even if was originally put on for a specific purpose, such as for children to dance to.

7.1   ***Rotated*** means that the musical materials accessible to children are changed periodically so that children can practice different skills, find new interests, and discover new ways of using things that they have used before. Rotating materials keeps children from becoming bored with the choices they can make for play and adds new learning opportunities. (See photos 18.7.1a-b.)

Rotation of musical materials should occur when children no longer show interest in the materials because they do not find them novel or challenging. The materials should then be put away and different ones brought out. Calling children's attention to a musical toy that is regularly accessible to children does not count as "rotating materials." For example, if staff take tambourines off the shelf where they already are accessible and place them on the table for toddlers to use, credit for "rotation" is not given. Credit is given only when new toys are brought into the classroom to add to or replace the existing toys.

Inaccessible materials can be made accessible as either special projects or for free play. The rotated music materials can be brought from storage, from other classrooms, or be newly purchased.

To give credit, at least two music toys or instruments should be rotated monthly or more often.

Indicator

7.2 Examples of ***various types of music*** are given in the indicator. Additional examples of different types include:

- vocal and instrumental music,
- children's songs,
- opera,
- classical,
- jazz,
- lively or quiet,
- rock,
- reggae,
- rhythm and blues,
- lullabies,
- rap,
- folk songs, and
- country and western.
- music characteristic of different cultures, some in different languages,

18.7.2 Various types of recorded music include classical, instrumental, children's songs, and music characteristic of different cultures.

Any music counted as a "type" for this indicator must be appropriate for use with children, that is, the music may contain no violent or sexually explicit material or language that is unacceptable according to accepted societal standards. Much of the music composed for adults is usually appropriate, as well as most children's songs. (See photo 18.7.2.)

To score this indicator "Yes," *at least three different types* of music must be used regularly with the children. Often this is observable, but to score this indicator, the observer should look through the recorded music options, such as records, tapes, and CD's. If these are not easy to find, ask staff the question given for Indicator 7.2 on page 34 of the ITERS-R, and score accordingly.

7.3 ***Staff encourage*** means that staff suggest that children react in some way to the music or participate with them in reacting to the music. This can be done in a large group, small group or individually and can vary depending on the child's age and ability. For example, a staff member may hold a baby and sing a verse or two and then pause for the baby to coo. For an older toddler, the staff member may put on a tape and say, "Remember this song?" and as she sings along says, "Isn't this fun?" For examples of movement activities, see the "General Information" section for this item and the examples listed for the indicator on page 34 of the ITERS-R. To give credit, staff encouragement must be observed at least once.

19 Blocks

General Information About This Item

Throughout the years, building blocks, like dolls and balls, have been one of the basic play materials for young children. They are so well associated with young children's play that we often see them depicted in illustrations for baby-related products, as the logo for child-related organizations, or as pictures in "baby's first words" books. Children follow developmental patterns in their use of these valuable traditional play materials. Block play for infants and toddlers is different from that of preschoolers. Older infants and young toddlers like touching and grasping soft textured blocks. They are mainly interested in the sensory characteristics of these new objects, such as how blocks feel, the bright colors, the different sides that are seen as they turn them in their hands, and what they sound like when two blocks are banged together. Toddlers are interested in using blocks for dumping and filling containers. They often throw them, watching how they fall and land, unlike round objects that act quite differently. Later, when toddlers develop more eye-hand coordination and muscle control they are able to manipulate many blocks. This usually begins with children lining blocks up horizontally and progresses to stacking blocks vertically. Finally, toddlers advance to the stage of block play where they build simple structures and use block accessories for pretend play.

19A The vinyl covered foam blocks are considered in scoring this item. The interlocking blocks are considered when scoring Item 15, Fine motor, but not considered in this item.

The materials required in this item are blocks and block accessories. Blocks are geometric shapes of various sizes and materials that have smooth sides, can be stacked, and are easily pushed over or fall, if they are not balanced properly. They are a building material limited only by the ability of the child to think of a final product and the skill to realize it by carefully balancing the various geometric shapes. The fact that blocks have nothing additional to hold them together (such as connecting rods or interlocking openings and protrusions) makes them a unique and challenging experience throughout the infant/toddler, preschool, and early school years. (See photo 19A.)

Because infants and young toddlers use blocks mainly as a sensory motor experience, they only need a small number of simple geometric shapes in sizes and weights they can mange safely. Older toddlers like the challenge of carrying larger blocks. (See photo 19B.) With the help of staff, they can build simple structures that can be used with accessories such as small vehicles and block people. Examples of materials that count as types of blocks are

19B With help from the teacher, these toddlers have built a road with large hollow blocks.

19C Soft cloth blocks are used by this infant as a sensory material.

listed in the "Notes for Clarification" on page 35 of the ITERS-R. Others that may be considered include:

- lightweight, hollow brick blocks made of cardboard,
- fabric covered blocks, (See photo 19C.)
- "ABC" wooden blocks larger than two inches,
- hard and soft plastic blocks of different sizes,
- geometric-shaped blocks used with shape sorters (but not other shapes, such as stars, hearts, animals),
- blocks with bells inside,
- homemade blocks made from empty tissue containers, or oatmeal boxes, covered with colored adhesive plastic or paper,
- large colored cubes that do not pose a choking hazard (over two inches), or
- wooden or hard foam unit blocks.

Other materials often categorized as blocks but which are *not* counted as blocks for this item include:

- building materials of any size that interlock in any way, such as Lego or Duplo (considered in Item 15, Fine motor);
- large, foam-filled, vinyl covered blocks used as gross motor climbing equipment (considered in Item 16, Active physical play);
- large plastic cubes that can be used as chairs (depending on use, considered in Item 2, Furniture for routine care and play, or Item 20, Dramatic play);
- blocks in mobiles or used as parts of other toys, in which the blocks cannot be freely manipulated, stacked, or knocked down (depending on use, considered in Item 5, Display or Item 15, Fine motor); and
- nesting blocks with one or more open sides (considered in Item 15, Fine Motor).

19D A container into which blocks can be dropped is considered an accessory.

19E Small toy people, animals and vehicles are considered accessories for block play.

19F [above] Big trucks that toddlers use for gross motor and pretend play are not considered block accessories because they interfere with block building.

19G [right] The plastic egg beater and carpentry tools are not considered block accessories because they are used as pretend play materials that hinder, rather than enhance, block play.

Accessories consist of appropriately-sized toys that can be used with blocks to extend block play. (See photos 19D-E.) Examples of accessories are listed in the "Notes for Clarification" for this item on page 35 of the ITERS-R. Other examples include:

- animals of various types, including farm animals, zoo animals, pet animals, or dinosaurs;
- sets of people, such as families of different races and ages or community helpers; and
- small vehicles, such as cars, trucks, or airplanes.

Accessories should be separated and stored in clearly labeled containers, and they should be placed near the blocks so that children know they are meant to be used with the blocks. Because accessories should not interfere with or interrupt block play, certain toys are not given credit as accessories. For example, big trucks, which are usually used by toddlers for gross motor activity, or a carpentry kit, which has plastic tools that are used for hammering on blocks and not for building with them, are not considered block accessories and should not be stored near the blocks. (See photos 19F-G.)

As the "Notes for Clarification" indicate, this item is scored "NA" if all children enrolled in the group being observed are under 12 months of age, even if blocks are accessible and used by the infants. However, if there are some children in the group under 12 months of age and some children 12 months and older, then this item should be scored. There are exceptions to this age requirement listed in the "Explanation of Terms Used Throughout the Scale" on page 7 of the ITERS-R. To determine whether the score of "NA" should be given, the observer should ask staff for the birthdates of all children enrolled and then collect information needed for scoring Blocks for those children 12 months or older. If an older child with a disability is enrolled, and all the other children are infants, the appropriateness of this item will depend on the child's abilities, not necessarily on the child's age.

19 Blocks

A closer look at each indicator

1.1   *Available* means that the materials are stored somewhere in the center and can be easily made accessible for use by the children. "Available" differs from the term "accessible," because it does not require that children can reach and use the materials by themselves. *No materials available for block play* means that there are no blocks stored in the classroom or in the center that are meant to be used for block play by the toddlers. This indicator does not consider accessories; it only requires blocks. Available blocks can be stored indoors or outdoors. Consider only appropriate blocks such as those listed in the "General Information" section of this item.

Score this item "Yes" if there are no blocks available for block play. If there is least one set of six or more blocks available that are designed to be used together, even if they are not accessible, then score this item "No."

3.1   A *set of blocks* is a group of blocks of the same type. The set must contain a minimum of six blocks of the same type so that children have experiences stacking, filling and dumping containers and building. (See photos 19.3.1a-b.) Examples of acceptable types of blocks are provided in the "General Information" section for this item and in the "Notes for Clarification" on page 35 of the ITERS-R.

The definition for *accessible* is listed in the "Explanation of Terms Used Throughout the Scale" on page 7 of the ITERS-R and means that the blocks can be reached and used by the children. To make blocks accessible they can be stored on low, open shelves so that children can easily reach and use them, or in open containers. The blocks may be located in the classroom or in other areas that children use on a daily basis.

Daily means every day except for rare occasions when the class is participating in a special event, such as a field trip. A minimum of one hour daily is required in programs of 8 hours or more. Less time is required in shorter programs and calculated proportionately. For example, in a program of 4 hours per day, ½ hour would be required.

If blocks or block play is not observed during the 3-4 hour observation, ask staff during the teacher interview or look at all areas used by the children to determine whether blocks are accessible in any other area.

To give credit for this indicator (score "Yes"), at least one set of six blocks must be accessible daily to the toddlers.

3.2   *Accessories* for blocks are toys used with blocks to stimulate or expand block play. Examples are included in the "General Information" section of this item. *Some* means at least five accessories of different types. (See photo 19.3.2.) Types of accessories include people, animals, or vehicles. For young toddlers who like to fill containers with blocks and dump them, containers are also considered acces-

19.3.1a   At the minimal level of quality a set of blocks consists of six or more blocks of the same type.

19.3.1b   Although there are more than six blocks in this set, this still represents a minimal level, because only one set of blocks is present.

19.3.2   Even though there are five cars and trucks, credit for "some" accessories cannot be given because only one type (transportation toys) is represented.

Indicator

sories. Accessories should be stored near the blocks. However, if the accessories are not stored near the blocks, they must be observed being used together during block play in order to receive credit. Score this indicator "No" if there is only one of the three different types accessible to the children on a daily basis, or if it is not evident that the accessories are used with the blocks.

3.3 This indicator requires that both blocks and accessories are accessible to the children for much of the day. There must be at least one set of blocks (see requirements for Indicator 3.1) and two accessories (see requirements for Indicator 3.2) accessible. The definition of **much of the day** is given in "Explanation of Terms Used Throughout the Scale" on page 7 of the ITERS-R. If there are the required number of blocks (one set of six or more blocks of the same type) and enough accessories, but they are not accessible for much of the day, then score this indicator "No." It is likely that if Indicators 3.1 or 3.2 are scored "No," this indicator would also be score "No."

5.1 **Two sets of blocks** are required for this indicator. For the definition of "a set of blocks," see Indicator 3.1. However, the number of blocks required in a set is higher at the "good" quality level. (See photo 19.5.1.) Each set must contain **10 or more blocks** of the same type. A classroom may have many blocks of different sizes, shapes and materials, but if none of them are of the same type they cannot easily be used together. If there are fewer than 10 blocks of the same type, then do not consider this as meeting the requirement for a **set** of blocks. Each of the two sets must be of a different type. The types are listed in the "General Information" section for this Item. The time requirement for accessibility is daily for **much of the day**. The definition of "much of the day" is provided in the "Explanation of Terms Used Throughout the Scale" on page 7 of the ITERS-R.

5.2 To score this indicator, the observer should look at the block shelves and containers before or after block play, and not just during block play. Children at this age tend to dump materials out of containers, mixing blocks and accessories, and often carry the items around the room. **Blocks sorted by type** means that different kinds of blocks (such as soft blocks, unit blocks, plastic blocks, and homemade blocks) are separated and stored on the shelf or in separate containers. If the blocks are scattered around the room and not replaced on shelves in their different sets at least once a day, then they cannot be considered **sorted by type**.

This indicator does not require that the blocks be organized by shape and size within a specific type. Only simple organization is required so that children are able to play with sets of blocks, all of the same type, and distinguish different categories of blocks. If different types of blocks are mixed together

19.5.1 At the good level of quality a set of blocks consists of ten or more blocks of the same type and at least two types must be accessible to children.

19.5.2a Accessories are organized in separate containers by type, animals, transportation toys and people.

19.5.2b In this classroom, block accessories are scattered on the floor and mixed with other materials making it difficult for children to select the accessories they want to play with.

for storage on shelves or in containers, then score this indicator "No."

Accessories sorted by type means that toys used with blocks are organized together, by type on a shelf or within separate containers. The accessories should not be mixed with blocks or other classroom toys. (See photos 19.5.2a-b.) The different types of accessories should be separated into categories. For example, wooden people are separated from animals and vehicles or the shape sorter boxes are stored with the blocks inside.

There are different ways to sort accessories by type, and as long as there is some clear organization, credit can be given. Examples of acceptable sorting might include:

- Small people and small vehicles are in separate containers; all animals are on a shelf

- Larger trucks are together on a shelf; small people and small vehicles are in one container; all animals are on a shelf.

- Small vehicles are in one container; little people (wood and plastic) are in one container; small animals are in one container; large animals are together on a shelf.

If both blocks and accessories are sorted and stored reasonably by type, score Indicator 5.2 "Yes."

5.3　***Space for block play*** can be floor space or table space, as long as it is appropriate for the blocks being used. Smaller blocks may be used on a table or on the floor, while larger blocks usually require floor space. All spaces used for block play must be out of traffic. (See photo 17.5.3a.)

Out of traffic means that children can play with blocks in an area without interruptions from children and adults walking through. For example, the middle of the classroom would not be considered out of traffic because other children who are moving freely around the room could easily step on or knock over the blocks. The block space should not be located near a doorway frequently used by children or staff or in the major pathways from one area of the room to another. (See photos 19.5.3b-c.) This indicator does not require that blocks be gathered in a special, separate interest area but that the space used for block play be free of frequent interruptions. If children must walk through the block space to access other kinds of toys on shelves shared with the blocks or surrounding the space, then the space would not be considered "out of traffic." If more than one area is used for block play, all areas must be located out of traffic.

A steady surface means providing a flat, level, relatively hard surface so that the blocks do not easily fall over when stacked. A steady surface might be on a low-pile carpet (not

19.5.3a This block area is out of traffic and has a steady surface for building.

19.5.3b Children using this slide often interfere with other children who are trying to build block structures because the two areas (gross motor and blocks) are not separated.

19.5.3c Block play is easily interrupted when it takes place near a doorway or pathway that children frequently use.

loop or high-pile rug), vinyl floor, wooden floor, or table. However, a thick mat, similar to those used for gross motor play, may not be steady because the mat easily goes up and down when children walk and crawl in the same area.

Score this indicator "No" if the space for block play does not meet *both* requirements for this indicator. For example, score "No" if the area is out of traffic, but it does not provide a steady building surface.

In the ITERS-R, *"NA permitted"* is listed in this indicator. However, this is a printing error and the indicator must be scored if the item is being completed.

7.1 **Three sets of blocks** are required to give credit for this indicator. Each set must **contain 10 or more blocks** of the same type. Each of the three sets must be of a different type. The types are listed in the "General Information" for this Item. The time requirement for accessibility is **daily for much of the day**. The definition of "much of the day" is provided in the "Explanation of Terms Used Throughout the Scale" on page 7 of the ITERS-R.

Score this indicator "Yes" if the required number of sets of blocks are accessible for the required length of time daily.

7.2 **Variety of accessories** means at least five materials from each of the following categories: transportation toys, people, and animals. (See photo 19.7.2.) Examples of **transportation toys** include trucks, construction vehicles, cars, motorcycles, trains, and airplanes. The transportation toys can be of different sizes, styles, and different textures, and made of cloth, plastic, or wood. Examples of **people** can include wooden figures of different races, ages and abilities, small plastic figures, doll house families, and small soft, flexible dolls. Examples of **animals** include dinosaurs, zoo animals, and farm animals. The **variety of accessories** must be accessible to children on a daily basis whenever blocks are used. There may be more in one category and less in another, as long as all categories of accessories are included.

The variety of accessories must be stored near the blocks, or they must be observed being used together. If any of the three categories (transportation, people, and animals) is not represented, then score this indicator "No."

7.3 Because children learn not only by exploring and experimenting on their own, but also by watching and imitating others, staff participation and guidance is important in expanding block play. Children usually play longer with materials when staff are actively involved in their play. The definition of **staff** is given in the "Explanation of Terms Used Throughout the Scale" on page 7 of the ITERS-R. Staff can also extend learning by using words to describe objects and actions during block play. **Simple block play with children** means that staff take the time to touch and use the materials alongside the children as they play. (See photos 19.7.3a-b.) This includes more than just observing and commenting on the children's play.

19.7.2 A variety of accessories means at least five materials from each of the following categories: transportation toys, people and animals.

19.7.3a

19.7.3b
19.7.3a-b Staff participate in block play but are careful not to take over or direct play.

19 Blocks

During an observation of 3 hours, at least one instance of staff doing simple block play with children must be observed to give credit.

When staff participate in block play with the children, this participation should not be seen as instruction for the children, but rather as an enjoyable experience where children learn informally. The adult must be careful not to take over or direct the play. Simple block play means that staff participate at the children's ability level, helping them to move gradually to the next step, but also accepting their existing skills. Simple block play should not include anything that would be too difficult, complex, or frustrating for a toddler.

The block play may be initiated either by staff or by children. For example, a child may take out some blocks and play on her own, and then be joined by a staff member. Or a staff member might stack a few blocks and see if children will join in the play.

As the "Notes for Clarification" indicate, at least one example must be observed during the typical 3-hour observation. If no example is observed during the 3 hours, but an example is observed later, credit is not given (score "No"). Examples that might be observed include:

- A child picks up a small foam block and looks at it. A staff member picks up a block just like it and says, "Here's another one for you." The child takes the second block and says, "More." They continue to look for more blocks together.

- Staff stack blocks for child to knock down. Then the child stacks blocks himself.

- A staff member talks about stacking blocks as she does this alongside a child, who is also stacking blocks.

- A child makes a row of three blocks and says, "Look." The staff member puts a fourth block down and asks, "Do you want me to help you build a longer road?"

- A staff member puts a small figure accessory on a rectangular block near a stack made by a child and says, "Look my doll is sleeping on her bed."

- A staff member builds a three-block bridge, talking about how to do this as a 2-year-old watches. Then she takes off the top bridge block and asks the child if he can build the bridge again.

20 Dramatic play

General information about this item

Dramatic play is pretending or making believe. Dramatic play for infants and toddlers begins with the child imitating something that he or she has seen some other person do, or something else, such as a dog or car, do. With the youngest babies, imitation takes place as part of social play, usually with a caring adult or older child. A baby might copy the mouth movement of the person playing with him, in a playful imitation game between the adult and child. Older babies, however, can imitate what they have seen or experienced, remembering and copying it at a later time. For example, a baby might pretend to take a toy spoon and stir an empty pot, having watched his mother or father cook at home. A child might put a doll into a doll bed and cover her up, just as her teacher has done for her so many times. Another child might play with a toy puppy, making barking noises.

Children tend to practice the words they know in their pretend play. Toddlers will say single words, such as "hat" as they put a hat on a doll's head, and later use several words together to add to their play ("Shopping, go shopping," while pushing a toy shopping cart, or making truck noises while pushing a truck on the floor). These are all part of the amazing development of intelligence. Dramatic play has a large role in encouraging such development.

There is also a strong developmental progression in the social-emotional component of dramatic play. Infants and younger toddlers tend to do their pretending all alone, in *solitary* play. However, they will pretend with an older child or especially an adult, if the older, more experienced person initiates the play and keeps it going. An older infant will pretend to talk on a toy telephone, if someone else shows him how and continues the play with him until he loses interest. Later he will do this activity by himself. Older toddlers tend to play side-by-side in *parallel* play, glancing at one another, sometimes copying what the other person is doing, but not really coordinating their roles yet, or working to create a story together. In *cooperative play*, we often see toddlers playing in the housekeeping area together, but still separate. It takes longer for children to develop the sophisticated abilities of cooperating while they pretend, as older preschoolers are able to do.

As children grow into older toddlers, they become able to do more complicated imitation, stringing together many different acts of imitation, and pretending that toys are the real thing, when they know they really are not. For example, a 2-year-old might pretend to wash a baby, and then dry her, *using simple, realistic props*, such as a baby bath filled with bubbly water and a towel. Older infants and toddlers also are able to imitate things they know about without having objects to use, just using their imaginations. A 15-month old might pretend to comb her hair, although she does not have a comb. She uses just the action of combing in place of combing with the object. A 2-year-old might pretend to wash a baby doll *even though there is no water or bathtub*. She can imagine that these things are present, and use them in her play.

Although older toddlers can act out a limited amount of play without the aid of any dramatic play materials, using more realistic materials (such as toy pots and pans, dolls, soft animals) and equipment (such as child-sized play furnishings, strollers, shopping carts) for dramatic play vastly increases children's opportunities for richer, *more detailed* play. The ability to combine props leads to what we call *meaningful play,* or more elaborate play.

Materials for infant and toddler dramatic play should be very simple. They should give the children their first experiences with learning to tell real things from pretend things. The young baby learns that a doll is like a person in many ways, but is not a person, or a toddler experiments to find out that a plastic piece of bread looks like a real piece of bread, but it cannot actually be eaten, and it does not taste the same when tried. Materials for toddlers should encourage a wider range of imitative play that has more options. With a variety of interesting materials and props, children practice many skills and attempt to show what they know about what happens in their world.

In this item, the ***materials*** used in dramatic play are sometimes called ***props.*** Both materials and props are the things children use to act out roles or pretend, just as props are used in movies. The best materials/props for the youngest children are those that represent the things with which they are most familiar. In their short lives, all infants and toddlers will have collected quite a bit of information about their routines (feeding, diapering, sleeping, bathing) and familiar people. Some will know about other things, such as going shopping, playing with pets, or riding in or driving a car. A high-quality early childhood program will provide the materials/props children need to act out what they know. ***Child-sized play furniture,*** which encourages dramatic play, is a requirement for classrooms with toddlers. Having ***no*** materials limits the type of play older infants and toddlers can carry out. Props stimulate and support play that has more meaning for children. A variety of props offers more options for what can happen in pretend play.

Meaningful play is more likely to occur when props can be used together. For example, if a child has a doll, she might act out the role of mommy by rocking the baby and pretending to care for him. But the possibilities are somewhat limited. If more props are added, she has more options about what to do with the baby. By adding a doll bed, blankets, stroller, doll food, doll bottle, dishes and cups, a little brush, and a doll diaper, the play options are increased.

If allowed, older infants and toddlers will almost always pretend in some way. It is natural for them to do so—it is an important part of their learning. This type of play usually takes place during free play times, both indoors and outdoors. The dramatic play of infants and toddlers can be enhanced by the participation of adults, who show children how to act things out, explain what they are doing, encourage imitation, and then step back to allow the child to play in his or her own way. ("Look, Emma. I am rocking the baby. She's going to sleep. Can you rock your baby?") Yet, to get the most out of dramatic play, children must be free to use materials/props in their *own* way, as part of their self-created make-believe. Thus, it should be noted that *activities used to teach children to follow specific sequences and not to use their imaginations, in order to properly complete household chores, such as table washing or clothes laundering, are not counted to meet the requirements of this item.* Although the same materials may be used, the intent of the activity and the children's experiences are completely different from dramatic play.

A closer look at each indicator

1.1 The term ***materials*** is defined in the "General Information" section for this item. Examples of materials are provided in the "Notes for Clarification" for Indicators 1.1, 3.1, and 5.1 on page 36 of the ITERS-R. More information on the material includes:

Infants:

- Dolls: Cloth, plastic, vinyl, wood; large or small, but of a size that children can handle; dressed or without clothes; with or without realistic hair, anatomically correct or generic, with identifiable faces; realistic or fantasy, but in human form, representing adults, children or baby. They must be intact to count as a doll for Indicators 3.1 and 5.1; just a head or arm would not count as a doll. (See photos 20A-B.)

- Soft animals: Realistic-looking toy animals, such as vinyl or rubber farm animals, zoo animals; plush animal puppets, small cloth or vinyl-covered grasping toys in the form of animals, such as smiling teddy bears, caterpillars of many colors, toy fish and fantasy animals. All must be soft to count.

- Pots and pans: usually plastic, but other safe materials are acceptable; includes pots, frying pans, kettles, tea pots (pot lids do not count as an example by themselves); may be realistic or fantasy (such as with a smiling face on the pot); may be accompanied by dishes or spoons, cups, but not required (but these do not count as an example for Indicator 5.1 because they do not substitute for the pots and pans required for the infants)

- Toy telephones: representing cell, portable, dial or push-button; must reasonably look like a telephone. Does not include telephone-type toys that do not look like any telephone a child might have experienced or could identify. May be realistic or fantasy (e.g., have a happy face); usually made of plastic, but other safe materials acceptable. Must have all parts—if the toy consists of two connecting pieces, both must be together. (See photo 20C.)

Toddlers

- Dress-up clothes

  Dress-up clothes enhance children's dramatic play by allowing them to wear different things for the different roles they might like to try out. For infants and toddlers only the simplest of dress-ups are considered age-appropriate, and they must be safe for very young children to use. This means that no dress-ups would permit tripping, strangulation, or blocking of the air passage. Appropriate dress-ups include :

  - Simple shirts or blouses for both men and women
  - Dresses, skirts, jackets of older children that have been shortened for older toddlers (24-30 months of age)
  - Simple footwear, such as adult slip-on shoes, sandals,

20A   Small soft dolls are appropriate dramatic play materials for infants because they can easily grasp and hold these light, stuffed toys.

20B   Dolls and doll strollers are considered dramatic play materials that children can use in pretend play.

20C   Toy telephones encourage children to talk while pretending.

slippers, shoes or boots made for older children that toddlers can put on

- Hats of many types, for men and women, including hard hats and other hats used in different jobs, hats for different kinds of weather, hats for leisure

- Purses, baskets with straps or handles that will not fit over a child's head so they are not a strangulation hazard

- Commercially produced costumes made to fit toddlers, representing community helpers or fantasy characters

- Child-sized house furniture

Toddlers quickly recognize child-sized house furniture and delight in pretending that they are carrying out the roles that are most familiar to them, those that are carried out at home. It is through such play that toddlers represent what they know about family life. They act out things that have happened in their own world, and also try out things that they have learned about but have not actually experienced. Child-sized house furniture may include:

- kitchen sink

- stove or oven

- washer or dryer

- refrigerator

- cupboard to store pretend pots, pans, dishes, foods

- ironing board with iron

- table and chairs

- soft couch or armchair

- place to hang dress-ups

- Cooking/eating equipment

Most toddlers have observed quite a bit of food preparation in their short lives, and done lots of eating. They have ideas about what to do with cooking/eating equipment that can be practiced with props such as these:

- pots and pans with and without lids

- toy microwave oven

- cooking utensils, such as big spoons, pancake turner

- play dishes

- safe and sturdy eating utensils, such as thick plastic or wooden spoons, thick plastic blunt forks, knives

- tea set

- wok

- toaster

- Play foods

Toddlers use play foods to explore differences between real and play objects. Quite often they try to taste or eat the play foods, showing that they know what they represent, but not really understanding the limits of pretending to eat. Older toddlers will use the foods as toys, and usually not try to eat them.

Play foods are usually made of sturdy plastic and are somewhat realistic looking. (See photos 20D-E.) Play foods are also represented as soft stuffed toys, such as a stuffed carrot or banana. The most common play foods include:

- fruits
- vegetables
- breads, including rolls, slices, pretzels
- examples of "fast foods" such as hamburgers, french fries
- ethnic foods, such as pizza slices, refried beans, tacos, rice, noodles
- baby bottles, food containers

- Dolls

Toddlers use dolls to act out what they understand about themselves and others. The most typical play with dolls is seen as toddlers pretend to care for the dolls—they feed them, put them to bed, hug and kiss them, and take them for rides in strollers or shopping carts. However, they also throw them around, drop them, and leave them, handling them as they do all the other toys they use. All the variations in dolls listed above for infants are considered as examples for toddlers as well, and include:

- baby dolls
- dolls representing adults and older children
- wooden people figures to use with blocks
- dolls showing racial diversity (variety of skin colors, hair types, eye shapes)

- Doll furnishings

Doll furnishings are props to be used with the dolls, and include:

- Doll furniture, such as a baby doll-sized bed, table and chairs, high chair
- Push toys to carry dolls, such as a doll stroller or shopping cart
- Other furnishings to use with dolls, including equipment used by people with disabilities, such as walkers or wheelchairs
- Other doll accessories such as clothes, vehicles for them to ride in

- Soft animals: See description under infant materials

- Small play buildings with accessories

- doll houses with furniture and people
- toy buildings, such as a farm, airport, schoolhouse with furnishings and people

- Toy telephones: See description under infant materials

20D Older toddlers understand that toy potatoes are pretend foods – not real.

20E This younger child is learning the difference between real and pretend.

Accessible means that children can reach and use materials by themselves. This term is defined in the "Explanation of Terms Used Throughout the Scale" on page 7 of the ITERS-R.

Observers should be sure to find out whether toys stored on open shelves are actually ***accessible*** to the children. It is usually apparent whether children are allowed or encouraged to take toys from open shelves or other storage areas to use, or whether they are not allowed to do so. Materials are not considered accessible if children are not allowed to play in the areas where toys and materials are located. For example, children who are kept in cribs, high chairs, swings, or in group gatherings are unlikely to have access to materials. In addition, when children do not seem to feel free, or are not able, to take out and use toys the observer must find out how and when materials are used by these children, and whether there are rules about special times when children are allowed to access materials. For example, toddlers may use some toys in one area of the room, but stay away from others that are also stored within their reach in other areas. The observer must determine how and when materials in those other areas are accessible, preferably by observing but also through questions asked of staff during the staff interview.

Dramatic play materials can be considered ***accessible*** *only* if it is *observed* that children can freely access and use the materials. In order to make materials accessible to *non-mobile* infants, staff must bring materials to the children or move the children to provide easy access to the materials. For example, a teacher places a non-mobile infant on a blanket located on the floor, brings over several soft dolls that the child can grasp and use if he wants.

To score Indicator 1.1 "No," children should have access to some dramatic play materials for some time during each day. It must be obvious that dramatic play materials are placed within reach of non-mobile children, if present. Materials must be accessible on a daily basis to score 1.1 "No."

Score 1.1 "Yes" if no materials for dramatic play, such as those described above, are accessible to all children, daily.

3.1   ***Accessible*** is defined in Indicator 1.1. ***Materials*** is defined in the "General Information" section for this item, and in Indicator 1.1.

Since the word ***materials*** is plural, ***some*** requires more than one accessible material. However, ***dolls*** and ***soft animals*** are required (see Indicator 1.1 for explanation of these toys). Since both dolls and soft animals are plural, it means two or more of each. (See photos 20.3.1a-b.) Therefore, at a minimum two dolls and two soft animals would be required to give credit for ***some***. Other dramatic play materials may also be included, but are not required to give credit.

Age-appropriate means that the materials are safe and interest children, matching their ages and abilities. For exam-

20.3.1a This child has access to one doll and one soft animal. An observer would need to determine whether additional toys are accessible for dramatic play.

20.3.1b Only if dolls and soft animals were among the props for dramatic play could credit be given for "some" materials accessible.

ple, soft dolls that babies can grasp, mouth, and squeeze are age-appropriate for young infants, instead of large baby dolls or the small plastic toy people used by older toddlers. Stuffed animals and dolls that have detachable pieces or removable parts pose choking hazards for infants and toddlers who explore objects by pulling and mouthing, and thus they are not considered appropriate for this age group. If there are problems with the safety of the materials, consider this also in Item 11, Safety practices, on page 26 of the ITERS-R.

To give credit for Indicator 3.1 (score "Yes"), some dramatic play materials, as defined above, that are safe and interesting to the children must be observed to be accessible at some point during an observation of three hours.

3.2 To give credit for this indicator (score "Yes") *some* materials credited in 3.1 must be *accessible* (see Indicator 1.1) for *much of the day*. In addition, this indicator applies to indicators at higher levels of quality, especially Indicator 5.1. In other words, the indicator applies to any materials that are credited as being accessible for this item.

The term *much of the day* is defined on page 7 of the ITERS-R, in the "Explanation of Terms Used Throughout the Scale." This time requirement includes all times when children are awake and able to play. It does not include times when children are involved in routine care activities, such as sleeping, eating, and diapering. The amount of time children actually can use materials will vary with the ages of children, with younger infants using more time for sleeping, eating, and diapering than for playing. When the children are not involved in routines, however, they should have access to the dramatic play materials.

The dramatic play materials can be accessible indoors and/or outdoors to count towards being *accessible much of the day*. Therefore, if children are outside for large portions of the day, without access to some dramatic play materials, credit cannot be given.

To give credit, it is not necessary that each child be observed using the dramatic play materials, but there should not be any restraints that prevent them from touching and using the materials. It is required that children have a reasonable chance to use the materials throughout the day at some time if they wish, including non-mobile children.

5.1 *Dramatic play materials* is defined in the "General Information" section for this item, and in Indicator 1.1. *Age-appropriate* is defined in Indicator 3.1. Accessible is defined in Indicator 1.1. The term *daily* means "daily for much of the day," as explained in Indicator 3.2.

The term many is defined on page 7 of the ITERS-R, in the "Explanation of Terms Used Throughout the Scale." Since this definition requires that there be enough materials so "children should have access without long periods of waiting or undue competition," the number of materials required will depend on the number of children in the classroom being observed.

The minimum requirement for many is provided in the "Notes for Clarification" for this indicator on page 36 of the ITERS-R. The quantities required in the Note are based on groups of no more than 8 infants and no more than 12 toddlers. If more children are enrolled, then more materials are required. For toddlers who enjoy doing the same things as their playmates, there should be enough materials so that children can use the same materials at the same time, without undue competition.

20.5.1a Many dramatic play materials are provided for toddlers in this housekeeping area, including dolls, doll furnishings, child-sized house furniture, cooking equipment, pots, pans, dishes and toy telephones.

20.5.1b Hats are included among the many pretend play materials in this classroom.

The materials should be plentiful enough to encourage meaningful play. (See photos 20.5.1a-c.)

Since **varied** materials means that they stimulate different skills, and have different characteristics, duplicates of the same toy do not count towards meeting the requirement of "varied," although they do count towards "many." To evaluate whether dramatic play materials are varied, note whether the materials provide choices for how children can use materials, and different possibilities for what they can pretend.

For infants, the requirements listed in the "Notes for Clarification" specify that three to five examples of the listed materials be accessible to give credit for Indicator 5.1. This is interpreted as three to five of *each* example, although there may be more of one example and fewer of another, as long as all examples are represented and the total number of toys required is accessible. The examples include dolls, soft animals, pots and pans, and toy telephones. To determine if the requirement for **many and varied** is met, the observer may want to keep a chart such as that shown below.

20.5.1c Simple dress-up clothes allow toddlers to extend their pretend play.

Chart for dramatic play materials for Infants

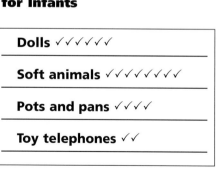

Dolls ✓✓✓✓✓✓
Soft animals ✓✓✓✓✓✓✓✓
Pots and pans ✓✓✓✓
Toy telephones ✓✓

In this sample chart, the requirements for **many and varied** are met and this indicator would be scored "Yes." This is true even though there are only two toy telephones accessible, because this shortfall is made up for by the presence of more than the required numbers of dolls and soft animals.

For toddlers, ***many and varied*** requires, at a minimum, two or more of each of the nine examples listed in the "Note for Clarification." As the note states, there can be fewer of one type of toy and more of another, as long as most types are represented. For "most types" to be represented, no more than two types of materials can be missing, and there must be more examples in the other types to make up for the missing types. In larger groups, as explained above, more materials than the minimum are required. To determine whether two or more items representing each example of toy are accessible, the observer should make a chart (like the one below) listing all of the examples and the items accessible for each.

Chart of Accessible Dramatic Play Materials for Toddlers

Dress-up clothes	Fireman hats (2) Boots (1 pair) Straw hats (2) Police officer uniform
Child-sized house furniture	Table (1) Chairs (3) Sink and stove combination (1)
Cooking/eating equipment	Pots (6) Pans (3) Wok (1)
Play foods	Fruits, vegetables, etc. (10) Cereal boxes (3) Oatmeal boxes (2)
Dolls	Baby dolls (5) People figures used with interlocking blocks (4)
Doll furnishings	Blankets (3) Doll bed (1) Stroller (1)
Soft animals	Small soft animals in cozy area (6) Stuffed dog (1)
Small play buildings with accessories	
Toy telephones	Toy cell phones (2)

In this case, credit would be given for "many and varied," even though not all examples of toys are represented. As state in the "Notes for Clarification," the ITERS-R requires examples of "most" materials. The lack of any small play buildings with accessories is made up for by having more toys than required in all other examples, and far more than the total number required, representing different play possibilities.

5.2   ***Props*** is defined in the "General Information" section for this item. Because infants and toddlers primarily act out roles and actions that they have experienced directly, it is important to encourage their dramatic play with props that represent what they are likely to know about. (See photos 20.5.2a-b, next page.) Examples of such familiar props are provided in the indicator.

The observer should consider the relevance of the props for the children. Certainly, props should represent familiar objects that children are likely to have experienced

20.5.2a Young children can act out the everyday routines they experience.

20.5.2b This boy can imitate kitchen chores he has witnessed repeatedly.

at home or in the community. Objects that represent less common, out-dated practices, such as a toy washboard for doing laundry rather than a toy washing machine, would probably not fulfill this requirement for most children, but might still be appropriate for some groups. Children in a very hot climate might not know what a toy snowman represents, having never seen snow or snowmen. Generally, fantasy materials, such as toys representing cartoon characters or costumes of superheroes, do not usually fulfill the requirement of this indicator.

To give credit, not all props have to meet the requirement of the indicator. However, the vast majority of materials should represent what children experience in their everyday life.

5.3 Children tend to play with materials longer when the environment and materials are organized. Because mobile infants and toddlers may carry objects around with them and scatter them throughout the room, organization also helps with clean up. *Organized by type* means, first, that the dramatic play materials are, for the most part, stored together in one area. Second, within the general category of dramatic play materials, the different subcategories or examples of materials (dolls,

20.5.3a The dress-up clothes and toys on this shelf are not organized, making it difficult for children to find the things they want to play with. An observer would need to see if materials were organized after play.

20.5.3b Most of the dramatic play materials are stored together in the housekeeping area and organized by type – plastic food, utensils, pots and pans are stored in separate containers on open shelves.

cooking/eating, dress-ups, foods, etc.) are stored together so that children know where to find what they need for pretending, and the materials can easily be put away without all being thrown into a confusing jumble. (See photos 20.5.3a-b.) Of course, when infants and toddlers have access to the materials, the materials will not remain organized by type for long. To give credit for this indicator, there should be evidence during the observation that staff reorganize the materials by type at clean-up times that occur throughout the day. For young children, each time the accessible toys are put back in an organized fashion, they seem new and exciting.

The organization does not have to be perfect to give credit. Some dramatic play materials may not be stored with the others, such as soft toy animal toys kept in a cozy area or book area, or people figures stored with the blocks. There can be a little mixing of materials, such as play foods stored with pots and pans, but for the most part, they should be organized in a way that makes sense. It should be obvious where to find things, because the materials and where they are stored should naturally go together (e.g., all dolls stored in the doll bed, toy foods in the refrigerator, pots/pans and dishes under the sink or stove). Give credit if the materials are obviously organized by type and are returned to their places periodically throughout the day.

5.4   This indicator is scored "NA" if no *toddlers* are enrolled in the group. For the definition of infants/toddlers, see page 7 of the ITERS-R, "Explanation of Terms Used Throughout the Scale." If an older child with a disability is enrolled, and all the other children are infants, the appropriateness of this indicator will depend on the child's abilities, not necessarily on the child's age. For this indicator, *play furniture* refers to any accessible furniture that is used in children's dramatic play.

Child-sized means that the furniture is appropriate for the height and size of toddlers. If a table and chairs are included as pretend play furnishings, children should be able to sit back in the chairs with their feet touching the floor and arms resting comfortably on the table. If children use a kitchen unit, they should be able to easily reach the unit and to manage play independently. Child-sized furniture used for toddlers may be smaller than furniture normally used by preschoolers. Observe children while they are playing with dramatic play furniture and materials to determine whether the children can play easily, reaching objects stored in furniture, and using the furniture as it was meant to be used. (See photo 20.5.4.)

Examples of such furniture are provided in the indicator, but also might include:

- tables and chairs
- kitchen unit with a stove and sink
- pretend play refrigerator
- pretend workbench
- vanity with mirror
- furniture for storing and organizing dress-ups
- outdoor playhouse with furniture

20.5.4   This child-sized kitchen unit with a stove, sink and refrigerator is the right height so that toddlers can easily act out what they see adults doing at home.

20 Dramatic play

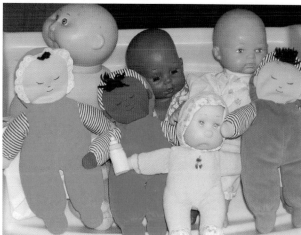

20.7.1a Dolls with different skin tones are accessible to children, and teach that diversity is an acceptable characteristic in people.

20.7.1b Diversity of abilities is shown in toy adaptive equipment for use with dolls.

7.1 **_Diversity_** in this indicator refers to the differences in people with regard to race, culture, ability, age, or gender. **_Props provided to represent diversity_** requires that materials associated with various groups are provided for children to use in their dramatic play. Props that represent the children in the group and their families should be included, but in addition, props associated with other groups must be included as well. Examples of such materials are provided in the indicator, but other examples might include:

- Dolls representing different age, gender, or ability, as well as race or culture (See photos 20.7.1a-c.)
- Dress-up clothing characteristic of different cultures, for men and women
- Play cooking and eating utensils from different cultures
- Play food characteristic of different cultures
- Toy tools representing work typically associated with men and women

20.7.1c In this classroom, diversity is represented in the different play foods children can use.

All props must be associated with a _positive image_ of the group represented. If any prop represents a group in a negative way, score Indicator 7.1 "No."

To score Indicator 7.1 "Yes," there must be dolls representing at least three races accessible and at least two other examples observed of materials showing diversity.

7.2 This indicator is scored "NA" if no **_toddlers_** are enrolled in the group. For the definition of infants/toddlers, see page 7 of the ITERS-R, "Explanation of Terms Used Throughout the Scale."

Active dramatic play can take place only when there is enough room for children to freely move about—walking, running, and moving in ways that are not tightly controlled due to lack of space, crowded conditions, or the need to be quiet.

Therefore, this indicator requires that a large area be provided for such play, either outdoors or in a large, uncrowded indoor space outside the classroom, where children can be noisy and move freely, such as a multi-purpose or gross motor room.

Within this space, accessible dramatic play props are required that must be complete enough to permit *meaningful pretend play, as defined in the "General Information" section for this item.* For example, just having a large empty playhouse outdoors would not be sufficient unless the house has furniture and other pretend play materials that allow the children to carry out more complex dramatic play. (See photo 20.7.2.)

Examples of props for more active dramatic play outdoors (or in a large, uncrowded space indoors) include:

- Large toy trucks with toy people or objects to transport
- Playhouses with furniture, dolls, or other props
- Riding toys that look like cars, with dolls to carry or a gas station or gas pump
- Toy strollers or shopping carts with dolls or stuffed animals to transport
- Water basins with baby dolls to bathe

Score "Yes" if examples of such dramatic play materials are observed to be accessible for outdoor play or for play in a large indoor space, outside the classroom.

If the weather does not permit children to use the outdoor space, be sure to visit the space to see what is accessible to the children. If it is impossible to tell what children have access to outdoors, ask staff about materials used. Such materials must be used daily, or almost daily, to give credit.

7.3   Although older toddlers and twos are able to carry out dramatic play competently on their own, their play can be extended and enriched by the input of an adult who facilitates play and adds resources. Infants and toddlers benefit from the involvement of adults in dramatic play because the adult often may provide a model to imitate in the pretending process, may join in as a more competent social player, and may entice a child to continue playing instead of wandering aimlessly. Staff also can guide children's social behavior with one another as they pretend with them, helping with disagreements about who is playing with what toy. Staff can extend children's language while participating in play, helping children learn words for objects and actions. For example, by pretending to talk on the phone with a baby, the teacher encourages the child to use language to communicate, provides a model for pretending, and if sharing issues come up, avoids serious disagreements by providing another toy telephone.

This indicator requires that staff be involved in pretending with children, facilitating dramatic play, adding language and extending children's ideas. (See photos 20.7.3a-b.) It does not mean that staff

20.7.2   Dramatic play props can be provided for outdoor play. Play houses must include materials, such as pots, pans, plastic foods or furniture so that children can have meaningful pretend play experiences.

20.7.3a

20.7.3b

20.7.3a-b Staff join children in dramatic play, adding language and extending children's ideas.

merely give children directions or commands, or set up materials and activities. To give credit, this indicator must be observed at least once during the observation.

Examples of staff pretending with children are included in the indicator. Other examples might include:

- Pretending to feed a doll
- Making animal sounds when playing with soft toy animals with a child
- Asking the toddler where he is going, if he's taking a doll for a ride in a stroller or shopping cart
- Pretending to eat and enjoy the foods children have pretended to cook
- Making doll crying sounds, and suggesting that the baby's diaper needs changing

21 Sand and water play

General information about this item

Sand and water are sensory materials that people of all ages can enjoy. By the time toddlers encounter water as a play material in a group setting, they have already had many experiences at home during their baths and when they have had their hands washed. Even if sand has not been as readily available a play material to them as water, most children take to it immediately. Because of the many health and safety concerns associated with using water and sand with infants and young toddlers, this item is not required for children under 18 months of age. If all children in the group are 18 months or younger, score this item "NA." If an older child with a disability is enrolled, and all the other children are under 18 months, the appropriateness of this indicator will depend on the child's abilities, not necessarily on the child's age. If sand or water is used for children under 18 months of age, this item should still be scored "NA," and any concerns regarding health, safety and supervision should be addressed in Item 10, Health practices, Item 11, Safety Practices, and Item 25, Supervision of play and learning. (See photo 21A.)

Sand and water play offer older toddlers opportunities to use their senses to discover the natural world. Because toddlers are constantly taking in information through their senses and trying to understand how the world works, sensory experiences with sand and water play an important role in their cognitive development. Water play gives children an opportunity to experiment, learning that water is a liquid which flows between their fingers and hands, and can be poured and splashed. Toddlers discover that sand is a solid that can be raked and shoveled but that it shares many characteristics with water. Playing with sand or water is also stress-reducing and relaxing for many children. (See photos 21B-C.)

There are other developmental benefits from sand and water play. By digging in sand and pouring water, children develop their eye-hand coordination and exercise small muscles. They also learn self-restraint and not to eat the sand and drink the water. Materials such as cups, buckets, and shovels enhance children's experiences with sand and water play. The various kinds and amount of materials required in this item increase with the levels of quality.

Because there are many health and safety concerns with sand and water play, close supervision is required for this item. Additional health and safety issues are also addressed in other items. (See

21A Sand and water play are not required for children under 18 months of age. However, if these activities are used with these younger children, issues related to health and safety should be addressed in Items 10, Health practices, 11, Safety practices and 25, Supervision of play and learning.

21B Sand and water play provide learning while being stress-reducing activities.

21 Sand and water play

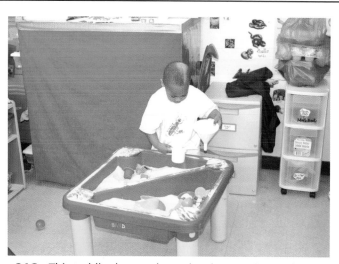

21C This toddler learns about the characteristics of sand while becoming acquainted with concepts of measurement.

21D Children in this program enjoy the sensory experiences of sand play provided in the outdoor play area. However, when outdoor sand is left uncovered there may be health issues, such as animal contamination, which are addressed in Item 10, Health practices.

photo 21D.) For example, washing children's hands before and after play at a shared water-play table is handled in Item 10, Health practices. Whether staff clean and disinfect the water containers and toys is addressed in Item 10, Health practices. Issues related to supervision and safety during water and sand play are addressed in this Sand and water play item, but some may also apply to Items 11, Safety practices and 25, Supervision of play and learning. Health and safety concerns are included in several items in the ITERS-R because children in that this age group are most vulnerable to germs and illnesses because they still have weak immune systems and have not yet developed the ability or knowledge to protect themselves.

A closer look at each indicator

1.1 *Available* means that staff have the equipment and materials needed for children to be able to play in sand or water. *Available* differs from the term accessible, because it does not require that children can reach and use the materials. In order to be available, the provisions for sand and water play, whether a small individual plastic container, a larger commercially made water table, or a sand box, must be located somewhere either in the building or outdoors near the building. The provisions/materials must be stored somewhere in the center so that they can be easily made accessible for use by the children. *Not available* means that there are no provisions in the center that are meant to be used for sand or water play by the toddlers. If sand play is available, observe whether there is enough sand or other similar material to dig, scoop, pour, fill containers, and experiment. This indicator does not require accessories, but it does require some type of container to use with either sand or a sand substitute or water, which is stored indoors or outdoors.

Consider as sand substitutes only appropriate materials such as those listed in the "Notes for Clarification" on page 37 of the ITERS-R. Others might include rice or birdseed. The "Notes for Clarification" also list materials that are unsafe and therefore not considered appropriate substitutes for sand. (See photos 21.1.1a-b.) Other inappropriate substitutes include finely milled sawdust, and baby powder which can be breathed in. Beans and styrofoam packing materials are also not con-

21.1.1a Dried beans are not an appropriate substitute for sand because of health and safety issues. A toddler may put beans in the nose or ear, where they can easily get stuck. Some uncooked, dried beans are toxic when eaten and present a choking hazard as well.

21.1.1b Staff should carefully consider what things to use as sand substitutes. For example, rice is safe and can be easily poured but using rice represents a waste of valuable food. The small sea shells may pose a choking hazard for young children.

sidered sand substitutes because these are considered hazardous for toddlers who may swallow them or stuff them up their noses and into their ears. There must be a sufficient quantity of safe sand-like material that children can dig, scoop, pour, fill, and empty containers. A sufficient quantity of water to permit similar play is required. Playing at the sink when washing hands or digging in dirt with a stick on the playground are not considered sand and water play activities, even if children are observed doing such activities.

Often, materials are observed in sand/water tables that *cannot* be used for digging, measuring, *or* pouring, such as shredded packing materials, natural objects (e.g., pine cones, acorns, leaves for children to examine), or gelatinous sensory materials (e.g., goop, jello). Such materials cannot be counted as sand/water substitutes.

There are various options for containers to hold sand and water. Examples include:

For sand play

- Outdoor sand boxes filled with sand
- Outdoor sand pits
- Various types and sizes of commercially-made sand tables, for indoor or outdoor use
- Dishpans with sand or sand substitutes
- Pails and buckets

For water play

- Hoses and sprinklers
- Dishpans for holding water
- Large outdoor water troughs
- Plastic bins used for water
- Buckets large enough to contain a sufficient amount of water
- Sinks (including trough sinks) used specifically for water play
- Specially designed water-play equipment

21 Sand and water play

If sand or water play is not observed, then ask the question provided on page 37 of the ITERS-R to determine if and when sand or water play is available for the children.

Score this item "Yes" if there are no provisions available for sand or water play. If there is least one provision available for children to have experiences with sand or water, even if it is made accessible to children only infrequently, for example monthly, then score this item "No."

"NA permitted" is a scoring option for the item but not for the indicator. "NA permitted" is printed in the scale under Indicator 1.1 but does not apply to this indicator if there are any children 18 months or older enrolled in the classroom being observed.

3.1   *Some* means that staff make accessible the equipment and material needed for children to be able to play with sand (or a sand substitute) or water, in a meaningful way.

Provided means that staff make the sand or water accessible to the children, so they can reach and use the provisions. The sand or water play can be provided either outdoors or indoors. If the material is located outdoors, then children should be able to freely access and use it when outdoors. If the water, sand, or sand substitute is stored in a closed space, it can be considered to be *provided* only if the staff bring the material out at some time for children to freely access and use. If weather does not permit use of either sand or water outdoors, then either sand or water must be provided indoors at least once every two weeks.

The sand or water play must be *provided at least once every 2 weeks*. Both sand and water are not required. If only one of these materials is provided, credit can be given. However, there must be a sufficient quantity of the material so that children can pour, fill, and empty containers.

3.2   Staff should closely supervise both sand and water play because of the potential dangers. *Close supervision* means that staff are in close proximity to children participating in the activity – they can see, hear, and easily reach children at all times while they play. (See photo 21.3.2a.) Water, even if it is only a few inches

21.3.2a   During water play staff should always be within easy reach of toddlers and adequately supervise to make sure children do not drink or fall into the water.

21.3.2b   In this situation staff do not closely supervise children to prevent them from eating the sand. This problem most frequently occurs on playgrounds where large areas are covered with sand.

deep, poses a safety threat to children, who can drown in less than an inch of water. Staff must also ensure that children do not drink water from the water table or eat the sand. (See photo 21.3.2b.) Staff should prevent or promptly stop children from throwing sand. Because indoor sand or water play can be messy, staff should make sure that spilled sand or water is cleaned up immediately to prevent slips or falls.

Observe staff and children during sand and water play to score this indicator. If there are any instances of children drinking water, eating sand, or throwing sand or water, or children falling on slippery floors, then score this item "No." As the "Notes for Clarification" on page 37 of the ITERS-R state, when sand or water play is not observed, then base your score on supervision provided during other activities and information gathered during the teacher interview.

3.3 ***Some toys*** means that there are at least two toys for children to use with the sand or water. (See photos 21.3.3a-b.) ***Toys to use for sand and water play*** include those that children can use to dig, scoop, fill, pour, and experiment with the material, as well as toys that extend sand/water play into the area of dramatic play, such as pots and pans or water to bathe baby dolls.

Examples of sand toys are included in the Notes for Clarification. Others include:

- measuring cups and other unbreakable containers
- funnels
- plastic tubes
- molds
- scoops
- pails, and shovels, rakes, sifters, sand or water-wheels, pipes, and toys that make patterns in sand, such as wide-toothed combs

Many of the sand toys listed above can also be used for water play, as well as:

- sponges
- things that sink or float
- turkey basters
- unbreakable spray bottles
- dramatic play toys, such as animals, sea creatures, dolls, and boats

Additional dramatic play toys that might be used with either sand or water include:

- animals
- dinosaurs
- small toy people
- large trucks and diggers
- unbreakable cooking props, such as pots, pans, pitchers, dishes, bowls, cups, and spoons

21.3.3a Children have access to three scoops and one bucket, meeting the requirements for Indicator 3.2.

21.3.3b Even though there are provisions (containers and water) for water play, there are no toys, causing Indicator 3.3 to be scored "No."

21 Sand and water play

21.5.2a In addition to cups used for pouring experiences, children are given sponges and brushes to use for bathing the small people toys. This variety in toys provides children with different experiences while using water.

21.5.2b The requirements of 5.2 are met because many different types of toys are provided for use during water play.

These toys must be accessible for children to use freely during the time that sand or water play is provided. If sand or water play is observed but children do not have access to at least two toys, then do not give credit, even if there are many toys available but not accessible (e.g., in a tightly closed container).

5.1 This indicator requires that children be given opportunities for **sand or water play** at **least once a week**. Provisions for sand or water play should be within children's reach and they should be given an opportunity to play freely. Both materials are not required; only one, either sand or water, is required. Either sand or water play can occur indoors or outdoors.

A combination of sand and water play meets the requirements for this indicator. For example, water play is made available one week and sand play is provided the next. As long as children have these experiences at least once a week, then credit for this indicator can be given (score "Yes").

5.2 The intent of the requirement for **variety** is that children have many different opportunities to experiment, explore, and learn while using sand and water. For **variety** consider the differences among the toys that children can use in sand or water play. Variety may be represented in the characteristics of the toys, such as, size, transparency, shape, color, or level of challenge. All these characteristics should be considered in determining whether variety is present, but differences in the function of the toys is the most important characteristic. (See photos 21.5.2a-b.)

The number of toys accessible for play is also considered when determining **variety**. For example, when fewer children use the toys at one time, fewer toys are required for **variety**, as long as the toys can be used for different purposes. When more children are present, more toys of different types are needed.

If there are duplicates of one toy (e.g. many shovels) but no other toys to use, then the requirement for **variety** is not met, because the children's experiences have been limited to the type of play that the one toy provides. For example, variety is not present when only buckets and shovels are available in the sand box or only cups in a water table.

If both sand and water are accessible, **variety** in toys must be provided for each, but many of the same toys can be used for both sand and water play. If provisions for sand and water are present both indoors and outdoors, a ***variety*** of toys is required in both locations.

The ***variety*** in toys does not have to be provided all at one time. If many different examples of one type of toy are used at a time, then variety can be provided through regular rotation of toys. For example, at the water table different types of measuring toys (e.g., pails and shovels, scoops, cups and spoons of different sizes) can be used on one occasion, and at another time the water table can be turned into an ocean with a variety of toy fish and boats in blue water. If the teacher reports that toys are rotated, then ask to see the toys. Find out how they are used and how often they are changed. If toys are actually rotated very infrequently, credit should not be given.

Score this indicator "Yes" if children have access to a variety of toys during sand or water play.

5.3   ***Activities set up to facilitate play*** means that the staff have provided the space, time and materials for children to benefit from the experiences of sand and water play. (See photo 21.5.3a.) Staff can select and set up equipment and materials that are easy for children to use and supervise closely, for example:

21.5.3a Staff provide this sturdy table and enough sand and toys so that children can have meaningful experiences. Staff also limit the number of children who can play at the sand table at the same time so that this area does not become too crowded or competitive.

- Using sturdy tables or tubs that prevent spills or tipping over.
- Limiting the number of children so that play is not crowded or competitive.
- Providing multiple smaller dishpans so children can freely explore without being interrupted. (See photo 21.5.3b.)
- Providing enough sand or water so children have meaningful experiences with pouring, digging, and filling.
- Making the equipment accessible to children who cannot reach, such as by using a lower sand or water table, providing equipment to child with physical disability.
- Choosing a space indoors where clean-up of spills is easy
- Setting up sand/water play out of traffic pathways
- Having a broom and dustpan or towels for clean-up ready
- Limiting the number of toys in the sand/water container to allow free use of sand or water
- Ensuring that there are duplicates of the most popular toys
- Ensuring that the area used for sand and water play allows room for props or toys, perhaps on another table nearby.
- Introducing new or different types of toys so children remain interested.

21.5.3b Staff set up water play so children have individual dishpans where they can explore without interruptions.

7.1   ***Provided daily*** means that children have some opportunity to participate in either sand or water play every day. There is no time requirement for accessibility, except that either sand *or* water play be provided daily for all children and the time allowed must be satisfying for the children. A combination of sand and water play meets requirements for this indicator. For example, if sand play is provided for children on Monday, Tuesday, and Wednesday and water play is provided on Thursday and Friday, then give credit for this indicator. In this situation, between

21 Sand and water play

the two, sand or water play experiences are provided daily. Sand or water play must occur every day, with only very few lapses (such as a special activity or a field trip that prevents the access). If sand/water play usually occurs outdoors, then it must be provided indoors during days when weather does not permit outdoor play.

7.2 ***Different activities*** with sand or water are required to give children broader experiences from which to learn and develop skills. To give credit, staff must provide a variety of materials and toys to change what the children can do with sand or water. Providing the same toys to use with sand and water every day does not meet this requirement, even if there is variety in the toys provided. The activities must give children many different experiences. This indicator requires different activities with either sand or water, and not for both. (See photos 21.7.2a-c.) However, if both sand and water are used with the children then different activities should be provided for each. Examples of different activities include:

21.7.2a   Snow in the water table.

Water

- Bubbles added
- Color added
- Wooden or plastic boats used
- Sink-and-float experiment done with water play
- Sponges and non-porous objects added at the same time to compare
- Shells or toy sea creatures added
- Small plastic water droppers and large basters used
- Water table used to wash baby dolls or doll clothes
- Sprinkler used on hot day
- Plastic pipes used to route water

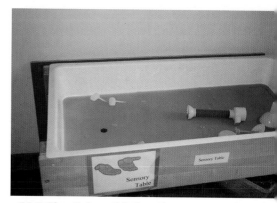

21.7.2b   Color added to the water.

Sand

- Wet sand used instead of dry sand, with toys that can be used to mold sand
- Cars and trucks added
- Small people added
- Substitute sand material used, such as bird seed that can be fed to the birds later
- Tools to make various designs in sand provided
- Small toy animals used

21.7.2c   Washing dishclothes and wringing the water out.

21.7.2a-c   Different activities provide a broader range of learning.

Note that giving credit for different activities does not ever require the use of foods as substitutes for sand or water or the use of any materials that would pose a safety threat to the children.

Score this indicator "Yes" if different activities are used with sand or water at least once a week. Ask the staff the questions provided for this indicator in the ITERS-R and score using the information given.

22 Nature/science

General information about this item

Young children are interested in everything they see around them, including natural occurrences and living things. Maybe this is because the natural world is still so new to them, full of surprises and details that adults often take for granted. For example, watching the fish in a fish tank swimming around can keep a toddler amused for a relatively long time, while most adults would be less fascinated. In this item, opportunities both indoors and outdoors with nature are required.

Opportunities for children to interact with nature begin by simply taking children outside. Being outside allows children to come into contact with natural things such as wind, trees, and grass. A young toddler will suddenly become fascinated with crawling in the grass when he discovers that it feels and smells different from what he has experienced indoors. (See photos 22A-B.) However, opportunities for children to experience nature can also occur indoors by adding living plants, animals and other natural objects, like leaves or pine cones. In addition to direct contact with nature both indoors and outdoors, this item also requires books, pictures and toys that realistically represent nature.

Since infants and toddlers use all of their senses to experience their surroundings, it is appropriate to include many hands-on experiences for learning about nature and science. This includes giving children opportunities to touch plants, smell flowers, or listen to the wind. For example, on a rainy day, staff urge toddlers to look outside the window and watch the rain make puddles instead of introducing rain by using a weather chart. It would be inappropriate to expect toddlers to learn about natural events and processes by using an academic approach with flash cards or other rote learning materials.

22 A　　　　　　　　　　　　　　　　**22 B**

22 A-B　Taking infants and toddlers where they can touch grass or other plants provides them with basic experiences with nature.

Staff input is also important in this item. Staff can expand children's experiences with nature by adding language to describe natural objects and processes. For example, when a child watches the class pet, the staff member may say, "It's a hamster. See his eyes, mouth and ears." When the baby notices a picture of a cat in a book, the staff member may say, "Meow, meow. That's a kitty like the one you have at home. Does your kitty say meow?" Since children learn by watching adults, it is important that the staff member serve as role models in the way they interact with nature. Staff should show curiosity about a bug that a toddler has discovered on the playground instead of modeling fear or dislike. Staff input and modeling help to expand on what the child is sensing.

A closer look at each indicator

1.1   *No pictures, books or toys* means that there are no displayed pictures, books or toys showing nature, located in the classroom. Examples of all three are not required but there must be at least one book, toy or picture for children to use. The example must *represent nature realistically,* which means that it shows what children would normally see or experience in the real world and does not represent nature in a fanciful way. For example, in many children's books, animals are portrayed with human features, smiling faces, walking on two legs, or talking. In this item, realistic drawings, photographs, or toys are required.

Pictures can consist of posters, photographs, or drawings that are displayed on the walls, backs of cabinets, on the floor, etc. To be given credit, pictures must be displayed in the classroom where children spend most of their time and not in hallways, bathrooms, gross motor rooms or other rooms where children spend a small amount of time during the day. Pictures should be placed where children can easily see them. Do not give photographs or illustrations that are found in books credit as pictures.

To give credit for **books**, they must be located in the classroom and be accessible for children to use. Books can be either commercially produced or homemade. Books must have realistic pictures or drawings or provide accurate facts about nature. Fantasy stories about animals do not meet the requirements for this indicator. (See photo 22.1.1a.) Books must be accessible to children even if this requires help from staff, for example for non-mobile children. (See photo 22.1.1b.) Do not give credit for magazines, coloring books, or ditto sheets. Books that are in poor repair (missing covers, backs, or torn pages) are not counted as books.

Toys must represent nature realistically, be safe for children to use, and be accessible to children. Example of *toys* include:

- realistic plastic or rubber zoo animals, farm animals, insects, (See photos 22.1.1c-d.)
- puzzles with realistic nature or science content, (See photos 22.1.1e-f.)
- scent boxes or "smelling" containers,
- realistic plastic vegetables and fruits, (See photo 22.1.1g.)
- an infant mat with realistic nature or science pictures displayed,
- realistic animal-shaped rattles, (See photo 22.1.1h.)
- mobile with realistic birds or butterflies that infants can play with, (See photo 22.1.1i.)
- large magnets that toddler can experiment with and safe things for magnets to attract, and (See photo 22.1.1j.)
- magnifying glasses for older toddlers (24-30 months of age) to use.

22.1.1a Both books show animals, but only the lower book represents animals realistically.

22.1.1b In this classroom, nature/science books on open shelves are accessible to children who are crawling and walking. However, to make these books accessible to non-mobile children staff take books off the shelves and bring them over for these young children to use.

22.1.1c

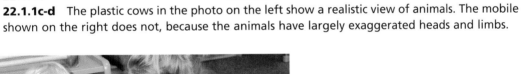

22.1.1d

22.1.1c-d The plastic cows in the photo on the left show a realistic view of animals. The mobile shown on the right does not, because the animals have largely exaggerated heads and limbs.

22.1.1e The puzzle showing a smiling dog, a purple cat, and a pink rabbit would not be considered a nature/science toy. The Mickey Mouse and smiling sun puzzles also would not.

22.1.1f These knobbed puzzles are easy to use, with some realistic and some fanciful animals.

22.1.1g Plastic vegetables and fruits are considered nature/science toys if they are portrayed realistically.

22.1.1h These rattles are not considered realistic because they do not look like real fish or insects.

22.1.1i Although this butterfly mobile is attractive to children, it is not considered a realistic nature/science toy.

22.1.1j Hands-on nature/science learning experiences include easy-to-use magnets and metal objects.

Indicator

Score this indicator "No" if at least one example of a book, picture or toy displaying a realistic view of nature is accessible to children. Score "Yes" if no example is found.

1.2 ***No opportunities for children to experience the natural world*** means that children are neither taken outdoors where they can directly access nature on their own, nor are there any experiences with living plants or animals or other natural objects indoors. Children are unable to directly access nature on their own by looking through windows that are not at eye level. Examples of indoor experiences with the natural world are included in Indicators 1.2 and 5.2 of the ITERS-R on page 38. Other examples include:

- collections of bird nests or other natural objects (e.g., seashells, pine cones),
- hatching chicken eggs,
- butterfly hatching kits,
- ant farm with ants,
- fish tank with living fish,
- terrarium with plants and animals, and
- crickets in a large container with plants.

Examples of outdoor experiences with the natural world are listed in the ITERS-R. Others might include:

- pointing out things in the sky, such as clouds, or the sun,
- noticing worms or insects,
- pointing out how the wind blows the leaves, and
- watching snow or rain fall.

Score this item "Yes" if children do not have any experiences with the natural world. These experiences can take place either indoors or outdoors. If the child's experience with the natural world takes place indoors and not outdoors, then score this item "No," since there is some opportunity to experience the natural world.

3.1 ***Some*** means at least two items from the categories of ***pictures, books or toys*** are accessible to children. (See photo 22.3.1.) Examples of pictures, books and toys are listed in the information provided for Indicator 1.1. At this level of quality at least two materials, in any combination from the three categories, which are developmentally appropriate must be accessible. These items must ***represent nature realistically*** as defined in the "General Information" section for this item.

22.3.1 At the minimal level of quality realistic pictures are displayed down low on the wall where toddlers can easily see them.

The ages and abilities of the children in the group should be considered when determining if these materials are developmentally appropriate. ***Developmentally appropriate*** means that the materials are safe, interesting and challenging for the children. What may be appropriate for a toddler may not be appropriate for an infant. For example, an older toddler may have the fine motor and cognitive skills to use magnets to pick up safe, metal pieces such as jar lids, but this may not be as appropriate for infants. Allowing a toddler to use an unsafe toy, such as a large rake to help with outdoor gardening, would be considered inappropriate. If there are problems with the safety of materials, consider this also in Item 11, Safety practices, on page 26 of the ITERS-R. In addition, any representation that is frightening or violent is not considered appropriate for infants and toddlers. This includes animals being hurt or shown hurting others and animals with mouths open baring their teeth.

Score this item "No" if only one picture, book, or toy, realistically representing nature in a non-frightening way, is accessible for children's use.

3.2 The *some pictures, books or toys* required in Indicator 3.1 must be *accessible* daily. The definition of accessible is provided in the "Explanation of Terms Used Throughout the Scale" on page 7 of the ITERS-R. The books and toys must be accessible to the children to be counted. Posters, pictures, and photos must be placed where the children can easily see them to be considered accessible.

A minimum of 1 hour daily is required in programs of 8 hours or more. Less time is required in shorter programs and calculated proportionately. For example, in a program of 4 hours per day, ½ hour would be required.

3.3 This indicator does not require that staff initiate a nature/science activity, but rather that children are allowed to experience natural objects or to interact with nature. *Some* means more than one opportunity exists daily. This opportunity can be informal and include viewing or touching grass, plants, a tree or just feeling the wind blow. Opportunities can occur either *indoors or outdoors*. (See photos 22.3.3a-e.) Examples are listed in the "Notes for Clarification" for this indicator in the ITERS-R and for Indicator 1.2 on page 38. Others might include:

- watching and listening to the rain and thunder,
- watching leaves fall,
- smelling flowers, and
- listening to the buzzing of bumble bees.

If there are no science/nature materials indoors and children do not go outside, viewing trees, grass and flowers through the window would count as having an opportunity to view the natural world, but only if these natural things are easily seen by the children. If children cannot easily see these things on their own from

22.3.3a Children enjoy seeing and feeling simple natural things, like grass, that many adults hardly notice.

22.3.3b Children in this classroom have some opportunities to experience nature by looking at and touching the trees located in the playground.

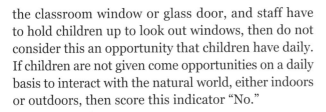

22.3.3c Inexpensive materials, like plastic soda bottles, dirt and plants are used to bring nature indoors.

22.3.3d Placing a fish tank on a low table provides children with indoor nature experiences. Children learn what fish look like, how they move, what they eat, and how to care for and respect them.

the classroom window or glass door, and staff have to hold children up to look out windows, then do not consider this an opportunity that children have daily. If children are not given come opportunities on a daily basis to interact with the natural world, either indoors or outdoors, then score this indicator "No."

5.1 An ***outdoor experience with nature*** means that children have some personal, up close opportunity with natural objects or materials while they are outdoors. The experience can vary, as long as it includes natural objects outdoors, such as trees, plants, stones, birds or insects, and these types of experiences are available to all children in the group at least two times a week. If some children go outside for nature experiences and some do not, then credit cannot be given for this indicator. For example, in a mixed-age classroom caring for both infants and toddlers, if the toddlers are

22.3.3e Credit can be given for Indicator 3.3 if children can easily view trees, grass, or flowers through the classroom windows.

taken outside everyday but the infants are never taken outside during the winter months, then the score for this indicator would be "No."

Some type of outdoor nature experience must be provided for all children on two different days each week, year round, except in very bad weather. Very bad weather is defined in Item 16, Active physical play, Indicator 3.2. There will be relatively few days in most areas when children will not be able to go outdoors at all. Even in climates with more severe weather, children should be dressed properly and taken outdoors unless there is a danger associated with outdoor exposure. The outdoor nature experience can occur anytime during the week, but do not give credit for two instances during the same day.

If the outdoor area does not contain any living plants or animals, then experiences with nature are too limited to give credit at the "good" level of quality, and this indicator should be scored "No." For example, some programs are located in a high-rise building and the space for outdoor play is located on the rooftop, con-

22.5.1 Enjoyment of flowers becomes a greater learning experience when staff add language. "You're touching the red flowers. Aren't they pretty?"

22.5.2a The aquarium in this infant class provides a daily indoor experience with plants and fish.

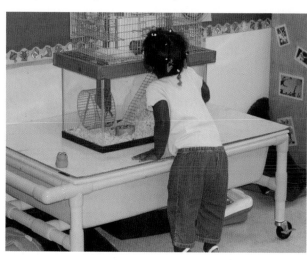

22.5.2b Having a classroom pet gives children opportunities to learn about living things.

taining a man-made concrete surface, without plants and animals. In this situation, credit cannot be given for the indicator.

The outdoor experiences with nature can be teacher- or child-initiated. Informally, children may be free to safely explore nature in the center's playground. Outdoor experiences can also include staff taking children for walks or stroller rides, where they draw attention to nature to increase children's awareness and interest. (See photo 22.5.1.)

Score "Yes" if outdoor nature experiences are provided two times each week, year round, weather permitting.

5.2 This indicator requires that either living plants or animals are located in the classroom or in an indoor area in the center that children visit on a daily basis. To give credit for this indicator, the observer must look to see that living plants or animals are in the areas used by the children. (See photos 22.5.2a-b.) They do not have to be located in the classroom normally used by the children and can be located in other areas throughout the center as long as children can experience them on a daily basis. For example, if children visit and feed the rabbit in the preschool room at least daily, then score this item "Yes." Taking children to the center's lobby to watch and help with the feeding of fish would be counted as an opportunity for children to have experiences with living animals indoors. This daily experience can be informal or teacher-initiated, but it must include some awareness on the part of the children or action by staff to draw attention to the living plants or animals. For example, the baby notices the hanging plant in the classroom and the staff member responds by brushing his hand across the leaves and talking about the plant. This indicator requires more than just having the plants or animals located indoors. Simply passing through an area with plants to arrive at the classroom would not be counted because this does not ensure that the children will notice the plants.

During the observation, the observer may not see examples of children's experiences with plants or animals. In this case, the observer should ask questions during the interview and look to see if there are plants or classroom pets located indoors in another area.

If there are living plants and animals accessible for children to view closely, but the opportunity occurs less than daily, then score this indicator "No." If there are no easily accessible living plants and animals indoors, then staff must draw attention to these things located outdoors if they are within children's view. In this situation, staff initiation is required to give credit for this indicator. This builds on the requirement at the minimal level of quality, where credit is given for having the outdoor natural world in easy view for the children through a window. However, at the "good" level of quality, some input or initiation from staff is required. To give credit, it must be clear from observation or report that such experiences occur daily.

22.5.3a Children take part in feeding the classroom pet everyday while staff point out characteristics such as the hamster's sleeping and eating habits.

5.3 ***Everyday events*** include the recurring routine and play activities that children regularly experience. For example, weather conditions and weather changes are everyday events. Also included are the seasons with their natural processes, such as new growth, blooming flowers, producing seeds, and dying back. If the program has a pet, cleaning its cage, feeding it, and watching its sleep-wake cycles would be everyday events.

Staff may point out or draw attention to these types of natural occurrences with children throughout the day, during routines and play activities, both indoors and outdoors. For example, the staff member takes an infant outside and says, "You're blinking because the sun is so bright today." When the toddler touches the sliding board, the staff member says, "The sun is shining on the slide. It's warm."

22.5.3b When helping children learn about the weather, staff use actual occurrences like pointing out the rain, instead of using flash cards or weather charts.

The baby turns its head when it hears the bird chirping and the staff member says, "See over there, it's a bird singing." Staff take advantage of occurrences such as these to help children to notice natural events, and learn a little about what they are, how and when they happen, and, to a small extent, why. The staff member may have brief, informal conversations with one child or several children.

Taking advantage of everyday events to help children learn about nature/science does not have to be planned. It can occur spontaneously if staff have a general awareness of helping children learn more about nature or natural events everyday. For example, when children notice an anthill in the play yard, staff can take advantage of this and talk to children about the ants and their habitat. Staff can point out the size and shape of the ants and talk about their similarities to other living things. Discussions can be formal or informal, teacher-directed or child-initiated, as long as they allow the child to learn about the many wonders of nature/science that are part of their everyday world. (See photos 22.5.3a-b.)

22.7.1a   **22.7.1b**
22.7.1a-b   After a snowfall, staff take children outside to talk about the snow and recent weather changes.

Examples of using everyday events as a basis for learning about nature/science are listed in the indicator in the ITERS-R. Other examples might include:

- talking about the color and shape of leaves during different seasons,
- describing the movement of objects while pulling or pushing,
- pointing out how children resemble their parents,
- pointing out clouds in the sky, and
- watching and talking about what happens as the bunny eats grass.

In order to give credit for this indicator, at least one instance must be observed.

7.1   Because young children learn by watching adults, staff serve as role models and send messages about how they value and feel about nature. Children imitate what they see adults doing, so it is important that staff show interest in nature. ***Interest in nature*** means that staff notice nature and show curiosity and appreciation. (See photos 22.7.1a-d.) For example, on a snowy day the staff member encourages children to look out the window and notice the snow. Later, she takes the toddlers outside and then brings in some snow so that children can watch it melt in the warm room. ***Respect for nature*** means that staff do not harm or destroy natural objects. For example, when children notice a spider in the classroom the teacher shows interest and talks about its features and characteristics as she carefully places it outdoors instead of killing it. Pets are carefully cared for and cages are clean. Respect for nature is also evidenced by staff caring for the earth, for example by not wasting water, by recycling materials, or by not littering. If enough information is

22.7.1c Some snow is brought indoors so that children can learn more about the coldness of snow and how it melts.

22.7.1d Making a paper cut-out snowman cannot substitute for a meaningful opportunity to learn about snow.

not available from the observation to score this indicator, ask the staff how they see the role they play in helping children enjoy and appreciate nature and science.

7.2   ***Well-organized*** means that the nature/science materials are grouped by type so that the children and staff know where to find them. Children and staff must be able to use the materials easily, and toddlers should be able to get these materials with little or no help from the staff. Materials must be organized so that staff can quickly make them accessible to non-mobile infants.

This does not mean that all nature/science materials must be placed together in one area. For example, nature/science puzzles can be accessible in one area of the room, and books on nature and science can be in the book area with other books.

Well-organized also means that the pieces for each game or activity and all parts of a set of toys should be stored together so they can be used as intended. For example, science puzzles should have all the pieces, the scent cans containing spices or other objects for the children to smell should be tightly closed and fresh enough to emit different scents. Perfection is not expected, but for the most part the nature/science games and materials should be organized.

In good repair means that books are not torn or missing pages or covers, puzzles pieces are complete, the water filter for the aquarium is working and the tank is clean, stuffed animals are clean and not torn. Almost all materials, books, etc., are expected to be in good repair, with only one or two minor exceptions. For example, if a piece of one puzzle has fallen underneath a shelf and cannot be found, then score this indicator "Yes." However, if an observer sees several puzzles with missing pieces, then score this indicator "No."

To score this indicator "Yes," almost all nature/science materials must be well organized and in good repair.

23 Use of TV, video, and/or computer

General information about this item

Recent research shows that watching too much TV is not good for young children and is associated with such risks as attention problems and obesity. Professional organizations, such as the American Academy of Pediatrics and the National Association for the Education of Young Children, suggest that TV use with very young children be limited, and some researchers think that it should be banned altogether in infant and toddler programs. This item appears in the ITERS-R, not to encourage the use of TV, videos and computers in programs caring for infants and toddlers, but to provide guidelines for those programs already using these types of media.

If a program does not use TV, videos or computers with children, then this item can be scored "NA." The scale does not require the use of audio-visual materials (TV, videos and computer), and low scores are given for programs that use them with infants, because children learn best from having many varied hands-on experiences with materials and other people in their surrounding world. Using computers, and watching TV and videos are passive activities that may provide children with good learning opportunities. However, activities associated with audio-visual technology often require forced participation in large groups, sedentary behavior, limited learning opportunities, and few opportunities to practice important social skills.

If audio-visual materials are used with very young children, it should be done in a developmentally appropriate manner, adding to children's experiences rather than limiting them in any way. When scoring this item, consider ***all*** audio-visual materials used with children, including television programs, movies, videos, and computer software. If you do not see a television or computer during the observation, ask the staff whether any of these materials are ever used. For example, some programs may use TV during the morning arrival time or just before departure, which may not be observed during an observation. This item must be scored if the classroom uses these materials ***at all,*** regardless of frequency. If the observer is unable to observe children using these materials, the questions provided in the ITERS-R on page 39 should be used with staff to obtain the information required to score this item.

A closer look at each indicator

1.1 ***Developmentally appropriate*** means that the materials and activities are right for the ages and interests of the children, do not encourage antisocial learning, or compromise the emotional security of any child in the group.

As noted in the examples provided in the indicator on page 39 of the ITERS-R, audio-visual materials containing ***violent content, frightening characters, or sexually explicit*** content are not considered appropriate. Children of this age

23 Use of TV, video, and/or computer

23.1.2 No child should ever be required to watch TV, with no alternate activity offered. Children in this class are free to leave and play elsewhere if they wish.

23.1.3 Item 23 is scored a "1" if computers, TV, and/or videos are used with children younger than twelve months of age.

often cannot distinguish between imaginary and real occurrences, and therefore can find violence upsetting. Young children empathize with imaginary people, animals, or other creatures that are depicted as the victims of violence and may become concerned for their own safety. Unfortunately, many children's videos or television programs contain violence and are therefore inappropriate, even though they have been created for the children's market. This may include some natural wildlife productions and cartoons. In addition, because children are not able to separate fantasy from reality, they are apt to copy violent acts depicted in audio-visual materials. This can lead to antisocial aggressive behaviors within the classroom.

Of course, not all children respond negatively when exposed to such materials, but chances are that some might do so. It is the responsibility of the early childhood program to protect **all** children from such exposure. There are many appropriate materials that should be used in place of the inappropriate ones.

Materials that depict a biased or prejudiced attitude towards any group of people (race, culture, religion, ability, gender, profession, etc.) are not considered to be **culturally sensitive**, and are also considered inappropriate in this indicator. These are materials that present certain groups only in a negative way. Children get definite messages from the audio-visual materials they are exposed to. They may not yet be able to put these messages into words, but they still learn from them. Therefore, staff must carefully select materials to encourage children is pro-social rather than anti-social behaviors.

Audio-visual materials are also considered inappropriate when they present too much of a challenge or require too little of the children. For example, a full-length movie is inappropriate for toddlers because it lasts too long, or a computer game designed for preschoolers might be too difficult for toddlers. Materials used should be interesting for the children, and not frustrating.

In scoring this indicator, all audio-visual materials used with the children should be developmentally appropriate. This includes videos and DVDs brought from children's homes, if these materials are used with the group. Ask staff whether any requirements for appropriateness are considered when materials are selected or brought from home. Ask whether staff become familiar with the content of all materials **before** allowing use in the program. Use the questions provided on page 39 of the ITERS-R as part of this item.

To score Indicator 1.1 "No," there should be *no* inappropriate materials used with the children. If any inappropriate materials are used, score 1.1 "Yes."

Some flexibility can be used in scoring this indicator in regard to the challenge level. If the difficulty level does not exactly match the children in the group and would not create problems for the children, then this would not contribute to a score of "Yes." However, this situation could be considered in Indicator 3.1.

1.2 Because some children may not be interested in participating in the classroom audio-visual activity, such as watching television or using the computer, there should be other choices available to them as alternative activities. (See photo 23.1.2.) An *alternative activity* is one that children are allowed to do if they choose not to participate in an audio-visual activity. The alternative activity can be teacher-initiated or child-initiated but must include an option, in addition to watching TV or using a computer, that the child would prefer. It cannot be something that the child would not like to do, such as sitting at a table with nothing to do or resting quietly on a cot. The alternative activity cannot serve as a punishment for not participating in the audio-visual activity. Acceptable alternative activities might include:

- quiet activities, such as looking at a book or doing a puzzle,
- choices of any activity areas (active or quiet) in the classroom,
- going outside for active play (with supervision, of course), and
- participating in activities in another classroom.

Children should be allowed to leave the audio-visual activity to select an alternate activity whenever they want to, whether it is at the very beginning or part-way through, when they become bored or restless. If children leave the audio-visual activity but staff call them back to the group, it is clear that the expectation is for all children to participate and no alternative activity is possible. This remains true, even if staff only encourage them to stay one time and the child is then allowed to leave. The staff, through their encouragement to stay, show an expectation of participation in an activity, and some children might feel pressured to comply.

Sometimes children are not required to participate in the audio-visual activity, but they are not given anything of interest to do instead. They may wander around without being allowed to use any materials or they may play with a friend's hair. This type of option is *not* considered an alternative activity in scoring this item.

If audio-visual materials are used during the observation period, base the score on what is observed. However, if this type of activity is not directly observed, scoring should be based on how staff answer the question provided for Indicator 1.2 in the ITERS-R on page 39.

If at least one alternative activity is provided, score Indicator 1.2 "No." If there is no choice for an alternative activity or if staff expect all children to participate and do not allow them to do other activities, score 1.2 "Yes."

1.3 Because infants learn by using a combination of senses, such as touching, smelling, seeing, and hearing, audio-visual materials do not provide them with the valuable opportunities needed for active, hands-on learning. Infants also lack the eye-hand coordination required for using computers, and the restraint and attention required to watch TV and videos. Therefore, if television, video, or a computer is used with children under 12 months of age, this indicator is scored "Yes." (See photo 23.1.3.) If all children enrolled in the group are 12 months of age or older, then this indicator can be scored "NA."

23 Use of TV, video, and/or computer

3.1 Materials that are violent and not culturally sensitive are discussed in Indicator 1.1.

In order to receive credit for this indicator (score "Yes") **all** of the materials considered for this item must be **non-violent and culturally sensitive, as well as developmentally appropriate.**

3.2 **Accessible** means that children can reach and use materials by themselves. A more detailed definition for "accessible" is given on page 7 of the ITERS-R.

Alternative activities are discussed in Indicator 1.2. This indicator requires that **at least one alternative activity** be accessible for toddlers to choose while the television (including video) or computer is being used. The alternative activities and materials used must be developmentally appropriate and engaging for the children.

In order to give credit for this indicator (score "Yes"), the alternative must be accessible as a clear choice that carries no negative message. Score this indicator "No" if the computer or TV is used as a whole-group activity, regardless of the frequency of use.

3.3 Because using computers, and watching TV and videos are passive activities, there should be relatively little time spent overall on such activities, leaving more time for participation in active involvement in play. The intent of this indicator is to ensure that toddlers participate in active play in which they can be creative, imaginative, move around, and have hands-on experiences with real materials rather than spending inordinate amounts of time watching TV, or video or using the computer. In other words, the time children can spend using audio-visual materials must be **limited**.

The amount of time given as an example in this indicator for watching TV and videos, is 30 minutes a day for a full-day program, operating 8 hours or more a day. This time limit is for the cumulative use throughout the day. For example, if the TV is used for 20 minutes during the morning arrival and again in the afternoon for 20 minutes during preparation for departure, this would exceed the daily time allowance of 30 minutes. The example for using computers is limited to 10 minutes per turn, which means that no child should be allowed to use the computer for more than 10 consecutive minutes. Computer time should be relatively short, compared to other activities. However, these requirements serve as a guide for limiting the time spent on using audio-visual materials and may vary, but only by a few minutes.

To score, the observer should keep track of the time children spend in these types of activities and consider the number of turns each child has and how much time is spent throughout the day. Staff may need to use a timer to remind themselves and the children of time limits, or staff may record the time children begin using the equipment and frequently monitor the length of time. Observe to see whether time limits are enforced. If children spend too much time involved in audio-visual activities, score Indicator 3.3 "No," even if a system is used to monitor time limits but is not enforced.

5.1 Materials can be developmentally appropriate, non-violent and culturally sensitive in terms of meeting the requirements provided in Indicators 1.1 and 3.1 of this item, and children may enjoy using or watching the audio-visual materials as well. However, they might not be considered **"good for children."** For example, a children's video might not be frightening, violent, sexually explicit, or show bias, and it might not be too complex or too simple for the children viewing it. Yet, it may not benefit children's development, such as by adding to their vocabulary, concepts, or physical exercise.

Certain materials are developed specifically to enhance children's learning and understanding. These are considered more educational and "good for children." Examples of such materials are provided in the indicator on page 39 of the ITERS-R. Other examples include:

- video version of a favorite book the children know,
- musical video for children to sing along, or dance to,
- video version of a story that is considered children's literature, and
- video showing how familiar things such as crayons or bread are made.

To score Indicator 5.1 "Yes," all materials (TV, video and computer) used with children must be considered "good for children."

5.2   ***Free choice*** means that the child is permitted to select materials and companions, and as far as possible manage play independently. When children are assigned to use a computer, this is considered an adult-initiated activity because the child has not chosen the activity or material. If children use a computer room during assigned times throughout the day, then this is based on staff planning and not children's free choice. In addition, situations in which the children are assigned to centers by staff, or staff select the materials that individual children may use, do not count as free play. For example, children use the computer software to complete a certain task and cannot move on to the next center until the task has been completed.

Free choice activities are those that children can select to carry out. The range of activities usually includes different types of play experiences offered to children, such as those listed in the Activities section of the ITERS-R (e.g., fine motor, art, blocks, music, science, books, sand/water, or active physical play).

Many means that free choice activities include enough different types of play so that all children may do things that are interesting to them, and they have the possibility of many kinds of experiences. To meet the requirement for many in this indicator requires at least three or more ***alternative activities*** be accessible while TV or computer is used. (See photo 23.5.2.)

During free choice activities, children can choose from TV, video, or computer and many other options, as long as children, not staff, make the choice themselves. Staff should offer enough materials so children have choices other than the computer or TV, and each can find something of interest among what is accessible. If this is true, score Indicator 5.2 "Yes."

Score Indicator 5.2 "No" if the computer or other audio-visual equipment is used only as a whole-group activity, for example, if children must use the computer as an assignment by staff, or if it is one of just a few (less than 4) interesting play choices.

23.5.2 Since some children may not be interested in watching TV, other choices have been provided for them.

5.3   When staff are ***actively involved in the use of TV, video, and computers***, they help children successfully use the media or extend the activity by adding ideas or language. It requires more action and thinking on the part of staff and more interaction with the children to extend learning introduced on the computer, television, or other audio-visual media. In many cases, staff provide the materials, and space and set up the equipment for children, but once children become actively involved, staff go do other things, leaving the child alone without any adult interaction. However, the expectation for this indicator is that staff facilitate the audio-visual activities, just as they would other activities, such as reading books or art. Turning on a video or computer would not be considered active involvement by staff, and just simply watching a video with the children without adding additional information or activities to supplement the audio-visual material does not meet the requirements. Examples are included in the indicator on page 39 of the ITERS-R. Others include:

- dancing and singing with children to a video,
- giving children musical instruments to use with video,
- describing what the child is doing while using computer, such as "You're clicking on the red bear,"
- reading a story and then playing the video version,
- noticing a child who is having difficulty on the computer and quickly helping to show the child how to use the equipment properly,
- noticing the content of computer software a child is using and showing child a related book or activity,
- stopping the video periodically to discuss what will happen next, and
- playing a game with a child on the computer if no other children are interested in playing.

If the staff have already taught the children how to use certain software on the computer and the children are able to use it on their own, staff must become actively involved with helping the children understand the content that goes beyond the initial teaching. In other words, once staff have taught children how to operate the audio-visual materials by themselves, they cannot then ignore the children using it. They must continue to interact with the children using the audio-visual material and be actively involved at some time in using the content of the audio-visual material to extend learning.

If audio-visual materials are observed being used, score Indicator 5.4 based on whether the staff are actively involved with the children for at least some time. Involvement does not have to be lengthy, but there must be some depth in terms of teaching and presenting children with learning opportunities. If no audio-visual material is observed being used, but staff have reported some use, ask what their role usually is while children use audio-visual materials such as the computer, TV, or video and base your score on the information provided.

7.1   ***Active involvement*** means that children participate in the audio-visual experience by either thinking, making decisions, or physically moving in response to the opportunities offered by the material being used. (See photo 23.7.1.) Some examples of how children can be actively involved are provided in the indicator. Others include:

23.7.1 Audio/visual experiences should include active involvement rather than passive activities. In this rainy day TV activity, children exercise with a video.

- playing musical instruments along with a music video,
- using the mouse to draw a picture on the computer,
- pausing a video at certain points and guessing what will happen next,
- solving problems presented by the computer software that go beyond simply clicking without much thought to make something happen, and
- doing the movements to finger plays demonstrated on a video.

If children simply sit and watch without actively participating in some way, credit cannot be given.

Most means that the *vast majority* of materials considered for this item (but not necessarily all), and those used most often with the children, encourage active involvement.

Score "Yes" if the vast majority of materials encourage active mental or physical involvement.

7.2   Materials *support and extend children's current interests and experiences* means that staff plan and use materials specifically to provide information on a current topic of interest, or are related to something the children in the group have recently experienced. (See photos 23.7.2a-c.) The fact that so much of a toddler's day is spent on routine activities, such as eating, napping and toileting, makes these events interesting to children. Videos can be used to show children about napping with a cuddly toy or blanket. In addition, staff should notice the things that toddlers are interested in and use this information when planning the use of audio-visual materials. For example, when the weather turns warmer and children go outdoors more often and for longer periods of time, staff may want to stimulate interest in the growing plants, grass and trees on the playground by showing a video about Spring, flowers, and the warm sun. The materials should relate to what children are actually experiencing in their real world. Examples of such use are provided in the indicator.

In order to get credit for this indicator, staff must use the audio-visual materials to expand on and develop what children have already experienced. This is not required as part of every curriculum unit or theme or new event with the children. If not observed, staff must report using such materials occasionally, for example, at least four times a year. Ask staff the questions in the ITERS-R for this indicator to get information for scoring.

23.7.2a

23.7.2b

23.7.2c

23.7.2a-c   Videos are used to extend the recent classroom activities and discussions about trucks.

24 Promoting acceptance of diversity

General information about this item

As our society becomes more and more diverse with people of various races, cultures and religions, so do the families and children served by child care programs. The early childhood classroom environment plays an important role in increasing children's awareness and acceptance of diversity through teacher guidance, the toys and materials that are used, and the pictures and photos displayed in the classroom.

In addition to this item, issues related to acceptance of diversity are found in other items of the scale. For example, Item 14, Using books, Item 18, Music and movement, and Item 20, Dramatic play all contain aspects of teaching acceptance of diversity. However, this is the primary item in the ITERS-R that looks at how well a program does in counteracting the growth of bias and encouraging constructive social attitudes.

Diversity in the ITERS-R refers to the differences found in groups of people with regard to race, religion, culture, ability, age, and gender. For example, all races of people do not look the same, in terms of features and skin color. People of different cultures will have different kinds of interaction styles, languages, and traditions. Unfortunately, many people make incorrect assumptions about a group that lead to discrimination and unfair treatment of people in those groups, and closed attitudes about differences. Such attitudes cause many problems in our world's societies.

Children are not born with attitudes that cause them to discriminate against others. However, they can quickly adopt such attitudes as they watch and learn from what others do and say. A child who is exposed to messages saying that certain differences are bad soon learns to believe and act according to those messages.

Thus, in an attempt to encourage children to view others as individuals, without preconceived notions; to see a positive side to differences, rather than a negative one; and to focus on similarities rather than on differences, high quality early childhood education provides experiences to infants and toddlers that encourage *acceptance of diversity*.

Acceptance of diversity means that instead of differences being viewed as a negative, they are seen as strengths, adding more flavor to life, allowing all to contribute in unique ways. Children learn that differences among groups exist and can be respected and enjoyed, rather than feared and disliked. In addition, there is a focus on the similarities that bind us together as humans, rather than a concentration on how we differ.

This item focuses on the environmental messages that infants and toddlers receive about different people in the world's societies. It considers the images that children experience as they participate in the program and also whether overt prejudice is handled appropriately.

24 Promoting acceptance of diversity

In some programs where there is little or no diversity represented in the children or staff, people often think that there is no need to represent diversity in materials. Staff may say that since there is only one group represented in the children in their classroom, they do not need to show anyone else in their materials. Certainly this gives the children a chance to see themselves represented, but it does not encourage learning about and accepting diversity. Therefore, the requirements of this item apply to all programs, whether they include or do not include variation in staff and children.

A closer look at each indicator

1.1 The **materials** considered in this indicator include all pictorial materials, all toys, and all print and audio-visual materials used by or with the children. Pictorial materials include pictures and photos found in books (both commercially made and homemade), and posters and photos displayed in the classroom. Toys include materials that children are allowed to play with, such as puzzles, puppets, dramatic play clothing, foods and dolls. Audio-visual materials include recorded music (tapes, CDs, or records), TV programs, videos, and computer software.

A careful assessment of all materials that are used by the children is required to score. For example, containers must be opened and the contents examined, all puzzles should be viewed, and shelves containing blocks should be searched for small figures that might represent different races.

For **materials** to **show racial diversity** means that more than one of the races or ethnic groups from the various continents are represented in some way.

Examples include:

- baby dolls with two different skin tones (one light and one dark), (See photos 24.1.1a-b.)
- posters showing people with different skin tones, facial features, and hair color and texture,
- photos of the various children in the classroom (if more than one race is represented), and
- books showing people with different skin tones or other facial features.

For **materials** to **show cultural diversity** means that the traditions of at least two different groups are represented in some way. Examples include:

- books showing cultural celebrations (holidays, weddings, birthdays), clothing, foods, or books written in various languages
- plastic play foods used in dramatic play representing specific cultures (rice, noodles, tacos), (See photo 24.1.1c.)

24.1.1a Children have access to dolls reflecting various races.

24.1.1b When only one race is represented in dolls, children do not learn about differences in race or culture as they play.

24.1.1c Plastic play foods represent diversity of cultures.

- posters showing people in their home-life settings (family sitting at table for dinner, family kneeling or sitting on the floor at table),

- dress-up clothing representing different countries and customs, such as hats, shoes, pants, shirts, and dresses,

- puppets representing people of different cultures,

- small toy people representing various ethnic groups, for use with blocks, or small play buildings or vehicles

- pieces of fabric or blankets typical of different cultures, and

- adaptive equipment used by people with disabilities, either actual or for use with toys.

For diversity to be ***observed in materials*** means that the observer should *not* have to search beyond what would be obvious to the children as they use the materials. For example, one picture showing diversity, found on a shelf serving as a storage space for diapers, would not be readily obvious to the children. An easy-to-see displayed picture or a picture in a book easily accessible to children would be considered *visible*.

The materials must be located in the room used most of the time by the children in order to receive credit. For example, a poster showing various races located in the hallway is not easily visible by the children in the classroom, where they spend most of the day, and would not count towards meeting the requirements for this indicator.

To score Indicator 1.1 "No," there must be at least two examples of materials that show diversity, either racial or cultural, that are obvious to the children. The diversity can be visible within a single material (such as several races represented in one poster, which would count as one example), or as a combination of two or more separate materials (such as two baby dolls, each representing a different race, would count as one example). The examples may show either cultural *or* racial diversity; both are not needed to score "No."

1.2 For this item, a ***stereotype*** is a standardized mental picture that is held about any group, representing an oversimplified view of the individuals within that group. (See photo 24.1.2.) Stereotypes cause people to say, "Everyone in that group is like that," without considering individual characteristics. Stereotypes can be either negative or positive generalizations. Examples of negative stereotypes include:

24.1.2 If people from different cultures were only represented in traditional costumes, this would present a stereotyped view of cultural groups. To counteract the stereotype, current representations are also needed.

- Boys are loud, girls are quiet.

- Blondes are dumb.

- Men are strong; women are weak.

- Old people are not competent.

- Fat people are lazy.

- Teenagers do drugs.

- Poor people steal things.

- Indians wear feathers and use bows and arrows.

Obviously these are not true statements, because if we look at the individuals within these groups, we would see little evidence to support such ideas. Yet, people make assumptions according to negative stereotypes, causing unfair judgment and treatment of many.

Negative stereotyped images may be found in the materials present in infant/toddler programs. Many are seen in old materials that are not up-to-date in terms of current social beliefs and practices. This is acceptable as long as there are more recent representations shown throughout the materials to balance the images that children are exposed to. For example, photos of women as doctors, and men as nurses are displayed in addition to men and women in their more traditional roles.

There are many negative stereotypes shown in children's toys. For example, the traditional "Cowboys and Indians" toys depict both groups superficially, implying that members of the groups only fight with and kill the other. Certainly, this is a limited view of cowboys and Indians, and it does not represent the more positive things that group members might do, either from a historical or current point of view.

To score, look for negatively stereotyped portrayals in all materials used by children. If groups of people are represented *only* as negative stereotypes, score Indicator 1.2 "Yes."

1.3   *Prejudice* means negative treatment of a group, or individuals within a group, because of a stereotype of the group's characteristics. The group or the individual is not judged by real evidence, but rather by preconceived notions of what they will be like. Examples of prejudiced thinking include:

- She cannot do the job because she is a woman.
- He cannot learn because he is slow.
- She is Jewish, so I cannot be her friend.
- Children with disabilities cannot function well in the group.
- They are stupid because they do not speak English.
- People of that culture do not care for their children well.

It is easy to observe extremely obvious prejudice, but far more difficult to know when more subtle prejudice is being shown. It is difficult to discern whether a behavior is a sign of true prejudice, shows insensitivity about some issues, or is the product of an over-sensitive interpretation by the observer. For example, if a child in a minority group appears to get less attention than other children, is this caused by prejudice on the part of staff or by other reasons? It could be that the observer is very sensitive to children from minority groups being treated unfairly, and so does not notice that there are many other non-minority children in the group who also get less attention than some favorites. It might also be that the child is truly getting less attention for some reason that is not attached to being in a minority group. However, it is also possible that active prejudice is occurring in the class. It is up to the observer to look at *all* the evidence before scoring.

Sometimes it might appear that staff are acting with prejudice, when in fact their behaviors are due to a lack of sensitivity about what is considered correct (political correctness) in our society. For example, in high-quality early childhood programs, it is not considered appropriate to ask children to sit "Indian style" because this is stereotyping the way in which Native Americans sit. It is likely to be insulting to someone who is a Native American. Many staff prefer the term "crisscross applesauce" to remind children to sit on the floor with their legs crossed because it is

Indicator

not potentially offensive. However, naive use of such commonly used terms cannot be considered prejudiced behavior unless a person intends to be offensive and insulting.

If, during the observation, including the staff questioning time, staff say or do anything that is an *obvious, clear* act of prejudice against others (either children or other adults), score Indicator 1.3 "Yes."

However, the observer should be cautioned to consider all evidence. What may appear to be prejudice might actually be a lack of knowledge on the part of the staff or an overly sensitive response on the observer's part. If in doubt about an instance that might be considered prejudiced, ask a question to get clarification from staff without accusing.

3.1 ***Racial and cultural diversity in materials*** is discussed in Indicator 1.1. Examples are provided in this indicator. To receive credit for this indicator, at least three examples of racial diversity or cultural diversity must be observed. All examples can be from one category, either racial or cultural, or a combination of both. (See photos 24.3.1a-b.)

The examples must be easily seen by the children and placed in spaces that are used for a large part of the day, to give credit. They must be located in the classroom where children spend most of their time, rather than in the hallway or in another classroom used for a short period. Materials such as toys must be accessible to the children. Posters, pictures, and photos must be placed where the children can easily see them. Music from various cultures would also receive credit as an example for this indicator, if children have this experience daily. (See photo 24.3.1c.)

An example of diversity can be visible within a single material (such as several races represented in one poster, which would count as one example), or as a combination of two or more separate materials of one type (such as two baby dolls, each representing a different race, or two different photographs, each showing a child of a different culture would each count as one example). It is the contrast of races or cultures shown within a type of material, that carries the message of accepting diversity.

To give credit, the three examples may come from one type of material (such as three books or three posters), or may be from various types (such as one book, two puzzles showing one contrast, and one poster).

3.2 Diversity in materials can be shown positively or negatively. Positive images give good messages about the characteristics of people; negative images give the opposite.

24.3.1a These two dolls with different skin tones represent one example of racial diversity. Indicator 3.1 requires at least three examples of materials showing either racial or cultural diversity.

24.3.1b Dolls representing at least three races are accessible to these toddlers.

24.3.1c Cultural and racial diversity are included in dolls, books and recorded music used daily with the children in this classroom.

For example, if toy soldier figures are only shown as people who use weapons to kill, and this is not balanced with other materials that show the wide range of soldiers' roles (protecting, helping others, as family members, in other job assignments), children receive only one message about what soldiers do—they kill others. Similarly, if members of certain groups are shown only as being poor, in certain types of jobs, or as people who take part in illegal activities, these are also negative portrayals of diversity.

Materials show diversity in a positive way requires that the messages depict people as good and do not stereotype members of any group. People are shown as humans who are pleasant, capable, and to be valued. (See photo 24.3.2.)

Score Indicator 3.2 "No" if any examples of negative images are included in the materials used by the children. Score "Yes" if all images are positive.

24.3.2 Books help encourage acceptance of diversity. This book contains positive images of different cultures and ages (young girl and her older grandfather), as well as words printed in two languages.

3.3 The meaning of ***prejudice*** is discussed in Indicator 1.3. For staff to ***intervene appropriately to counteract prejudice*** requires that:

- Staff do not ignore any prejudice that they observe.
- Staff are aware of situations involving possible prejudice (e.g., a child who speaks another language, a child with a disability, a child whose family celebrates different holidays from those of others in the group) and give those situations special attention.
- Staff take immediate action when they observe prejudiced behavior, either by children or other adults, and make it clear that such talk or behavior is not acceptable.

With very young children, it is unlikely that staff will need to respond to prejudice shown by infants or toddlers in the class. The most constructive response staff can have with older toddlers is to stop behavior and discuss it in simple terms, explaining why it is not acceptable. Children should be helped to recognize the feelings of others and the effects of their actions. Modeling the appropriate behavior is the most effective method to use with very young children.

It is more likely for staff to see prejudice shown by other adults but difficult to respond to appropriately. However, this must be handled by staff if prejudice by adults comes up during the observation. For example, a parent might say to the staff, "Well, what do you expect of the child? Those people are always like that!" In this case, the teacher would be required to discuss the inappropriateness of such a statement with the offending adult, making it clear that prejudice is not shared or tolerated. This would have to be handled in a non-confrontational, constructive, professional manner.

If ***no prejudice*** is observed, and the observer sees plenty of evidence that such behavior would be very unlikely, score Indicator 3.3 "Yes."

If prejudice is observed during the observation, either from staff members, parents or children, and staff are (or should be) aware of it, score Indicator 3.3 "No" if staff do not intervene appropriately.

24.5.1a Many books are accessible to children including those that represent people of different races, ages, abilities and gender in non-stereotyping roles.

24.5.1b Puppets are considered and given credit as "materials" for Indicator 5.1.

5.1   For this indicator, **books** include all books that are accessible to or used with the children. (See photo 24.5.1a.) Magazines or other books that are obviously not accessible to the children are not considered in scoring. **Pictures** include displayed pictures, picture cards, photos and posters that are located in an area where children can easily see them. **Materials** include puzzles, dramatic play food, clothing or props, and puppets, but it does not include dolls. (See photo 24.5.1b.) Dolls are addressed in Indicator 5.2

Diversity is described in the "General Information" section for this item. The example given in the indicator on page 40 of the ITERS-R contains a list of categories representing diversity, all of which are required for this indicator.

As stated in the "Note for Clarification" for this indicator, **many** means that there are at least 10 examples for children to easily experience, without having to complete a difficult search. Examples of diversity depicting non-stereotyping roles should be from the following categories:

- Races
- Cultures
- Ages
- Abilities
- Gender

Not all categories of diversity need to be included. The presence of diversity in the books/pictures/materials should be obvious. However, an observer should carefully look through the books that children use, opening pages, and looking at pictures to find examples. If there are large numbers of books, the observer can select a sample of books to look at.

Books/pictures/materials must be located in spaces children use for most of the day, such as their main classroom. If no main classroom is assigned to the group being observed, materials in all spaces used should be considered to score. Books/pictures/materials located in spaces used only for relatively short periods (e.g., hallways, entry way, lunch room, early AM or late PM classroom) are not counted to meet the requirements of this indicator, nor are they considered in scoring any other indicator in this item.

24 Promoting acceptance of diversity

24.5.2a Small toy people that are often used with blocks are considered "dolls," and can be given credit in Indicators 3.1 and 5.2.

24.5.2b In order to make these dolls accessible to this non-mobile infant staff have placed him on a blanket where he can easily reach the dolls.

An example of diversity can be visible within a single material (such as several races represented in one poster, which would count as one example), or as a combination of two or more separate materials of one type (such as two puzzles, each representing people of a different race, or two different photographs, each showing a person of a different age, would each count as one example). It is the contrast of races or cultures shown within a type of material that carries the message of accepting diversity.

To give credit, at least 10 examples showing diversity must be observed in all three types (books, pictures, and materials, excluding dolls), meeting the requirements stated above.

5.2   ***Dolls*** are figures that represent humans that infants and toddlers use for pretend play. Dolls for infants include soft, stuffed dolls; dolls for toddlers can include traditional baby dolls, small (but safe) wooden or plastic people, usually used with blocks or play buildings. (See photo 24.5.2a.) Puppets are not considered in scoring this indicator, but are considered for Indicator 5.1. For this indicator, dolls ***representing three races*** must be accessible. (See photo 24.5.2b.) Race is easily shown by various shades of skin tones, but race can also be represented in facial features, hair texture, and eye color. To be considered in scoring, the differences must be obvious to the children.

All of the three examples must be accessible to children, (see the definition of ***accessible*** on page 7 of the ITERS-R). Dolls that are located in other classrooms, on high shelves as displayed items, or in closed cabinets are not considered accessible to children.

7.1   ***Non-sexist images*** go beyond what is considered the historical or traditional role for men and women and show both men and women in similar roles, reflecting our modern day society. (See photo 24.7.1.) For example, a poster of a woman playing professional basketball, traditionally thought of as an activity for men and boys, would be a non-sexist image. Similarly, a picture of a man holding and feeding a baby would be considered non-sexist.

Sexist images are common in our society, and they may be found in the materials located throughout infant-toddler classrooms. They are more likely to be seen in older materials that are not up-to-date in terms of current social beliefs and practices. For example, out-of-date pictures of people in jobs often systematically show men in certain roles (professionals, roles associated with physical strength) and women in others (housekeepers, nurses, teachers).

To receive credit for this indicator, examples of non-sexist images must be shown in pictures or books. There can be other images, as well, showing males and females in more traditional roles but credit cannot be given if materials are observed showing only traditional roles. **Pictures** include displayed posters or photos, which are easily visible to the children. **Books** include all books that children can easily reach and use, as well as books that staff may use or read to the children. At least two examples of non-sexist images must be found throughout the accessible pictures and books. If the pictures are present but not easily seen and the books are not accessible, then score this indicator "No."

7.2 In this indicator **cultural awareness** means that the traditions of various groups are represented and recognized in the classroom.

24.7.1 Non-sexist images go beyond what we traditionally think of as specific male and female roles: for example, showing girls as firefighters or women as basketball players.

Showing cultural awareness **in a variety of activities** can be observed in play experiences when staff provide materials throughout the classroom that show cultural diversity. For example, puzzles may depict people from various cultures in both traditional and current dress or work; puppets may represent people of different cultures; there may be books with pictures showing and telling about cultural customs, with some books in different languages; dramatic play props may represent different cultures, any of which could be counted for Indicator 5.1, but required across the classroom for credit here. In addition, cultural awareness in a variety of activities can be provided in routines, such as:

- Staff use some words in different languages to talk about routines.
- Music from various cultures is used at naptime.
- Staff say hello or goodbye in different languages.

Special activities can also be used to help meet the requirements of this indicator, such as:

- Children dance to music of a specific culture.
- Musical instruments representing various cultures are used with toddlers.
- Children celebrate winter holidays of many different cultures.
- Staff sing songs in various languages
- Toddlers try on shoes people wear in different countries.

Cultural awareness activities can take place within daily activities (routine or play) or be special activities that do not take place on a daily basis. Therefore such activities do not have to be observed, but can be reported by staff.

The representation of various cultures in accessible materials throughout the class must be observed and is required for a score of "Yes." In addition, however, staff must report at least one routine or special activity for a score of "Yes."

Interaction

25 Supervision of play and learning

General information about this item

This item examines the attention and guidance given to children by the staff during all play and learning times. *Supervision* requires that staff can easily see, hear, and reach the children, and that they are actively attending to them. Note that all three (see, hear, and reach) are required. Obviously, staff must be physically present and alert in order to supervise children appropriately.

For staff to be able to *see* the children means that staff members can glance at all locations where children are playing and clearly make sure that children are safe. If there are more than one staff member in the room, they must together be able to see all the children, but this is not required of each one separately. There can be no barriers that prevent at least one staff member from being able to see each child. For staff to be able to easily *hear* children means that the noise level in the room allows staff to hear the sounds children make, either their verbal communication or other sounds they make. For children to be *within easy reach* requires that by moving a relatively short distance, staff can reach a child in only seconds; it does not require that all children are always within arm's reach of a staff member.

In some cases, accommodations are made to help staff see and hear children who are out of immediate view and hearing. Devices such as mirrors and audio or visual monitors might, but do not necessarily, help staff to see and hear the children under certain circumstances. For example, a mirror might be placed so that staff who are diapering children might be able to see the children playing in the space hidden by the diapering table. Or an audio sound monitor might be placed in a separate play area. These provisions should be considered in evaluating the ability of staff to supervise, but counted positively only if they are effective in doing what is needed to allow staff to see, hear, and reach children. The observer must try out the provisions to see if they really allow staff to know clearly what is happening to the children. Sometimes the provision may help to meet the supervision requirement and at other times it may not. For example, the presence of a sound monitor may help staff hear a child crying, but it may not be able to detect that a child has stopped breathing. Therefore it would not substitute for the staff being able to glance over to check on a baby who is playing out of sight.

25A If children can play in this separate nap room, staff must be able to supervise them. Supervision of sleeping children, however, is considered in Item 8, Nap.

This item considers supervision during all times that children are not involved in routines and able to participate in play and learning. It does not apply to the supervision of any child who is involved in routine care (see Items 7, Meals/snack, 8, Nap, or 9, Diapering/toileting), since supervision for these activities is handled under the respective items. (See photo 25A.) For this item, the quality of supervision of play and learning should be evaluated in the classroom, in any other indoor spaces used with the children, and outdoors.

A **lapse in supervision** means that staff cannot easily see, hear, or reach the children, or are not attending to them. (See photo 25B.) A **momentary lapse in supervision** means that staff are in the space used by the children but cannot see, hear, or reach children, or are not attending to the children, for a period of less than 1 minute. Staff can often handle more than one task at once, attending to the children while doing something else as well. For example, a staff member may prepare a bottle but keep an eye on the group by frequently glancing at the children, or watch and be prepared to intervene while talking to a parent. If the staff member is doing one task, but also supervising the children, this is not considered a lapse in supervision.

In this item, **staff** refers to those adults who are considered program staff and have formal responsibility for children. This includes adults who are in the classroom for short periods of the day, or who are usually a part of the classroom. For example, if a therapist, "floater," assistant, parent volunteers in a cooperative program or director of a program comes into the classroom and interacts with children for short or irregular periods, they are responsible for supervising the children and count in scoring this item. However, a parent who is in the classroom to visit or drop off their child would not assume responsibility for supervising children and does not count in scoring this item.

25B When no staff member can se any child, there is a lapse in super sion. Momentary lapses are acceptab when children are in a safe place.

To score this item, consider *all* observed adults supervising play and learning activities, indoors or outdoors. Concentrate primarily on the staff and children in the group being observed, but if several classrooms are regularly combined during play times (for example, if active physical play takes place with several groups of children outdoors, or if groups are combined in the early or late parts of the day), consider *all* observed staff and children of similar ages and abilities as those in the group being observed. Notice whether there are enough staff to supervise the children and whether adults are supervising the most hazardous areas and activities adequately. In some cases, state-mandated staff-child ratios might be met, but there still may not be enough staff to supervise adequately because of the size or configuration of the play space, the children's abilities, or the attention to one child that is often required by routines such as diapering or feeding.

The score for this item must be based on what is seen throughout an observation. No questions should be used to gather information required to score this item. The observation must be long enough to provide a range of circumstances, including quiet and more active times, group times (if used) and free play, indoor and outdoor times, and more and less stressful periods of the day. For example, to score accurately, the observer should see supervision early in the morning, when children and staff are fresh, and continue to observe during the more stressful times of the day, such as when many children become hungry at once or when people are tired.

It should be noted that a less harsh and more responsive approach to supervision is associated with more positive child development. This does not mean that staff should move to the other extreme by being overly permissive, and not protecting children adequately or not helping them to learn and practice growing abilities. Instead, the indication seems to be that all supervisory interactions with children must be carried out in a positive way rather than in a cold, harsh, more detached or restrictive manner.

Indicator

A closer look at each indicator

1.1   ***Insufficient supervision to protect safety*** means that staff severely compromise children's safety needs by not watching, guiding, or intervening as required by the children's abilities or the nature of the hazards present. (See photos 25.1.1a-c.) The most diligent supervision is required for infants and toddlers because they are extremely dependent on adults and know very little about protecting themselves from danger. They quickly develop physical abilities that are far ahead of their knowledge about safety.

Because of the intense need for close interaction, this age group needs much supervision at all times. This does not mean that staff should always be "on top" of the children, tightly controlling them, but rather they should be observing them closely without interrupting their play, keeping them safe, and helping, teaching, responding or providing comfort at the right moments. Not even a ***momentary lapse*** in supervision (defined in the "General Information" section) can occur when risk of danger is high. (See photo 25.1.1d.) For example, staff must have children in sight and within easy reach when they are playing on a climber, taking a short walk around the neighborhood, going down stairs, or playing in an area with major hazards.

25.1.1a-c [below]   Staff must watch carefully and intervene as needed to protect children's safety.

25.1.1a

25.1.1b

25.1.1c

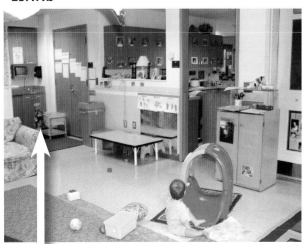

25.1.1d   Staff must stay close to this child playing at the water table, because of the higher risk.

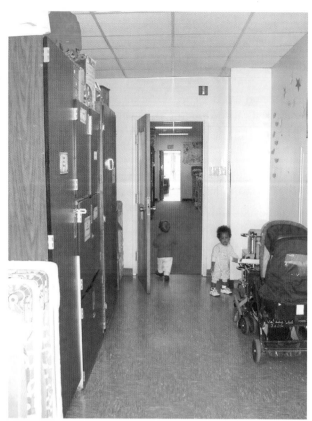

25.1.1e   **25.1.1f**

25.1.1e-f If staff do not go after the children immediately, supervision is insufficient.

Since routine care, such as feeding babies or diapering toddlers, requires the close attention of one adult, the observer should be especially aware of how the other children are supervised while one staff member works with a single child or a small group of children. Although the children involved in the routine may be adequately supervised, the other children may not be. For example, in a room with two staff, if one changes diapers, there may be a fairly large group of children who are left with inadequate supervision, especially if the other staff member is also involved in routines (such as getting cots out for nap or cleaning up after lunch).

This indicator is always scored "Yes" if staff leave children, and no adult is present (or awake) to supervise them, even for short periods of time. For example, score "Yes" if the staff member leaves the children alone in the room to talk to another person in the hallway, or the staff member goes into the building to get her coat, leaving the children unsupervised on the playground. (Note that this would not be considered a momentary lapse in supervision, because staff are not present and alert to the children's needs). Inadequate supervision will also be true (scored "Yes") when there are too few staff to meet the supervision needs of children, there are hazards present, or staff are frequently inattentive and ignore children or attend to other interests instead of to the children's needs.

Similarly, when a child leaves the area that is visually supervised, goes where he cannot be seen, and is not noticed for a while by the supervising staff, score this indicator "Yes." (See photos 25.1.1e-f.) For example, a child wanders out of the classroom unnoticed and no adult realizes the child's absence, goes around the corner of the building when on the playground, or goes into another area of the room and her absence is not noticed by staff. Do not score "Yes" if a staff member goes immediately after the child and the lapse is for just a few seconds, unless going after the child leaves all other children completely unsupervised.

If there are only a few momentary lapses in supervision, do not score this indicator "Yes." However, if there are many momentary lapses, or one lapse in supervision of over 1 minute, where staff cannot easily see, hear, and reach a child at all, score 1.1 "Yes."

3.1 The requirements for **c**hildren being within sight, hearing, and easy reach of staff are provided in the "General Information" section for this item and in Indicator 1.1. ***Momentary lapses in supervision*** is defined in the "General Information" section for this item. This indicator requires that there are enough staff present to watch children during play. The staff must be positioned to see all areas where children are playing, move around as needed to keep a close eye on children, and remain attentive to children's basic safety needs. There must always be an adult present supervising, and children are never left unsupervised for any amount of time.

To give credit for this indicator, staff must intervene when problems occur that could seriously compromise a child's safety (for example, to stop children from hurting themselves or others, to keep all children within view of adults, or to help a toddler climb up on the stepstool to wash hands). They must pay extra attention in more hazardous situations, such as when children are using small objects, participating in water play, or using climbing equipment. (See photos 25.3.1a–c.)

*A **few momentary lapses*** in supervision are permitted when scoring this indicator "Yes." A ***few*** means no more than five lapses during the 3-hour observation. If even one ***momentary lapse in supervision*** is observed when risk of danger is high, score this indicator "No." For example if staff do not supervise water play closely for a short period of time, this indicator would be scored "No."

3.2 ***Caregiving responsibilities*** include attending to the needs of children both for routines and for play and learning. (See photo 25.3.2, next page.) Caregiving responsibilities do not include staff attending to personal needs, social interactions that take away from meeting the needs of the children, or other responsibilities that are part of the job but not related directly to the children in the group. These are things that should be done while on a break from classroom responsibilities. For example, caregiving responsibilities would include serving food to the children in the group being observed, but not preparing or serving food to other children enrolled in other classes. Talking briefly to the parent of a child in the group would be part of caregiving responsibilities, but socializing with other friends would not.

To give credit for this indicator, the vast majority of staff attention must be on meeting the needs of the children in the observed group.

25.3.1a A momentary lapse in supervision should not happen when children climb in an area that does not have an appropriate fall zone.

25.3.1b

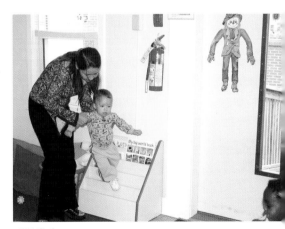

25.3.1c

25.3.1b-c Toddlers move quickly and children must be within easy reach for staff to be able to protect them.

25.3.2 Although children are not being closely supervised in the more hazardous area of the classroom, the staff member is involved in caregiving responsibilities.

25.5.2 When the toddler was upset after going down the slide, the staff member was quick to respond to him and provide reassurance.

Very little or no attention should be given to other work or interests that do not directly involve the well-being of the children in the group. This does not mean that staff cannot interact with other staff, visitors, or children, but these interactions should be infrequent across the observation time, and momentary. Staff who are responsible for the group should not be pulled from the class to perform other tasks for the center without a substitute being provided.

Score 3.2 "Yes" if staff are attentive to the children in the group with few or no momentary lapses.

5.1 First, this indicator requires that staff respond to things that happen in the total area or classroom used by the ***whole group*** of children. Second, the indicator requires that this "whole area supervision" be done even when staff are ***working with one child or a small group***. It must be obvious during the observation that staff watch, listen to, and remain aware of what is happening in the entire area used by children. Evidence of meeting the requirement includes:

- Staff frequently scan the room, even when working with one child or a small group.
- All staff members coordinate their supervision, so that no area being used by children is left unsupervised.
- Staff generally notice where children are located and what they are doing.
- Staff interrupt work with a small group or an individual child to respond when needed to prevent problems or to give help.

The indicator is not met (score "No") when staff are so involved with individual children or small groups that they miss obvious problems and do not take action because they have not scanned the whole group.

5.2 For staff to ***react quickly*** means that children do not have to wait an unreasonable amount of time for staff to respond and meet their needs in a way that satisfies them. In considering what is reasonable, the observer must see the waiting time from the child's point of view, not from the point of view of the staff, who may be working as quickly and hard as they can but still cannot answer a child quickly enough. Moderate periods of waiting are acceptable if the child is not terribly upset and if the staff reassure the child in a way that satisfies him or her. However if a child continues crying strongly or is obviously upset, the wait for a satisfying response must be very short.

To ***solve problems in a comforting and supportive way*** requires a positive response that consoles and satisfies the child. (See photo 25.5.2.) Staff should be able to judge what the child is trying to communicate (such as hunger or thirst, tiredness, being bored, wanting affection or attention) and respond accordingly. If they misjudge what the child wants, they should continue trying other options that might help the child. They do not give up or stop responding, leaving the child upset. Admittedly, this can be difficult when caring for a group of infants or toddlers. There are many conflicting needs. Nevertheless, this indicator cannot be scored "Yes" unless children's needs are positively met with very little waiting. A score of "No" for this indicator may mean several different things. For example, "No" might indicate that:

- There are not enough staff to properly meet the needs of the children in the group and that extra help is required at especially demanding times.

- Staff have not worked out the systems required to meet the needs of the children effectively and cooperatively.

- Changes in the physical setting are needed so staff can work more efficiently.

Whatever the reason, if the children's needs are not positively met with little waiting, this indicator is scored "No."

5.3 This indicator requires, first, that staff ***play*** with the children, meaning that they participate in the children's play and learning activities, as opposed to doing only routine care tasks. (See photos 25.5.3a-c.) In some cases play might take place as part of routine care, but the play that is considered here is associated with non-routine care. This may occur as staff initiate play activities with children, or join in and follow the child's interests as he plays. It is not to be confused with directing or taking over children's play in an intrusive manner. Rather, it should consist of a partner-like interaction, in which the adult is responsive to what the child is interested in doing.

Second, the indicator requires that staff show ***interest in or appreciation of*** what the children do. (See photos 25.5.3d-e, next page.) This means that staff know when children attempt to practice or learn skills as they play, and respond positively to whatever the children do. This recognition can come in many forms and may not always be delivered to the child verbally. The interest or appreciation should be provided regularly, even when children's efforts are not successful.

25.5.3a The child and staff member play "dress-up" together.

25.5.3b The staff member helps these toddlers to take turns, while acting as the bridge.

25.5.3c Staff use puppets with the babies as part of playing together.

25.5.3d Child and staff member celebrate the amazing crayon, and all it can be used for.

25.5.3e Beyond supervising closely for safety, this staff member is also very interested in what the children are doing as they play.

Some examples of staff behaviors that meet the requirement for **showing interest in or appreciation of what children do** include:

- looking at the what the child is doing or talking to the child about it;
- showing nonverbal delight in what a child has done or is doing (e.g., smiling at the child, clapping, patting on the back, or hugging);
- praising a child verbally for what he or she has done or for the effort shown ("You rolled the ball to me. Thank-you!" "I like the way you moved so she could ride past us."); and
- describing in a positive tone what the child has done or is trying to do ("I see you put the dolly to bed. She was sleepy." "You built a tower with three cardboard blocks. Oh, now you knocked it over!").

To give credit for this indicator, no specific number of examples must be observed. However, it must be evident that playing with the children is a usual and positive practice of the staff, and that a sufficient time of the day can be given to this aspect of supervision. If the vast majority of staff time is taken up in routine care, credit cannot be given for this indicator, even if staff play with the children for a brief portion of the observation.

5.4 To **give children help when needed** requires that staff set up toys and activities to make it possible for children to play as independently as possible, then watch children to see when they need help, and provide help as needed. (See photos 25.5.4a-c.) To give credit, there should be evidence that adults step in and offer help when children seem to be having trouble or are frustrated, for example, in using equipment or materials, in getting along with others, or in getting involved in play. Some positive adult-child interaction must be observed during the children's play to give credit, even if it is not "helping" but rather showing interest, which is encouraging. Credit should not be given if staff help is usually intrusive and interferes with children's play.

The extent to which children need help will vary by child and the activity in which he or she is involved. Some children simply need more help than others, and they should not be forced to do things on their own before they are ready. Younger

25.5.4a Encouraging children to participate in simple "clean up" is part of helping children.

25.5.4b Making toys accessible to non-mobile children is an example of helping children in their play.

infants or toddlers, children with certain disabilities, or those who do not feel secure will need more help in activities than others. Staff can help by providing simpler tasks or materials or by adapting tasks and activities to allow the child to have success. Some examples of giving help when needed include:

- making sure the children have the things they need to be successful in activities (e.g., making sure the grasping toys are within reach of the baby, adding materials to provide new interest, removing barriers to toys, putting books on the shelf with covers facing outward so that children can choose easily, ensuring that children can access toys stored in bins by removing covers);

25.5.4c Without staff help, these two children would not have the skills needed to play a roll and catch game together.

- providing simpler materials to work with when more complex ones are too difficult (e.g., shortening long paint brush handles so a toddler can manage them more successfully, adding pop beads to the fine motor toys if toddlers have trouble stringing large beads, putting out large cardboard blocks if children cannot stack smaller blocks);

- showing children how to do a task or use materials (e.g., making blocks balance, using the funnel to fill a container with a small opening, moving a puzzle piece until it fits, holding on to the railing when climbing up the steps of the slide);

- guiding children by talking them through the steps needed for success (e.g., helping children figure out how to clean up an activity area by breaking the task into many small steps and talking them through each step, talking a child through balancing a block structure or figuring out a puzzle, guiding a child through the steps for using a bubble wand); and

- helping children work out problems with others (e.g., redirecting children away from continuing problems, helping a child walk around another child's play, helping a child find a duplicate toy, helping a child understand what another child is trying to communicate).

To **give children encouragement when needed** requires that staff observe children at play and show positive interest in what they do or try to do. Encouragement does not have to be enthusiastic "cheerleading" nor does it have to consist of praise. Instead, it can be a consistent, supportive attitude that tells the children that their play is valued, it is fun or interesting to try new skills or practice established ones. Encouragement can be verbal, for example, a staff member says, "Reach, I know you can get the doll." Or it can be nonverbal, for example, a staff member smiles as the child looks for reassurance when trying something new. The message given is that children are competent and staff trust that they can deal with challenges.

To give credit for this indicator, no specific number of examples must be observed. However, it must be evident that the requirements of the indicator are a general practice used by staff throughout the day.

7.1 **Staff watch carefully** means that staff are vigilant and alert to the children's needs throughout the observation. They miss very little, in terms of what happens to the children as they play. **Act to avoid problems before they occur** means that staff realize there will be a negative effect if things progress, among the children or with the physical setting, and they make changes in the social group or the physical setting before children get into trouble. (See photos 25.7.1a-c.) Examples of such practice are provided in the indicator. Additional examples include a staff member who:

- removes toys from the fall zone of a climber before children fall and get hurt,
- intervenes when a child is grabbing a toy from a child who is ready to defend herself by biting,
- sits next to a non-mobile baby to protect him from more active children who have entered the play area,
- moves with the children on the playground to be near them at all times,
- removes art materials requiring more supervision when she is needed in another area, or
- stays next to the water table whenever any child is using it.

To give credit for this indicator (score "Yes"), some examples of such practice must be observed. Since the term **usually** is used, it must be evident that the requirements of the indicator are a general practice used by staff throughout the day. There should be few, if any, examples

25.7.1a Staff notice that children are choosing to play near one another.

25.7.1b To provide enough materials for the group of three, this staff member brings out a new container of toys.

25.7.1c Then the children can play side-by-side without undue competition.

25.7.2a Staff individualize supervision of this infant, ensuring that he enjoys play and learning.

25.7.2b As staff see a need for change in activity, the non-mobile infant is moved to participate in different activities.

when staff did not meet the requirements of this indicator and allowed problems to occur that could have been avoided by preventive action on their part.

7.2 *Individualized* supervision means that the watching, protecting, and interacting with the children varies according to the specific needs of each child, each activity, or the hazards in the environment. (See photos 25.7.2a-c.) In other words, supervision is not the same for everyone and everything. Examples of such supervision are provided in the indicator. Additional examples include staff who:

25.7.2c This ensures ongoing, fun learning with little boredom.

- stay closer to a child who is more aggressive,

- give more comforting attention to a child who is not feeling well,

- bring out a more difficult puzzle for a child who does simple puzzles very well,

- hold a non-mobile baby more than the active crawlers who want to move about,

- handle more gently and speak more softly to children who startle easily or who are more sensitive, or

- show more overt enthusiasm and excitement with children who are alert and want to have fun.

To give credit for this indicator (score "Yes"), examples of such individualized supervision must be observed. It must be evident that the requirements of the indicator are a general practice used by staff throughout the day.

7.3 The *differing requirements of activities* are related to the relative hazards, complexity, and difficulty associated with the play. The abilities and personalities of the children must be considered when determining the requirements of an activity. (See photo 25.7.3, next page.) For example, rolling a big ball would not have high supervision requirements if a robust toddler was doing the activity. However, the requirements would change dramatically if the toddler was rolling the ball to an unsteady baby who was just learning to stand up. In addition to the examples in the indicator, variations in supervision include:

- Staff limit the number of children who may participate in a messy art activity at one time.

- While some children are sleeping, staff spend time with the children who are awake to do activities requiring closer supervision.

- There are always toys accessible on open shelves that are safe and easy for toddlers to manage by themselves with minimal supervision by staff.

- Activities that require closer supervision take into account the best time to do the activity, which staff will supervise, which children participate, and what the other children will be doing (e.g., playing outside, sleeping, playing independently).

25.7.3 While the more experienced children scribble independently, this staff member knows that the younger child requires more help.

To give credit for this indicator (score "Yes"), examples of such varied supervision must be observed with regard to play activities. It must be evident that the requirements of the indicator are a general practice used by staff throughout the day and that the supervision of all activities is not handled in the same manner.

26 Peer interaction

General information about this item

The title of this item, *Peer interaction,* refers to the relationships children have with one another—how well they play near, or with, one another and whether they fight or get along peacefully. However, this item does not evaluate how well children get along, but what staff do to encourage the learning required to do so.

Helping children develop the social skills needed to get along well with other children is a major task faced by the staff in early childhood programs. Infants and toddlers in group care are at a particular disadvantage, because they have barely started to develop the abilities required to get along well with others. They usually play best alone, do not understand that their actions may hurt another child, and often use other children as objects to experiment with, poking, mouthing, pulling, and pushing them to see what happens. None of this is meant to hurt others. Infants and toddlers simply do what comes naturally, and this would work well if all their interactions were restricted to adults and older children, who do have the social skills needed to get along well. However, grouping babies or toddlers together with peers who share the same level of social development requires special understanding and skills of staff.

It takes a long time and lots of patience to help children learn necessary social skills, such as recognizing their effect on others, cooperation, sharing, and understanding another's feelings. In addition, children need time to grow and develop physically before they gain the skills to interact well.

Because infants and toddlers have immature social skills, the methods staff use to encourage positive social behavior among infants and toddlers is of great importance. Forcing good behavior on infants or toddlers would require that the children be kept separate, for example each in a playpen, or that the children be tightly controlled, so that there is no opportunity for trouble to break out. Restricting children, so they rarely get to interact naturally, might keep children from being troublesome to their *peers* (the other children in the group), but it does little to help them learn to get along well. Staff who work with infants and toddlers must clearly understand this stage of social development, act to minimize problems without restricting the children, model the social behaviors that these youngest of children need to learn, and help the children understand the effects of their actions on other people.

Although infants and toddlers do not usually get along particularly well with one another, they are definitely interested in other children. Their eyes brighten and they become excited when other babies come into view. For many toddlers, the word "baby" is one of the first they use. The interest is there, but the skills are not. They do not understand why a child grabs a toy, nor does the "grabber" know that taking the toy is not socially appropriate. There are specific methods that have been proven to be effective in helping infants and toddlers develop social skills.

These include:

- Staff give children many chances to interact—to play near one another, to communicate, either verbally or non-verbally—but avoid putting children into impossible situations with others that they do not have the ability to handle. For example, infants and toddlers cannot share without lots of direct help from an adult. Therefore, the need to share must be minimized, and sharing should never be required.

- Staff supervise children's interactions closely so that when problems come up (as is natural), staff can step in to help children work things out. Staff must stay very close to infants or toddlers who tend to hurt others (for example, by biting, poking, or pushing) and must actively protect children from hurting one another.

- Staff model the way to interact positively with others, but do not expect children to have such advanced social skills.

- Staff point out and talk about the effects of a person's actions on others and about feelings, sharing, cooperation.

- Staff act as "social interpreters" for the children by explaining the intentions of others.

- Staff accept the feelings of the child and of others, even if the behavior cannot be accepted. For example, if a toddler is angry with another child and hits that child, staff need to make it clear that they understand the anger, but will not allow the hitting.

These are the ideas represented in the indicators of this item. At the lower levels of quality, it is required that children have chances to interact with one another, and that when problems come up, the staff intervene.

At the higher levels of quality, staff play a stronger teaching role, modeling what is needed and providing children with the learning opportunities that will eventually allow them to get along well with others all by themselves.

Information required for scoring the indicators in this item must be observed. No questions should be used to gather information required to score the item.

In this item, **staff** refers to those adults who are in the classroom and work with the children daily (or almost daily), for a substantial portion of the day. This can include volunteers, if they are in the classroom for the required amount of time. Adults who are in the classroom for short periods of the day, or who are not a regular daily part of the classroom, do not count in evaluating whether the requirements of the item are met, *unless they are observed to interact very negatively with children.* For example, if a therapist, parent, or a director of a program comes into the classroom and interacts with children for short or irregular periods, these interactions do not count in scoring the item, unless they are negative with the children. But in programs where the usual daily staffing pattern includes different people as teaching assistants or "floater" staff (including parent volunteers in parent co-operatives or students working in lab school settings), these assistants should be counted as staff during the observation.

An observation period of at least 3 hours should be completed before scoring to ensure that a range of conditions, requiring varying types of staff responses, is observed. For example, the observer would want to see what interactions are like during both relaxed and more stressful times of the day and in routines and in play.

26.1.1a

26.1.1b

26.1.1a-b   Babies and toddlers kept separated are safe from one another, but do not have the opportunity to learn how to get along peacefully.

A closer look at each indicator

1.1   *Peer interaction,* as stated above, refers to the relationships children have with one another, not with adults. It includes how infants and toddlers play near one another, and, as they approach preschool age, how they play together, their communication, and whether they fight or get along peacefully.

The term *appropriate peer interaction* means the kinds of socializing that these youngest children are able to do, based on their developmental abilities, without being forced into situations that are beyond their social skills. Since infants and toddlers are not yet able to play cooperatively, they require a setting in which they are able to play alone, but near others, with the necessary protection of a supervising adult.

26.1.1c   Sitting "not-too-close" for lunch allows some social interaction. However, if children were required to spend much of the day at the table, they would miss opportunities to learn to play well together.

In classrooms where *little or no* appropriate peer interaction is *possible*, children are either kept separately or in extremely controlled groups so they cannot interact. (See photos 26.1.1a-c.) If allowed to interact, there is little support provided by staff or within the environment to help children get along with one another. Some examples are provided in the indicator. Other examples include:

- Children spend much of day at a table and are not free to play and move around, interacting with one another.
- Children are kept in individual playpens.
- No help is provided from adults to guide children in their interactions.
- There are too few toys so children must compete.

Score Indicator 1.1 "Yes" when appropriate interaction among children is rarely possible. This means that during all or the vast majority of the observation staff do not allow children to interact or that the environmental conditions make it impossible for the children to interact appropriately.

1.2   *Negative peer interaction* occurs when children are not getting along well. Examples would be grabbing or fighting over toys or space, biting, pushing, poking, or other physical or emotional harming of others. Since this type of behavior happens naturally with young children, constant supervision by staff is needed, with an immediate, appropriate response.

To score Indicator 1.2 "No," negative peer interactions cannot usually be ignored by staff. Ignored means that there is no response to comfort children who have become upset or hurt by others, nor is there a response to help the children who caused the upset. It is possible that some negative peer interactions will be missed by staff, because the behavior is sometimes hard to notice and staff are busy elsewhere. For example, a child might grab a toy from another child, and although this is not pleasant, no one gets very upset. This would not necessarily count as "staff ignoring" the problems, as long as staff respond most of the time, not missing issue after issue, and never missing an instance where children are really hurt.

For negative peer interactions to be **handled harshly** means that staff respond with shouting, handling children roughly, punishing, or labeling the offender as a "bad" child in any way. In other words, staff are modeling the behavior that they do not want from the children. Score this indicator "Yes" if even one instance of such a response is observed.

Score Indicator 1.2 "Yes" if negative peer interaction is ignored as the usual practice or handled harshly even once. Be sure to consider how all negative peer interactions were handled, throughout the observation to provide a sound basis for the score.

If no negative peer interaction is observed during the observation, and children are allowed to interact, score 1.2 "No."

3.1   **Peer interaction is possible** means that there are opportunities for children to play, communicate, and get along with one another. (See photos 26.3.1a-e.) The peer interaction that is possible must be considered appropriate (see Indicator 1.1) to give credit. Examples of how staff can make peer interaction possible are provided in the indicator. Other examples include:

- taking non-mobile infants out of cribs, playpens, swings, etc., and allowing them to play close to others, with staff supervision;
- providing considerable time in the schedule when mobile children are allowed to play freely and choose their own companions;
- maintaining a relaxed, rather than strict, atmosphere that makes children comfortable enough to interact with one another;
- helping children become involved with or near one another in play or routines;
- helping babies and toddlers play near one another, in small groups rather than all together;
- preventing children from being crowded into small areas; and
- providing enough materials and choices to avoid competition for toys.

Much of the day is defined in the "Explanation of Terms Used Throughout the Scale" in the ITERS-R on page 7.

Score Indicator 3.1 "Yes" when children are free to interact appropriately with one another in play, and in routines (for older babies and toddlers) for much of the day. If it is not possible for children to interact with one another for most of the time that they are awake and not involved in individual routine care, score this indicator "No."

26.3.1a During free play, a couch for two encourages toddlers to play near one another.

26.3.1b Placing non-mobile babies near one another for play allows simple interaction.

26.3.1c Including a child with a physical disability with peers requires that toys are accessible to every child.

26.3.1d Outdoors, these babies play near one another on a mat.

3.2 *Negative peer interaction* occurs when a child harms another child, emotionally or physically. For staff to *stop negative peer interaction* means that they notice and intervene to put an end to the negative behavior. (See photos 26.3.2a-c, next page.) This intervention must happen within a reasonable amount of time to keep things from getting out of control or to prevent a child being hurt. *Usually* means that staff intervene in at least 75% of observed instances of negative peer interaction. Furthermore, to give credit, staff can never fail to intervene in a prolonged occurrence where one child is really hurting another child. In addition, the intervention cannot be *harsh* (see Indicator 1.2).

Score Indicator 3.2 "Yes" when it is observed that staff stop most (75%) of the minor negative interactions between children, in which children are not really being hurt, and they stop all major problems. It is possible that staff will miss some of the negative interac-

26.3.1e These toddlers spend much of the day in free play. They can choose to play alone, or together, depending on preferences and interests.

26 Peer interaction

26.3.2a

26.3.2b

26.3.2a-c When children are given the freedom to play near one another, some problems will occur naturally due to undeveloped social abilities. It is up to the staff to intervene quickly and stop the problem.

tions that the observer notices. If negative interactions are major and recurring (causing a lot of hurt to a child) and frequently ignored or missed, then credit cannot be given. However, if only a few minor negative interactions are missed, or if they are resolved with no intervention from staff, credit can still be given.

26.3.2c

There may be times when the children being observed get along very well with one another. In this situation, the indicator may be scored "Yes," and the assumption is made that staff manage children's behavior well so there are few occurrences of negative behavior.

5.1. The intent of this indicator goes far beyond what is required in 3.2. Here staff must not simply stop negative interactions (without being harsh). Rather, they are required to help children develop positive interaction with peers. ***Positive peer interactions*** are seen when children play well next to, or with, one another, without interfering in the other child's play. Positive interactions are also seen when older infants and toddlers pleasantly participate in routines together, such as eating snack in a very small group, when appropriate.

To facilitate positive peer interaction means, first, that staff remember that the children are extremely limited in their social skills; second, that they arrange play and any group routines to avoid conflict and allow interaction; and finally, that they guide children through interactions with one another. (See photos 26.5.1a-c.) They help children achieve behavior that is within the range of what children will be able to do without facing impossible odds. Examples of setting up the environment to facilitate positive peer interactions include:

- Children are given lots of space so that they can choose to play alone if they wish, or play with another child, and do not have to compete for play space.

- There are plenty of toys and duplicates of favorite toys, so alternative choices are available when there is conflict.

26.5.1a Placing these young infants close to one another, and paying close attention, is a good introduction to getting along well with peers.

- Non-mobile children are moved to where they can be included in play with others and are still protected by staff.
- Times of stress, such as when children are tired or hungry, are minimized to limit grumpiness among children by careful scheduling of routines.
- Transitions are handled smoothly, and there is always an adult supervising children who may get into trouble with one another.

Examples of staff guiding children in their interactions are provided in the indicator. Other examples include:

- Children are not expected to share, except where sharing would be enjoyable, such as rocking in a rocking boat or rolling a ball back and forth to one another, with an adult who helps ensure that when one child rolls the ball, that child will get it back.
- Shy or isolated children are not expected to find friends to play with on their own, but with plenty of help from the staff.
- Staff remind children of the simple rules, and gently redirect them to more appropriate behavior (for example, by saying "Gentle touch" when redirecting baby from hair pulling; or "He has the toy now. You can use it when he is done with it" when redirecting child from grabbing a toy).

Score Indicator 5.1 "Yes" if examples of staff facilitating positive peer interactions through setting up the environment and of staff guiding children in their interactions are seen during the observation. Score "Yes" only if what is observed is a regular practice and not an unusual instance.

26.5.1b Setting up simple activities that toddlers can do together helps teach the beginning of how to cooperate. Close adult attention is required for successful learning.

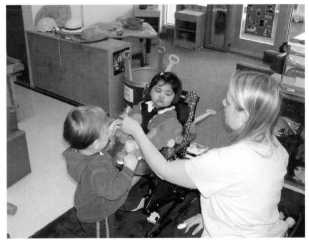

26.5.1c An adult is needed to help the two children use this toy together.

26 Peer interaction

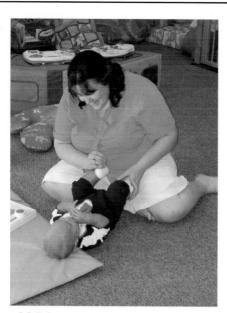

26.5.2b

26.5.2a

26.5.2c

26.5.2a-c Staff who are interested, gentle, appropriately affectionate, and cooperative give children powerful messages about positive social interaction.

5.2 To *model positive social interactions* means that staff are responsive, polite, interested, and cooperative with every person the children see them interacting with. This includes all children, other staff, parents, and others who become part of the children's environment.

Children copy what they see adults doing. If adults are physically and verbally aggressive with others, then it is likely that the children who see this will also act out the same behavior. When adults are kind, gentle, and respectful of others, children will be more likely to copy this type of behavior. It is often said, "Children do what we *do*, not what we *tell* them to do." This emphasizes the power of using modeling as a teaching tool.

Usually *staff model positive social interactions* when interacting with other adults. However, they are less likely to show children the same kind of respect. When staff ignore children, yell at them, boss them around, shout demands, spank or punish, show impatience, are cynical, tease to belittle, or do other things that the children find unpleasant, they are *not* modeling good social skills.

Of course, it is necessary for staff to maintain control in a group—to be the adult. But this can be done with respect, sincere interest, politeness, and gentle guidance. (See photos 26.5.2a-c.) When such positive social interactions are used consistently among all staff, then credit can be given for Indicator 5.2 (score "Yes"). To give credit, no staff member can be observed modeling negative social skills.

7.1. Because infants and toddlers are so focused on their own needs and interests, they can barely notice their effect on other children, let alone understand that their actions cause a reaction on the part of another child. (See photos 26.7.1a-c.) This is why we so frequently see a toddler shoving, or walking through, the place where another toddler is standing, and the child who has been knocked down usually will not have seen the danger in time to move. Similarly, we will see an infant pulling a bow in another child's hair, not realizing that that pretty object is attached to a child

26.7.1a Sharing the telephone cannot last long with these toddlers.

26.7.1b When they each want to use it alone, trouble begins.

who will suffer pain from that action. And of course, the infant with the bow will not know what is going to happen, and does not protect herself. It is up to staff to not just stop this type of peer interaction, but to help children begin to understand what is going on. Then, eventually, as they become older toddlers and preschoolers, they will have more of the understanding required to behave appropriately with others. This important teaching process is what is considered in this indicator.

When staff ***explain children's actions, intentions, and feelings*** to other children, they put into words why children have done something, what they intended to do, and why the other child responded in a particular way. The observer will usually see such explanations when children have difficulties with one another, but also at other times when emotions need to be explained.

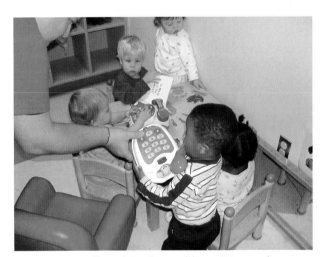

26.7.1c Staff explain the problem. "You each want your own phone. Here's another one for you to use."

It is important to listen carefully in order to hear what is being said to give credit. Examples of what might be heard include:

- "Bobby is crying. He's sad that his Mommy left. Maybe he will be happier if we look at the birds on the bird feeder."
- "Marta didn't knock you down on purpose. She was trying to get to the dolls. I'll help you up."
- "You are making Keisha angry. She wants to finish using the telephone before you can use it."
- "Move over here, Emma. See Jimmy? He wants to get by on the trike."
- "Nassar is so happy. He has a big smile."
- "Rachel wants you to throw the ball to her. See how she is reaching out her hands?"
- "Oh, that noise scared Tyler. I'll hold her so she isn't afraid."
- "Look out for Noah. He does not want you to fall on top of him."

- "He didn't step on your hand to hurt you, Evie. He was trying to sit with us. Let me see your finger. Look at Evie's finger, Jon. You stepped on it by mistake. Would some ice help?"

- "Look Nate, she wants to give you the piece of playdough. See how she is holding it out to you? Can you take it? Thank you, Ellen."

Simple statements such as "Look out," "Get out of her way," "He didn't mean it," or "You're okay" do not count as examples of the requirement, since they do not clearly explain sufficiently to children what has happened.

As the "Note for Clarification" for the indicator states on page 42 of the ITERS-R, the observer must see at least two instances in order to give credit. The two instances must be observed during the first 3 hours of the observation, and not later, if a longer observation is being completed.

7.2. In this indicator, staff help children notice the positive social interaction (pro-social behavior) that occurs around them. (See photo 26.7.2.) This is distinguished from staff helping children understand other children's actions, intentions and feelings required in 7.1. To ***point out and talk about*** means that the staff help children focus attention on the positive social interaction that other people do. It is important for the observer to listen carefully throughout the observation in order to hear staff communication needed to give credit. Examples of the practice are provided in the indicator. Additional examples of what staff might be heard saying follow:

- "Gillian just gave the telephone to Sarah. She's sharing the telephone!"

- "Thanks for moving over, Lisa. Now Cathy has a place to sit. See how Lisa moved to make a place for you Cathy?"

- "David's hugging Charlie. He wants Charlie to feel better. Hugs are nice."

26.7.2 When these toddlers hug one another, staff quickly notice and talk about how nice gentle hugs are.

- "Ms. Harris brought us our milk. She didn't want us to be thirsty. Thanks, Ms. Harris."

- "Thanks for helping to clean up, Jesse. See how Jesse helped put our blocks away?"

As the "Note for Clarification" for the indicator states, the observer must see at least one instance in order to give credit. The instance must be observed during the first 3 hours of the observation, and not later, if a longer observation is being completed.

27 Staff-child interaction

General information about this item

To really thrive, infants and toddlers require close, loving relationships with the adults who care for them. Such relationships allow the children to bond to, or form attachments with, their caring adults. (See photo 27A.) Such close relationships are shown to have a strong association with children's developmental success across a wide range of outcomes.

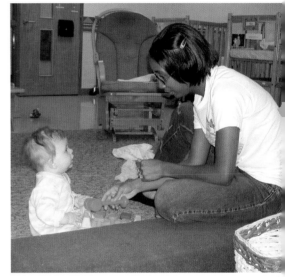

27A A close, loving relationship helps to ensure children's developmental success.

Since infants and toddlers are so dependent on adults for protection, opportunities for learning, and positive social-emotional relationships, the ITERS-R includes requirements about staff interactions with children in many items. For example, in Item 20, Dramatic play, at the excellent level of quality, it is required that "staff pretend with children in play." Similarly, in the good level of quality in Item 7, Meals/snacks, it is required that "staff talk with children and provide a pleasant time." These indicators clearly assess how staff relate to children. In many of the ITERS-R indicators, such as Item 7, Indicator 3.1, "Meal/snack schedule meets individual needs," it is the responsiveness of the adult to the child that determines whether this is true. In fact, interaction, or developing positive relationships, is one of the major areas that the ITERS-R examines in many items throughout the scale, along with protection and appropriate learning opportunities. The Interaction subscale has four items that look at how staff relate to children, each from a different perspective. It is in this item, however, that the ITERS-R focuses most specifically on staff-child interactions.

Information required for scoring the indicators in this item must be observed in order to score. No questions should be used to gather the information required to score this item. An observation period of at least 3 hours should be completed before scoring, to ensure that a range of conditions, requiring varying types of staff responses, is observed. For example, the observer would want to see what interactions are like during both relaxed and more stressful periods of the day.

For this item, *interaction* refers to the ways in which staff relate to the children. These interactions can be expressed through physical contact and other non-verbal communication, such as gestures, the kinds of touch staff use when holding or meeting children's needs, the focus of attention, or facial expressions. Interactions can also be expressed in the verbal communication that occurs between staff and children.

Interactions are classified as being negative, neutral, or positive. **Negative** interactions often carry messages of anger, coldness, disrespect, impatience, or unhap-

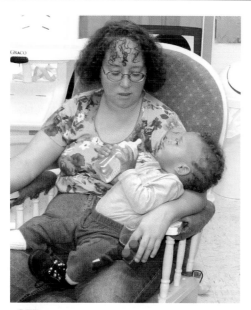 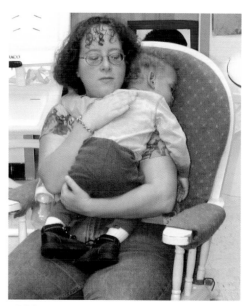

27B   **27C**

27B-C   This more neutral moment during feeding quickly turns into a positive interaction of comforting closeness.

piness. When received by others, they make the recipients feel less valuable, less competent, less appreciated, or less loved. ***Positive*** interactions are the opposite, carrying messages of being happy, content, relaxed, patient, respectful, and interested, helping the recipient to feel more valuable, competent, appreciated, and loved. *Neutral* interactions do not give strong messages of any type—they are neither harmful nor supportive. (See photos 27B-C.)

In the ITERS-R, the impact of negative interactions on the recipient is considered to be stronger than the impact of either positive or neutral interactions. Thus, for purposes of scoring, negative interactions should be given more weight because it takes many positive interactions to balance the effect of one negative interaction.

Interactions can also be characterized as ***warm*** or ***harsh***. Warm interactions may be expressed in appropriate physical contact, such as holding and cuddling or putting an arm around a child. Warmth can also be expressed by smiling, looking pleased, making eye contact, sharing an interest, or using a pleasant tone of voice. Harsh interactions may be expressed through rough physical contact or through verbal communication that reprimands, abruptly orders children about, shouts, or uses other unkind tones.

It helps to consider the climate of classroom interaction in terms of the warmth or coldness that the children feel, and then consider whether the setting is warm enough for each child to be comfortable. For example, think of each staff member as a heater, whose job it is to keep the classroom at a comfortable temperature. One might be extremely warm, putting out enough heat to keep the classroom warm enough, even though another staff member tends to be neutral or slightly cold in interactions. However, if one staff member is like an air conditioner in the room, often blasting out cold air, then it is unlikely that the warmer teacher would be able to counteract this effect on the classroom temperature.

It is likely that positive/warm, neutral, and negative/cold interactions will be observed in differing amounts. It is up to the observer to see the overall effect of all interactions on all children in the group.

When there are different staff members with different interaction styles, or if one staff member uses different types of interactions throughout the observation, the observer must see whether the overall interaction climate sufficiently meets the needs of the children.

In some cases, classrooms might assign a "primary caregiver" to each child, meaning that although there are several staff in the room, one staff member handles the needs of a specific smaller group of children, while other staff meet the needs of their own groups. The intention is to provide more personalized care. This is fine as long as all caregivers are fairly equal at providing high quality. However, problems with quality might occur when the staff are not equally skilled. Since requirements in the ITERS-R apply to all children in the group being observed (see ITERS-R page 6, "Scoring System") the average of what all children receive in the form of interactions must be considered. Thus, if one primary caregiver meets the requirements of the item, but the children in other primary-caregiver groups within the observed classroom do not regularly benefit from this, credit would not be given for the indicators that are not met by each of the staff.

In addition, be sure to observe the effects of adult interactions with any of the children on all the children. Remember that even when a negative interaction is directed at only one of the children, the others experience the interaction second-hand. The other children can become fearful or anxious, thinking that such negative interactions might be directed at them, or they might take such negative behavior as an example of how to act towards others.

In all items involving any type of interaction, *staff* refers to those adults who are in the classroom and work with the children daily (or almost daily), for a substantial portion of the day. This can include volunteers, if they are in the classroom for the required amount of time. Adults who are in the classroom for short periods of the day, or who are not a regular daily part of the classroom, do not count in evaluating whether the requirements of the item are met, *unless they are observed to interact very negatively with children.* For example, if a therapist, parent, or a director of a program comes into the classroom and interacts with children for short or irregular periods, these interactions do not count in scoring the item, unless the visitors are negative with the children. But in programs where the usual daily staffing pattern includes different people as teaching assistants or "floater" staff (including parent volunteers in parent co-operatives or students working in lab school settings), these assistants should be counted as staff during the observation.

A closer look at each indicator

1.1 *Impersonal* interaction is detached or disinterested. The "personal touch" that all of us enjoy so much is missing. Staff may be unresponsive and uninvolved with children, and thus might appear to have their minds on other things and not on the children. They might show that they do not share the children's interests or do not consider what children want to be important or necessary. Staff might ignore the children. They will not respond to what children need, or if they do, it is done in a mechanical way, where the child is handled like an object, not like a person. (See photos 27.1.1a-b, next page.)

Negative interaction is defined in the "General Information" section for this item. Usually an observer will be able to tell if an interaction is negative by watching the response of the child. But this is not always reliable. Inevitably there may be some

27.1.1a If staff rarely respond to children who are upset, interactions would be impersonal.

27.1.1b Fortunately, staff respond right away, so impersonal interactions do not occur.

interaction that a child perceives as being negative that was not negative at all. For example, if a staff member prevents a toddler from grabbing a toy from another child, even if the preventing was done in the nicest of ways, the child might respond by being upset. Thus, for the purpose of scoring this item, it is the staff negativity that we consider. We strongly consider the child's response, but tempered with the reasons for the staff action and whether it could have been done in a more positive way, under the circumstances.

Examples of indications of impersonal or negative interaction are provided as part of the indicator. Others include:

Impersonal

- ignoring or not answering a child's obvious cry or communication,
- paying little or no attention to the children's more subtle verbal or non-verbal communication attempts,
- providing routine care with little eye contact, talking to the child, or gentle treatment,
- rarely using children's names, or not knowing who children are,
- paying no attention when a child shows what he has done in play,
- not checking a child who is showing signs of being sick or very uncomfortable,
- continuing a group activity when it is clear that children are not interested,
- ignoring children when they compete over toys or hurt one another,
- not reacting to children's signs of being tired, hungry or needing to be changed,
- ignoring a child who shows a need for physical affection, or
- spending much time on tasks not involving the children.

Negative

- reprimanding a child who is crying,
- belittling children's fears,

- teasing a child who is upset or embarrassed,
- punishing a child rather than using a more positive approach,
- trying to make children do things they cannot really be expected to do,
- forcing a child to do something he or she does not want to do, when it is not absolutely necessary for protection,
- using a strict, unnecessarily restrictive approach,
- telling children "No" frequently,
- yelling at children,
- handling a child roughly, or
- using an angry or threatening facial expression or "look" to control children.

27.1.1c Some impersonal interaction will always occur, but it should be rare.

There will always be some ***impersonal interaction*** (lack of response) when staff are working with groups of children. However, such examples should not be observed regularly throughout an observation. They should be the infrequent exception, rather than the general behavior of the staff. (See photo 27.1.1c.)

Score Indicator 1.1 "Yes" if staff, on average, show a lack of response or personal involvement with the children, or if much negative interaction by staff is observed. This means that there is much ignoring of children, with many examples such as those listed above or many negative interactions observed.

1.2 ***Positive attention*** is staff attention to children that includes supportive and warm interaction. Such interaction is defined in the "General Information" section for this item.

All children deserve the same amount of positive attention from their caring adults. Each child needs to be loved, nurtured and supported. Staff who work with children can easily fall into the trap of liking one child more than another, and showing this in obvious or subtle ways. That child becomes a favorite, is held more, talked to more, and given more opportunities. Parents may also do this, causing problems with sibling rivalry. Professional staff, however, must ensure that the amount of positive attention they provide is evenly divided among all children, with no one child receiving more or less attention than another.

To give an ***uneven amount of positive attention*** means that some children do not get what they need for their well-being, and this is a sign of inadequate quality. To determine whether staff give ***an uneven amount of positive attention***, it is best to observe not only which children get attention but also which children do not. It also helps to notice the type of attention children are given, positive, neutral or negative. In some cases a staff member may give a favored child more positive attention, while others receive more neutral treatment.

Of course, in some cases, a child may get more attention because he or she demands more. The fussy baby may require more holding than the mobile child who is out and about, exploring the room. This might cause the observer to assume that one child is getting more positive attention that the other. However, positive attention can be given in ways other than just holding. To score the observer must consider the following:

- Are other forms of positive attention being used, such as commenting on what the child is doing or is interested in?

- If the staff gave more close attention, would this intrude on a child's play?

- When the child approaches the staff member, is there a pleasant interaction or is the child ignored?

- What is the proportion of positive, negative, or neutral attention each child receives?

- Are there any children who are not getting the attention they want or need?

- If a child appears to be a favorite, is this actually because staff are meeting children's differing needs for attention appropriately, and the child is not a favorite after all?

- Do children who cause more disruption in the class get the amount of positive attention they require?

- Are there any children who wander aimlessly, with little attention from staff throughout the day?

Score Indicator 1.2 "Yes" if there is a very large difference in the amount of positive attention that any child receives, to the detriment of the other children in the group. Smaller differences are acceptable due to differing child personalities, but no child should receive a far greater amount of positive attention than the rest of the group, and no child should receive far less. Do not score this indicator "Yes" if all children get similar amounts of inattention or negative attention.

1.3 ***Physical contact*** includes any instance of staff touching children. This includes contact to handle children during routines, to control children, or to show affection, interest, or support. Allowing the child to touch or get close to the staff is also a type of physical contact.

Warm physical contact is touch that shows appropriate affection, acceptance, and support to the children. (See photo 27.1.3a.) It is often gentle, but sometimes may be more energetic and playful, but never to the extent that it becomes unwanted by the child such as chasing or tickling that is not enjoyable to the child. (See photo 27.1.3b.) Examples include gentle hugs, patting, putting a hand on the child, picking the child up, softly wiping a child's face, or carefully putting the child down to prevent a bump.

Responsive physical contact is touch that appropriately answers what the child wants. (See photo 27.1.3c.) For example, if the child reaches up her arms, the touch she most likely wants is to be picked up. If the child holds onto the adult's legs, to hide behind the adult when a stranger is present, he most likely needs touch for reassurance and protection. If a child wiggles and squirms to get off the adult's lap, he probably wants to end the touching, and go off to do something else. If a baby is obviously not feeling well, she is unlikely to want the kind of touches associated with energetic, less gentle physical play. Continuing any physical affection a child does not want or enjoy, such as forcing a child to accept kisses, is not responsive.

Harsh physical contact is rough, often with the intention of controlling or hurting. Examples include grabbing and pulling a child; pushing a child away but not gently; any physical punishment such as slapping, squeezing, yanking, forcing; and using rough movements while attending to children's routine care needs. ***Harsh*** is not

Indicator

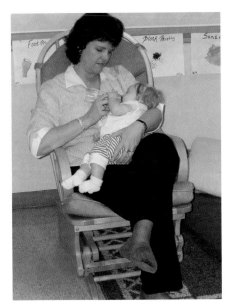

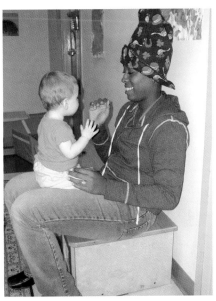

27.1.3a Warm physical contact includes gentle holding during feeding.

27.1.3b Warm and responsive physical contact that is more energetic is often observed during play.

27.1.3c How this staff member responds to this unhappy child will help the observer determine how physical contact is used.

to be confused with the energetic, playful touch that children often enjoy, such as whisking up into the air, although this touch would not be considered "responsive" if the child showed fear or discomfort.

Warm and responsive physical contact is usually very acceptable to the child, unless the situation is unpleasant, for example, a staff member gently cleans a cut or needs to look at an injury. Harsh physical contact is intrusive to the child. To score, the observer should watch not only how the staff use physical contact, but also how children respond. If the child pulls away or shows a facial expression that suggests dislike or discomfort, then the contact is perceived as being negative.

To score this indicator, pay attention to the kind of physical contact (touching) used by staff throughout the observation and especially to the children's responses to that contact. Keep track of when physical contact is used, the staff intention, and the children's responses to determine the usual practice.

Score Indicator 1.3 "Yes" when most of the physical contact is not warm or responsive or is harsh, as described above. Remember that this negative type of physical contact would need to be the usual practice, rather than the exception, to score "Yes."

3.1 The ***smiling, talking and affection*** required in this indicator are all meant to be positive for children, rather than neutral or negative. In other words, the child enjoys this action by staff. Therefore, the smiling must indicate real pleasure, without hidden threat or disinterest behind it. The talking cannot include reprimanding or controlling children; the affection must be welcomed by the children.

Occasional means that these actions on the part of staff are not necessarily frequent, but appear regularly, as a normal part of practice. They are not the unusual circumstance. (See photos 27.3.1a-e, next page.) The requirement that these interactions occur ***throughout the day*** can be judged based on what is seen and heard during the normal 3-hour observation. This amount of time is considered an appropriate sample from which to draw the conclusions needed to score.

27.3.1a

27.3.1b

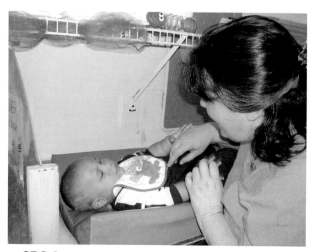

27.3.1c

27.3.1d

27.3.1e

27.3.1a-e Pleasant interactions should be seen during play and routines. They may be calm, supportive, exuberant, or interested, but neither negative or neutral.

To give credit for throughout the day (score "Yes"), the required interactions should be sprinkled relatively evenly across both play times and routines and *all* children should be likely to receive some.

3.2   For information on this indicator, see the "Note for Clarification" for this indicator on page 43 of the ITERS-R. As the note indicates, to ***respond sympathetically*** means that staff notice and validate a child's feelings, even if the child is showing emotions that are often considered unacceptable, such as anger, crying, or whining. (See photo 27.3.2.) The staff respond in a kind and gentle manner, not with rejection or anger. The feelings of the child should be accepted, although any inappropriate behaviors, such as hitting, biting, kicking, or throwing things, should not be allowed. Often, when a child's feelings are validated through a sympathetic response by staff, the problem a child is having is vastly reduced, and the problem can be solved more easily than if the staff had responded with anger or impatience. A negative response by staff only lets the child know that he or she is not understood and that no one cares.

27.3.2 This crying child receives quick, responsive comfort from staff.

A sympathetic response should be provided in most, but not necessarily all, cases. If children are able to solve minor issues for themselves, then staff response is not needed. For example, if a toddler falls down and makes a very small complaint ("Oh!"), and quickly gets up and moves on happily, no staff response is needed. A very strong sympathetic response, especially when attached to anxiety or fear, can be unsettling and give the child a message that does not reassure. Another example of when a sympathetic response might not be needed would be a baby who cries for a few seconds as part of going to sleep. The infant will not benefit from a sympathetic response that prevents settling down. However, if the child cried for a few minutes, then a sympathetic response would be needed.

It is rather typical for staff to respond sympathetically when they feel the child deserves such attention because of an acceptable problem. Usually staff respond sympathetically to a child who is hurt. However, sympathetic responses to children who are upset about something that staff do not believe deserves sympathy are more rare. For example, some staff might believe that the child needs to get used to a parent's leaving without crying. They believe that if they show sympathy, the child will never get used to the reality of life. Similarly, staff rarely give sympathy to the child who became angry and hit another child. Instead they react with rejection. However, such negative responses to children's needs or feelings compound the problem, because children do not learn the more appropriate behavior, and in addition, learn that their feelings are considered either "bad" or unimportant. Thus, staff are required to respond sympathetically to all children who are really upset.

Indicator 3.2 is not true (score "No") when staff most often discount children's feelings as being unnecessary, inappropriate, or incorrect. This is usually shown by ignoring the child, reprimanding the child, or punishing for what are perceived as unacceptable feelings. The sympathetic response must be the usual practice in order to score "Yes." As the "Note for Clarification" for this indicator states, there can be some responses that are missed, "but if minor problems persist, or if staff ever respond in a negative manner, give no credit for this indicator."

3.3   The meaning of the term ***harsh*** is provided in the "General Information " section for this item and also, with regard to physical contact, in Indicator 1.3. Since

27.3.4a

27.3.4b

27.3.4a-b It is the little unnecessary hugs or touches that show these children how much they are valued.

harsh treatment of children has never been proven to put a permanent stop to inappropriate behavior, and sets adults against children, creates anger or hurt in the child, may lead to child abuse, discourages the use of more appropriate teaching, and presents an antisocial message to children, this indicator requires that **no** harsh staff-child interaction is observed. Not even one instance of verbal or physical interaction that is harsh can be observed to give credit for this indicator.

3.4   **Warm and responsive physical contact** is defined in Indicator 1.3. **Warm and responsive physical affection** is touch where the main purpose is to show love or appreciation of the child. It goes beyond the physical contact that is required to provide routine care or to simply move or control children, which should be positive, as required for Indicator 1.3 to be scored "No." For example, with regard to routine care, a diaper can be changed with physical contact that is warm and responsive, but when the staff member adds a little hug as she picks up the baby, or counts his toes, touching each one playfully, warm and responsive physical affection is being observed. Similar physical affection is seen when a teacher helps a toddler to sit in his chair to work on a puzzle, and then adds a soft pat on the head before she moves to join another child. (See photos 27.3.4a-b.)

To give credit for this indicator, some extra touches, added for the purpose of showing children they are valued and appreciated, are required in routines or in play.

Examples of such behavior are provided in the indicator in the ITERS-R and above. Others include:

In routines, staff:

- stroke the baby's head while feeding the bottle,
- pat the baby's back softly while she is going to sleep,
- give a big hug after buttoning the child's coat, before the child runs off,
- pat child's clean cheeks after wiping the toddler's face, or
- pick up and hug the child at greeting.

In play, staff:

- cuddle a child who has taken a break from play and is watching others,

- put arm around child in small group activity,

- allow child to run into her arms during active physical play,

- pat child on back as she shows her scribble picture,

- smooth a playing child's hair, but not because it is messy, or

- place head close to child's while looking at birds on bird feeder together.

The physical contact does *not* always have to be extremely obvious to the observer. An example of obvious contact is when a teacher enthusiastically hugs or cuddles with a child, and the contact lasts for more than just a second or two. However, affectionate contact is also seen in the more subtle, less obvious actions such as the quick, unnecessary touches of children (smoothing hair, touching a hand or shoulder, sitting close enough to touch, holding hands, or gently touching while guiding or controlling a child). Such touches let children know the teacher is present and supportive.

Some means that such physical affection on the part of staff are not necessarily frequent, but appear regularly, as a normal part of practice. They are not an unusual circumstance. The requirement that these interactions occur **throughout the day** can be judged based on what is seen and heard during the normal 3-hour observation. This amount of time is considered an appropriate sample from which to draw the conclusions needed to score.

To give credit for this indicator (score "Yes"), the required interactions should not be unusual and should be observed at least during play or routines, and all children are likely to receive such treatment, even if it is not observed.

5.1   *Positive staff-child interaction* is discussed in the "General Information" section for this item. Examples are provided in the indicator in the ITERS-R on page 43. The requirement that these interactions occur **throughout the day** can be judged based on what is seen and heard during the normal 3-hour observation. This amount of time is considered an appropriate sample from which to draw the conclusions needed to score.

To give credit for **frequent**, there must be many pleasant, supportive interactions observed between the staff and the children. The many interactions may be staff-initiated, or in response to children's initiations. They must be the usual practice that is easily observed at just about any time. (See photos 27.5.1a-e, next page.) The positive interactions must outweigh the neutral, and there can be no negative interactions observed. The required interactions must be observed during both routines and play, and all children should be recipients, to score this indicator "Yes."

5.2   In an infant/toddler classroom, sometimes it seems that the requirements of this indicator would be impossible to meet—one in which everyone seems to be relaxed, with pleasant voices and frequent smiling. There always is crying and upset with very young children as they communicate their needs in the most effective way they know. However, in a classroom that is "good in quality," where children do not have to wait too long to have their needs met, where there are enough staff who know how to soothe or satisfy all children, where children are well protected and can learn, scoring "Yes" for this criteria is entirely possible, because the indicator uses the word **usually**. (See photo 27.5.2, on page 345.) Although this term means 75% of the time in some items, it is defined in the "Explanation of Terms Used Throughout the Scale" (page 8 of the ITERS-R) as the common or prevalent prac-

27.5.1a

27.5.1b

27.5.1c

27.5.1d

27.5.1e

27.5.1a-e Positive interactions with staff occur frequently for these children.

tice observed, one that is carried out with only a few lapses. Thus a percent rule is not provided for **usually** in this indicator.

Usually, for this indicator, means most of the time for each child and for each staff member. It is expected that one child or another will have a time of upset, and there will be times when staff are not relaxed. However, to score 5.2 "Yes" the overall tone or feeling perceived throughout the observation should be one of satisfying, interesting, and pleasant experiences for both staff and all children, both in routines and play. The observer must be able to consider special circumstances, such as the presence of a new child in the group who might be more upset than usual, as long as staff handle the child appropriately in a soothing manner within the confines of what is possible for the child. Do not score "Yes" if stress and upset are not quickly resolved under normal circumstances.

27.5.2 Although there may be a few short hectic periods, staff and children are relaxed and happy most of the time.

5.3 To understand the requirements for this indicator, the observer must be familiar with terms used in Indicators 1.3 and 3.4. This indicator requires staff to use physical contact or physical affection in a positive way to show **warmth**, which gives a positive message of affection, encouragement, appreciation, interest, or support to the child. (See photos 27.5.3a-b.)

To give credit, any such physical contact must be used **appropriately**—the contact is pleasant and not intrusive to the child or likely to result in problems. Such contact can often be identified by watching the child's response. Some children, for example, will not want to be hugged tightly, kissed, gently tickled, or cuddled. If the child does not pull away or show a facial expression of dislike or discomfort, then the contact is perceived as being positive. Overly enthusiastic physical contact often causes things to get out of control, and staff are then unable to calm children without having to resort to negative interaction. For example, staff allowing children to "climb all over them" would not be considered appropriate if it led to rough play where people got hurt. And of course, any physical contact considered sexual in nature would not be appropriate.

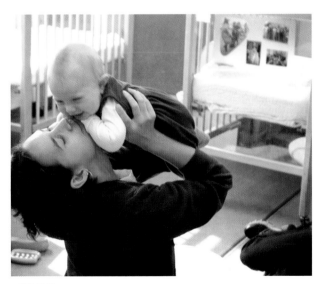

27.5.3a

27.5.3a-b Physical warmth can be very obvious to the observer or seen in more subtle examples.

27.5.3b

27.7.1a

27.7.1b

27.7.1c

27.7.1a-c Staff know that when this baby wakes up, he needs gentle treatment, until he becomes fully alert and ready to play.

27.7.1d

27.7.1e

27.7.1d-e The staff in these classrooms recognize and respond appropriately to children's needs.

There is a range of what is acceptable to meet the requirements of this indicator, as long as it is positive from a child's point of view and does not lead to rough play or misinterpretation.

To give credit for **throughout the day,** staff should be observed providing this type of contact regularly and frequently throughout the 3-hour time in the classroom. Not all children need to be observed receiving the same amount of physical contact. However, warm physical contact that includes holding and patting should be part of what all children are observed to receive during the observation.

7.1   In indicators at lower levels of quality, the term **responsive** has been used to label a type of physical contact used with children. In this indicator, at the excellent level of quality, **responsive** goes beyond physical contact, and is applied not only to the characteristics that differ from child to child, but also within one child at any specific time. For example, one baby might be quick to startle or become upset, while another might be more complacent. These two babies would obviously do better with different styles of interaction from the staff, with the sensitive baby requiring calmer treatment and the complacent baby being able to enjoy a more active approach. In addition, in the morning a toddler might be clingy, while after a nap in the afternoon, she is ready to go off and conquer the world. Obviously different interaction approaches would be required for the same child, based on her mood.

When staff modify how they treat a child, based on each child's current physical and emotional state, they are providing **interaction that is responsive to each child's moods and needs**. (See photos 27.1a-e.) Examples of such interaction are provided in the indicator. Others include:

When responding to changes in one child

- being calmer with child who has become fearful or angry,
- slowing down for child who was running but then stops to inspect something,
- ending looking at book when child gets wiggly,
- hurrying through diaper change for toddler who dislikes the procedure,
- turning wiping nose into a fun game for child who resists, and
- being reassuring and supportive to child who is uncertain about new experience.

When responding to differing children

- using louder voice with more resilient child and quieter voice with child who is more sensitive,
- cuddling tired child outdoors while others do active play,
- providing closer supervision to more impulsive child,
- encouraging active child to use active play equipment in room,
- actively encouraging social child to join in group play while allowing less social child to observe until comfortable, then gradually encouraging child into group,
- sitting closer to child with more difficulties feeding self while giving more skillful children more independence, and

- because of differing transition to sleep patterns, putting one child in crib for nap while still awake and rocking another to sleep before putting in crib.

Give credit for Indicator 7.1 (score "Yes") when all children are not handled in the same way, and staff respond appropriately based on needs and mood of each child.

7.2 In many cases, staff "do" things abruptly to children, such as picking them up, pulling a pacifier out of their mouth, taking away a toy, wiping their nose, handing them to another person. Usually these are done as part of the tasks required in routines, but they may also be done in carrying out play. If an adult had to experience such treatment without warning or explanation, it is very likely that the adult would complain or feel insulted or mistreated. This indicator, at the excellent level of quality, requires that staff approach children from a more sensitive point of view, letting them know ahead of time what will be happening, and giving them some time to adjust to whatever will be done to them.

27.7.2 This staff member tells the baby, "Night, night," and supports his head, before moving him to his crib.

Such treatment usually requires some kind of communication on the part of the adult to let the child know what will be happening. (See photo 27.7.2.) Examples are provided in the indicator. Additional examples include staff:

- saying "Can we put your pacifier away now? Are you ready to let go?" and wait for a positive response before taking it from the child's mouth;

- holding out hands towards child, letting him read the gesture before picking him up;

- asking the toddler if her Mom can leave yet, when the child is having trouble separating, and encouraging the mother to stay until the child shows she is ready;

- asking the baby if he is ready to go to sleep before picking him up and putting him in the crib, and giving the child time to process the idea; and

- holding out a hand when asking the child to give up a toy, and respecting child's response whenever possible.

Usually, for this indicator, means most of the time for each child. It is not likely that every child's wishes will be honored and each task that must be done with each child handled sensitively. For example, a child who dislikes having his diaper changed will not be likely to drop his toy and eagerly head for the diapering table when the teacher explains what will be happening. However, to meet the requirements of the indicator, the explanation should be given, and the experience made as palatable as possible for the child.

Much of the evidence needed to score this indicator will be observed in what staff say to children or in the nonverbal communication they use. When staff talk frequently to children, describing what is going on as it happens, and showing a response to the child's reaction, the requirements of this indicator are being met.

28 Discipline

General information about this item

Discipline carries many meanings in our society. Some interpret the word to mean "punishment." To others, it carries the meaning of "guidance." In all cases the intention of discipline is to help children learn how to behave according to the established rules of conduct. In this item, ***discipline*** means the methods used by staff to manage children's behavior.

For young infants, many of us wonder how this item could be applied. Infants do not usually have the behavioral issues that require discipline found in older children, who can fight, yell, ignore requests, or act in a destructive way. Nevertheless, people do discipline infants. For example, some people do not pick up an infant when he is crying because they believe he will become spoiled. This is actually a form of discipline, because it is a method that people use to manage a child's behavior. However, once infants begin to move about and start getting into things, once they start becoming more independent and able to walk away from an adult who wants to impose an unwanted action upon them, discipline issues grow.

The perceived need for certain types of discipline depends on the adult's expectations for the child. ***Expectations*** for behavior are what staff think children should be capable of doing successfully. These expectations determine what they try to get children to do and how they handle non-compliance. There are many kinds of expectations for what children should know, understand, and be able to do intellectually, physically and socially. Different adults may have different expectations for the same child; some will expect more and some will expect less. It is important to relate expectations to where children are in their actual development, to what they can really understand and do.

Thus, staff who work with infants and toddlers should understand that children learn and develop gradually. Adults cannot expect infants and toddlers to be "instant" preschoolers, or to act older and more mature than they really are. Expectations are ***inappropriate for the age and developmental level*** when staff think that children should be able to do what they cannot yet actually do. ***Inappropriate expectations*** can also come from staff thinking children are unable to do what they actually can do.

Inappropriate expectations, or when young children are expected to do what older children or adults can do, have been shown to be the reason why many adults mishandle children. Adults who misinterpret children's behavior as defiance often discipline them harshly or too strictly, sometimes leading to child abuse. If an adult thinks that a child is able to do something but does not do it, the conclusion too often is that the child is just being negative or disobedient. Thus children are punished with the expectation that they will obey next time, but when they are not able to do so, stronger punishment is used. In fact, most often the children do not do what is required of them because they have not yet developed the ability to do so.

It is not impossible to get the typical infant or toddler to do what an adult thinks is necessary, even though the expectation does not really match the child's developmental level. For example, toddlers can be taught to sit and be quiet for long periods of time if the adult works very hard to do this. However, the effort that is required for a toddler to comply with such a demand makes the child lose out in other developmental areas. If the child has to sit quietly for long periods, this means she will not get to do all the more valuable things needed to develop socially, physically, and intellectually. By demanding behavior that does not match the child's needs, the adult who forces it takes away other options needed for developmental success. And for the less compliant child, the results will be disastrous, with a cycle of negative interaction growing that creates emotional issues that last the child's lifetime.

Discipline requires, first, appropriate expectations of the children and, second, adult guidance that has long-term positive effects, rather than short-term positive effects that lead to long-term problems. At the lowest level of quality, discipline is either too strict or too permissive, so that children have few opportunities to receive the kinds of guidance that allow them to learn to manage their own behavior within reasonable limits. For a child to develop self-discipline takes time, learning, and maturation on the part of the child, as well as a lot of patience and effort on the part of the adults who care for the child. But all of this is well worth it, because once self-discipline is a part of the child, less external guidance is needed to enforce rules. Children who master self-discipline can follow rules on their own and make their own choices about how they will act, based on their understanding of how their actions affect themselves and others.

Discipline that is too strict allows adults to manage the behavior of most infants and toddlers through fear or harshness. This may appear to work in the short term, but at some point in the lives of most children, fear is no longer something that controls them. They learn that they can behave inappropriately when there is no one watching or no one stronger around to control them. They do not develop self-discipline because they have learned to rely on discipline from outside.

Discipline that is too permissive, or lax, does not help children learn that they are responsible for their actions. Often, adults who do not exert reasonable control fail to make clear to children what the rules and expectations for behavior are. Without proper guidance, children do not learn self-discipline either.

There is a middle ground between the extremes of **strict** and **lax** discipline that has been shown to work best in helping children develop the skills required for eventual self-discipline. In this middle ground, rules are clear, expectations for behavior are age- and developmentally appropriate, and guidance is non-punitive and educationally sound. Children need to learn about rules, limits, and being responsible. But these behaviors cannot be forced upon them with long-term success.

At the higher levels of quality in this item, the emphasis is on teaching self-discipline to children in a realistic way—without demanding what children are not yet able to do. In addition, strategies are required for minimizing situations that lead to problems with infants and toddlers, and for encouraging behavior that is safe and productive.

In this item, **staff** refers to those adults who are in the classroom and work with the children daily (or almost daily). This can include volunteers, if they are in the classroom for a substantial amount of time. Adults who are in the classroom for short periods of the day, and who are not a regular daily part of the classroom, do not count in evaluating whether the requirements of the item are met, *unless they are observed to interact very negatively with children.* For example, if a therapist, parent, or a director of a program comes into the classroom and interacts with children for short or irregular periods, these interactions do not count in scoring the item, unless they are negative with the children. But in programs where the usual daily staffing pattern includes different people as teaching assistants or "floater" staff (including parent volunteers in parent co-operatives or students working in lab school settings), these assistants should be counted as staff during the observation.

Information required for scoring all indicators in this item, except Indicator 7.3, must be observed in order to score. Questions should be used only to supplement or confirm uncertainties, and to gather information needed to score.

An observation period of at least 3 hours should be completed before scoring. This is to ensure that a range of conditions, requiring varying types of staff responses, is observed. For example, the observer should see the discipline methods used during both relaxed and more stressful periods of the day. Keeping notes throughout the observation is helpful when deciding on a score.

A closer look at each indicator

1.1   **Strict** discipline is that in which any severe methods are used to control and punish infants and toddlers. These methods are associated with hurting children either physically or emotionally. Such methods are considered harsh and which, if frequently used, have been shown to be both harmful and ineffective in helping children develop self-discipline and positive feelings about themselves. (See photos 28.1.1a-c.)

28.1.2a   Any type of physical punishment would be considered a severe method.

28.1.2b

28.1.2b-c   Isolating any infant or toddler in "time out" is considered using a severe method. The observer must determine whether the child is sitting alone by choice or whether he is in "time out."

28.1.2c

Usually, staff use harsh methods of controlling children when they lose their own control and become angry, causing them to handle children in a way that they would never want to be handled themselves. If children acted in the same way, they would certainly be punished. Strict discipline is also used when the adult forces her will on a child when it is not really called for. A frequently-seen example is the staff member who angrily tells a child to stop crying when the child is upset about being left by her mother, saying, "Be quiet. There will be no crying here. You need to get over it and behave." Another common example is the staff member who says about the baby, "Just let him cry. Don't pay any attention. He is just trying to get what he wants."

Examples of strict discipline of infants and toddlers include:

Physical punishment:

- hitting, spanking, biting back, pinching, yanking, or pushing,
- throwing into a crib or onto a cot,
- burning with hot water, hot stove, or cigarette,
- exposing to cold or other discomforts,
- tying up or holding very tightly,
- having another child hit or physically punish a child, and
- washing a child's mouth out with soap or putting "hot sauce" on tongue

Other **severe methods** would include:

- isolating any infant or toddler for any period of time due to perceived bad behavior, or isolating a 2-year-old child for longer than just a few minutes, such as with "time out," standing in the corner, being made to eat alone, sitting in the corner, confining in a closet, or having to stay on a cot or mat;
- embarrassing, teasing, or taunting a child;
- yelling or shouting at a child;
- withholding food, drink, or sleep;
- restricting a child from an activity, such as keeping a child inside at outside time;
- forcing a child to eat or drink something he or she does not like; and
- forcing a child to repeat any disagreeable task numerous times, such as walking across the classroom over and over to make the child remember not to run.

There are certainly other harsh methods that are used to discipline infants and toddlers. The observer should watch carefully to be sure to understand how discipline is handled.

When **discipline is so lax that there is little order or control,** staff generally pay little or no attention to children's behavior or the methods that they use to maintain order are not effective. Examples of **little order or control** include constantly allowing children to endanger themselves or others, or to destroy materials and equipment. Children are often allowed to hurt other children or the staff, destroy toys and materials, or engage in unsafe activities, all with little or no effective intervention on the part of the staff.

Naturally, there will be times when control is less successful, but staff should be able to re-establish control without having to use strict discipline.

This indicator is to be scored based on the prevalent discipline practices observed during the 3-hour observation. If no harsh discipline methods are observed, if it is obvious that such methods would never be used, and if discipline permits staff to handle children in a reasonable way, score Indicator 1.1 "No." If it is difficult to tell whether or not strict discipline is ever used, ask staff the question provided as part of the item. However, what has been observed should carry most of the weight in scoring. If much of the observation is characterized by overly strict or lax discipline, and either appears to be the prevalent practice, score Indicator 1.1 "Yes."

1.2   Examples of **severe methods** are provided in Indicator 1.1. This indicator should be scored "Yes" if any such methods are ever observed being used or reported to be used with the children.

3.1   If *no* **physical punishment** *or* **severe discipline** is observed and staff report it is never used (in response to the question in the ITERS-R), score "Yes." (See Indicator 1.1 for definitions.)

3.2   To **maintain enough control to prevent problems** requires staff to watch carefully and intervene to stop infant and toddler involvement in dangerous or harmful behavior. Problems include children hurting one another or adults, endangering themselves, or being very destructive.

Usually means that staff maintain the control required to keep children from getting involved in problems most of the time, with only a few exceptions during the observation. The term *usually* is defined on page 8 of the ITERS-R to "indicate the common or prevalent practice observed, that is carried out with few lapses." This means that staff actively supervise the children and minimize being involved in activities that prevent them from supervising the children.

Staff should not be observed being overly restrictive with children to give credit for **maintaining enough control**. The amount of control should be appropriate to the developmental abilities and expectations of the children. For example, if a toddler is observed to be tearing the page of a book, staff would not necessarily be out of control of children, because toddlers tend to experiment with paper to see what is possible to do with it. One instance of inappropriate tearing would be acceptable, but if all books were torn up and unusable, this might certainly be a sign that control was lacking. Since the requirement of *usually* is given some flexibility in scoring, the relatively small amount of destructive behavior should be evaluated along with whatever the usual practice is.

Often observers are tempted to accept more harmful behavior when children who have less physical self-control are in the group. For example, if toddlers or children with behavioral disabilities are present, the observer may be tempted to allow more hurting. However, this is not acceptable in scoring this indicator because no children should be expected to accept being hurt, but rather should expect to be protected by the staff. It is the responsibility of the staff to protect the children, and children must know that they are in a safe place where they will not be hurt by others.

Score "Yes" if there are few problems observed during the observation.

28 Discipline

The term *expectations* is discussed in the General Information section for this item.

Realistic expectations based on age and abilities of children are appropriate expectations. Examples are provided in the indicator. Realistic expectations consider the age and developmental stage of a child when determining how the environment will be set up and what demands will be placed on a child. One result of realistic expectations would be "childproofing" the environment in which a mobile infant or toddler spends time. Sensible adults recognize that infants and toddlers are curious little explorers, who have not yet developed knowledge of the world needed for self-protection. Another result of realistic expectations would be to closely supervise toddlers playing near one another and to be sure there are enough toys, because toddlers are learning about possession and must do so before they can ever be expected to start sharing.

Unrealistic expectations demand too much or too little of the children. They allow adults to encourage baby behaviors far beyond the baby years. Or they let adults forget how young an infant or toddler really is, and to expect too much. Examples of unrealistic expectations that overestimate what children should be capable of, include expecting infants and toddlers to:

- do without their comfort objects, such as pacifiers or "blankies,"
- be able to control their emotions, without crying, having tantrums, or getting upset,
- understand and respond appropriately or quickly to what they are asked to do,
- sit quietly in a large group for any amount of time without someone wanting to leave,
- understand and avoid dangers, such as busy streets, high unprotected places from which falls could happen, sharp objects, and poisons,
- understand the effects of their actions, for example, if they climb up on a chair they might fall or if they grab another child they will cause the child to be angry or hurt,
- have mature social skills, such as sharing, taking turns, and cooperating, and
- have self-help skills before they are ready, such as using the toilet, eating without making a mess, or cooperating at naptime.

Unrealistic expectations that underestimate what children should be able to do are also harmful to children's development. If expectations do not challenge children, the children are less likely to progress well. Believing that a baby will grow up just fine as long as she is not wet, hungry or tired leads to unrealistic expectations that hold a child back developmentally. Examples of such low expectations would be that infants and toddlers do not need:

- adults to talk to them and explain things, even though they cannot talk themselves,
- books to look at and to have an adult read to them, even though babies mouth books and cannot read,
- many different kinds of toys to play with that challenge but do not frustrate,

- to go outdoors almost every day, even though they may seem so fragile,

- to explore and find out about the world, even though they cannot walk or keep themselves safe, or

- many positive interactions with other children, even though they do not have the social skills to get along with their peers.

Of course, among infants and toddlers of the same age there will be differences in what can be expected of a child. There is great developmental variation among typically developing children of the same age, and children with disabilities may not have developed all the same abilities as their typically developing peers. Realistic expectations should take all these differences into consideration.

Indicator 3.3 is true (score "Yes") when the expectations are **generally realistic** for the children in the group. This means that *most* of what each child is required to do or understand during the observation matches the child's abilities. No children are under a great deal of stress to perform what is too difficult, nor are any children unchallenged to the extent that their development is being compromised.

The term **generally** is much like the term **usually**. It means the normal practice, with only a few lapses. Do not score "No" if there are only a few examples of inappropriate expectations observed, especially if these do not cause significant problems for the children. For example, children may be asked to sit for longer than is optimal at feeding time, but this does not cause big problems, resulting in adults mistreating children or children suffering.

28.5.1a Problems are minimized when children are not crowded and have plenty of choices of interesting activities.

5.1 Certainly, the best discipline strategies prevent problems from even coming up, or at least minimize problems that are likely in groups of infants and toddlers. Staff in a program that is **set up to avoid conflict and promote appropriate interaction** understand what very young children are able to do well and what causes problems among them. They then arrange the children's environment to allow children to get along well with one another, without unnecessary restriction or "booby-traps" that cause difficulties. (See photos 28.5.1a-b.) Some discipline strategies that are preventative include:

- *Maintaining a dependable routine*

  More problems are likely, and more discipline is needed, when children are grumpy. If reliable classroom routines that meet the children's individual needs are in place, then children do not become stressed and irritable. For example, a reliable schedule means that the schedule is relaxed, individualized for infants (and younger toddlers if needed), and dependable. Children eat at regular times, they get rest when needed, and routines are not handled in a regimented way. All of these practices help keep young children from becoming irritable or stressed, so discipline problems are less frequent.

- *Having enough staff and coordinating their tasks*

  In rooms with babies and toddlers, much staff time must be used to deal with individual routine needs, such as diapering.

28.5.1b Small groups, supervised closely by a staff member, help prevent problems.

In a room where there are four children to one adult, much of the time is actually spent with a ratio of one adult to one child and no adult to three others. As groups become larger, and more than one staff simultaneously attempt to do tasks that require significant individual attention, the numbers of less-well supervised children increase. Therefore, it is important to set up the program with sufficient staff to complete all required work, and for those staff to coordinate their work, to ensure that all children are adequately supervised at all times. For example, one staff member should not set out cots while another is changing a child's diaper, because this would leave too many children minimally supervised. Children may get into trouble with one another unless a very restrictive approach was used to control them.

- *Setting up spaces to meet children's differing needs*

  In infant and toddler rooms, there are inevitably children who are likely to get "run over" by the more mobile or active children, and there are mobile, active children who get into trouble when they disrupt the play of others or become a danger. Differing needs and abilities must be considered so that rooms are arranged to provide quiet and active spaces, where children will be able to act appropriately without getting into trouble.

- *Keeping children busy, challenged, and interested*

  Many strategies focus on avoiding problems by keeping children interested and busy. For example, having many attractive materials and activities for children to choose from each day, with new things added regularly, helps keep children engaged so there are fewer problems. Also, staff make sure children have lots of time for active play so they can use their energy in a positive way.

- *Avoiding competition and crowding*

  Infants and toddlers do not do well with competition. They become aggressive or hurt, and they do not have the social skills needed to solve the problems that come with having to compete. Therefore, if staff provide plenty of materials and duplicates of popular toys, then children do not have to compete over things. Staff also ensure that children are not crowded, are not lined up, or grouped closely together in other ways. This helps minimize fights over territory and possessions.

Score Indicator 5.1 "Yes" if the program is set up to avoid problems and thus runs smoothly.

5.2   ***Positive methods of discipline*** are those that allow staff to control and guide children without harming them, emotionally or physically. These methods are more likely to pay off in the long term to help children learn self-discipline (how to behave positively) and to cause less anger and hurt. Positive methods of discipline do not include what is typically thought of as punishment. Isolating infants or toddlers using "time out" is interpreted by such young children as being a punishment. Thus it is not counted as a positive method and should never be used with children under 2 years of age. Examples of non-punitive discipline methods are provided as part of the indicator on page 44 of the ITERS-R.

Redirection

Redirection is, by far, the most effective and positive means of guiding infants and toddlers, because their actions are not usually determined by the kinds of under-

28.5.2a   **28.5.2b**   **28.5.2c**

28.5.2a–c The positive method of redirection is used to solve the problem of two children who both want to use the same toy.

standing that an older child or adult will have learned. They are much more reactive and self-centered in their actions, not understanding that what they do might be dangerous or have an effect on others. So the best method to use is one in which they learn what to do, not just what not to do. **Redirection** means that when a child acts inappropriately (doing something not wanted by others), staff help the child focus on something else to do that is appropriate to achieve his or her goal. (See photos 28.5.2a–c.) For example, if a toddler grabs a doll from another child, staff point out that there are plenty of the same dolls to use in the baby bed and help the child get one of those instead. Or if a child is throwing toys and staff recognize that the child really wants to practice throwing, they encourage her to throw bean bags into a box. If a child is wandering aimlessly (and heading for trouble), staff help him to become involved in an activity he enjoys. If a child climbs on furniture, staff redirect her to another acceptable activity, such as climbing on a safe piece of active physical play equipment. Giving alternatives to aggression that are peaceful, such as touching gently rather than pulling another child's hair, is also an example of redirection.

Intervening and working it out

Sometimes staff can solve problems that come up between older toddlers by suggesting a solution, for example, by telling them who will ride a tricycle first and starting a "waiting list" for turns. The children then go along with the "judge's" decision and a conflict is avoided. Both children are happy with the solution.

Intervention by an adult can also result in punitive action that does not teach a positive way to solve problems. For example staff might see a toddler grabbing a doll from another child, and the tussle for possession causes a fight. A staff member intervenes and says, "If you two cannot share the doll, then I will put it away." The children cry harder as the staff member takes the doll and puts it up high on a shelf.

In some cases, the solution may not be satisfying for a child but it enforces an appropriate rule that protects others. In the example just given where the toddlers are fighting for the doll, the staff member might say, "Jasmine had the doll. She was not finished playing with it. You cannot take the doll from her. Here is another doll you can use." The other toddler might continue to want the doll held by Jasmine and not be satisfied with the solution. In this case, the way to continue with the positive method would be to reassure the child, accepting his feelings, and help him to find some other fun activity to do (redirection).

Non-punitive methods must be used ***effectively*** if they are to ensure that children get along well in the group, not be dangerous to themselves or others, and not be destructive in any way. ***Effectively*** means that the non-punitive methods work reasonably well to maintain the level of control of children's behavior that is necessary for order and safety in a classroom.

For any method to be effective, staff may need to follow up with extra attention, help, and guidance. For example, if staff ask 2-year-olds to "use your words" to tell another child to stop annoying them, the staff must observe to be sure the children's words have the desired effect. If the child who is doing the annoying pays no attention to the children's words, the adult must step in to call the child's attention to the verbal request and to help the child engage in constructive activity.

The observer should be careful to objectively judge the effect of the ***non-punitive*** methods used by staff. In many cases, staff may choose a method that the observer would not have chosen. If the method used by staff is non-punitive and effective in managing the children's behavior, credit should be given (score "Yes"), even though the observer might have handled the problem in a different way.

If there are no discipline problems observed and punitive methods are never used, obviously the discipline methods being practiced are working well, so score Indicator 5.2 "Yes."

If there are many disruptions and staff are too often not able to control children to maintain order and safety, or they use methods of discipline that are negative, score 5.2 "No."

5.3 Children enjoy getting positive personal attention from adults. Giving children attention while they are behaving in a productive manner makes it more likely for them to repeat such activity or to continue it longer. Just showing enjoyment or interest is one of the most powerful tools adults can use in helping children learn about acceptable behavior. (See photos 28.5.3a-d.)

It is best if this attention does not usually come as verbal praise (e.g., "I like how Ben is playing" "You're really paying attention. Good girl."). Verbal praise is often empty of meaning if given too often, making children devalue it or, on the other hand, perform only for the praise. Instead, giving attention for good behavior must genuinely show the children that they are appreciated as individuals. For example, when a staff member shows interest in what children are doing, shows them affection or sympathy, listens to them express ideas, has fun or relaxes with them, or helps them, a bond is created so that children trust, listen to, and want to please that adult.

When most of the personal attention children get is for undesirable behavior, then children may do more of such behavior because it gets attention, even if the attention is not pleasant. However, when they know that they will get plenty of personal

28.5.3a

28.5.3b

28.5.3c

28.5.3d

28.5.3a-d Children are less likely to be disruptive when they enjoy positive attention from staff while behaving well.

attention for doing acceptable things, then they are far more likely to use the positive behaviors that get attention.

Score Indicator 5.3 "Yes" if children who are behaving well are rewarded with lots of positive interest from staff, such as staff joining in their play, sitting and talking with them at meals, smiling and explaining things at diaper-changing times, or cuddling while reading a book. Do not give credit (score "No") if positive attention is usually given for completed routine tasks, or if negative attention is given for unwanted behavior.

5.4   For staff to *react consistently to children's behavior* means that there is a similarity in the way staff respond to and handle situations and children. The basic rules for positive behavior in a group, (e.g., not hurting oneself or others, staying safe, and not being destructive) are enforced equally by all staff. The same rules are used for all children and by all staff. For example, one staff member cannot ignore biting while the other responds to stop such behavior. Consistency also means that things are handled similarly at different times, for example, staff stop certain behaviors during calmer times as well as during busier times.

This does not mean that there can be no flexibility in the way staff handle the children. But the flexibility cannot affect or change the important basic rules. Beyond the basic rules, there may be *some* differences in expectations for each child, based on the child's abilities. For example, a very active child might not be expected to sit in a large group for as long as others. He would be allowed to leave, while others would be expected to stay. However, this child would still need to be held to the basic rules—no hurting or harmful behavior.

Staff may also differ in personality. One might be a calmer, quieter person, while another might be more enthusiastic. They might talk to children in somewhat different ways, using different kinds of words. Such differences are acceptable as long as they use similar methods and consequences for the same reasons. For example, redirection should be used by all staff when there are problems over toys, but the staff might differ in the specifics of how they positively handle the redirection, based on the child's characteristics and their own personalities.

To score, watch carefully to see how all staff handle children's behavior throughout the observation. If differences in the handling of specific children or among different staff members are minor and do not seem to cause unfairness or give mixed messages to children, score Indicator 5.4 "Yes." If problems are observed due to a lack of consistency between staff, score "No." For example, if one staff member has the difficult task of handling all the problems because the other is not involved, or one child is, for some reason, allowed to hurt others, while the rest of the children are not, or if one staff member is punitive while the other uses positive non-punitive methods, score "No."

7.1 Infants and toddlers have little understanding that their own actions impact other people differently from the way that they affect objects. When an infant pulls another baby's hair, she only knows that she is reaching for something that is shiny and attractive. She is curious to see what it does when she grabs it, just as she is curious to see what happens when she pulls the string on a toy. She does not really connect the crying noise she hears with the pulling of the hair. A responsible adult needs to ensure that she does not treat others as objects, while encouraging the learning that is needed to understand her own effects on others. Similarly, the toddler who yanks another child from the tricycle he wants only perceives the other child as an object that is in the place where he wants to be. He does not think about the personal consequences of pulling the other child from the tricycle; he only focuses on his goal. For toddlers, the attractive goal is very often what another child is doing, because toddlers are great imitators in their learning.

The infant/toddler characteristic, of being unable to understand the effects of actions on others, often leads adults to misinterpret children's intentions. They see the troublesome behavior as being "bad," so they resort to punishment to stop it, which causes physical or emotional pain for the child and weakens the bond between child and adult. This indicator requires that staff use the action by a child that affects others as a positive learning opportunity to encourage the development of self-discipline.

Helping infants and toddlers **understand the effects of their own actions on others** means that in addition to intervening positively to solve a problem, the adult calls the child's attention to his or her effect, explaining the response or feelings of the other person. (See photos 28.7.1a-d.) Since infants and toddlers do not intend to hurt others, they are less likely to do so as they begin to realize that what they do has had a harmful effect. Examples of staff helping children are provided in the indicator. Other examples include:

28.7.1a When this child grabs the doll blanket, she does not understand the effect of that action.

28.7.1b The children look to the staff for help with the problem.

28.7.1c The staff member gently explains that the other child was using the blanket, and she was upset when it was taken away. However, they can find another blanket if she wants to play too.

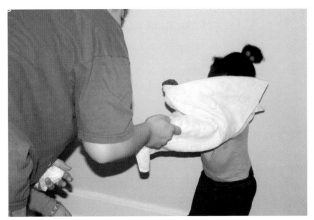

28.7.1d The child understands, and willingly hands the blanket to the staff member.

- A mobile infant pulls on a sleeping baby, and as the baby wakes and cries, a staff member intervenes, saying "Look, Thomas. You woke up Roberto. He doesn't want you to pull on him. See his face. He wants to sleep. I'll pat his back and you can see him go to sleep. Then we will go and play."

- A child grabs the pacifier from another child's mouth and a staff member responds, "Erica, Molly wants her pacifier back. See her sad face? Look here [calling Erica's attention to Molly's face]. We can wash this pacifier and give it back to Molly. Your pacifier is in your cubby. Do you want yours?"

- A child stretches out a hand to retrieve the marker taken by another child. When the other child does not respond, the staff member says, "Look at Emma, Charlie. She is asking you to give the marker back. See her hand? Can you give it back? She got angry when you took it."

To score "Yes," at least one example of an explanation of a child's negative effect on another person must be observed during the 3-hour observation to demonstrate that helping children, as described, is a regular part of discipline practice. If there are no negative effects of children's actions observed, explanations of positive effects are acceptable to give credit. For example, if a child hands a toy to another child and the staff member says, "You really made Ajah happy, Leah. See her smile?," credit would be given for Indicator 7.1.

7.2 Although infants and toddlers do not intend to hurt others, they do learn that hurting is an effective way of getting some things that they want. For example, a toddler who bites another child to get a toy soon learns that biting works (as long as she does not get caught). Such negative behaviors may continue if adults do not intervene appropriately to teach that communication is the more effective, and in the long-term a more satisfying means to an end. The biter does not realize that no one will like him if the biting continues, and that there are other problems with hurting others. He can only focus on what he wants, right at that moment.

It takes effort and intelligence on the part of staff to teach children that using communication is the more effective strategy to use in getting along well with others. The earlier this is started with children, the better the results as children get older. (See photos 28.7.2a-b.)

Certain practices are required in teaching children the skill of using communication rather than physical aggression to solve problems. Staff must:

- First, intervene in a timely fashion when there is a problem of aggression

- Second,

   —For a child who cannot talk, encourage the gestures that help communicate the child's need while providing the words to be used in place of aggression;

   —For a child who can talk, help by encouraging the use of words and appropriate gestures; and

- Third, ensure that communication attempts made by children are effective in getting what the child wants. Otherwise, children will go back to using what works, even if it is not acceptable.

Examples of this practice include situations such as the following:

- Noah tugs on Jesse's shirt, trying to move past him to reach a toy. Jesse shoves Noah in the face to stop him. Noah falls over and cries.

   The staff member responds, "You did not like Noah pulling on your shirt, did you Jesse? But you can't push him. You can say, 'Stop.' Put up your hand and say 'Stop.' That's right, 'Stop.' And Noah, next time you need to walk around Jesse. See, you can go around him this way."

- Cathy grabs a crayon from Thelma, and hits her as Thelma reaches to take it back.

   The staff member responds, saying, "Thelma, are you OK? You did not want Cathy to take that crayon. You are still using it. Cathy, you wanted that red crayon. You need to ask Thelma if she will let you use it. Hold out your hand and say, 'Crayon.' Now wait to see if Thelma will give it to you. No, she is using it some more. Try again. Now she's giving it to you. Thank you Thelma. Thank you for sharing the red crayon with Cathy!"

To give credit for Indicator 7.2 (score "Yes"), at least one example of staff helping children learn to use communication rather than aggression to solve problems must be observed. If no use of aggression is observed, give credit if staff help children use either nonverbal or verbal communication skills with one another in other circumstances.

7.3 In some cases, it helps to get assistance from an outside expert when particu-

28.7.2a There has been a fight over the toy camera. Staff intervene immediately to help the children solve the problem.

28.7.2b Staff help children by giving the words they could use to solve the problem: "Can I have the camera when you are done?"

lar problems cannot be handled well by staff. Teachers sometimes need another point of view that is not found within the classroom or the center. For example, something in the program might be causing great challenges for a child who has difficulties getting along with others. The staff might not be able to tell that the issue could be resolved with some environmental changes. Another professional is likely to look at the child and the environment more objectively and help the staff see the child from another point of view.

Because staff may not always have the answers, this indicator requires that they *seek advice from other professionals concerning behavior problems*. This is most necessary when the behavior problems are serious, endangering the child or others.

In most cases, *other professionals* means someone from outside the program who specializes in the area of concern. Examples of such professionals include mental health specialists, psychologists, social workers, special educators or therapists with special training, and pediatricians. In some cases, however, a program staff member can count as the "other professional" if the person has a specialization in the area of concern and can give an unbiased perspective.

To get information needed to score this indicator, ask staff the questions provided in the ITERS-R. Score "Yes" to Indicator 7.3 if the staff have used outside professionals to help with behavior problems. If no other professionals have ever been used, score "Yes" if staff can provide the name of an agency or practitioner they would use if needed. If staff say that outside help is never used or would never be needed, do not give credit (score "No").

Program Structure

General information about this item

When it comes to scheduling to meet personal care needs, even adults vary (becoming hungry, tired, or needing to use the toilet at different times), and they are most comfortable with having flexibility in how time is used. Unlike adults, however, infants and toddlers do not have the control and understanding that adults have, and their needs are far more pressing because they are so young. Therefore, in a high-quality early childhood program, flexibility, combined with dependability, is provided in the daily schedule used with these young children.

Infants require individual handling for care and play because infants vary greatly in terms of when they are alert and when they require routine care, such as feeding, sleep, or diapering. When their needs are not met according to their own inner clock and they are forced to adjust to one shared schedule, they go through a period of upheaval until they adjust. They may not thrive because they are not being fed when they are hungry, or they may not be alert during play times because their sleep patterns have been disrupted. In addition, they are given the message that their own requirements are not important, and this affects the sense of trust in caring adults that must be developed during the earliest years.

Young toddlers also require far more flexibility in their schedules than older children, because they still vary greatly, although not as much as young infants. It takes a long time to make the physical changes that allow comfort while being required to follow a group schedule. Older toddlers, like preschoolers and adults, can usually manage a group schedule, as long as there is some flexibility possible.

For this item, **schedule** means the sequence of events that infants and toddlers actually experience (or live) each day, in terms of how time is used. The score is based completely on how the children spend the time in the classroom, rather than on what appears on a written schedule. In fact, there is no requirement for a written schedule in this item, even though it is important to have such support to help staff and substitutes provide what is needed in a dependable way and to let parents know what to expect for their children.

To score this item, focus on the sequence of events and the use of time in the classroom. The observer will have to document what happens at different times of the day, by taking notes on what happens during the observation. This is called the observed schedule. The amount of time spent on each activity (routines and play) should be noted, as well as what the children do and the types of materials they use.

If a **written schedule** is present for the group being observed, this can only be used as evidence when it reflects reasonably well what actually occurs during the observation. Small variations from the written schedule are acceptable, but not great differences. If the written schedule matches what has been observed, it can be used to gather reliable information about the rest of the day that is not included in the observation.

Information from the observed schedule always takes precedence over the written schedule in determining the score for the item. For example, if a written schedule shows that the children go outdoors every day in the morning, but it is observed that children do not go out even though the weather is fair, then score based on what is observed. Similarly, if the written schedule indicates that the infants' routine care needs are met on individual schedules, but the children's routines are observed to be handled as a group, with children being fed, diapered, and put down for nap on the same schedule, then score based on what is observed.

If the written schedule cannot be used to figure out the amount of time usually spent on the different activities during the whole day (because it does not reasonably match what was observed), then questions must be used to get the needed information from the staff.

A closer look at each indicator

1.1 A schedule that is **too rigid** ignores the flexibility in time that is needed during the day to meet the individual needs of infants and toddlers. A rigid schedule may rarely allow children's routine care needs to be met according to each child's needs. Signs that a schedule is too rigid include:

- All toddlers are required to nap at the same time, even though some of the children obviously need a nap much earlier.

- Toys are made accessible to infants only during certain times, and if children are sleeping or being fed at that time, they will miss play activities.

- 2-year-olds must complete play activities in the same amount of time, making some wait for the others to finish, while some do not get to finish at all.

- Children must go outside to play whether they are ready or not, or all babies are taken for a buggy ride outdoors, and some fall asleep while others cry from hunger.

- Toddlers get upset when interrupted in their play to participate in an art activity.

- Toddlers are required to participate in circle time, even though most are not interested.

- A toddler falls asleep on the floor, and staff wake him up to get him through lunch time, though he barely eats anything.

Infants and toddlers who are forced to follow an overly rigid schedule, which does not allow for individual needs, will often show their distress by crying, whining, throwing tantrums, or showing frustration or apathy. The observer must consider all experiences of all the children when determining whether the schedule is so rigid that it is **not satisfying the needs of many children**, and should not score this indicator based on just a small part of what happens. (See photo 29.1.1.)

At the other extreme, a schedule that is **too flexible** provides too little dependability or structure to the day. Children will have no idea what is supposed to happen or what they are supposed to do next. Staff will also appear to be uncertain, and the atmosphere in the classroom will usually be chaotic. For example, a staff member might begin feeding an infant, and then stop before the baby is satisfied,

29.1.1 When all babies are fed, have naps, are diapered and play at the same time, the schedule is too rigid.

29.1.2 If crying due to hunger typically goes unanswered, children's routine care needs would be unmet. This baby, however, will get a prompt response.

so she can handle something else that requires her attention. Or the staff may direct children to wash their hands for snack and then change plans and take the children outdoors instead. Meals might be very late, too early, or unexpected, so that pre-meal preparation cannot be completed. Children may have to wait long periods with nothing to do.

To score "Yes" for Indicator 1.1, the schedule must generally be either very rigid or too flexible. If there is a reasonable balance of flexibility with dependability, or if there are minor problems that do not affect children too severely, score 1.1 "No."

1.2 For infants and toddlers, ***children's routine needs*** consist primarily of feeding, nap, and diapering and toileting.

This indicator is true (score "Yes") when the meeting of any one of the routine care needs is generally not satisfactory for most of the children, in terms of the schedule (e.g., not carried out 75% of the time for all children), or if most of the needs of any one child are consistently ignored. (See photo 29.1.2.) Do not score "Yes" because a routine is not carried out as required in other items of the ITERS-R. For example, if sanitary requirements are not properly completed for diapering/toileting, this is handled in Item 9, Diapering/toileting. Score "Yes" only if the routines are usually not done at all as would be required for basic care, or if they are not done when needed by the children.

1.3 In some cases, staff are able to meet the routine care needs of the children, but this takes most of the time, leaving no opportunity to provide activities or to supervise children involved in play. Score "Yes" if the staff spend so much time in routine care that there is no opportunity to supervise children at play. To score "No," staff must have the time to supervise playing children, while they are not doing routine care tasks. For example, if a staff member is changing a diaper and keeping an eye on other children who are playing at the same time, for the purposes of scoring this indicator, this would not count towards "supervising children at play."

Do not score "Yes" if the staff do not supervise children at play for other reasons, such as:

- Staff are uninvolved with children except when completing routine care tasks, and attend to other interests while children play.
- Lack of accessible materials makes play impossible for children.

29.3.1a Meeting the needs of infants means that the majority of children have naps when they show they are tired.

29.3.1b These babies are on individual nap schedules.

3.1 ***Schedule meets the needs of most of the children*** means that the schedule allows every routine care activity to be completed for each child as required, with only a few minor lapses. In addition, the amount and timing of play activities is satisfactory for almost all of the children. (See photos 29.3.1a-c.)

To score "Yes," no routine care task can be systematically ignored, nor can most of the routine care for any one child be ignored. On the whole, the schedule must meet most of the needs for most children. Examples of minor lapses include:

29.3.1c These toddlers usually respond well to an early lunch, followed by nap. All are on the same schedule, and this meets most of the children's needs.

- All infants are fed, but a few must wait a short time, even though they are obviously hungry.

- Toddlers are all seated at the table, ready for lunch, but lunch is 5 minutes late, so they must wait.

- Children's diapers are all changed, but one child's diaper was overlooked until much later.

- One child is tired at lunch, but manages to get through it without falling asleep.

- At nap, one toddler is obviously not tired enough to go to sleep right away; he would rather be playing.

- One active toddler would profit from active play outdoors, but her needs are not met until group outdoor time later in the day.

3.2 Infants and toddlers do much of their learning by playing with materials or toys, participating in activities, and, as they approach the preschool years, playing with one another. It is during play that children develop knowledge and the physical, cognitive, language, and social skills needed for later success. They do this through exploring, experimenting, and discovering, as well as imitating what they see. Therefore, ***play activities*** are required ***as part of the daily schedule***. Routines should not take up most of the time, nor should children be required to be quiet and passive for long periods of time. (See photos 29.3.2a-c.)

During ***play activities***, children must be actively involved, allowed to use toys or other materials, and be able to interact with others if they wish. Play activities

29.3.2a Play is offered to these babies whenever they are awake and interested.

29.3.2b These toddlers are free to play much of the day.

29.3.2c Even when everyone else is sleeping, this baby is ready for play, and encouraged to do so.

should not be confused with more passive group times (such as circle times, when children mostly listen to a staff member, or time spent watching TV or videos), or times when children are required to work on specific non-play tasks, such as coloring alphabet ditto sheets. Routine care times do not count as play activities, even if they are done playfully. Play activities can be:

- part of free play, in which the play is child-initiated and toys or playmates are self-selected,
- teacher-initiated activities,
- either indoors or outdoors
- offered with many choices of toys or with a more limited selection,
- done individually, in a small group, or in a large group, and
- active or more quiet.

To give credit for Indicator 3.2 (score "Yes"), the schedule must provide play opportunities for all children for much of the day, because most play materials required in the items in the Activities subscale (Items 15–24) are required for this time period at the minimal level, and this time requirement also applies in other items that include play. ***Much of the day*** is defined in the "Explanation of Terms Used Throughout the Scale," on page 7 of the ITERS-R. This means that staff make toys or other play materials accessible to the children throughout the day, and that inactivity or lengthy participation in routines cannot take up most of the time in the schedule.

5.1   The ***basic routines*** consist of feeding, taking a nap, and diapering or toileting for the infants and toddlers.

A dependable schedule for routines allows staff to know what they must do and provides security to the children. To be ***flexible*** within the dependable schedule for basic routines provides the time required to meet the care needs of all children in the group, while also allowing for special circumstances. Flexibility helps to make

29.5.1a

29.5.1b

29.5.1a-b In both these infant classrooms, evidence is observed of individualized schedules for play and routines.

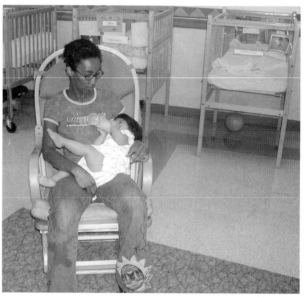

29.5.1c Each child's personal needs are met by the schedule.

29.5.1d A longer, relaxed feeding time is permitted when schedules are individualized.

29.5.1e Flexibility in the schedule means that all toddlers do not have to finish eating at the same time.

29.5.1f An extra snack helps this toddler through the long morning.

29.5.2a Because of typical indoor restrictions, active toddlers need lots of time outdoors.

29.5.2b Freedom of movement and fresh air are satisfying and healthful to these toddlers.

things in a classroom more relaxed, because the staff can accommodate to the infrequent occurrences. An ***individualized*** schedule allows the needs of ***each*** child to be met with little or no waiting, based on each child's preferences. This means that the use of time can be customized to satisfy children in a very personal way. Infants are fed, changed and allowed to sleep when they are ready to do so. (See photos 29.5.1a-f.) Examples of a flexible and individualized schedule are provided as part of the indicator. More specific examples include:

- A toddler, who is not feeling well, can sleep longer than usual.
- Several toddlers show that they are very hungry before lunch time, so staff have lunch earlier or provide a small snack to help children wait.
- An infant is still hungry after having her bottle, so she is fed some more.
- Children who eat more quickly are allowed to do so and move on to play when they are finished, while the slower eaters are given all the time they need.
- A baby who dislikes the diapering procedure is diapered more quickly than another who enjoys the personal attention.

Score Indicator 5.1 "Yes" if routine care is provided to meet the personal needs of each child in the group. This is generally more likely to be observed in infant groups and less likely for toddlers and twos. The observer should be especially aware that toddlers often still have very differing needs for routine care. If the schedule for routines causes difficulties or distress for any child, score this indicator "No."

5.2   A ***balance of indoor and outdoor activities*** requires, first, that children have opportunities for both indoor and outdoor play every day. In addition, to give credit for this indicator, the amount of time in the each area (indoors and outdoors) must be satisfying to the children and promote their well-being. Since all children profit from being outside, outdoor activities should be provided as a daily event, except in very bad weather. However, the amount of time provided outdoors, as stated in the "Note for Clarification" for this indicator, will depend on the ages of the children, their abilities, their moods and the weather. For example, active toddlers, especially those who are older, will need longer periods outdoors. (See photos 29.5.2a-b.) Very young infants, however, with their greater needs for sleep and more time required for feeding and frequent diaper changes, may require more indoor time. (See photos

29.5.2c Babies enjoy play indoors, but they need fresh air, also.

29.5.2d A ride in the baby buggy is a quiet outdoor activity.

29.5.2c-e.) More time outdoors should be provided in nice weather, and less on the very cold days or when the grass is wet.

Score this indicator "No" if infants or toddlers do not have outdoor time daily, with the exception of those rare days of bad weather. (It is assumed that they will have sufficient indoor time, but if not, then score "No.") In addition, score "No" if the children do not have a reasonable amount of time indoors and outdoors, based on their needs.

In some cases, a program will not be able to take children outdoors due the circumstances under which the program operates. For example, there may be no safe, appropriate outdoor area for very young children to use; one child's parents might have requested that an infant be kept indoors, so it would be impossible to supervise all children with one inside and the rest outdoors; or the individual schedules of infants prohibit children from going out. In all such cases, a score of "No" is given for this indicator, because in a higher quality program, the necessities required to meet all children's needs must be provided.

29.5.2e This more active play is also an outdoor activity.

5.3 Infants and toddlers enjoy and benefit from both quiet and more active play. ***Quiet play*** includes activities that do not require much large muscle, physical effort. For infants such play might include manipulating toys with the hands, looking at pictures, listening to someone who is singing to them, or social play with an adult, such as peek-a-boo. For toddlers, quiet play might include using fine motor toys, art materials, sand or water play (such as scooping or pouring), or books. Quiet play is done without lots of noise or excitement, and is thought of as being more soothing and relaxing than active play. Less energy is spent in quiet play. (See photos 29.5.3a-b.)

29.5.3a

29.5.3b

29.5.3a-b Children in this group can always choose either active or quiet play.

Active play, depending on age and ability, includes movements, such as reaching, kicking and batting at things, rolling over, crawling, walking, running, jumping, climbing, throwing, catching, riding wheel toys, or dancing. Social play can also be more active, for example when a baby is encouraged to become excited, laughing and waving arms and legs. This type of play is associated with exuberance and noise far more than quite play, and results in more energy being spent.

Either type of play can be done:

- indoors or outdoors,
- individually, in small group, or in a larger group,
- child- or adult-initiated.

Both active and quiet play must not be confused with routine care activities or passive non-play activities such as sitting in a big group with little active involvement, watching TV, or waiting for the next activity.

For quiet and active play to be *varied to meet children's needs* means, primarily, that staff allow children to choose the type of play they wish to do from both quiet and active alternatives accessible to them. In addition, it requires that staff be able to modify how they play with each child, responding to the messages each child gives. For the more alert child, for example, more active play would be encouraged. (See photos 29.5.3c-e, next page.) For the child who is becoming tired, a quieter play option would be provided. Similarly, for a baby who startles easily, social play would be soothing, while for the more robust baby, an excited tone would become part of the play.

To give credit for Indicator 5.3 (score "Yes"), both types of play (active and quiet) must be provided each day, and staff must vary children's opportunities depending on what the child requires. In addition, not all children can be handled in the same way, doing active play at the same time, or doing quiet play at the same time, unless this obviously meets the needs of each child in the group. Otherwise, there must be both quiet and active options for children, and staff must vary what they do with children in play, based on the child's needs and preferences.

29.5.3c

29.5.3d

29.5.3c-e Because toddlers are working on developing many gross motor skills, active play options should be provided both indoors and outdoors for children to choose.

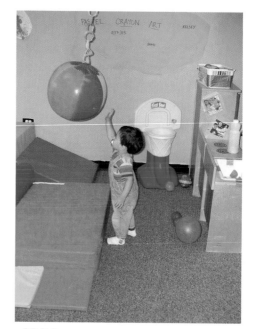

29.5.3e

5.4 To give credit for this indicator, the schedule must be organized so that there are no long periods of waiting during transitions between daily events. A **long period of waiting** means waiting without any activity for 3 minutes or more or a waiting period that results in obvious distress or problems for children. During long periods of waiting, when children have nothing positive to do, learning time is wasted and problems with discipline may come up, often forcing staff to control children unnecessarily. (See photos 29.5.4a-d.)

Transitions are times when children change from one activity period to another. Usually a number of steps are needed to end one activity (whether routines or play) and prepare to move to another. For example, a transition from eating to play would require that toddlers' hands and faces be washed as they finish eating, and that they be moved to a play space with toys. A transition from diapering to play would require that staff complete all sanitary procedures with the child, put the child down to play without contaminating any surfaces, then return to finish the sanitation tasks required.

This indicator refers only to periods of waiting that occur **during transitions between daily events**. This means waiting between one activity period and another, rather than waiting **within** any activity period. For example, if a toddler wants to paint at the easel but has to wait for another child to finish, and the child chooses to wait rather than to do something else, this is considered waiting within an activity period and is not considered here. However, if toddlers help clean up toys, wash hands for lunch, go to the table, and then wait for more than 3 minutes with nothing to do before the food arrives, this is a **long period of waiting between daily events.** During this time children are waiting for the

29.5.4a Any period of waiting can cause distress in infants and toddlers, but they recover if answered quickly.

29.5.4b If children have to wait at the table for more than 3 minutes, this would be considered a long period of waiting.

29.5.4c It is unusual for all children to be asked to line up and wash hands in this class, because it causes difficult transitions.

29.5.4d Getting coats on to go outdoors can often cause a long period of waiting.

next activity with nothing to do. Similarly, if a non-mobile baby, who has had her diaper changed, must sit with nothing to do for 3 minutes while the staff member completes the remaining diapering tasks, this would be a long period of waiting.

Staff can usually provide something for children to do while they have to wait. They can sing songs with the children, place them near accessible toys, read books to them, or play other games. In this case, children are not considered to be waiting with nothing to do, unless the waiting time is so long that the activity no longer interests the children.

To give credit for Indicator 5.4 (score "Yes"), there can be *no* long periods (3 minutes or more) of waiting between daily events observed. If it seems that children have to wait a long time during a transition, keep track of the amount of time they wait to see how long it actually is.

29 Schedule

7.1 A flexible and individualized schedule of routine care is required in Indicator 5.1. In this indicator, additional flexibility is required by adjusting the schedule or changing the schedule to meet the current needs of the whole group or to meet individual needs throughout the day.

Varying the schedule of play activities to meet the needs of the children is considered in this indicator.

Some examples of such adjusting of the schedule are provided in the indicator. Other examples include:

- As young infants stay awake for longer periods, toys and play materials are offered to them much of the day.

- A non-mobile baby who becomes bored with one toy is moved to a new play area or given different toys to use as needed.

- A 2-year-old who is not tired at nap time may do quiet activities instead of having to stay on his cot.

- A toddler who is especially involved in an activity may continue working, even though it will soon be lunch time.

- A child who is not feeling well may do quiet activities instead of going outdoors for active play.

- Older toddlers who show signs of not wanting to listen to a group story are allowed to find an alternate activity.

- Children are allowed to stay outdoors longer on a day with fine weather, if the children seem to have extra energy.

- Play time is shortened on a day when toddlers seem hungrier and more tired than usual, so lunch and nap can begin earlier.

- Staff change outdoor play time to avoid the predicted rain or very hot weather.

Score Indicator 7.1 "Yes" if staff are observed making adjustments in the play schedule for either the whole group of for individuals with needs that differ from the group. This can be evidenced by staff allowing children to make choices from among many options (providing free play) or by making changes in the play schedule based on the requirements of special circumstances, such as the weather.

7.2 ***Transitions between daily events*** are times when children change from one activity to another. The change might be from one routine to another, from a routine activity to play, or between play activities. Transitions also include arriving at and departing from the class at drop-off and pick-up times.

When children must change from one activity to another, adults are often occupied with managing the tasks that are required to make the move. Because the staff are often involved with specific children at such times or taking care of other transitional tasks (such as cleaning the table and floor after snack, picking up and re-shelving toys, or talking to parents), children are less well supervised than usual. Often the children have nothing of interest to do or miss the attention they usually get from adults. Troublesome behaviors can occur, such as babies getting upset; toddlers getting into fights, wandering away, or running around uncontrolled. Transitions are difficult times to handle unless staff have thought through how to make these times go well. (See photos 29.7.2a-b.)

Indicator

29.7.2a Staff coordinate their tasks so that the transition between lunch and nap goes smoothly.

29.7.2b Lunch can be unrushed when staff coordinate supervision responsibilities and provide flexibility.

Smooth transitions between daily events means that children flow smoothly from one activity period to the next, without long waits or troublesome behavior. Transitions work best when staff have planned ahead, avoid having children wait, and keep them actively involved as much as possible. Examples of smooth transitions include:

- providing individual nap schedules for infants, so all will not require the same type of care at the same time, i.e., children are placed in cribs as they become tired;

- having a few toddlers complete a task such as handwashing at a time, rather than having the whole group wait for each one to finish;

- using staff in a coordinated way, so that one helps children through transition tasks while the other moves those who are finished on to the next activity;

- having toys and materials needed for the next activity ready and accessible so children can become involved right away;

- making clear to toddlers what the transition tasks are and guiding them through each step; and

- allowing children to stay actively involved until the next activity is ready.

Score Indicator 7.1 "Yes" if transitions are usually smooth and relatively trouble-free. Perfect transitions are not required, but children should not have to wait for long periods with nothing to do. Moreover, changes should *never* be chaotic, with children fighting or getting upset. Also, transitions should *never* require harsh treatment of children to avoid trouble and force compliance. If any of these is observed during any transition, score Indicator 7.1 "No."

30 Free play

General information about this item

Free play, according to the definition page 46 of the ITERS-R, means that the "child is permitted to select materials and companions, and as far as possible, manage play independently. Adult interaction is in response to the child's needs. Non-mobile children will have to be offered materials for their free choice and moved to different areas to facilitate access." Situations in which mobile children are assigned to centers by staff, or staff select the materials that individual mobile children may use, do not count as free play.

Infants and toddlers naturally want to do their "own thing." They learn by exploring their environment and experimenting with the materials they discover. They will play with something that captures their interest, get all the learning they can from it at that time, and then move on to new experiments and discoveries. Their attention spans vary widely, with some paying lots of attention for longer periods, and others moving on frequently to something new. Some children prefer adult interaction as they play, while for others it seems less important. What infants and toddlers attend to, and for how long, depends on individual personalities, learning styles, and the skills that they are developing at the time.

Having sufficient free play is important in infant and toddler programs because it is during free play that children can:

- make their own choices, tailoring their learning to their personal needs,
- interact with others to the extent that their preferences determine and their limited social skills allow, and
- choose to play and learn in the way that is most effective for their own personality, following their interests and working on the skills that they really need to develop.

Free play does not mean a "free for all" with no rules and "anything goes." Instead, free play requires an organized structure provided by staff, where the choices are clear to children, safe options are plentiful, and staff supervise carefully to promote productive and engaged behavior. These provisions ensure that a wide range of learning opportunities can take place.

Free play does not mean that all areas of the classroom must be open at one time, with all materials accessible. Although fewer choices may be available, free play will still take place as long as children are allowed to choose with what and with whom to play.

30 Free play

When observing a classroom with mobile children, look for these characteristics of free play:

- Children are playing in various activity areas of the room or outdoor play space, with access to all, or almost all, areas.
- Children are playing in self-selected small groups or individually. They may move from one social group to another when they wish.
- Children may choose toys, other materials, or equipment to use, either indoors or outdoors.
- Children may move from one area to another when they wish to.

When observing a classroom with non-mobile children enrolled, look for these characteristics of free play:

- Children have access to many toys, which are changed as children lose interest.
- A variety of toys are moved so they are accessible to children, or children are moved to different areas of the room to play with different toys.
- Children are not kept in swings, infant seats, or other equipment without toys to use or with only a very limited selection of toys.

Staff have important roles in supervising free play, for example to:

- ensure the children's health and safety,
- ensure proper, non-destructive use of materials,
- encourage positive interactions among children,
- help children learn to use materials and see new possibilities for what they can do,
- read to the children,
- interact socially with children as they play, providing comfort, security, or interest as needed, and
- maintain organization so play spaces do not become cluttered, and involve older children in helping with clean-up.

30.1.1 If more than just this momentary lapse in supervision were observed frequently during free play, especially in hazardous activities, free play would be considered inadequately supervised.

A closer look at each indicator

1.1 *Little opportunity for free play* means that children can participate in free play for less than 1 hour a day in full-day programs. Less time is required for programs operating less than 8 hours a day (see Indicator 3.1). The vast majority of time each day is spent in routine care activities and whole-group or small-group times, where children can make few choices about what to play with, for how long, and with whom.

Much of day spent in **unsupervised free play** means that children choose activities and spend time in different types of play, but staff are relatively uninvolved in supervising the

30.1.2 A lack of toys to use prevents free play from being a rich learning experience.

30.3.1a

30.3.1b

30.3.1c

30.3.1d

30.3.1a-d All these children have daily free play, indoors and outdoors, unless weather is extremely bad.

children. (See photo 30.1.1.) Staff may be absent at times during free play, or they may not pay attention to the children, even to the extent that children's major health and safety needs are not ensured.

Score Indicator 1.1 "Yes" if either of the situations described above occurs during the observation or if, during the questioning time, the staff report such a situation.

1.2 ***Inadequate toys, materials, and equipment*** means that there are not enough play materials for children to use without undue competition. In addition, there are too few play materials to interest the children, challenge them, and encourage extended play. (See photo 30.1.2.) Materials may simply be lacking, there may be too few materials for the number of children in the group, there may only be one type of material, or toys may be in such poor repair that they cannot be used constructively.

When scoring this indicator, be sure to consider the materials that are ***accessible for children to use*** during any observed free play periods, indoors and outdoors. Sometimes materials are present in the children's play areas, but the children are not allowed to use them during free play times.

If the materials that children can use during free play are inadequate, as described above, score Indicator 1.2 "Yes."

3.1   Some *free play*, at the minimal (3) level, means that each child can participate in free play for approximately 1 hour a day in full-day programs. (See photos 30.3.1a-d.) The 1 hour may take place at one time, or be a combination of times throughout the day. Less time is required for programs operating less than 8 hours a day, with the amount of time calculated proportionally, based on the ratio of 1 hour for programs of 8 hours or more. For example, if a program operates for 6 hours a day, this would be ¾ of a full-day program, so the time required would be ¾ of the 1 hour. If the program operates 4 hours a day, the requirement would be ½ hour. The hour requirement is modified for programs where a very young baby is enrolled and sleeps most of the time in the program, so that 1 hour is not available for play. In this case, the baby must have some play time while awake and not involved in routines, but less than the required time would be allowed.

To give credit, a portion of the free play must happen **indoors** and a portion must happen **outdoors** for each child enrolled in the group. The indoor and outdoor times can be combined to satisfy the total amount of time required. Outdoor play is required, **weather permitting**, which means that the outdoor free play must be carried out if the weather allows children to play outdoors. There will be relatively few days in most areas where children will not be able to play outdoors at all. Even in climates with more severe weather, children should be dressed properly and allowed to play outdoors unless there is a danger associated with outdoor exposure. To an extent, whether children should be allowed to play outdoors is a location-related consideration. For example, people who live in very rainy climates will be more likely to take children outdoors on wet days than people who live in drier climates. Or people who live in cold climates are more likely to take children outside on snowy days than are those for whom snow is less usual. In some areas, pollution levels can become dangerous to the health of children on certain days. On those unusual days, children should not play outdoors.

If the required amount of time for free play is not provided to all the children, or if free play is provided either indoors *or* outdoors, but not in both locations, score Indicator 3.1 "No."

3.2   Staff must supervise children during free play, at the minimal level, to protect their basic safety and to facilitate play. **Some supervision provided** means that staff are present in the area being used by children and are usually paying attention to them as they play. (See photo 30.3.2a.) **Protect children's safety** requires that staff watch and guide children to minimize *major* safety hazards (e.g., children are supervised so that they do not mouth small objects, hurt one another, wander away, or have access to dangerous materials, such as poisons or sharp objects).

At this quality level, it is not required that staff take part in intense educational interactions with the children, but that they do **facilitate play**. Facilitate play means that staff help children access toys and materials and help children who become upset or uninvolved. (See photos 30.3.2b-d.) For example, if a non-mobile child drops a toy he is using and has nothing to do, staff place more toys within the child's reach or move the child to another play area where there are toys to use. If a toddler is wandering aimlessly, uninvolved in play, staff help the child become engaged with something that is interesting. If two children are fighting over a toy, staff step in and help the children come to a solution that is satisfying to them.

As stated in the ITERS-R "Note for Clarification" for this indicator, do not score "No" unless supervision during free play is extremely lax. If staff are present during free play, paying attention to prevent major problems, and helping children to remain productively involved, score this indicator "Yes."

30.3.2a At this moment of free play, staff are supervising to protect children's safety.

30.3.2b Staff facilitate play by initiating some activities and helping with others.

30.3.2c Staff make materials accessible to non-mobile babies as part of facilitating play.

30.3.2d Showing intense interest in children's play helps to extend free play.

3.3   ***Adequate toys, materials and equipment*** means enough for children to use in free play without undue competition. In addition, there must be enough materials so that children can make some satisfying choices about what to play with.

Toys, materials, and equipment must be ***accessible*** to the children—children must be able to reach them and be allowed to use them during free play. There can be no barriers to using the materials. Materials that are present, but that cannot be used for any reason, are not counted among the accessible materials. Materials must be made accessible to non-mobile children. (See photos 30.3.3a-c, next page.)

The materials must be in usable condition to be counted for this indicator, so that children can actually do what is required for play. (See photos 30.3.3d-e, next page.) For example, there is paper for toddlers to use with crayons, there are enough snap-beads stored together, there are enough rattles for all infants who want to use them, there are enough things in the housekeeping area so toddlers can pretend, there are some books with pages and covers, some balls are inflated, and wheel toys have wheels. If free play is provided in a space that is not used during the observation (another classroom or outdoors, for example), the observer must be sure to look at and evaluate the materials children can access during free play.

30.3.3a This crawler has fascinating toys accessible to choose.

30.3.3b Staff make a selection of toys accessible to this non-mobile baby.

30.3.3c When there are adequate toys for free play, children will choose the toy that is challenging and interesting.

30.3.3d Dramatic play materials are part of the accessible toys for this boy.

To score this indicator, observe to see the range and quantity of materials children can use during free play, both indoors and outdoors. If free play is not observed, ask the staff about whether free play is provided, and if so, what materials children can use during that time, indoors and out. If non-mobile children are enrolled, ask how toys are made accessible to them. If the materials meet the requirements described above, score Indicator 3.3 "Yes."

30.3.3e These puzzles are in good condition indicating that staff value the learning that occurs during free play.

5.1   ***Much of the day*** is defined in the "Explanation of Terms Used Throughout the Scale," on page 7 of the ITERS-R. It means that children can participate in free play most of the time they are awake and able to play, and are not involved in routine care. (See photos 30.5.1a-c.) When awake, children cannot be restricted to groups or kept in spaces where there is no access to toys or play materials for lengthy periods. If long periods of time are unnecessarily spent in routine care activities or transitions between activities (especially

30.5.1a Whenever babies are awake and ready to play, free play is available.

30.5.1b Children get many opportunities to explore and experiment during lots of free play.

30.5.1c Gross motor options are included in the free play choices this child can make.

30.5.1d During most of the day, toddlers can choose what to play with and with whom.

30.5.1e Snow is a wonderful play material during the outdoor play for these toddlers.

when children are required to wait with nothing to do), credit cannot be given for this indicator.

To give credit for Indicator 5.1, children should spend most of the time they are awake in free play activities. Therefore, children should be observed involved in free play throughout much of the observation. (See photos 30.5.1d-e.) If they are not, score this indicator "No."

30.5.2a Providing stability for an unsteady infant is part of facilitating free play.

30.5.2b Sometimes it helps when staff show how to make a toy work.

30.5.2c Each child will require different amounts of help, depending on the child's abilities and the nature of the activity.

30.5.2d Helping to clean up periodically, to avoid clutter, is part of facilitating play.

5.2 ***Facilitating children's play*** means supervision in which staff *help* children during free play, but without intruding. (See photos 30.5.2a-d.) Examples of staff facilitating children's play are provided in the indicator. Other examples include:

- making accessible the materials each child needs for play, especially for non-mobile children who can access materials only with help,

- showing children how to use new or unfamiliar materials,

- calling the child's attention to a toy that might be interesting,

- stopping negative interactions among children,

- ensuring that each child has a safe place to play, or

- maintaining organization so play spaces do not become cluttered, and guiding older children in clean-up.

Facilitation of children's play is in addition to the basic supervision of children's safety required in Indicator 3.2. The requirement for this indicator goes beyond the facilitation of children's play, also required in 3.2, in that the staff must be ***actively involved*** in providing help, and this help must be provided frequently, ***throughout the day***.

Since the facilitation of children's play described above is required **_throughout the day_**, the observer should be able to score Indicator 5.2, based on observation. Score "Yes" if during the observation staff actively help children's play go well. If free play is not observed, or if staff do not usually facilitate children's free play during the time observed, score 5.2 "No."

5.3   **_Ample and varied toys and materials and much equipment_** means that children have *many* choices of appropriately challenging and interesting toys, materials, and equipment to use during free play. (See photos 30.5.3a-e.)

Varied materials and equipment are required so that each child can find a satisfying challenge within the free play environment, and when finished with one experience, can change to another interesting thing to do. Because infants and toddlers have different learn-

30.5.3a   Non-mobile babies are provided with many toys to choose from. In addition babies are moved so they can access different toys.

30.5.3b

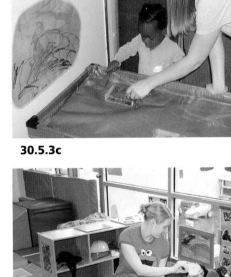

30.5.3c

30.5.3d

30.5.3e

30.5.3b-e   In this room children have safe choices of blocks, fine motor, gross motor, books, dramatic play, and science.

30.5.3f Within the many fine motor materials there are varied choices that represent different challenges.

30.5.3g Within the many dramatic play materials, there are varied materials that encourage pretend play.

ing styles, work on different skills at different times, and have special interests, ideally free play should be a time when all children can take advantage of the opportunities offered and learn in the way best suited to their individual personalities and developmental levels. Therefore, a *variety* of activities must be provided. (See photos 30.5.3f-g.)

Free play areas must offer many different types of play choices, including materials for both quiet and more active play. Most, but not necessarily all, types of activities included in the ITERS-R Activities subscale should be represented in what the children can choose to do (books, fine motor play, active physical play, art for toddlers, music/movement, blocks, sand/water for older toddlers, dramatic play, and nature/science). There should usually be at least three to five choices (depending on the number of children in the group) of *different* things to use within each of the types of materials and equipment provided, although some types of activities may have fewer choices.

Score Indicator 5.3 "Yes" if there is evidence that the requirements described above are met during free play times. Note that not all types of play have to be accessible to children at the same time during free play. For example, gross motor equipment might not be provided during indoor free play, or one area of the room might be closed for one of the several free play periods offered. However, many types of activities for children to choose from are required during any free play period, and variety (different types of choices) must be provided throughout the day.

7.1   ***Supervision that is used as an educational interaction*** means that staff encourage extra learning to come from the children's free play activities, but they do so without intruding. Examples of using supervision as an educational interaction are provided in the indicator. Other examples occur when staff:

- talk with children socially during their play,
- show children how to use a toy in a new way (see photo 30.7.1a),
- read to children,
- play or pretend with them (see photo 30.7.1b),
- help toddlers think through problems encountered with materials, not just by showing, but by cooperatively finding the solution (see photo 30.7.1c),

30.7.1a Demonstrating how a toy works is an educational interaction.

30.7.1b Staff involvement in dramatic play helps these toddlers imagine and act out household tasks, but also provides a model for social interaction.

- help children work out conflicts with one another, talking through the problem and coming to a satisfying solution,
- give suggestions about play,
- ask questions and provide answers, or let more able children provide the answers on their own,
- have toddlers explain what they are doing or thinking about in their play, and
- add new words and ideas to what the children are doing.

30.7.1c Seeking the missing pieces to the puzzle together is part of problem solving.

The score for this indicator must be based on observation of free play. Score Indicator 7.1 "Yes" if staff demonstrate educational interactions at least twice during observed free play, as required in the "Notes for Clarification" on page 46 of the ITERS-R. Remember that these interactions must occur during free play and not during group "teaching" times. If staff do not interact educationally with children during the observed free play time, score 7.1 "No."

7.2 ***When staff add materials to stimulate interest*** they increase children's learning opportunities, widening their knowledge and encouraging new discoveries. (See photo 30.7.2.) Even with ample toys and materials regularly accessible, infants and toddlers benefit from novelty. They gain from playing with toys that are completely new to them, and also from familiar toys that are reintroduced after a time. Examples of new materials being added for free play include:

30.7.2 Introducing a young infant to a new toy provides new interest during free play.

- new books added to represent current topics of interest to children in the group, or the things staff want them to notice, such as the seasons of the year,

- puzzles introduced as infants become toddlers,

- new props added to the dramatic play area so children can pretend about a variety of roles,

- supervised art activities offered regularly with toddlers as an option during free play,

- fine motor materials changed to create new interest and allow the practice of emerging skills, with sets of materials with many pieces being rotated,

- new pet added for children to watch or help care for,

- different types of toys used with sand/water play,

- different portable gross motor equipment added outdoors regularly, and

- indoor materials, such as art materials, fine motor toys, or books added to the outdoor play area.

In order to give credit for this indicator (score "Yes"), new materials or experiences must be added to the free play opportunities *at least once a month,* and preferably more often. To determine whether new materials are added, observe to see if obviously unfamiliar toys are being offered (the children's response should be a good clue). Also, check curriculum or activity plans, but only if the plans are followed during the observation. In addition, ask staff the questions on page 46 of the ITERS-R and base the score on what is reported.

31 Group play activities

General information about this item

Some practitioners believe that having infants or toddlers participate in *group activities* is good for them, because it prepares them for school. However, getting children ready to learn from group activities requires the development of many prerequisite or preparatory abilities and skills before they can actually learn in groups, and not just sit and behave as if they are learning. Those children who have developed the prerequisite social, language, and cognitive skills through appropriate individual learning experiences during their infant and toddler years will be ready for the next developmental step of learning in groups, without help. This ability will come with far less failure and stress if children have been able to learn according to their abilities when very young, and have not been pushed into the more mature behaviors too early. They will be able to learn in groups, not just look as if they are learning while they sit passively in a group.

The prerequisites for being able to learn efficiently in a group situation can be compared to the prerequisites for being able to drive a car. To teach a toddler to drive a car might be possible, if enough time and effort were used, and a small enough car was provided. However, we all would understand that the child was not really ready to be "out there" with the rest of us on the road. The toddler might have the superficial, obvious abilities of being able to make the car stop and go, and to steer, but not the more subtle skills required to do all that is needed to be a safe and responsible driver. The same is true for very young children's participation in group activities. Some children may be able to produce the easily observed behaviors of being part of a group activity (they can sit and be quiet), but this does not mean that a group activity is the best method to use to foster learning, based on their development.

Generally, group activities do not promote the type of learning from which young children benefit most because they are not individualized, hands-on, flexible, and self-directed. Having children participate in group activities, where all do the same thing at the same time, requires them to set aside their own interests and participate in a setting where individual needs are not emphasized. Although some young children may be able to do this, many children are at a disadvantage in such groups. Infants and toddlers are even less likely to have the skills required to benefit from the types of interactions and teaching methods that usually occur in a group. For example, infants and toddlers:

- require intense, personal interactions as they learn communication skills; therefore they are unable to benefit from the lecture style of teaching often used in groups, where staff talk to many children at the same time;

- learn best through hands-on play, in which they explore and experiment with objects in their own personal ways; therefore much learning time is wasted in activities that require all children to do the same thing at the same time;

- have vastly differing learning styles and developmental needs; therefore anything presented to them in just one way will not match many of the children's learning requirements; and

- have not yet developed the social skills or control to remain in a group setting without being forced (or constantly encouraged); therefore they often receive a message of failure that affects their long-term sense of how competent or valuable they are.

Although preschool-aged children are able to participate in large- and small-group times, these periods must be quite limited so children do not face inevitable failure, in terms of meeting staff expectations. Even school-aged children and adults profit from a more intense, personal approach to learning, though they usually have the skills to take what is required from group teaching methods. At times, however, a tutor, who gives very close, personal attention to a learner may be required, even for adults who are not getting what they need from group methods of teaching.

Since infants and toddlers are developmentally far from being able to profit from group teaching methods, such practices are not required in the ITERS-R. Instead, this item evaluates the appropriateness of any group play activities that might be used with very young children to be sure that children are not inappropriately pressured to conform to expectations that would be used with much older children.

As the "Note for Clarification" on page 47 of the ITERS-R indicates, the focus of this item is on play and learning activities that are carried out in groups, and does not include routine care activities, such as meals or nap. The Note provides a definition of *group play activities* as being "staff-initiated" with "an expectation of child participation." If this type of activity is not used in the infant/toddler group being observed, then the item is scored "NA."

Often observers are somewhat confused about whether they are observing a *group play activity* in an infant/toddler classroom or not, because, quite frequently, children of this age "flock" together, going where something of interest is happening. It may be that the staff are doing something of interest that children notice, or that a child has found an attractive toy, which becomes a magnet to the others. The result is that the children may come together for a time, all tending to focus on the same thing. However, when infants and toddlers are allowed to do what comes naturally, such temporary, spontaneous groupings dissolve as the children move away to the next thing that captures their attention. Such groups that tend to form and dissipate periodically in infant/toddler classrooms do not count when scoring this item.

This item does not apply to the less formal group activities that usually occur during free play in which children participate in groups because they are interested in doing the same activity at the same time." In other words, this item considers only activities that the staff initiate and direct with a group of children. Group play activities do not include:

- an activity that the children have initiated on their own, unless staff take over the activity and direct it with a group of children who are expected to participate; or.

If group play activities are used in the classroom being observed, then this item must be scored. Group play activities, when used sparingly and tailored to meet the needs of each child expected to participate, can be a positive experience, especially for older toddlers. The observer should consider the frequency of group play activities, whether the activities are appropriate and interesting, and the amount of pressure placed on children to remain with the group.

Scoring should be based primarily on what is observed. However, if no group play activity is observed but there is evidence that such activities are used with the children (e.g., circle time is listed on a displayed schedule, a group activity is shown on a curriculum plan), ask questions during the staff interview and score based on what is reported by staff. Ask:

- Do you ever use group activities, such as circle time, story time, art, or music with the children in your group? If the answer is "Yes," ask:
- What kinds of activities do you usually do with the children during group times?
- How are these usually handled?
- What is done if any child does not want to take part in the group activity?
- Are there other play options children can choose if they do not want to participate?

A closer look at each indicator

1.1   A ***staff-directed activity*** is one that is started and controlled to a great extent by staff. Staff-directed activities are the same as the ***group play activities*** considered in this item when two or more children are required to participate. Two examples are provided in the example for the indicator in the ITERS-R. Other examples of staff-directed activities include:

- Staff start a game of "Ring around the Rosie" with a small group.
- All children must leave what they are doing and watch a video that the teacher has selected.
- Children listen to a story selected and read by staff.
- Staff lead children in marching or singing with recorded music.
- Staff set up and direct a finger-painting activity at a table, supervising closely.
- Staff bring out a set of interlocking blocks for all to use at the same time.

It should be noted that if these examples are offered as options that children can freely choose to join or leave, they would not be considered group play activities, even though they are staff-directed.

Children must often participate even when not interested means that children are routinely forced or strongly encouraged to participate on a daily basis, even though they show signs of wanting to leave the group, being bored, frustrated, interested in something else, or unhappy. (See photo 31.1.1a-b, next page.) If children show that they want to leave, and staff tell them that they must stay, physically keep them in the group, or control children in any manner so that they have no understanding that leaving is a possibility, then they ***must participate***.

Score Indicator 1.1 "Yes" if it is observed during the observation that children who

31 Group play activities

31.1.1a

31.1.1b

31.1.1a-b If frequent participation is required in group play activities, even when toddlers are not interested, Indicator 1.1 would be scored "Yes". However, these children are free to play elsewhere.

are not interested must participate in a group play activity and staff take action to ensure that they do, as described above. If children are expected to participate, and all children obviously enjoy the activity, with no child becoming unhappy, bored or upset, score 1.1 "No."

If no group play activity is observed, but there is evidence that such activities are used with the children daily, or almost daily (e.g., circle time is listed on a displayed schedule, a group activity is shown on a curriculum plan), ask questions provided in the "General Information" section for this item and score based on what staff report.

1.2 The type of experience provided during a group play activity will have a great impact on whether the children will wish to participate. **Appropriate** group play activities are those in which children:

- are interested in the content of the activity, (See photo 31.1.2a.)

- can be more active (such as singing or dancing, pointing to pictures in a book and talking about them), rather than activities that require children to be quiet and passive, (See photo 31.1.2b.)

- each have close interactions with the staff, and do not have to wait long periods of time for individual attention—very small groups work best,

- can participate in a meaningful way, for example, can clearly see a book being read, can do own art, and can understand the content, (See photo 31.1.2c.)

- do not have to share materials, but each has his or her own to work with,

- are not crowded, and (See photo 31.1.2d.)

- are challenged by what is done, but not frustrated.

Group play activities that are inappropriate would not be characterized by the attributes listed above. For example, activities such as the following would be inappropriate:

- A large group of toddlers is crowded together as the staff member reads a very small book that few children can see clearly.

- All infants/young toddlers sit at the table together to do an art activity that requires skills they have not mastered.

31.1.2a Babies are very interested in this group activity, but are free to leave if they wish.

31.1.2b Music time, in which children can actively participate when they wish, is an appropriate group activity for these toddlers.

31.1.2c Toddlers enjoy active participation in the appropriate activity of books and songs.

31.1.2d Children are not crowded during this book activity so they are more likely to enjoy the short story.

- A teacher places a set of interlocking blocks in the middle of the group of toddlers and all children are supposed to use them together.

- All children in a 2-year-old group must listen quietly during "Show and Tell," in which each child will take a turn.

- All toddlers must sing while sitting in their chairs, as they wait 10 minutes for lunch; many try to get up and leave.

To score, the observer should pay close attention to the content of any group play activity that takes place during the observation. If no group play activity is observed, but there is evidence that such activities are used with the children (e.g., circle time is listed on a displayed schedule, a group activity is shown on a curriculum plan), ask questions provided in the "General Information" section for this item and score based on what staff report.

If the activities used during group play are usually inappropriate (about 75% of the time) score Indicator 1.2 "Yes."

31 Group play activities

1.3 For staff to **behave negatively** means that their interactions with the children carry messages of anger, coldness, impatience, or lack of respect. When this behavior is directed at infants or toddlers, the children learn to feel less valuable, competent, appreciated, or loved. Negative behavior is often associated with using a harsh or loud tone of voice, rough treatment, teasing, unpleasant expressions, criticizing or punishing the child. Such behavior is considered for this indicator when it is displayed in response to a child who does not wish to participate in a group play activity. The observer should note the child's response to what is considered to be negative behavior on the part of staff.

31.3.1 Since no one is forced to participate, just three dancers are participating at this moment. Other children are involved in free play.

Score Indicator 1.3 "Yes" if it is observed that any child is responded to with negative behavior by staff because the child does not wish to participate in a group play activity. If no group play activity is observed, but there is evidence that such activities are used with the children (e.g., circle time is listed on a displayed schedule, a group activity is shown on a curriculum plan), ask questions provided in the "General Information" section for this item and score based on what staff report, combined with information on how staff treat children who are not compliant during the observation. It is unlikely that staff would use positive behaviors with non-compliant children at group play times if they use negative behaviors in many other situations.

3.1 **Forced to participate**, in this item, means that children are strongly encouraged or made to participate, even though they show signs of wanting to leave the group, being bored, frustrated, interested in something else, or unhappy. If children show that they want to leave, and staff tell them that they must stay, physically keep them in the group, or control children in any manner so that they have no understanding that leaving is a possibility, then they are **forced to participate**.

To score this indicator "Yes," no instance of forcing a child to participate in a group play activity can be observed or reported by staff. (See photo 31.3.1.) This is true, even if staff only encourage a child once to participate, if the child does not become interested and engaged in the activity but must stay. This is because staff expectation of participation in an activity may pressure many children to comply. For example, a toddler sitting in the group at story time, is not interested in the book. As she begins to stand up to move away, the staff member says, "Sit down so you can hear the story." The child then sits passively but never becomes engaged in the activity.

3.2 **Appropriate** is defined for group play activities in Indicator 1.2. This indicator requires that at least 75% of the activities used with children during group play times be appropriate. Often, a group time will consist of several activities. For example, at circle time, children may first sing songs, then listen to a story, and then staff may tell children which centers are open. Each activity (not the group time as a whole) should be considered. Children's responses to the activities, the extent to which they are interested, involved, engaged, and content, should be used to determine the appropriateness, and how well it meets children's developmental needs.

3.3 **Positive** staff behaviors are the opposite of negative staff behaviors, defined in Indicator 1.3. They give children the message that they are happy with the children, and seem content, relaxed, patient, respectful, and interested, helping each child

31.3.3a Story time is over when the children lose interest, and teachers respect children's needs to move on.

31.3.3b Staff are positive and everyone enjoys music time, because expectations for participation are appropriate.

to feel valuable, competent, appreciated, and loved. Staff who are neutral in their interactions do not give strong messages of any type--they are neither harmful nor supportive. ***Acceptant*** means that staff do not try to get children to do what children are naturally incapable of doing. They understand where each child is, in terms of development and personality, and think little of no child. Instead staff take each child where he or she is, understanding that with appropriate guidance and teaching, the child will progress. (See photos 31.3.3a-b.)

To determine whether staff are positive and acceptant with children, for this indicator, no instances of negative behavior towards any child can be observed during a group play activity. Positive and acceptant behavior must be observed 75% of the time, with neutral behavior accounting for any other interactions with the children.

If no group play activity is observed, but there is evidence that such activities are used with the children (e.g., circle time is listed on a displayed schedule, a group activity is shown on a curriculum plan), ask questions provided in the "General Information" section for this item and score based on what staff report, combined with information on how staff treat children who are not compliant during the observation. It is unlikely that staff would use positive behaviors with non-compliant children at group play times when they use mostly negative or neutral behaviors in many other situations.

5.1 ***Staff are flexible and adjust activity as children join or leave the group*** means that they adapt to the children's preferences and interests, meeting the needs of each child. For example, because mobile infants and toddlers tend to flock to novel activities, they will frequently join a group activity that the staff initiate. Then some will want to stay and others will drift away, as their attention is captured by another interesting learning opportunity. Another child, who was not interested initially, may join the others later. Children will naturally join and leave the group periodically. Staff who can respond positively to these "comings and goings," and who can carry out the activity successfully, will get credit for this indicator. They do so by adjusting the ***activity*** to the number of children who are present in the group. Examples of how this might be done are provided in the indicator. Others include

31.5.2a This very small group, working closely with one staff member, ensures individual attention during group time.

31.5.2b Reading a book to just two babies is an enjoyable, intimate experience in which children are relaxed and have the greatest chance for learning.

- Staff have additional adults join in the supervision of the group when more children are participating, and leaving the group to supervise children who drift away.

- If the group gets too big for productive interactions, starting another group doing the same thing at another place, for example, putting out the same art materials for children to use at another small table, or setting up another place for water play if one becomes too crowded.

- Staff changing the pace or content of activity if children's interest begins to lessen, for example, putting away a book if children are not listening and having children do exercises to music instead

31.5.2c This larger group, even with plenty of adults, makes the experience far less meaningful to these very young children.

When a group play activity is observed, score this indicator "Yes" if children are allowed to join and leave group play activities freely, and staff modify how the group is handled, based on the children's participation.

If no group play activity is observed, but there is evidence that such activities are used with the children, ask questions provided in the "General Information" section for this item and score based on what staff report, combined with what is observed regarding how staff treat children and handle activities during the observation.

5.2 To learn from adults, infants and toddlers require more direct and intense interactions than older children. In addition, younger children have less developed social skills that make interactions with their peers in groups less meaningful. The younger the child, the greater the need for intense adult interaction. Younger children do better if they have fewer peers with whom they must share the adult. In addition, activities that need lots of supervision, such as sand play or art (where staff need to prevent children from eating the materials), require fewer children. Therefore, to make group play activities beneficial to infants and toddlers, they must be in very small groups. (See photos 31.5.2a–c.)

Indicator

Suggestions for the appropriate *size of group* for group play activities are provided in the example of this indicator. However, a group size that works successfully will depend on the characteristics of the children in the group and the nature of the activity being done. For example, if children are actively involved in the activity, such as in dancing to music, then a larger group size might work well. However, if a staff member is reading a very small book to infants, a smaller group might be needed, or the activity might not work well at all with more than one child.

31.5.3 When not choosing to participate in a group activity, children have many choices for free play in the rest of the room.

To score, the observer should watch any group play activity that occurs to determine whether the size of the group allows all participating children to benefit. The response of the children will be the best indicator. If any child is bored, unhappy, or not interested and engaged, due to the size of the group, score Indicator 5.2 "No." If all children are happily interested and engaged, score 5.2 "Yes," because obviously the size of the group matches the type of activity and the needs of each child.

If no group play activity is observed, but there is evidence that such activities are used with the children, ask questions provided in the "General Information" section for this item and score based on what staff report, combined with what is observed regarding how staff group children during the observation.

5.3   An *alternative activity* is another option for play that children are allowed to choose if they do not wish to participate in the group play activity. The alternative activity can be teacher-initiated or child-initiated, but it must be an interesting option that the child would prefer. It can be a choice of another group play activity, and not necessarily a free play option, as long as the child can choose something that is engaging. It cannot be something that the child does not like to do, such as sitting at a table with nothing to do or resting quietly on a cot. The alternative activity cannot serve as a punishment for not participating in the group play activity. Most frequently, the alternate activity is what the child does who leaves the group and has free access to many toys.

Since the word activities is in the plural, to score "Yes" there must be more than one interesting option for the children to choose. Score "Yes" if more than one alternative play option is available to any child who chooses not to participate in any group play activity. (See photo 31.5.3.) The presence of a selection of accessible toys that the child is allowed to use would result in a score of "Yes."

If no group play activity is observed, but there is evidence that such activities are used with the children, ask questions provided in the "General Information" section for this item and score based on what staff report.

7.1   For group play activities to be *set up to maximize children's success* requires that staff consider the characteristics of the children who will be participating and tailor the experience so that it will be appropriate for the children (see definition of appropriate in Indicator 1.2), the size of the group will not hinder children's participation, and the staff and children can manage the complexity of the task being used.

Basically, if a group play activity goes well (children are interested, content, and engaged) and children want to participate, the activity will have been set up to meet the children's needs. (See photo 31.7.1.) The observer will notice that each child can be involved in a meaningful way. This does not mean that children quietly sit and behave according to staff expectations, but rather they are enjoying the experience, and it is interesting to them. Children want to join, and remain with, the group because it is satisfying to do so.

Examples of some basics needed for infants and toddlers to be successful in group play activities are provided in the indicator, and other examples have been discussed throughout the indicators at the lower levels of quality. Score "Yes" if group play activities go well for most of the children (e.g., most children are able to participate successfully, and those who cannot are allowed to do something else). If group times are chaotic, and children are not interested or meaningfully involved, score "No."

31.7.1 Children's success is maximized by the small group, the positive staff who ensure all can participate, and the "surprise boxes" that interest the children. In addition the group time will last only as long as children are interested.

If no group play activity is observed, but there is evidence that such activities are used with the children, ask questions provided in the "General Information" section for this item and score based on what staff report about how group activities are set up.

7.2 Group play activities that work well for one infant or toddler will not necessarily work well for another. This indicator requires that staff adjust what they do to meet the needs of a child who has difficulty participating in an activity that would otherwise be appropriate and beneficial, and who could be helped by a simple change in how things are handled. Examples are provided in the indicator for such accommodations. Other examples include:

- Staff position themselves next to children who cannot do an art activity successfully without extra help.
- Staff read a story used in larger group to a smaller group who need more direct staff attention.
- A special chair is used for a child who has trouble sitting on rug, due to a physical disability.
- A child with a visual impairment is placed closest to the flannel board being used.
- Children who do not get along well are not placed next to one another.

Score "Yes" if there is evidence of any adjustments in group play activities for a child who needs a little extra help to be successful. The help provided must make the activity satisfying for the child, rather than only keeping the child in the group without causing problems.

If no group play activity is observed, but there is evidence that such activities are used with the children, ask questions provided in the "General Information" section for this item and score based on what staff report and staff behavior during the observation.

32 Provisions for children with disabilities

General information about this item

In the ITERS-R "Notes for Clarification" for this item, it is stated that this item should be used only if a child with an identified disability is included in the program.

A child with an identified disability is one who has completed a formal assessment procedure and is receiving (or is eligible for) early intervention services.

The assessment procedure must have been completed by professionals who specialize in psychology, pediatrics, physical therapy, early childhood special education, or other appropriate areas, and who have formally assessed the abilities and needs of a child who does not appear to be developing typically. Upon completion of the assessment, the child has been classified as having a disability, usually categorized by either a specific condition, (such as Down syndrome, cerebral palsy, hearing impairment, or autism), or by the type of disability, such as physical/sensory, cognitive/language, social/emotional, or a combination of these.

If no assessment has been completed on any child who is thought to have disabilities, score this item "NA."

An infant or toddler might be diagnosed and classified as "at risk" for a disability, without being classified with a specific condition. If a child who has been diagnosed in this way is enrolled in the group being observed, and is *receiving early intervention services*, then the item should be scored.

If a child is diagnosed with a disability (or is diagnosed as being at risk for a disability), then intervention services (such as physical therapy, occupational therapy, or speech and language therapy) will usually be provided, or the child might be waiting for services to start. In either case, this item is to be completed for the one or more children enrolled in the group being assessed. Usually, a plan with goals defined by a team of people interested in the child's progress (such as parents, special educators, classroom staff, and doctors) will be developed to guide the services to be provided to the child. In the United States, such a plan for infants or toddlers is called an Individualized Family Service Plan (IFSP). An IFSP is not required to begin scoring the item, but a plan with goals must be used if requirements of the higher quality levels are to be reached.

To find out whether a child who meets the requirements is enrolled in the group being assessed, question program staff (usually the director or classroom staff) *before* the observation begins. Fill in the information collected in the space provided on the first page of the ITERS-R score sheet. In this item some indicators will be scored based on observation, while others will depend on what is reported by classroom staff.

Observers are cautioned to make sure that the child in question has *already* been evaluated and diagnosed, and that staff are not simply reporting their own informal concerns about the development of a child. Although program staff are often among the first people to express concern when a child does not seem to be developing typically and are often proven correct in their informal assessments, an official diagnosis is required to score the item. Many of the requirements in the indicators are based on the premise that the diagnosis and services are in place.

Whether the classroom meets the needs of any child in the group being observed, including those with disabilities, is examined in all items in the ITERS-R. This item, however, focuses primarily on issues relating to how information from the assessment is used and the extent to which the child with disabilities is included in, as opposed to excluded from, regular classroom activities.

To score the item, a combination of observation and questioning of staff is needed. If the child with special needs is easy to identify in the group, the observer should evaluate whether the child is handled in a way that would promote development. For example, the child is not segregated from peers but included with the other children to the extent possible, and any necessary adaptations are provided so the child can participate in classroom activities as fully and positively as possible.

Do not ask the program staff to give any information that a child's parents might consider private. The staff do not need to point out the child in question or tell about the particulars of the disability being considered, in order to adhere to confidentiality requirements. If the child is not easy to identify, always assume that parents prefer to have their privacy protected, and simply ask the questions needed to score this item without having the child identified.

A closer look at each indicator

1.1 This indicator is scored "Yes" when program staff report that a child meeting the requirements discussed above is enrolled in the class being observed, and staff report that they do *not* try to find out assessment information and know nothing about the child's special needs or the results of the formal assessment. No one (such as parents) has communicated the necessary information to the staff, nor have staff attempted to find out about the assessment.

If staff report that they are aware of the diagnosis, but have not had the opportunity to talk with parents or to find out about the assessment, then score Indicator 1.1 "Yes." Also, if program administrative staff report the enrollment of a child with a diagnosed disability in the group being observed, but classroom staff report not being aware of the child's special needs or condition, 1.1 is scored "Yes."

1.2 ***Attempts to meet children's special needs*** may take many forms, depending on the nature of the needs. In some cases, for example, when a child is at risk for a disability due to premature birth or lack of appropriate early stimulation, a child's special needs might be met by providing a good, stimulating early childhood program alone. For children with more specific disabilities, special action by staff or early interventionists will be required. For example, staff might need to handle the learning needs of the child in a special way, specific accommodations might be needed in the furnishings or classroom, the schedule might need to be adapted, or therapy activities might need to be implemented. Being able to meet a child's special needs requires that the staff know what the special need is and what it requires from them.

Indicator 1.2 is true (score "Yes") if classroom staff report that a child in the group has special needs (the child has been evaluated and diagnosed and is eligible for special services), but they do nothing to meet the child's special needs within the program. However, remember that the provision of a *good* quality program, in itself, may meet the special needs of some children with disabilities, and that no accommodations beyond that provision are required. In case no special accommodations are needed, score the indicator "No."

1.3   For this indicator, ***involvement of parents*** means that parents (or other responsible adults who have the parenting responsibility) share information with staff about their child's special requirements (***needs***) and the ***goals*** set for the child. The goals for the child (usually the steps or milestones parents want their child to work towards) may be in the form of an IFSP (see "General Information" section for this item) or less formally set. If no communication takes place between parents and staff about what the child's disability requires and how to best meet the special needs of the child, score Indicator 1.3 "Yes."

Sometimes parents choose not to share information about how to best meet the needs of their child. Some reasons for this lack of communication might be that the parents do not communicate willingly with others, they cannot find the time for such communication, they are uncomfortable talking with staff, or they do not speak the language the staff speak. If for any reason Indicator 1.3 is true (score "Yes") if no involvement or communication between parents and staff takes place. This is considered inadequate because the child's development is compromised when parents and staff do not work together to meet a child's needs. Even if staff have put significant effort into encouraging parental involvement, if such efforts are unsuccessful, 1.3 is still scored "Yes."

1.4   When a child with disabilities is segregated from other children, learning opportunities are missed by the child who is segregated and by the other children as well. Therefore, it is desirable to have children with disabilities included with their peers as much as possible during the play/learning activities and routines. This is what is meant by ***involvement*** with other children, or the rest of the group.

The extent to which children with disabilities can be involved with other children in the group is determined by the social skills of children in the group. If the class has only very young infants, not much social interaction would be expected among peers, although children might be interested in one another. Toddlers, on the other hand, tend to play near one another, but they are not able to communicate well with one another or cooperate. The observer should observe to determine whether the child with disabilities is segregated from the rest of the children in any way, or whether the child is handled as the other children are. (See photos 32.1.4a-d.) When it is difficult to tell which child in a group has a disability, based on the way the child is handled by staff (rather than on physical or developmental characteristics), it is likely that the child is being well-integrated into the group. (See photo 32.1.4e.)

Sometimes it is easy to involve a child with disabilities in all the children's activities. In other instances, it takes more thought and effort on the part of the staff to figure out how a child can be included. For example, a child with reduced physical abilities may need a ramp to take part in active physical play on a climber or slide. Or

32 Provisions for children with disabilities

32.1.4a

32.1.4b

32.1.4a-b   If these two photos represented most of what this child experiences, there would be very little involvement with the rest of the group.

32.1.4c

32.1.4d

32.1.4c-d   The amount of segregation used will determine how well the child is involved with other children. A simple change turns this into a far better experience for everyone.

a child whose social skills are developing less rapidly than those of her peers may require an adult's help to participate in play with others.

Very little involvement means a child with disabilities does not usually participate with others in the class and is segregated from the other children most of the day.

Indicator 1.4 is true (score "Yes") when a child with disabilities is usually separated from peers in the group, for example, eats separately, is not included in play times, naps in a different place, or does not go outside with the others. Staff do not ensure that the child is included with others as much as possible, or the child is needlessly segregated.

32.1.4e   When it is difficult to tell if there is a child with a disability in the group, it is likely the child is well-integrated.

Indicator

3.1   See the General Information section of this item for the definition of ***assessments***.

This indicator is scored "Yes" when a child meeting the requirements, discussed in the "General Information" section for this item, is enrolled in the class being observed, and staff report that they know about the child's special needs and the results of the formal assessment. Someone (such as a parent, special educator, or therapist) has communicated the assessment information to the staff. Staff should be able to describe, in general terms, the child's disability. The staff do not have to have read the written report--verbal communication is sufficient to score Indicator 3.1 "Yes."

3.2   ***Minor modifications made to meet the needs of children with disabilities*** include small changes that take place in the regular classroom operations and staff behaviors. Minor modifications should not require intense, regular, specialized help from professionals or extra staff members. They may require small changes in a classroom, such as in the furnishings, room arrangement, how people interact with a child, the amount of attention given to a child, what is taught, or the schedule. (See photos 32.3.2a-d.)

32.3.2a

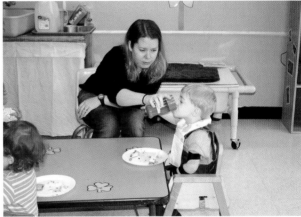

32.3.2b

32.3.2a-b   A special chair and extra help at breakfast are examples of modifications made for these children so they can eat with their peers.

32.3.2c   Equipment taken from the infant room is used to help this child play.

32.3.2d   Arranging furniture to accommodate the wheelchair is a modification made by staff.

Here are some examples of minor modifications:

- Special foods are served to a child who may have problems eating due to a disability.
- Staff provide more help to a child who has difficulty playing.
- A more flexible schedule is used to accommodate a child's need for less rigid time periods.
- Toys that meet the child's special requirements are included with regularly available materials.
- Staff stay closer to a child who has more difficulty getting along with others.
- Diapering facilities are provided for a child who is taking longer to become toilet trained.
- Pathways in the room are widened to allow a toddler using a walker or wheelchair to access the various play areas.

To score this indicator, the observer can depend on two sources of information. First, if the observer can identify the child in the group and knows something about the child's disability, modifications might be observed during the observation. Second, staff can describe any modifications that are carried out to meet the needs of the child during the staff interview.

3.3   See Indicator 1.3 for definitions of *parent involvement* and *goals*.

To score "Yes" for this indicator, the parent(s) of the child with disabilities and the classroom staff must communicate in some way to decide on the goals for the child. Involvement of center staff who are *not* a regular, daily part of the child's classroom (such as the director, assistant director, or therapist) does not meet the requirement of this indicator, even though such staff can provide helpful, positive input into goal-setting for a child.

Some involvement by classroom staff can take place through formal meetings, informal conversations, phone, or written communications. At this quality level (minimal), the involvement does not have to be extensive, but it does have to take place, and goals for the child must come from the communication.

3.4   See Indicator 1.4 for a definition of *involvement in ongoing activities with other children.*

Some involvement means a child with disabilities sometimes participates with others in the class, and at other times does not. The child may be segregated from the other children at some times, but not at all times of the day.

Indicator 3.4 is true (score "Yes") when the child with disabilities sometimes (but not necessarily always) participates in play or routine care activities with peers in the group. For example, the child may eat separately but is included in play time and naps in the same place, or she goes outside with the others but does not play on the same equipment.

5.1   All classroom staff, and other professionals who work with children, can profit from sharing ideas that come from others. This allows new perspectives to influence the work done with children. In the case of teaching children with disabilities, the recommendations from others who specialize in treating disabilities can make a big difference in the ability of classroom staff to better meet the special needs of a child. A cooperative, collaborative approach works best.

There are specialized **professionals** who have the experience and knowledge required to make recommendations for the care of children with disabilities. For example, a psychologist can help a child with a social/emotional challenge; a speech and language therapist can define what a child with communication difficulties needs; or a physical therapist can determine the experiences that will best help a child improve motor skills. **Classroom staff** can gain knowledge by finding out what specialists recommend for a child and by **following through** with their suggestions.

Recommendations are usually suggestions for activities or interactions that will help the child meet the challenges caused by a disability. (See photos 32.5.1a-c.) For example, an occupational therapist might suggest that a child who has difficulty coordinating his hands be given a special spoon at meals and snacks so he can feed himself. Or a speech and language therapist might recommend that staff consistently make eye contact with a child who has hearing difficulties and speak more clearly and simply than with other children. Special activities and interactions are often recommended for both routines and play.

To give credit for Indicator 5.1 (score "Yes"), staff must either be observed using special activities or interactions with the child, or, during the teacher interview, staff must describe the special recommendations made for the child and how these are carried out in the classroom.

If staff are not observed doing special activities or using special interactions with the child or report that they do not know about recommendations made by specialists, score Indicator 5.1 "No."

5.2   **Modifications** in this indicator, at the "good" level of quality, include *any* changes **needed** to allow the child with disabilities to participate in many of the classroom activities with others. In some cases these modifications may not be particularly demanding, but in others, they may require a lot of creativity, new arrangements, additional staff, and resources. (See photos for Indicator 7.2.)

Modifications in the environment include changes in the facility (the building or classroom), furnishings and equipment, or arrangement of spaces used. Examples of such modifications are:

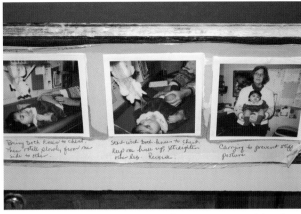

32.5.1a   Therapists' instructions are posted in the room to guide staff.

32.5.1b

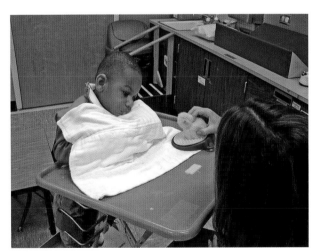

32.5.1c

32.5.1b-c   Play activities are also part of the recommended practices that staff use.

- providing a ramp or elevator to access the building,
- providing special lighting,
- rearranging classrooms to provide wider pathways,
- installing special accessible play equipment on playgrounds,
- providing specialized furnishings, such as chairs or standers, to allow a child to access materials and play with them,
- providing equipment needed for routine care, such as special feeding equipment or sleep surfaces, and
- adapting space for therapists to work with the child.

Modifications in the program include changes in staff-child ratio or group size; the provision of special activities, toys and materials; using different teaching or behavior management practices; including therapists as part of classroom staff; and more intensive parent/staff cooperation and communication. There is a great number of modifications that might be needed to allow a child with a disability to participate in activities with others. A limited list of examples includes:

- reducing class size to better meet the needs of all children enrolled,
- adding an additional staff member to provide extra attention for the child with a severe disability who requires more intense help,
- providing either more structured or less structured activities, depending on the special needs of the child,
- providing a greater range in difficulty levels of play activities,
- targeting activities to help a child practice very specific skills,
- using special modes of communication, such as signing, word boards, switches, or photographs,
- using special equipment, such as hearing devices, glasses, or medical equipment, and
- giving special medications.

Modifications in schedule include changes in the sequence of events experienced by the children, but also in the schedule for attendance at the center. Examples of such modifications are:

- providing a more flexible, individualized rest time for a child who tires easily,
- allowing longer feeding times for the child who has difficulties eating,
- allowing a child with a disability to attend for half a day in a full-day program, or
- freeing staff from classroom responsibilities so they can attend meetings with parents, therapists, and other professionals involved in the care of the child.

The modifications required to allow a child to participate in many (but not most or all) activities in the regular classroom will depend on the needs of the child. If little or no modification is required for the child to participate in many activities, score 5.2 "Yes."

If the possibilities for participation in many activities are not met reasonably well because obvious, needed changes are not being made in the environment, program, or schedule, do not give credit for Indicator 5.2 (score "No").

5.3   To score "Yes" for this indicator, the communication described in Indicator 3.3 must take place **_frequently_**. Daily (or almost daily) informal communication is required, and formal meetings, in which issues can be handled in more depth, should take place at least twice a year.

The content required in the indicator (sharing information, setting goals, and providing feedback on how the program is working) does not have to be covered every day. However, it should be included often enough to ensure that staff and parents work as partners in meeting the child's needs. Conversation specifically related to the child's disability is not required every day. Instead, parents and staff can share information about the child's experiences or progress that is not bound to the disability. If not observed, ask the questions on page 48 of the ITERS-R for this indicator, and base the score on what is reported by staff.

7.1   **_Professional intervention_** consists of activities designed specifically to optimize the development of a child with disabilities. The activities can be carried out during routine care or play times and will help a child reach the goals set by those who are most interested in the child's well-being, such as parents and classroom staff. For example, activities might be designed to help a child with physical disabilities learn to feed himself with a spoon or to walk. Or activities might be developed to help a child who has unusual difficulties getting along with others to form friendships and to play with others.

Intervention activities have been shown to be most effective when they are carried out as a usual part of a child's home or classroom experiences. When **_most_** of the intervention is incorporated into regular classroom practices, a child gets more chances to develop the skills being targeted.

To give credit for Indicator 7.1 (score "Yes"), a specialist who provides intervention must usually carry out most of the intervention activities **_within the classroom setting_** (indoors or outdoors). Only under unusual circumstances should the activities be carried out in a segregated setting.

Credit can also be given for Indicator 7.1 when classroom staff carry out the intervention activities. To be sure the activities are being implemented properly, it is preferred that professionals, such as therapists, explain and demonstrate the activities to regular classroom staff before the staff take over.

7.2   In many cases, children with moderate disabilities can be so well integrated into most classroom activities that the observer has to search hard to identify the child. This is a sign that the requirements for Indicator 7.2 are being met.

To score this indicator, consider the nature and severity of a child's disability. Look to see how well the child with disabilities blends into the group and determine whether the child is being excluded when he or she could be included. (See photos 32.7.2a-i, next page.)

A child with disabilities should be included in most play activities and routines, just as every other child is, with special modifications or interventions being carried out as smoothly and inconspicuously as possible. Remember that most therapies or interventions should be carried out as part of the regular classroom activities that include both the children with disabilities and their typically developing peers. Only in relatively unusual cases, when a child has extremely severe disabilities, should the child be segregated in any way, and no child should often be segregated from the group.

32 Provisions for children with disabilities

"Inclusion of All Children"

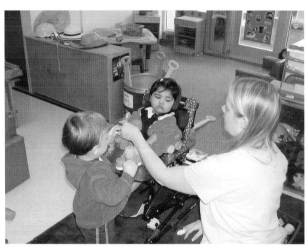

32.7.2a

32.7.2b

32.7.2a-b Making toys accessible, where others can join in play, promotes participation with peers.

32.7.2c Outdoor play is for all children in the group.

32.7.2d The musical toy on the wheelchair tray adds to the dancing experience.

32.7.2e

32.7.2f

32.7.2e-f Children enjoy many informal story times together.

Indicator

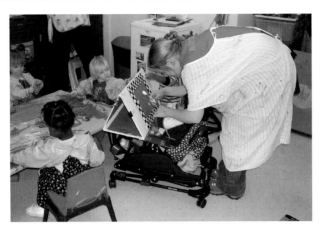

32.7.2g

32.7.2h

32.7.2g-i Inclusion in art requires more modifications.

7.3 Like parents, classroom staff have significant knowledge about how a child is progressing and ideas for activities that will help promote the child's development. Classroom staff see the child in a different environment, where he may not behave in the same way as at home or during a formal assessment in a strange place. Having *all* the responsible adults in the child's life give input about the child to determine his developmental level and make plans for the future gives the child a better chance for success.

32.7.2i

To score this indicator, ask staff if they participate in the assessments of the child's developmental status and help in creating the intervention plans. If staff can describe participating in these activities, score Indicator 7.3 "Yes."

Parents and Staff

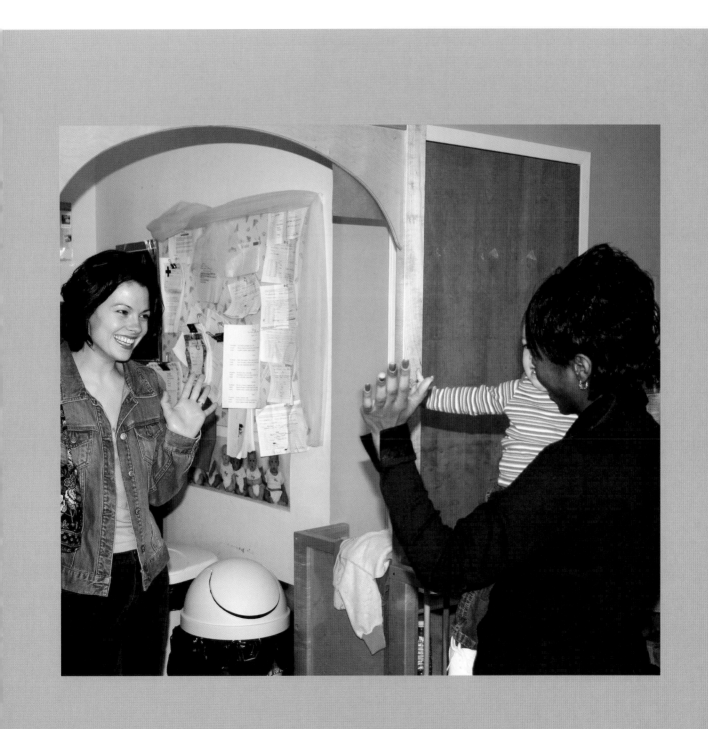

33 Provisions for parents

General information about this item

When the parents of young children send their child to an infant/toddler program, they need help in adjusting to the new situation as much as their child does. For many parents this may be the first time they have entrusted their child's care to a stranger for many hours every day. They may have concerns about their child's safety and the ability of staff to supervise so many young children, about whether their child will be picked up promptly or allowed to cry, whether their picky eater will eat anything away from home, and whether the staff's way of handling discipline will coincide with their own. Along with these fears there is a sense of loss because now someone else will be watching the first step, hearing the first word, dealing with the sad moments, and getting the warm hugs. From this uncertain, somewhat reluctant initial relationship, parents and staff will need to gradually build a trusting partnership. We all know that things go more smoothly for a child when the key caring adults get along well and act as a team. As the professional partner in the team, it is the responsibility of the staff to reach out to parents with information about the program and to extend a warm welcome to participate as actively as they can. Staff need to remember that the parents come into an unfamiliar program and may be uneasy at first about leaving a young child who cannot tell them if anything is wrong. It is the staff's responsibility to help the parents feel at ease so they can start to trust.

At the other end of the spectrum are parents that staff perceive as being altogether too relaxed about having someone else care for their child. However, these are parents about whom no assumptions or value judgments should be made. Each parent may respond differently to leaving a child with someone else. All must be encouraged to form the partnership with staff that will promote the well being of the child.

Each parent must be treated with respect by the staff and administration. If staff set a high standard of behavior, parents will follow suit and behave with respect towards the staff in return. A free exchange of information about the child forms a good basis for teamwork between parents and staff. Although programs vary in their involvement of parents, all programs must have an "open door" policy, so that parents are free to visit at any time.

Parents will vary in the amount of time they have to be involved in the program and in the ways they express their interest. This item focuses on what is offered to the parents by the program, not how the parents respond to the provisions made for them by the program.

Providing information about the program is a good beginning for building a relationship. Before enrollment, parents must have key administrative information in writing about the program, such as fees, hours of operation, or rules for exclusion for health reasons. But they will need to know other programmatic information as well. For example, parents should be informed about the caregiving practices, the discipline policy, and the activities provided for the children. In addition to this general information, parents appreciate ongoing communication about how their child is doing in the program through both informal conversations and periodic conferences. If needed, referrals to other professionals should also be available.

In addition to an ongoing information exchange, provisions for parents must include many ways for parents to be involved in the program. At the most basic level, parents need to be able to bring their child into the classroom and feel free to visit at any time, which is known as an "open door" policy. Other ways for parents to be involved might include visiting the program and sharing talents and interests with the children, assisting with simple field trips (for older toddlers), joining in a pot luck or clean up/fix-it day with other parents. As parents become partners with the staff, they can give helpful feedback through evaluations requested by the program, and by serving on committees and boards to share responsibility in decision making roles.

This item addresses these three aspects of provisions for parents, information sharing, involvement, and playing decision making roles. Much of the information needed to score this item must be collected by asking questions of program staff. Ask the classroom staff the necessary questions first, and if they are not able to give the answers, then the director or other program administrators may be asked. There are sample questions printed in the ITERS-R to guide the interview. Whenever possible, look for concrete evidence to determine whether an indicator is true. For example, ask to see the written materials provided to parents, if staff report they are used.

Additional information related to the interaction between parents and staff is assessed in Item 6, Greeting/departing.

A closer look at each indicator

1.1 This indicator is scored "Yes" if no information is given to the parents about the program *in writing*. Verbal information can be misunderstood and there is no proof about what was actually told to parents. Therefore, giving information about the program only verbally is considered inadequate and scored "Yes." Score this indicator "No" if any program related information is given to parents in writing. Ask to see the written material in order to score "No."

1.2 This indicator assesses whether parents are discouraged from participating in the program. Programs that discourage parents from observing or do not allow them to become actively involved cause families to feel anxious and alienated. Not being allowed to observe also causes parents to be misinformed about their child's experience.

Parents receive reassurance and a better understanding from visiting to see how their child and others are being treated. Such visits can form a basis for trusting the classroom staff and program administrators. Excuses for excluding parents, such as telling parents that their child will adjust more quickly if they do not visit, often prolong a child's adjustment period, or have a lasting negative emotional effect on the child. Putting excessive demands on parents to make appointments to visit only at certain times or on certain days makes it difficult for parents to visit and should be considered examples of discouraging parents from visiting. If the program has parents drive up and drop off their children at the curb, the observer should watch to see if parents and children are greeted. If some parents are observed bringing their children in while others use the curb drop-off, score 1.2 "No." If no parents are observed bringing their children into the classroom, score 1.2 "Yes."

Parents can be **_discouraged_** from taking part in the program in several ways including through policies such as:

- having a policy prohibiting parents from participating in the classroom

- having a no observation policy

- asking parents to make an appointment several days beforehand to visit during specific "visiting hours"

- installing a curb or front desk only drop-off policy so that parents are not allowed to bring their child into the classroom

Or through practices such as:

- staff reacting in a cold or unfriendly way when parents drop in or drop their children off

- never asking parents to participate in or to be involved in the program

- refusing politely by citing the school policy or philosophy if parents offer to help, visit, or participate

Score this indicator "Yes" if the program has any policies or practices such as those listed above.

3.1 At a minimum, parents must be given **_administrative information in writing_** before they enroll their child. The administrative details, such as fees and when they are due, hours of service, absence policy, and health rules for attendance, should spell out clearly the responsibilities of the program and the responsibilities of the parent. Prototypes of forms are sometimes available from child care licensing or resource and referral agencies and child care provider organizations.

If staff report that such materials are provided to parents in writing, ask to see a copy to assure that most of the basic administrative information is covered.

Parents whose primary language is not the language used in the written materials or who cannot read, may need help with accessing the information. It is essential that all parents receive the information about the program and are clear about the content.

33.3.1 This handbook, containing both administrative and program content information, is reviewed with the parents when their child is enrolled. Translation is provided if necessary.

Thus, to give credit for this indicator, the observer also needs to find out whether all parents of children in the group being observed are able to read the materials. (Are there any parents who do not speak the language used in the materials? Are there any parents who are unable to read?) If any of the parents fit the criteria, the staff must take responsibility for ensuring that parents have the information they need, for example by making sure that arrangements have been made to have someone read or translate the materials for those parents. A question should be asked to find out whether staff have ensured that parents can access the information. Acceptable help might be provided by another parent, an older child who is bilingual or can read well, or a staff member who speaks the required language. (See photo 33.3.1.)

Score 3.1 "Yes" if written materials are given to all parents, meet these requirements, and staff have ensured that all parents can understand the information.

3.2 ***Some communication of child related information*** must occur between parents and staff to be given credit for this indicator at the minimal level. This can consist of:

- informal communication between parents and staff at arrival and departure times
- written notes or phone calls to parents who do not bring their children
- conferences with staff at the parents' request
- parenting information available for parents to take or check out, in languages used by all parents

33.3.2 Every day parents and staff share information informally at drop-off and pick-up time.

Check to see if such sharing of information occurs when parents and staff interact during the observation, for example at greeting and/or departing time. (See photo 33.3.2.) If neither greeting nor departing is observed, ask the staff the questions provided in the scale for this indicator, and base the score on their answers. Score this indicator "Yes" if at least one parent communication activity occurs as a regular part of the program.

3.3 ***Some possibilities to be involved*** means that at least two different types of possibilities are offered to parents or other family members to contribute to the children's program. Being ***involved*** in the children's program requires active participation on the parent's part, not only sharing information, as in 3.2. (See photos 33.3.3a-c.) Examples include:

- Inviting parents to attend a potluck dinner
- Inviting parents to have lunch with the children
- Finding a place for a mother to breast feed her baby
- Having the parents bring a treat on their child's birthday
- Helping at a class party
- Donating clothing the child has outgrown to be used in the classroom as extra clothes to change children
- Donating some scrap materials for art projects
- Assisting the teacher in the classroom (reading a story, helping with a messy art project)
- Serving on a committee or an advisory board
- Editing a class newsletter
- Assisting staff when the group takes a field trip
- Sharing a family cultural custom with the class
- Collecting materials needed for sand/water play or the dramatic play area
- Shortening dramatic play clothes
- Bringing a special visitor, such as a family pet or a new baby
- Playing a musical instrument so children can sing or dance to it

33.3.3a Parents are invited to stay and participate in the program.

- Helping with fund-raising events (yard sale, bake sale)
- Participating in a clean-up or fix-up day
- Helping to provide a "teacher appreciation" event
- Sharing skills such as carpentry or sewing to make something for the group

To score 3.3 "Yes," at least two possibilities for parent involvement must be present.

3.4 ***Generally respectful and positive*** means that interactions between staff and parents are pleasant, with very few exceptions. (See photo 33.3.4.) If the assessor has the opportunity to observe greeting and/or departing, a judgment can be made based on how the staff and parents interact. Do staff members greet the parent in a pleasant tone; does the parent respond in kind; have there been any complaints or serious conflicts?

If the scale is being used as a self-assessment by the staff, it is important for staff to be as honest and objective as possible in order to achieve a baseline for planning improvement. It helps to pay particular attention to the staff's interactions with parents who arrive later when the staff are busy. Often, these parents are ignored.

In scoring this indicator, note the word ***generally***. This means that an occasional lapse in respectful and positive interaction between parents and staff should not cause a score of "No." Score Indicator 3.4 "Yes" if the staff and parents deal positively or neutrally with one another with only an occasional lapse. However, *no* strongly negative interaction can be observed or reported.

33.3.3b

33.3.3c

33.3.3b-c A birthday party is a festive occasion that brings parents, and sometimes even grandparents, into the classroom.

33.3.4 Staff treat parents with respect so that daily interactions are usually positive.

33 Provisions for parents

5.1   A good program invites parents to ***observe the group*** that their child will be attending ***prior to enrollment***. Parents need to be able to make an informed decision before they place their child in a program. This can only be done if the parent is not only invited to observe, but the program strongly advises or requires it. (See photo 33.5.1.)

Ask whether the program has a policy that actively encourages parents to observe before enrollment, and if most parents do so. Score "Yes" if the policy is in place and practiced regularly.

5.2   Making parents aware of the ***philosophy*** and child development ***approaches*** used in the program is important because it adds information that parents need in order to decide whether the program is the right one for their family. To give credit, information can be shared verbally or provided in writing, but it should be noted that the combination is most effective. (See photo 33.3.1.)

Major discrepancies in child rearing approaches can cause serious conflicts between parents and staff. Parents should be informed about the discipline policy and the general educational philosophy as well as the types of activities in which their child will be involved. Discussion of these issues during the initial contacts and coverage of them in a clearly written handbook that is given to parents might avoid later problems.

To score this indicator, look at documents provided to parents such as the parent handbook, and use information reported by staff in response to the question provided in the ITERS-R, for this indicator. If any parents cannot read the information, arrangements must be in place to provide help as described in Indicator 3.1.

5.3   ***Much sharing*** requires daily informal conversations with all parents at drop-off and pick-up times. (See photos 33.5.3a-b.) In addition, at least once a year a planned conference must be offered to the parents of each and every child. Parent conferences provide time for staff and parents to discuss the child's progress and strengths as well as any difficulties the child or family may be having. Conferences should deepen the relationship between parents and staff and help in joint planning for the child's development. (See photos 33.5.3c.)

33.5.1 Parents are urged to observe, prior to enrolling their child, in the classroom their child will attend so that they can make an informed choice.

33.5.3a

33.5.3b

33.5.3a-b Staff share specific and helpful information frequently with parents.

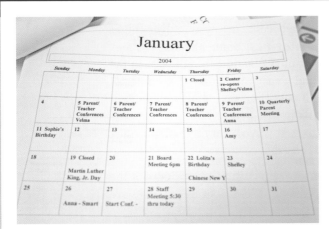

33.5.3c Staff conduct a yearly conference for the parents of each child.

33.5.3d

33.5.3e

33.5.3f

33.5.3d-f Parenting information is available for parents to consult on-site or to check out.

A good program also provides other communication opportunities, such as:

- Group meetings for parents
- A parent library with parenting information to check out
- A parent bulletin board
- Daily notes sent home to parents with information about routines (feeding, nap, toileting) and play activities
- A newsletter containing information about the other children and their families as well as current activities

To score "Yes" the following are required:

- daily informal communication
- a planned individual conference at least once a year
- a parent handbook
- one additional ongoing print communication material
- a parent meeting

If any parents cannot understand the information due to language or reading difficulties, arrangements must be in place to provide help as described in Indicator 3.1. (See photos 33d-f.)

33 Provisions for parents

5.4 In order to increase the possibility that parents can become involved in their child's program, the center offers a *variety of alternatives*. Some alternatives may require parents to help in the classroom, others might be done at home or in the evening. For example, working parents might find it easier to attend an evening pot luck dinner, while a parent who attends school part-time may want to volunteer in the classroom during the program's operating hours. Because different parents will have preferences for how they would like to be involved, varying options must be provided. See Indicator 3.3 for examples of possible options.

The score for this indicator is based on the variety of possibilities offered, not the degree to which the parents take advantage of them. At least four alternatives are required to give 5.4 a score of "Yes."

7.1 An *annual evaluation* by parents is requested by the program in order to make sure that parents have a way to express their opinions about the program. Parent evaluations should be treated as a source of new ideas as well as a forum to allow parents to express concerns.

It is difficult to get honest evaluations from parents because they might feel a negative response would affect the care their child receives, or feel guilty about leaving their child in a program they are not happy with. Despite the difficulties involved, excellent programs conduct evaluations by parents in an effort to find out if changes are needed. Making parents' evaluations anonymous often helps. This can be done if all evaluations are gathered by one or two parent representatives and presented as ideas from the parent group. (See photo 33.7.1.)

In some cases, a parent might chair an evaluation discussion for parents only, with no staff present. The purpose would be to gather parent concerns and suggestions to present to the staff in writing from the parent group.

33.7.1 Parents are asked for a written evaluation of the program every year.

To score "Yes" for 7.1 evidence must be present that a formal parent evaluation is requested from parents at least once a year. Staff should be able to show any evaluation form used and describe the process.

7.2 During the early years, timely *referrals* to specialists may avoid later, more serious problems. This indicator requires that *referrals are made to other professionals* by the staff when they feel it is needed for the well being of the child.

The program staff have the opportunity to see a child among his peers in many different situations that offer varying perspectives. Because of their wide experiences with very young children and their early childhood education background, staff can often see problems that are missed by the parents or by the child's physician, who is usually the only other professional with whom the child comes into contact. Providing referrals and assisting in the diagnosis and treatment of child development-related difficulties are important roles that staff sometimes must take on.

It is essential that a staff representative (often, but not always, the director) talks to parents if the classroom staff feel a referral may be needed. The staff representative should come prepared to such a parent conference with specific information about the issue that is causing the concern and some suggestions for how the parents and/or staff can access the right services for help. (See photo 33.7.2.)

As parents develop trust in the staff and administrators, they may also seek advice about broader family matters such as concerns about their other children, harmonizing work and family responsibilities, or financial problems. It is important to remember that early childhood program staff should not be expected to provide advice outside their professional area of expertise, but rather to provide referrals to qualified agencies or individuals.

Since each state organizes its services differently, the state licensing consultant for the center is a good initial contact for information about available services for different types of concerns. A brief description of the various local agencies available, the services each one offers, and some contact information is helpful for center administrators to have on hand, in case it is needed. The most important thing in making a referral is to be supportive, helpful, and non-judgmental.

Credit for 7.2 should be based on the answers of the staff and/or administrators to questions such as those included in the ITERS-R. If referrals are made when needed, credit should be given (score "Yes"). Credit can also be given if no referrals have ever been required or made, but staff show that they are well informed and willing to provide this service.

7.3   Parents can be actively involved in ***decision-making roles*** by serving on the program's advisory board or on various committees that have an advisory role. For example, Early Head Start mandates the involvement of parents at all levels, from participation in the classroom to serving on advisory boards. Many other programs also involve parents at all levels including parent cooperatives, some demonstration programs, laboratory schools, and exemplary programs recognized by various state or local agencies.

33.7.2 Staff and parents discuss the child's progress before referrals to other professionals are made.

Parent Representatives

Each class has a parent representative who volunteers to keep parents up to date on things that are happening in the classroom and around the school. Communication among parents is typically through email.

If you would like to be included on the class distribution list, please put your information on the posted sign-up sheet. You may also email your class's parent rep directly using the information below. Please tell the rep your name, your child's name, and your email address. If your spouse or the child's grandparents would be interested in receiving these emails, sign them up too. If you don't have email but would still like to be included, please let your parent rep know and she/he will print out a copy of each email and attach it to your score sheet.

The parent representative for our class is:

33.7.3 Parents can contribute to the improvement of the quality of care for all the children in the group by serving on a centerwide committee or board.

This indicator, at the highest level of quality, addresses the need for parent input into decisions that affect all the children in the center, not only the decisions that affect their own children or the group being observed. Parents have a unique perspective that can contribute to the general quality of the program. (See photo 33.7.3.)

To gather information required for scoring this indicator, staff should be asked the suggested question provided for this indicator in the ITERS-R. Score 7.3 "Yes" if it is reported that any parents are currently involved on advisory boards or in other decision-making roles at the center. To give credit, the parents do not have to have a child in the classroom being observed, but they must have a child currently enrolled in the program.

34 Provisions for personal needs of staff

General information about this item

Working with infants and toddlers is a demanding job that requires intense concentration and considerable physical strain while the staff are responsible for the care of the children. Therefore, staff need breaks to maintain their focus, energy and good humor. It is necessary to plan for appropriate coverage for those times when staff need to be out of the room for personal reasons. Personal reasons for staff to be relieved of responsibility for the care of children include times for morning, midday, and/or afternoon breaks for refreshments, meals, or bathroom breaks, and time to handle other personal matters requiring a short period, such as answering an emergency telephone call.

The number of breaks and the length of break times should be suited to the number of hours the staff member works daily, the number of staff present, the required staff-child ratio, and the children's schedule. Break times should be planned so that they do not interfere with the children's program. Although most breaks should be planned in advance so that competent staff who know the children can be scheduled in the classroom as substitutes, someone who knows the program must always be available on-site for short, unscheduled emergency breaks, if these are needed.

Some flexibility should be possible in break times so that staff who prefer to leave early in lieu of breaks or who need one longer break instead of several shorter ones, should be able to have such needs met, if this is arranged in advance and does not adversely affect the children's program. At a minimum, a 15-minute break for every 3 hours worked in the classroom should be provided to staff. Staff should also have a meal break if they work a full day.

In addition to time away from children, classroom staff need an "adults only" restroom, and a safe, convenient place to store personal belongings, such as a coat or purse.

Staff who have their personal needs met are more likely to feel respected as "people" by the administration of the program. They can also do a better job with the children because they are under less stress when their personal needs are being considered and met.

When scoring this item, ask the classroom staff (not administrative staff) for information needed to score.

34 Provisions for personal needs of staff

34.1.1 In this room, staff must put their personal belongings wherever they can find space.

34.3.1 A separate adult restroom is available for staff to use.

A closer look at each indicator

1.1   *No special areas* means no space, separate from that used by the children, is available for staff to use when meeting their personal needs. This includes not having a restroom separate from the restroom used by the children, a place to sit down and take a break, or storage for personal belongings, such as a coat or purse. (See photo 34.1.1.)

Score 1.1 "Yes" if *no* such accommodations are made for the staff who work in the classroom being observed.

1.2   *No time away from the children* means that the staff do not have breaks from being responsible for the children, nor time when another person takes over this responsibility. This can cause staff to be tired, irritable, or non-attentive to children.

If classroom staff report having *no* breaks at all, including no break for a meal for full-time staff, then score 1.2 "Yes."

3.1   *Separate adult restroom* means that no children use this restroom area and that the toilet and handwashing fixtures are adult-sized. This restroom may be shared with other adults who work in or visit the facility. (See photo 34.3.1.) To score "Yes" ask to see the restroom to assure that it is within a reasonable distance to use during break times. If the restroom is not reasonably convenient to the classroom, for example in another building, score "No".

3.2   *Some adult furniture available* means that staff have access to some adult-sized seating separate from the children's play area but reasonably close to it, so that staff can use it within the allowed break time.

To score 3.2 "Yes," the adult-sized furniture for staff may be in the program office or in the entry lobby if there is no teacher lounge, but it cannot be located in a children's classroom.

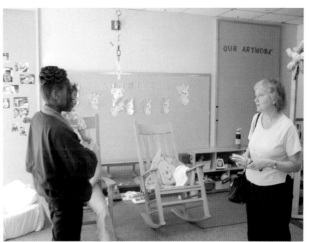

34.3.4 Staff breaks from the children are provided daily by having floaters relieve regular staff of their duties.

34.3.3 Staff coats are hung on a rack in the hallway.

3.3 *Some storage for personal belongings* means that staff have some place to hang coats and store purses and other personal items. At this minimal level, only the space is required, but no specifications are included as to the adequacy of the provision. Thus, using a hook in the classroom or a drawer in the director's office, even though it is not convenient or private, meets this indicator. (See photo 34.3.3.)

3.4 This indicator requires that *staff have at least one break daily*. A break is time when a staff member is relieved of the responsibility of caring for the children. The break should allow enough time to visit the restroom, have a little quiet time, or make a short phone call. A minimum of 15 minutes should be provided for a break. (See photo 34.3.4.)

To score, ask classroom staff if they have any breaks, and base the score on their response. To score "Yes" on 3.4, full-time staff who work at least 8 hours a day, must each have at least one break of 15 minutes.

3.5 If any staff member in the program has disabilities of any kind, *accommodations* need to be made to meet the individual's needs. The accommodations needed to make a facility accessible to individuals with disabilities are handled under Item 1, Indoor space. Other accommodations that might be needed are books with large print for staff with visual impairment, a fire alarm system with flashing lights for staff with hearing impairment, or handrails in the restroom. A score of "NA" is permitted if no staff member has a disability that requires accommodations. To score "Yes," appropriate accommodations for the particular disability of the staff member involved must be made.

5.1 A *lounge* means an area, separate from the space used by children, with *adult-sized* furniture, where the staff may sit and relax when not responsible for the children. The lounge does not have to be used only for this purpose, but can have another use as well. The *dual use*, or other use, can be as an office, conference

34.5.1 Staff use the couch and chairs in the director's office as their lounge area.

34.5.2a Staff store their personal belongings in a convenient closet in the room.

room, or other area that adults use. It must be clear that staff may use this area as a lounge in order to score 5.1 "Yes." (See photo 34.5.1.)

5.2   *Convenient storage* means a place that is within easy reach for staff to keep their personal belongings, such as a coat, purse, extra shoes, books, or briefcase. A place is considered *convenient* if it does not require the staff to leave the classroom or neglect the care of the children to get to their belongings.

Security provisions when necessary means that staff can lock belongings away so that they are safe from tampering by others. Security provisions are required only if there is any danger that tampering or theft may occur.

Ask classroom staff where they can store their personal belongings, and whether this causes any problems. If needed, ask staff to show the place(s) used for storage. If the storage for their personal possessions is convenient and safe, score "Yes" for Indicator 5.2. (See photos 34.5.2 a-b.)

34.5.2b Due to the close monitoring of the entry to the building and the safe neighborhood, this latch and notice provide sufficient security.

5.3   Sufficient time away from the children must be *provided daily* so that staff can take short breaks to meet personal needs. Breaks of 15 minutes in the morning and afternoon and an hour midday lunch break are required to meet this indicator for any staff who work at least 8 hours per day.

Sometimes state regulations specify the length of breaks based on hours of service. If the state regulations are less than the requirements given for this indicator, and the program only provides that amount of time away from the children, score this indicator "No."

If the classroom staff say they receive the required amount of time, or more, credit should be given for 5.3.

34.5.4 Basic provisions for use during breaks and lunch time are available for staff use.

34.5.5a This building has a ramp access as well as a staircase.

Some flexibility in timing is allowed in this indicator, so that staff can arrange with the administration to leave early or take a longer break at midday, in lieu of three shorter breaks, if that is mutually acceptable. If the combined breaks equal the time requirements in this indicator, score 5.3 "Yes."

5.4 *Facilities provided* means that basic provisions, such as refrigerator space, a stove or microwave for cooking or heating meals, and a place to eat meals with adult-sized furniture, are accessible for staff use. If classroom staff report that such provisions are available and can be used, give credit for 5.4. (See photo 34.5.4.)

5.5 In order to meet the national requirements for *accessibility* in all public facilities in order to ensure equal access for people with disabilities, all child care facilities must adhere to the requirements specified in Item

34.5.5b A handicapped-accessible toilet with handrails is required, even if there are no staff members, parents, or other adults needing such accommodations currently involved in the program.

1, Indoor space, Indicator 5.3. These requirements must be met even if there are no staff members, parents, or other adults needing such accommodations currently involved in the center. (See photos 34.5.5 a-b.)

To score this indicator "Yes" the facility and at least one adult restroom must meet the requirements for accessibility stated under Item 1, Indoor space, Indicator 5.3.

7.1 *Separate adult lounge* area means that the space is used only as a staff lounge area. To give credit for 7.1, the staff lounge must be separate not only from the children's program, but also from dual use by other adults (such as for an office) during the time the staff may use the space.

7.2 *Comfortable* adult furniture means that the furniture is not only of the appropriate size, but also suits the various intended purposes well. Thus, chairs and tables for meals and snacks or reading and record keeping should be sturdy and properly proportioned (elbows fit above tables, knees underneath tables, feet on floor). There should be soft chairs or couches for resting or reading in the lounge area. The requirement in this indicator is for functionality and comfort, not for aesthetic appeal. The furniture should, however, be serviceable, clean, and generally in good enough repair to cause no major problems, in order to give credit for this indicator. Before scoring, be sure to observe the furniture in the staff lounge. (See photo 34.7.2.)

Score this indicator "Yes" if all requirements are met.

7.3   ***Some flexibility*** in deciding when to take breaks means that there is some leeway so that the staff can decide when to take breaks, within reason. This usually requires that there are enough staff in the center to cover break times during the day. Substitutes to take over groups may include the director, other administrators, or a floater who serves as a relief person for breaks as well as an "extra hand" for special projects or during busy times, such as the children's lunch time.

34.7.2 A separate lounge area with comfortable furniture is set aside for staff use.

Base the score on the answer given by classroom staff about whether there is any flexibility possible in break times.

35 Provisions for professional needs of staff

General information about this item

In order to do a professional job as a staff member in an infant/toddler program, space, furnishings, and some equipment are required to meet professional needs as well as personal needs. This includes space to prepare and store the materials used with the group and to keep information on file for each child. When individual conferences are conducted with parents or with other staff, suitable space is needed, separate from that being used by the children, with some provision for privacy. Group meeting space, for staff and/or parent meetings, with suitable adult-sized furniture is also needed. Group meeting space should not interfere with the ongoing program for the children.

Relatively few early childhood programs are conducted in purpose-built facilities. Even those that have good space to conduct the children's program often lack suitable space for the staff and parents to use. As plans are developed for custom-built facilities, the planners need to be sure to include the space needed to meet the professional needs of staff. Space to make materials, store materials, hold individual conferences and large group meetings are all necessary to support staff as they implement a high quality program for children.

A closer look at each indicator

1.1   *No access to phone* means that there is no telephone within reasonable access for staff to use. For example, if the telephone is on a different floor or in another building, access may be so difficult that it prevents the use of the telephone. Also, if the phone is located in an office, and staff sometimes cannot access it because the office is locked or being used by someone else who cannot be interrupted, then there is no reasonable access to the phone.

Necessary professional use of the phone includes incoming and outgoing communication with parents, reporting the need for urgent services for the classroom, as well as handling emergencies that might arise with staff or children.

At this level of quality, the phone does not have to be located in the classroom, but it must be readily accessible. Score 1.1 "Yes" only if there is no telephone, or if the telephone is difficult for classroom staff to access.

1.2   *No file or storage space* means that the staff does not have any file or storage space anywhere in the facility to store information or materials needed for preparing or conducting classroom activities. *Staff materials* that require storage might include:

- Books and toys for use in the classroom
- Supplies to make or repair materials
- Files containing information about the children
- Parent education materials for the families included in the group

Indicator

Storage space in the room, such as high open shelves or closed cabinets not accessible to the children, count as storage for staff professional needs, if appropriate materials are stored there. Also, any other storage space in other parts of the facility, for example, file cabinets in an office or in a reasonably accessible closet, may count as storage for professional needs of staff, if such materials are stored there. Storage space for routine care supplies such as juice, paper cups, and paper towels, does not count to meet this indicator.

Even if no file or storage space is seen in the classroom, the observer should ask the staff whether they have access to any file or storage space, to describe where it is, what is kept there, and whether the space is "fairly limited" (information needed to score Indicator 3.2) or "ample" (information needed to score Indicator 5.1).

If storage space is reported to be available, ask to see the space and what is stored there, in order to give appropriate credit. Score 1.2 "Yes" only if there is *no* file or storage space for staff materials. (See photo 35.1.2.)

35.1.2 Staff resource books are kept on the children's toy shelves because there is no file or storage space for staff professional materials.

1.3 This indicator addresses the need for **individual conference space** when children are in attendance. If there is any space that has some privacy that can be used by staff for a confidential conference with parents or other staff members during school hours, this indicator is scored "No."

The space does not have to be used solely for conferences, but dual use should not interfere with the privacy or concentration required for an individual conference. For example, if the only space available during program hours is in an empty classroom, but the conference will not be interrupted, this indicator should be scored "No" because *some* space is available, even though it is not completely satisfactory. Score 1.3 "Yes," only if *no* space is available while children are in attendance.

35.3.1 A telephone in the classroom is convenient for emergency calls or brief but necessary communication with parents.

3.1 **Convenient access** means that staff have a phone in the room for emergency calls or for brief conversations with parents. A portable or cell phone is acceptable if it is easily accessible to all staff in the classroom. (See photo 35.3.1.)

If a staff member is observed talking for a long time on the telephone, with serious negative consequences to the supervision of children, consider this under Item 25. Supervision of play and learning.

3.2 **Some file and storage space** means access to even a little space to store professional materials. Note that *both* some file space and some storage for other materials is required to score 3.2 "Yes." See 1.2 for examples of such space.

3.3 **Some space available for individual conferences** means that while children are attending the program there is a place where staff can sit down with parents or other staff for a confi-

35.3.3 While the children are using another space in the center, a staff member can have a conference with parents in the empty classroom.

35.5.1a

35.5.1b

35.5.1 a-b There is a large enough space for staff to store files and materials.

dential, private conference without fear of being over-heard or interrupted. (See photo 35.3.3.) Any space that can be arranged during the children's program to provide the privacy required is acceptable to score 3.3 "Yes."

5.1 *Ample file and storage space* means there is a large enough space to comfortably store professional materials of classroom staff without the crowding or disorganization caused by insufficient space. (See photos 35.5.1 a-c.) See 1.2 for examples of space for files and storage of other professional materials.

5.2 In order to give credit for this indicator, there must be a *separate office space*, *on site*, used for the administration of the program. The director's office in a child care center or the office in another facility where an infant/toddler program is housed, is considered separate office space for the program, as long as the classroom is housed at the same site as the office. Credit can be given for Indicator 5.2 if the office is located in a different building on site, as long as it is reasonably accessible to classroom staff. (See photo 35.5.2.)

5.3 At the good level, satisfactory space for both individual conferences *and* adult group meetings is required. *Satisfactory space for individual conferences* means that the space:

- Provides both visual and auditory privacy
- Is protected from interruptions
- Contains adult-sized furniture
- Can be used while children are attending
- Is relatively easy to schedule for a conference, even if the space is used for other purposes at other times

35.5.1c Ample, well organized storage space makes it easy for staff to access materials for use with children.

35.5.2 There is a separate office space on-site used for the administration of the program.

35 Provisions for professional needs of staff

35.7.1 A well-equipped office has the necessary equipment to conduct the administrative functions efficiently.

35.7.2 Separate, conveniently located space used only for conferences and group meetings avoids problems of scheduling.

Satisfactory space for adult group meetings means:

- There is enough space for the number of adults in the group
- There are enough adult-sized chairs, tables, and other furniture needed for the meeting
- It is relatively easy to schedule group meetings, even if the space is used for other purposes at other times.

Thus, an evening meeting for parents and staff might be held in space used by children earlier in the day, if the space can be sufficiently cleared of the children's furniture to accommodate enough adult-sized furniture. This accommodation would be considered satisfactory space for adult meetings and 5.3 would be scored "Yes," even though a lot of work is required for set-up and clean-up.

7.1 ***Well-equipped office space*** means that the office has the necessary equipment to conduct the administrative functions of the program efficiently. Examples of such equipment include a telephone, an answering machine that takes messages 24 hours a day, 7 days a week, the furniture needed for office work, a photocopier, sufficient computer capacity, and a fax machine. The intent of this item is that the office has the capacity to serve the needs of the staff for communication, clerical tasks, record keeping, and reproducing materials. (See photo 35.7.1.)

To score this indicator "Yes," all examples listed are not required. However, the basic necessities for efficient program operation are required, including a telephone with answering machine, office furniture, and basic office supplies.

7.2 At the excellent level, the space used for individual conferences *and* group meetings must be ***conveniently located***, which means easy for staff and parents to get to, ***comfortable***, which means furnished to be comfortable for adults, and ***separate from the space used for children***, which means space used only for adults.

Having space that is ready to be used for individual conferences and group meetings avoids the problems of scheduling and rearranging space caused by dual use. Separate space for conferences and group meetings makes it easier for a program to conduct these important support functions for parents and staff. (See photo 35.7.2.)

If the space that staff describe and show the observer meets all of these requirements, score 7.2 "Yes."

36 Staff interaction and cooperation

General information about this item

Staff members working with the same group of children need to work closely as a team in order to best meet the needs of the children for whom they jointly provide care. Teamwork requires developing a shared context for care and education based on information about the children, their families, the curriculum, program policies, and daily procedures. In the ITERS-R, the word *staff* means all the people who work directly with the children in a particular group for much of the day, most days of the week. Additional adults who work in the classroom, such as practicum students, volunteers, and/or therapists, may be counted as staff only if they work with the children daily or almost daily for much of the day. One exception to this definition of staff occurs in parent cooperatives or lab schools, where different people are present every day to serve as assistants to the permanent staff. Since the regular staffing pattern in such classrooms includes different people daily for much of the day, they are counted as regular staff during the observation.

In all other cases, adults who come into the classroom and interact with the children for shorter periods of time or for fewer days of the week are not counted as staff unless the observed effect is *extremely negative*. This includes student teachers, volunteers, therapists/ specialists, or administrative staff who come into the class-room for short periods and/or to work with specific children.

Since we want our sample of how staff interact with one another to be typical of what the children experience on a daily basis, it is not wise to count the positive or neutral interactions with temporary helpers that might be observed, because it does not contribute information about the nature of the ongoing interaction among the staff. However, any negative interactions among adults should be counted since it adversely affects the general atmosphere of the classroom. Negative interactions include angry voices or actions, or demeaning remarks.

The word "staff" in this scale is always plural because few classrooms have only one staff member. If there is only one staff member with a group all day and no one else regularly cares for the children at any time during the day, this item may be scored "NA." However, if two or more staff members work with the same group at different times, or at the same time, this item must be scored. For example, if one staff member has responsibility for the early arrivals in a class until the regular teacher arrives and takes over the responsibility for the group, then the item must be scored. This is also true if the regular teacher leaves before the end of the day and another staff member takes over the group for the end of the day.

Communication among staff members about the children, as well as the curriculum and environment, is essential in order to provide consistency in the program.

Daily informal communication of specific information is needed about practical matters, such as:

- A change in the drop-off or pick-up times for any of the children
- A different adult who will be picking up one of the children that day
- Unusual behavior on the part of a child that might signal possible illness or emotional stress
- Information shared by a parent about family problems or other events that might affect the child's behavior
- Additional tasks that staff must remember to complete before they leave
- Last minute changes in the schedule or in a planned activity

However, such informal communication is no substitute for regular planning, which is also essential in order for staff to conduct a high quality program.

The interpersonal relationship among staff members affects their work as a professional team. If staff members are too friendly with one another, they might spend a lot of time relating to one another rather than to the children. On the other hand, staff members need to be helpful, respectful, and pleasant to one another to create a wholesome and efficient working situation. As with many other aspects of program quality, achieving a balance between one's personal interest and professional responsibilities is necessary.

In addition to observing how staff communicate and get along with one another, questions must be asked of classroom staff to get the specific information needed to decide on a score for this item.

A closer look at each indicator

1.1 *No communication of necessary information* among staff means that even essential information of immediate practical importance is not clearly communicated to each staff member. For example, if a parent has told a morning staff member that she will be picking her child up before nap, and this has not been communicated to the afternoon staff member, the child may be put down for his nap and not be ready for departure. Communication of other information concerning children's health, safety, social/emotional, and learning needs must also not be neglected. If the observer is present to see whether information is communicated when necessary, then the score can be based on what is observed. If the evidence is not observed, classroom staff should be asked whether any information is exchanged among staff responsible for the group, and if so, how this is this done. The suggested questions in the ITERS-R may be used to elicit information.

Score this indicator "Yes" only if *no* child-related information is communicated in any way, verbally or in writing, among staff.

1.2 This indicator describes a negative condition where the staff's **interpersonal relationships interfere with** or hinder the staff in carrying out their caregiving duties. This may be caused by the staff being overly friendly so that they are distracted by personal conversations much of the time and neglect the children during either indoor or outdoor activities. In infant/toddler classrooms, staff who do not value observing and responding to very young children who are not yet verbal, resort to conversation among themselves because they find it more interesting. This can result in neglecting the children's care in a number of areas including personal care routines, language stimulation, or conducting activities. (See photo 36.1.2.) The other extreme, namely staff who behave in a hostile or curt manner with one another, may also cause lapses in caregiving, because they do not work as a team to meet children's needs.

The information needed to score this indicator must be based on observation. If no problems are obvious, score 1.2 "No."

1.3   ***Staff duties*** need to be ***shared fairly*** in order to maintain good relationships among staff as well as to fulfill all the staff responsibilities for conducting the program. ***Sharing work fairly*** means that a similar amount of effort or work is put into meeting the various needs of the children by the various staff members. In any team effort (and staff members make a team), the skills, interests, and abilities of the various team members, as well as the organization of the team (the job descriptions), will play a part in how work is divided. The important thing to observe is whether the work is shared in such a way that all staff members are busily involved and the work gets done.

36.1.2   Staff interpersonal relationships should never interfere with the care of the children.

There are many different kinds of tasks involved in providing group care and education for children. Some are associated with routine care such as meals/snacks, nap, and diapering/toileting. Others are associated with conducting activities, such as reading to the children, interacting with them as they play with various materials, and managing transitions. Both types of tasks require preparation and clean-up as well as interacting with children to help them enjoy and learn from their experiences.

Staff that communicate and work well together as a team have various ways of sharing duties fairly including:

- Staff rotate routine tasks, such as preparing for and cleaning up after lunch or putting out the mats for nap.

- To avoid contamination and cut down on illness, one staff member handles diapering/toileting tasks while another handles tasks associated with food.

- Preparation of materials, such as paint, play dough, and special activities, is rotated among staff members and assigned during the staff planning time.

- Each staff member takes primary responsibility for particular play areas for a specified amount of time, including gathering appropriate materials for a new activity, rotating materials, removing materials that are incomplete, in poor repair, or no longer appropriate, and ordering new materials when needed.

- One staff member takes responsibility for ensuring routine care activities are done properly, while the other takes responsibility for organizing the play and learning activities.

- Each staff member contributes her own particular interests and areas of expertise, including new ideas from early childhood education courses, for example on healthier ways of conducting routines for infants and toddlers, better ways of handling discipline problems with older toddlers, or activities that can be introduced to the children.

36 Staff interaction and cooperation

36.3.1 Health related information is posted so that all staff and substitutes are informed.

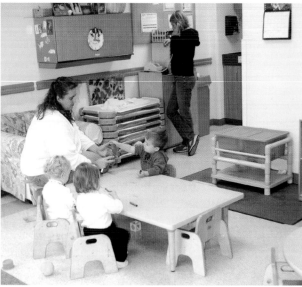

36.3.3 Staff duties are shared fairly. While one staff member works with the children the other handles necessary phone calls to parents of children who are absent.

Observe to see if there is a sensible balance of work, with each staff member contributing towards meeting the needs of the group. This indicator should be scored "Yes" only if problems are observed.

3.1 **Some basic information is communicated** means that, at a minimum, staff share information to meet children's health needs or other information of immediate concern. If such communication is not observed, ask classroom staff the sample questions in the ITERS-R to elicit this information and score the indicator based on their answers.

Health-related information, such as proper diapering/toileting and food-related hygiene, individual children's allergies or medications, must be written and communicated to all staff and substitutes. Other information of immediate concern, such as a child needing to leave early, can be communicated verbally or in writing. (See photo 36.3.1.)

Score 3.1 "Yes" if information of immediate concern that could cause serious problems is communicated.

3.2 Observe to see whether the **interaction among staff** is pleasant or at least neutral so that it **does not interfere** with the caregiving responsibilities of the staff described in 1.2.

To score "Yes," this indicator requires only that the interactions are neutral and do not interfere by being too friendly and social, or hostile.

3.3 **Staff duties shared fairly** means that there seems to be a balance of effort on the part of the staff members so that the needs of the children are met. The skills and job description of each staff member should also be considered here. Score 3.3 "Yes" if staff seem to be similarly involved, not necessarily both doing the same tasks, but putting out a similar amount of effort to meet the needs of the group being observed. (See photo 36.3.3.)

5.1 At this level, communication is required among staff of **child-related information** that is of educational and developmental significance. During the observation,

Indicator

36.5.1 Staff have brief, informal conversations to share child-related information of educational and developmental significance.

36.5.2 Staff have a warm, supportive relationship while they are meeting children's needs.

look to see whether staff talk informally about specific interests of various children or suggest activities related to a child's emerging skills. (See photo 36.5.1.) Supplement the observed information by asking classroom staff the questions suggested in the ITERS-R. Note that this indicator requires **daily** communication of child-related information and that all children need to be considered, but not each child each day. This may be done verbally or in writing, depending on whether staff schedules overlap and verbal communication is possible.

36.5.3 Staff responsibilities are shared so that both care and play activities are handled smoothly.

5.2 This indicator must be based on observation of **staff interaction**. Look for a warm, supportive, positive feeling and an easy relationship among staff members while they are concentrating on caring for the children's needs. Although some interactions may be neutral, no negative interactions among staff may be observed to score 5.2 "Yes." (See photo 36.5.2.)

5.3 The result of sharing duties fairly should be that **both care and play activities** are handled smoothly, with no long delays or problems, even during transitions. When staff members communicate effectively and work together to meet commonly held goals, the program usually runs smoothly for the children.

The score for this indicator should be based on what is observed. (See photo 36.5.3.) Score 5.3 "No" only if it is obvious that care and play activities suffer because work is not properly shared by staff.

7.1 **Planning time** is required for the staff working with the same group or in the same room. The staff should be able to meet together to refine procedures for routine care, organize activities and materials for their group or to discuss approaches needed for specific children or families. During their planning time, the staff members should be free of caregiving responsibilities so that they can concentrate on planning. Therefore, if staff are responsible for supervising children during naptime and might be interrupted, this cannot be considered planning time.

36 Staff interaction and cooperation

It is helpful for as many as possible of the staff members who work with a group to plan together. For example, if there are two staff members working with the same group during the major part of the day, and one comes early and the other stays later when fewer children are present, their planning time should take place when both are there and can be free of caregiving responsibilities. (See photo 36.7.1.)

In cases where a number of part-time assistants, student teachers, or volunteers assist the lead teacher in a classroom, the staff member or members who are there most of the time should be involved in making plans, but all the adults working with the group should be informed about the plans, so that their interactions with the children can be helpful and relevant. Although it is not required for this indicator, a weekly written activity plan that is posted in the classroom can help inform part-time assistants about planned activities for the group and for individual children.

36.7.1 Staff who work with the same group have planning time when they are free of caregiving duties and can concentrate.

Some programs gather children together from various classrooms in a combined early morning or late afternoon group. Often, this fact is ignored when planning occurs for the individual classrooms. This omission is counter-productive because the children's experiences throughout the entire day are valuable play and learning opportunities.

In the ITERS-R, the "*much of the day*" required for many of the activities is based on the total time the program is open daily, not only on the time spent in the group's main classroom. Therefore, all time should be planned with children's developmental needs in mind. The staff that take major responsibility for a particular group should know what is accessible to their children during the time spent in other classrooms. Some sharing of program content, across the various staff members that are responsible for the same group of children at various times of the day, is essential if the program is going to provide consistency in routines and play activities. The staff members from various classrooms need not plan together, but they should know something about one another's plans and approaches if they share children at any time.

When classroom staff have time to plan together they can make decisions on key matters including:

- Major focal points for the next few weeks
- Various materials and activities needed to meet the rapidly changing needs of infants and toddlers
- Dividing the work to implement the activities for the upcoming week or two.
- Evaluating how each of the various activities and different areas indoors and outdoors are functioning and making plans for improvements
- How routines might be handled more efficiently
- How to better meet the needs of children or parents who are having a difficult time

Planning time is required at least **every other week** to meet this indicator.

Base the score on the answer given by the classroom staff to the question about planning time in the ITERS-R. The perceptions of the classroom staff and administrative staff may differ on the availability of planning time.

Score this indicator "Yes" if classroom staff report that they have planning time together at least every two weeks.

7.2   In order to assure that the program runs smoothly, staff duties and **responsibilities should be clearly defined**. This does not mean that the same staff member must always handle the same tasks, but it does help to have some level of continuity. For example, specific tasks might be assumed by a staff member for a specific period such as a month at a time, then rotated, if desired, in order to prevent boredom. During the planning time, specific responsibilities can be selected by each staff member.

36.7.2 Staff duties are clearly defined so that the program runs smoothly.

Having staff members take responsibility for daily routines is particularly important to keep the schedule running smoothly. Thus, one staff member might be the assigned "greeter" while another either sets out materials or prepares breakfast. The "greeter" will continue to watch the entryway and greet latecomers, even after the program is underway. Similarly, one person might be in charge of preparing the room for nap while the other is reading a story to the children; one might be in charge of diaper changing while the other deals with food related tasks as much as possible.

Since there are many different, sometimes competing activities going on in a classroom every day, each staff member will need to assume and follow through on a number of responsibilities to keep the program running smoothly. For example, although daily clean-up of materials is the responsibility of the staff member who is conducting a particular activity, it helps to divide the activity centers among all the staff members for major weekly clean-up duties. At the end of every week each staff member then has certain centers to get ready for the coming week. Materials may need to be changed for next week's activities, depleted materials replenished, additional materials ordered, or materials/equipment no longer developmentally appropriate stored and new ones brought out. When staff members work together to keep the facility functioning smoothly, they assume joint ownership of the program.

Staff responsibilities need to be clearly defined for the upkeep of the facility, planning of the curriculum, and conducting the daily program. Base the score for this indicator on observation and the answers given to the questions in the ITERS-R. (See photo 36.7.2.)

7.3   Staff members are people as well as professionals, and early childhood is an emotionally and physically demanding field in which to work. Therefore, it is necessary for programs to **promote positive interactions** among staff members if they want a high level of performance from them.

Social events, such as recognizing and celebrating staff birthdays, organizing occasional social events such as luncheons during training, or facilitating group

36.7.3a Professional and recreational trips staff take together help promote positive staff interaction.

36.7.3b Organizing occasional social events helps create a pleasant atmosphere for staff.

attendance at professional meetings, create the social ties that promote positive interaction. (See photos 36.7.3 a-b.)

The information for this indicator can be obtained by asking the classroom staff the questions suggested in the ITERS-R. Credit can be given if classroom staff report that the administration encourages some social event at least two times a year.

37 Staff continuity

General information about this item

Whenever infants and toddlers experience a change in their group, room, or caregiving staff, they face a break in continuity that requires them to make many adjustments. The new staff will undoubtedly have some differences in interaction styles and expectations to get used to. The new room environment will have different sights, sounds, materials and equipment. The new group will have different children to learn to get along with. Some changes might delight a child while others may result in increased distress, but all will require adjustment.

The children are not alone in having to make adjustments to changes. Their parents and the new caregiving staff will also have to find out how to work together as a team, and the staff will need to become acquainted with the needs and interests of their new group of children.

Even though changes may be challenging, if they are properly handled, they can foster growth and bring new rewarding experiences. This item focuses on what programs can do to ease the disconcerting aspects of transitions by providing proper support for young children. It examines issues such as how frequently children are required to make adjustments to change, what procedures the program uses to ease the transitions, and what is done to provide stability and continuity of care.

A closer look at each indicator

1.1 A *stable* person to care for children means that there is at least one person who is with the group daily for much of the day, on whom the children and parents can rely. If there are many staff members who rotate through the group for short periods daily or if children are arbitrarily moved from group to group in order to meet staff-child ratios, it is difficult for both children and parents to form trusting relationships with the staff. It takes some time for children to *adjust* to or become comfortable with the different personal styles and ways of doing things that different staff members have. Therefore, having many people to adjust to in rapid succession can cause children to become insecure and clingy, unattached to any adult, or defiant and test limits. Also, if many staff members deal with the children for relatively short or irregular periods the staff may not get to know the children well.

Score this indicator "Yes" if there is not at least one stable person who cares for the children for more than 50% of each day, and children must adjust to many caregivers on a daily or weekly basis. Ask staff the questions in the ITERS-R scale to get information to score this indicator.

37 Staff continuity

1.2   When children are **changed** to a different group they usually are faced with adjusting to new staff, new peers and/or a new physical environment. Changes in grouping are often based on the needs of the program, rather than on the needs of the children. For example, staffing patterns may require that children are put into different groups on a short-term basis to maintain the required staff-child ratios, or the facility may arbitrarily move children by "promoting them" to the next group, when they achieve certain milestones (eg. walk, have a birthday that places them into another age group). The occasional need to change an individual child to another group based on the needs of the child is not considered here. If group changes occur more than twice a year as a regular practice, score this indicator "Yes." Ask staff the questions in the ITERS-R scale to get information to score this indicator.

1.3   **Transitions to new groups or staff members** means moving children to another group with new staff and/or new children, or replacing familiar staff with new staff members in an established group, thus interrupting the stable arrangement and requiring a new adjustment period. (See photo 37.1.3.) **Abrupt** transitions are changes in staff, room, or companions that children have not been prepared for.

37.1.3 Transitions from one teacher to another must be handled sensitively, understanding that learning to trust a new adult can be difficult for infants and toddlers.

Some ways to ease transitions for children are:

- gradually introducing children to a new staff member by having the new staff join the group along with the familiar staff members, so the children can become comfortable with her, before the change in staffing takes place

- taking children in very small groups to visit the new group/room/staff for a short time, initially, then for progressively longer periods

- selecting times to visit the new group when things are relatively calm and interesting, and avoiding more stressful times such as meals, naps, transitions in the schedule, or when children are tired

- taking the whole group to visit the new room when it is empty (eg. when the other group is outside) so that the children can see all the new things that they will have to play with

- having the parent visit the new group/room/staff with his child for a short time

- having the new staff member visit the child in his home

Score this indicator "Yes" if transitions are abrupt, with no preparation, such as the examples listed above, for easing the transition to a new group or staff. Use the questions in the ITERS-R scale to get information from the staff to score this indicator.

1.4   **Substitutes** are people brought in to replace regular staff members who are unable to work with the children. If substitutes are used who do not know the children, then the children may be uneasy about being cared for by strangers. This is especially troubling in situations that require close contact, such as diapering/toileting and feeding, or that require specific comforting behaviors such as patting a restless toddler's back or humming a favorite song as he falls asleep. Problems may also occur if a substitute does not know the way the program usually works. For example, routines may be done in an unfamiliar way or be done too early or too late. Important interactions, such as discipline or rules for accessing materials may be handled in a contradictory way.

Frequently means that at least 75% of the time when substitutes are used, they are people who either do not know the particular children in the group, or the practices used in the program.

Score this indicator "Yes" if using substitutes who do not know the children or the details of the program is a usual practice. Use the questions in the ITERS-R scale to get information from the staff to score this indicator.

37.3.1 Although there are many adults supervising these children on the playground the children know exactly who their stable teachers are, and prefer to be near them.

3.1   ***Continuity*** means that the same lead staff and consistent practices are present every day. Having one or two ***stable*** or unchanging lead staff in a group, assures that the children will know and be able to rely on at least one familiar staff member at all times. This can be accomplished if the staff schedules are arranged so that at least one lead staff member who knows the children and program well is assigned to the group throughout the day. Different staffing patterns may be used to establish continuity, including having two lead staff members, one taking morning duty and the other taking afternoon duty with overlapping midday schedules; having one lead staff and one well qualified assistant in A.M. and P.M. shifts whose schedules overlap; having one lead staff who is present during the hours when most of the children attend the program, assisted by stable, part-time morning and afternoon/evening staff members. (See photo 37.3.1.)

Score "Yes" if the group has a few (one or two) constant or stable caregivers who lead the group daily for the majority of time during the day. Ask staff the questions in the ITERS-R scale for information to score this indicator.

3.2   This indicator focuses on providing a stable group for children by ***rarely*** or very infrequently changing children from one group to another group ***more than twice a year***. If it is either the policy and/or practice for the center to frequently change any child from one group to another more than twice a year, this indicator must be scored "No." Score "Yes" if the policy and practice is to consistently limit the number of times any child is changed to another group to two times a year or less. More frequent changes made on a rare occasion because of the unique needs of a particular child, should not influence the score. Ask staff the questions provided in the ITERS-R scale to get information to score this item.

3.3   A ***provision*** is a preplanned strategy practiced by a program to avoid problems when children experience change in groups or lead staff. (See photos 37.3.3a-c, next page.) Since ***transitions***, or changes from one group or lead staff to another, can cause problems for children, programs often use strategies to ease or minimize the disruption children feel. For a list of provisions or strategies to ease transitions see Indicator 1.3.

If transitions are never abrupt and at least one provision (such as described in Indicator 1.3) is made to minimize the disruptions of a group or staffing change

37.3.3a This toddler's transition to a new class and teacher is eased as she goes to visit. She is accompanied by her current teacher and friend.

37.3.3b She gradually makes friends with the new teacher and other children.

for children, credit can be given for this indicator. Ask staff the question in the ITERS-R scale to get information needed to score this indicator.

3.4   *Substitutes* are people brought in to replace regular staff who are unable to work. In order to have the program operate with the least disruption, the substitutes should know the children, and the practices of the program. Children are most comfortable with people whom they know and who know them. They also are reassured if their daily routines, expectations for their behavior, and the rules for access and use of materials, continue in the same way. It is especially important that any substitute who is left in charge and who is mainly responsible for determining how the group functions, is someone who knows both the children and the program.

37.3.3c   When the actual move takes place, she will be ready.

Score this item "Yes" if substitutes who are left in charge of the program are almost always (with only rare exceptions) people who know both the children in the group and the program. Ask staff the questions provided in the ITERS-R scale to get information needed for scoring this item.

5.1   Young children find it easier to become friendly and trusting with familiar people, people with whom they have had pleasant and predictable experiences. Not only is it important for them to have a small, stable, reliable staff with whom they become relaxed and on whom they can rely, but the number of additional adults who *work* with the children as helpers should also be limited. (See photo 37.5.1.) The additional adults who work with the children may include volunteers, parents,

37.5.1   Two stable staff members are with the children in this group during most of the day, and one is always present. They are assisted by other staff who are familiar to the children.

student teachers, senior citizens serving as "surrogate grandparents," or floaters who substitute for staff during scheduled breaks. Observers who do not interact with the children are not considered here.

The number of such classroom helpers should be limited to two or three at most, in order to maintain a high level of consistency in the program.

Ask staff if there are any additional adults who come in to work with the children such as volunteers, students, or floaters and if so, how many there are, and how often they come. Score this indicator "Yes" if there are no more than two or three additional adults who work with the children on any day.

5.2 This indicator requires that it is the usual practice for children to remain with one staff member and the same group for at least a year. This means that moving a child to another group or to the care of a completely new staff would be done only in very unusual circumstances. Generally, children in this program would have a continuing relationship with at least one of their teachers and a group of familiar companions for at least a year.

Score "Yes" if the practice is to allow children to remain with at least one staff member and the same group for a minimum of one year.

5.3 Children need an ***orientation*** or introduction to the new group/room/staff they will be joining. This applies not only to when a child is moved to a new classroom, but also when a classroom is assigned a new staff member. The orientation period is a time for the child to get acquainted with the new situation and/or people in a way that is as secure and comfortable as possible. A ***gradual*** orientation requires that:

- The child is given sufficient time to adjust prior to any change.
- The changes are introduced in small, easy steps.
- The child is with a familiar adult.

In addition to the examples given in the ITERS-R item, see the strategies for easing transitions listed in Indicator 1.3. The main purpose of providing a gradual orientation is to ease the child's transition to a new situation.

Score this indicator "Yes" if the program consistently provides a gradual orientation for children. Ask staff the question in the ITERS-R scale to get the information needed to score this indicator.

5.4 A ***stable*** group means that the same relatively small number of people always serve as ***substitutes*** for the regular staff. This permits the program to properly train the substitutes so that they:

- use proper health practices in children's personal care routines,
- follow the schedule in each group,
- meet the expectations for supervision, interaction and discipline set by the program, and
- conduct appropriate activities for the age and abilities of the children.

Another advantage is that a stable group of substitutes will be used frequently enough so that they get to know the children and the children can become familiar with them. ***Always available*** means that the program never has to go outside the ***stable group*** of substitutes to hire people who have not been properly oriented to the program and/or who do not know the children.

Score this indicator "Yes" if the same group of substitutes is always available and substitutes used for the center are limited to this stable group. Ask staff the questions in the ITERS-R scale to get information to score this indicator.

37 Staff continuity

7.1   A ***small group*** of infants/toddlers means a ratio of one caregiver to two or three infants and young toddlers up to 18 months of age, and one caregiver to three or four toddlers 18-30 months of age. The total group is divided among the staff into smaller subgroups. (See photo 37.7.1.) ***Primarily caring for*** means that each staff member takes the major responsibility for the small group assigned to her, including:

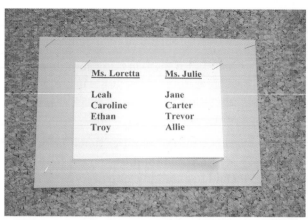

- carrying out most of their personal care routines
- planning special activities they (and the total group) might enjoy
- keeping notes about each child's day and progress made towards specific goals
- accompanying the children in preparations for transitions
- communicating informally with parents
- preparing the report for parents about each child's day including routines and play interests
- participating in the parent conferences
- participating in the child's IEP or IFSP if needed

37.7.1 In this group of eight children, half are assigned to each primary caregiver, who takes personal responsibility for ensuring that their needs are

Whenever possible, children are assigned to a primary caregiver to whom the child is attracted and who is attracted to the child. Despite the special bond that might develop, serving as a primary caregiver for a small subgroup should not supplant each staff member's sense of responsibility to care for all the children in the group and to share duties fairly with the other staff member(s). For example, if a child who is in one staff member's group needs a diaper change and her primary caregiver is busy, another caregiver who is available takes responsibility for changing the diaper.

Score this indicator "Yes" if each staff member is assigned a small group of children and serves as a primary caregiver for them, performing some of the functions described in the indicator. Base the score on observation, supplemented by information reported by the staff.

7.2   Continuity of care for more than a year is made possible by some programs by keeping children together in the same group with the same staff. Making such an ***option*** available means that the continuity group is a possibility for some children, but may not be the only possibility. If remaining in the same group with the same staff is not a good solution for some of the children, another option should be available.

Score 7.2 "Yes" if the option to remain with the same group of children and the same staff for more than a year is available. Ask staff the question in the ITERS-R to get the information needed to score this indicator.

7.3   One way of assuring that all the substitutes used by the program know the children and the practices of the program, is to employ ***enough staff*** so that ***only*** staff are used as substitutes. Enough staff must be hired so that the program continues to maintain appropriate staff-child ratios at all times, even on days when some regular classroom staff are absent. Some options for achieving such a staffing pattern are to employ:

- several floaters who assist with the most busy times and work with individual children when they are not needed as substitutes
- students in early childhood education for half-day positions as floaters and potential substitutes
- retired teachers or parents who want to work two or three days a week
- multi-talented staff who can assist with office or administrative tasks as well as serving as substitutes

Score this indicator "Yes" if enough staff are employed to use only staff as substitutes. Ask staff the questions in the ITERS-R scale to get the information needed to score this indicator.

38 Supervision and evaluation of staff

General information about this item

A high quality program for infants and toddlers requires competent staff. Regular supervision, observation, and evaluation of all classroom staff, timely and complete feedback, and planning for and implementation of corrective action, are needed for staff to continue to grow as professionals. When staff feel valued by the administration, and their strengths as well as their weaknesses are identified during the evaluation, some of the tension involved in the evaluation process may be lessened.

If the program is conducted by one person alone with no other staff, then this item must be scored "NA."

It is best to obtain the information to score this item from the classroom staff member who is being supervised rather than from the supervisor. However, if the classroom staff member states that she does not know whether staff are supervised, for example, because she is new to the facility, then ask the director of the program. The reason it is preferable to ask the person who is being supervised is because only that person knows how the supervisor is being perceived. The supervisor might think that her feedback is being given in a helpful and supportive way, but the recipient of the feedback may not perceive it that way. The perception of the person being supervised is very important in the feedback process.

Both formal, planned evaluations with written feedback and shorter, more informal, ongoing observations with feedback are valuable, and considered in this item. It is important to engage staff in active participation in the evaluation process by working cooperatively to find solutions to problems they perceive as well as those perceived by the supervisor. Feedback that is given in a helpful, calm, supportive manner, where both supervisor and supervisee cooperate to find a solution, is a more positive experience for both parties. It is important to stress that the purpose of supervision is to improve the program for children.

A closer look at each indicator

1.1   *Supervision* means that a member of the administrative staff, or a representative chosen by them, observes a classroom staff member in action with the children, in order to see how well the staff member is performing her duties. The supervision may be quite informal, for example, through a daily visit to see if everything is all right. In order to score this indicator, ask classroom staff the suggested questions in the ITERS-R, and base the score on their answers.

Score 1.1 "Yes" only if *no* supervision is provided.

38 Supervision and evaluation of staff

1.2   ***Feedback or evaluation*** means giving the person being supervised information about his or her performance, based on the observation done by the supervisor. If no feedback is given, either about strengths or weaknesses, score this indicator "Yes."

3.1   ***Some supervision*** means that classroom staff are observed by administrative staff at some time while staff are working with children to see how well they are performing their duties. This indicator is at the minimal level, so supervision for any reason is acceptable. This might be a short observation in the classroom as part of a director's daily routine, or an informal observation of a new staff member. Ask classroom staff the questions in the ITERS-R, and base the score on their answers.

3.2   ***Some feedback*** means that the supervisor reports back to the person being supervised about what was observed. This feedback may be done verbally or in writing, and may be fairly general to meet the minimal requirements of this indicator. (See photo 38.3.2.) Comments such as, "You've reorganized the soft area. It's much better to have a bigger area," or "Let me get my camera to take a picture of your new bulletin board for parents. It's so colorful," can be considered favorable feedback. "It would help if you came in at least half an hour earlier to get things set up before the children arrive," or "Mary needs to be getting set up for breakfast, not you, because you need to be free to talk to parents," can be considered suggestions for improvement. Base the score on the answers

38.3.2 The director supervises teaching staff everyday, through informal observation, and provides verbal feedback.

of the classroom staff to the questions printed in the ITERS-R for this indicator. If any feedback or suggestions are given at all based on observation by the supervisor, score 3.2 "Yes."

5.1   The ***annual supervisory observation*** required in this indicator is intended as a safeguard to assure that all staff members continue to perform at a high level of quality. This observation should be of sufficient length (at least 1-3 hours) and done at a time when the children are awake and active. Short, informal observations such as a director's daily walk-through, cannot be used to satisfy this indicator, which requires a more formal, sustained observation of considerable length.

Each staff member should receive an ***annual*** (once a year) ***supervisory observation.***

If two or more staff members have joint responsibility for a group and work together most of the day, credit can be given if the supervisor observes them both during one longer observation or each during separate observations. However, the supervisor will have to be careful to note in detail each staff member's strengths and weaknesses, in order to give personalized feedback to each one.

During the annual observation, the supervisor should focus on the important aspects of the particular staff member's performance, such as whether:

• Both verbal and non-verbal interactions with children, parents, and other staff members are generally upbeat and positive

• Action is taken to protect infants and toddler's health and safety both indoors and outdoors

• The arrangement of active and quiet play areas and most of the materials in them are functional and inviting

38.5.2a

38.5.2b

38.5.2a-b   The director provides feedback through an annual written evaluation, supplemented by a meeting in which the evaluation is explained.

- Hands-on activities to encourage fine and gross motor development, and promote independence are plentiful
- Appropriate language stimulation for children through reading, conversing, and explaining occurs throughout the observation

Although, in this indicator, it is not required that the supervisor use a recognized process quality assessment instrument to conduct the annual supervisory observation, many administrators find it very helpful to do so. There are a number of commonly used assessment instruments that the supervisor could consider in order to select the best one for his or her particular early childhood program. It is also acceptable if the program wishes to develop its own guidelines for the supervisory observation.

Score this indicator "No" if some, but not all, classroom staff members are observed, if the observation is less than 1 hour in length, or if it is completed less than yearly. To give credit for this indicator all staff members must be observed yearly, each for 1-3 hours, in a formal, sustained observation.

5.2   This indicator requires that a *written evaluation is shared with each staff member at least yearly.* (See photos 38.5.2a-b.) To give credit, staff performance must be observed while they are working with the children (as described for Indicator 5.1), and a written evaluation must be based on the observation.

If two or more staff members, who have joint responsibility for a group and work together most of the day, are observed at the same time, a separate written evaluation is required for each. The supervisor must give personalized feedback to each. Any suggestions for improvements needed in the classroom environment, for which they are jointly responsible, such as for adding new materials, updating the display, or rearranging the daily schedule, should be given to both staff members since they will need to work together to make these changes. The suggestions for improving teaching performance, including interactions, language, discipline methods, staff cooperation, supervision of children, and facilitation of play, will need to be handled separately. It is probably best to arrange to provide feedback on teaching performance personally to each staff member, although the classroom suggestions may be handled together.

A copy of the evaluation must be given to the staff member, and a copy must be kept by the administrator in the staff member's file. Having an evaluation in writing leaves less room for misunderstanding and also preserves what has been observed that particular year, so that it can be compared with earlier or later observations.

Base the score for this indicator on the answers given by the classroom staff to the questions in the ITERS-R. However, if classroom staff have been employed a relatively short time and have not had a supervisory observation, the administrative staff should be asked to explain their procedures and to show an example of a written evaluation done recently for another staff member in the facility.

5.3 Identifying *strengths of staff as well as areas needing improvement* gives support as well as constructive criticism. Staff may feel discouraged if they only hear criticism in an evaluation. On the other hand, if only praise for strengths is given, change may not occur because areas of weakness are not acknowledged. To give credit for 5.3, a balanced report is required because it has the best chance of resulting in a willingness to work to improve practice.

Score "Yes" for Indicator 5.3 if classroom staff indicate that both aspects of performance, the strengths and areas needing improvement, are presented in the evaluation.

5.4 This indicator addresses how evaluation gets translated into change. It requires that *action is taken to implement the recommendation of the evaluation*. The sample questions printed in the ITERS-R may be used to gather information to score this indicator. In order to give credit, look for concrete examples of implementations, such as descriptions of training sessions that were given to correct some shortcoming or materials that were purchased so improvements could be made.

Additional examples of possible corrective action that might be taken after an evaluation are:

- Additional children's books showing cultural diversity and inclusion are purchased or borrowed from the library, to round out the classroom collection.

- Lunch is scheduled earlier because the toddlers become too hungry.

- A floater is assigned to the classroom to ease the transition between lunch and nap.

- Staff members who work together rearrange their break times to avoid the disruption that seems to be causing unhappiness for the infants.

- Various in-service workshops are organized to correct similar weaknesses in a number of classrooms (e.g., on discipline, health and safety practices).

- Policies that seem to be misunderstood by classroom staff are spelled out more clearly, and some new policies are articulated.

- Several staff members who show unusually strong skills in certain areas are asked to share these with the whole group through presentations at staff meetings and other on-site training sessions.

The question in the ITERS-R should be used to get information from the staff to score this indicator. If needed, additional questions may be asked about specific examples of actions that have been taken to implement changes in the program. However, if staff have been employed a relatively short period of time and have not had an annual supervisory observation, ask the administrative staff to explain how implementation of evaluations are carried out.

38.7.1a Staff participate in self-evaluation so the way in which teachers see their practices is part of the conversation.

38.7.1b All staff are encouraged to participate in figuring out how to improve the classroom environment.

7.1 Being evaluated is difficult for everyone, because it forces individuals to see themselves from another's point of view. The shock of an impersonal, objective view of oneself can be softened if the ***staff member participates in self-evaluation*** and gains some experience in looking more objectively at his or her own performance. (See photos 38.7.1a-b.)

Self-evaluation has become an accepted part of many program improvement efforts, including NAEYC accreditation and CDA credentialing. Often the staff member uses the same instrument for self-evaluation that the supervisor uses to evaluate staff. In this case, the two evaluations can be compared and discussed before recommendations for improvement are made based on a joint decision.

Score 7.1 "Yes" if self-evaluation is part of the annual (or more frequent) supervisory evaluation.

38.7.2a The director frequently observes and provides feedback, at varied times during the different days.

7.2 ***Frequent observations and feedback*** make it possible to make improvements in small steps. This approach also has the advantage of getting staff accustomed to being observed, so that they start to feel more comfortable. (See photos 38.7.2a-b.) Frequent observations can be less formal and shorter. Score this indicator "Yes," if in addition to the annual supervisory observation, staff report that observations and feedback are provided about every other month. Some variation in the number of observations is permitted, based on the

38.7.2b She involves staff as partners in solving any problems that need to be addressed.

needs of individual staff members. More frequent observations may be needed for new staff, less frequent ones for more experienced staff.

7.3 This indicator emphasizes the importance of the manner in which the feedback is given. If feedback is given in a ***helpful, supportive manner***, much of the threat of disapproval and failure is neutralized. Then the staff member can feel that the supervisor is going to be part of the solution. Score "Yes," if classroom staff report that the tone used in giving feedback meets this requirement.

39 Opportunities for professional growth

General information about this item

In order to deliver consistently high quality care and education to children, programs require well trained, professional classroom staff. This item addresses the various steps a program can take to stimulate and support the professional development of their classroom staff.

Staff at all levels of expertise, from the novice to the highly trained professional, benefit from ongoing opportunities for professional growth. When a new staff member is hired, he or she must be oriented to the philosophy, policies, practices, and procedures of the center. Over time, through regular staff meetings that include staff development activities and cover administrative issues, a cohesive team can be built with commonly held beliefs and consistent practices. By encouraging and supporting staff to utilize both on-site and community educational resources, each classroom staff member can be helped to continue to learn and grow professionally as an early childhood educator.

In order to score the indicators in this item, the observer will need to ask the classroom staff to answer the questions in the ITERS-R. If the classroom staff has been employed for less than three months and state that they do not know some of the answers about the indicators on the 5 and 7 levels of quality, the administrative staff need to be asked these questions. It is preferable to get the information about opportunities for professional growth from the classroom staff because in order to improve, the classroom staff must know about and make use of these opportunities.

A closer look at each indicator

1.1 An *orientation* to the program means that all new staff are given a systematic introduction that covers their basic responsibilities and requirements for carrying out the program with the children. Basic orientation includes, at a minimum, the emergency, safety, and health procedures required. More thorough orientation includes guidelines for interaction with children and parents, discipline methods, and instruction about appropriate activities for the children.

In-service training means training provided *while* the staff are working in the program. In contrast, pre-service training is training that is required *before* an individual is allowed to work in the program. The person might be employed by the program, but cannot take responsibility for the tasks assigned to his or her position before the pre-service training is completed.

Score 1.1 "Yes" only if classroom staff who have been employed for 6 weeks or longer report that they have not received any basic information about the program including emergency, health, and safety procedures.

39 Opportunities for professional growth

1.2 ***Staff meetings*** are meetings conducted by the director or other administrative staff to discuss center concerns, which are attended by classroom staff and any other employees invited by the administrative staff. Staff meetings can cover a variety of issues including:

- Administrative concerns, such as changes in days and hours of operation, variation in daily or weekly schedule, purchasing of materials and equipment, assignment of staff and part-time assistants, or changes in children's grouping patterns

- State licensing and other regulatory issues, such as changes in state regulations, status of center license, or upcoming regulatory visits

- News items, such as introducing a new employee, new children enrolled, an honor the center has received, or inclusion of the center in a newspaper article

- On-site in-service education including a guest speaker, presentations by staff members who have attended a course or a conference, or meeting time for staff members working with the same age group in different classrooms

- Announcements about training opportunities in the community, such as courses offered by community colleges or resource and referral agencies or local, state, and national conferences

- Display of and discussion about new books or other teaching resources and educational materials added to the on-site professional library for all staff to use

To decide on a score for this indicator, use the classroom staff's answers to the questions in the ITERS-R for Indicators 1.2, 3.3, and 5.3. If staff, who have been employed less than 6 weeks, state that they do not know whether staff meetings are held, ask the administrative staff. Score "Yes" on 1.2 only if no staff meetings are held by the center for classroom staff.

3.1 ***Some orientation*** means that, within 6 weeks after the start of employment and before they are put in charge of a group of children, new staff receive information about crucial issues such as emergency, health, and safety procedures. (See photo 39.3.1.) This orientation should occur when staff are not responsible for care of children and can give their undivided attention. All staff newly employed by the center must receive a basic orientation (approximately 8-10 hours in duration) even if they have been previously employed by another center, have been in another child development related profession, or have considerable academic training. (See sample of documentation of staff orientation, next page.)

Score 3.1 "Yes" if all new staff are required, within 6 weeks of employment, to attend orientation that covers, at a minimum, the emergency, health, and safety procedures of the center. Base scores on the answers given by classroom staff, using the questions in the ITERS-R.

3.2 ***Some in-service training*** means that, *at least once a year*, training is provided by the center, and the classroom staff are expected to attend. This training may be conducted on-site, for

Procedures

- Upon arrival, all children must be accompanied inside the facility by an adult.

- Staff must be notified of the child's arrival.

- Upon the child's departure, an adult must come inside the facility and notify staff that the child is leaving.

- Authorization is required in writing when anyone other than the designated adult arrives to pick up the child.

- When a child is transported by the facility to the child's home, an adult must be available to receive the child from the bus or van.

- Children must never be left unattended .

114 • Resource Section

39.3.1 Orientation includes the basic procedures for protecting children.

Documentation of Staff Orientation

Employee_____   Date Hired_____

In the first six weeks of employment, each new employee shall receive a minimum of 10 clock hours of on-site orientation. Employee will attend training on topics below. The trainer will sign and indicate the hours of orientation training provided on each topic.

TOPIC	TRAINING PROVIDER	HOURS	DATE
Review of Personnel Policies			
Review of individual's job-specific duties and responsibilities/job description			
Review of child day care licensing/NAEYC accreditation standards			
Review of Center's history/purposes/goals			
Review of Center's operational policies/ parents handbook, including discipline policy			
Health and safety standards/emergency procedures			
Child Abuse reporting procedure			
Special services component and reporting requirements			
Observation of Center operations			

I have received training in the topics listed above.

_____

Employee Signature

_____

Date

Adapted from FPG Family & Child Care Program, "Documentation of Staff Orientation."

example by inviting guest trainers or by using video training, or off-site, if the center administration arranges for classroom staff to participate in a community training workshop.

To give a score of "Yes" for Indicator 3.2, classroom staff must describe examples of in-service training they have attended, or administrative staff must show documentation of in-service training that occurs at least yearly.

3.3 *Some staff meetings* means that, *at least two times a year*, staff meetings are held by the director and/or administrative staff, and the classroom staff are expected to attend.

Administrative concerns, such as those listed under the first two bullets for Indicator 1.2, are required to be included in the staff meetings, although additional matters may also be discussed.

Score 3.3 "Yes" if classroom staff describe the staff meetings held at the center at least two times a year, or if administrative staff document a sufficient number of staff meetings that cover, at a minimum, administrative issues.

5.1 *Thorough orientation* means that new staff are provided a longer basic training (at least 16 hours) to introduce *sound social/emotional practices*, such as supportive interaction with children and parents, and effective discipline methods, as well as *programmatic issues*, such as ways to conduct appropriate activities.

Base the score for this indicator on answers given by classroom staff to questions in the ITERS-R for Indicators 1.1, 3.1, 3.2, 5.1, and 5.2. Ask specific questions if needed to get further information about the nature of the orientation provided for new staff. If staff have been employed at the center for less than 6 weeks and state that they do not know, ask the administrative staff about the length and content of the orientation and to provide documentation for their answers.

5.2 For the definition of *in-service training*, see Indicator 1.1. *Provided regularly by program* means that training is provided for all classroom staff *at least two times a year*, either on site or in community workshops.

To give credit for this indicator, attendance by classroom staff must be required at the twice yearly in-service training sessions.

In-service training might be conducted for all the classroom staff together, such as training on reporting child abuse and neglect, or for subgroups of staff members on age-appropriate topics, such as effective language development for infants and toddlers. The score for 5.2 should be based on classroom staff's answers to the questions in the ITERS-R for this indicator. If staff have been employed for less than 6 months and state that they do not know about any in-service training, ask administrative staff to describe the center's in-service training program and document that it is being carried out. Documentation can include a dated training agenda, a description of a recent community workshop attended by staff, or a record of attendance at various in-service sessions by staff at the center.

5.3 *Monthly staff meetings* means at least one staff meeting a month, for the portion of the year the program is in session. In order to get credit for including *staff development activities* as part of the staff meetings, each staff meeting must include at least one activity (e.g., short presentation and discussion) that adds to the competence of the staff, such as:

• A staff member gives a book report on a new professional book that has been added to the center's library, and other staff ask questions and discuss.

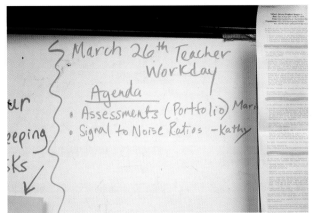

39.5.3a All staff are expected to attend monthly staff meetings, which are scheduled for teacher workdays.

39.5.3b Notes of staff meetings are provided for staff to review.

- A staff member shares some practical ideas she has tried from a course she is taking on a curriculum topic such as age-appropriate art, music, language stimulation, or relating to parents.

- A center-wide monthly parent newsletter that each group contributes something to is discussed, and new features are added.

- Some new materials or games that are being added to the on-site resource library are introduced, and staff discuss how to use them.

- A short educational video is shown and discussed.

- Staff visit a classroom in the center that has conducted a particularly successful parent program, to see the bulletin board and talk with the staff member whose class it is.

To give credit for 5.3, use the answers classroom staff give to the questions printed in the ITERS-R for Indicators 1.2, 3.3, and 5.3. Further questions may need to be asked about whether staff development activities are included in the monthly meetings. (See photos 39.5.3a-b.) Ask for examples of such activities to score 5.3 "Yes."

5.4   ***Some professional resource materials*** means *at least 25 books, pamphlets, or AV materials* in good condition that staff can use as resources for their own professional development, and several issues of at least one early childhood focused magazine or journal (for example, *Young Children*, NAEYC's journal). (See photos 39.5.4a-b, next page.)

The resources must be ***on site***, which means at the center(for example, in the director's office or in the staff lounge), and ***available*** for staff to use. These resources can include some materials that have been borrowed from another library, but when they are returned, other materials must be made available.

Ask to see the professional resources, if the classroom staff (or administrative staff) respond that there are such resources (use the questions in the scale for 5.4 and 7.2). Look through the resources to see whether the topics are appropriate for the staff. Professional resources might include:

- Curriculum activity books for use with various ages from infancy through school-age, suited to the age range served at the center

39 Opportunities for professional growth

39.5.4a A variety of books is among the professional resource materials that teachers of infants and toddlers use.

- Books or pamphlets on child development topics such as language development, discipline, literacy, health, inclusion of children with disabilities, encouraging acceptance of diversity, working with parents.

39.5.4b In addition, videos are provided on infant/toddler care and education. To score, the observer would need to find out whether child-focused magazines were used.

- Videos on various curriculum areas and child development topics (If staff may not borrow the AV resources from the library, there must be suitable equipment for them to use at the center for viewing.)
- Copies of professional journals such as *Young Children* and magazines such as *Parenting* or others designed for infant/toddler staff.
- Labeled file folders with articles clipped or copied from professional magazines and journals

7.1 In order to encourage staff to participate in courses, conferences, or workshops provided in the community, **support** or help should be made available by the program to enable staff to participate. Various types of help may be given credit to meet this indicator including:

- Staff are given released time to attend a program during work hours, and substitutes are provided to take over their childcare responsibilities.
- Travel costs are reimbursed, or the program provides transportation in their school van, so that staff may attend a workshop or conference.
- Scholarships covering course enrollment and books are available.
- Scholarships covering conference fees are available for classroom staff to attend local, state, regional or national conferences.

To score 7.1 "Yes" at least two ongoing provisions yearly for support should be described by classroom staff (or administrative staff) in response to the question in the ITERS-R for this indicator.

7.2. A **good professional library** is one that contains **current materials**, meaning that most of the books in the library have been published within the last 10 years, and the journals and magazines are issues from the past 2 years. Books, such as the work of Piaget and Erikson are exceptions, since they are classics on which many of our current ideas are based.

The library should contain at least 60 books and 3 series of periodicals (magazines and journals) that belong to the center. The library should have a balanced collection of books on a *variety* of early childhood subjects including:

- Curriculum and activity books containing practical classroom ideas for children of the ages enrolled in the center
- Books and articles on child development theory and practice (e.g., ages and stages, discipline, language development)
- Materials on working with families, diversity, or inclusion

Ask to see the library to decide on a score for this indicator.

7.3   ***Formal education*** means education that is awarded credit and can be applied to a degree, credential, or other recognized certificate of completion. Although attendance at workshops and conferences is important in developing professional competence, working towards a particular certificate of completion such as the GED (General Education Diploma), a credential such as the CDA (Child Development Associate) or a Birth through Kindergarten teaching credential, or a degree such as an AA (Associate of Arts) or BA (Bachelor of Arts), requires a longer period of study and a more comprehensive, systematic set of courses. Although more sustained work is involved, the rewards are also greater. As the early childhood field grows in professionalism, staff members will be required to have degrees and credentials in order to serve as lead teachers. Requiring staff with less than an AA degree to continue their formal education will benefit both the staff members and the center.

"NA" is permitted for this indicator if all staff have an AA degree or higher.

Give credit for 7.3 (score "Yes") if the center has a policy requiring staff with less than an AA degree to continue their formal education. Base scores on the answer given by classroom staff (or administrative staff) and documentation of implementation of the policy.

KAPLAN
EARLY LEARNING COMPANY
Professional Development Services

Enriching the education and Quality of child care programs one training at a time.

With Kaplan's Professional Development Program, you can create your own training program as part of a comprehensive plan for your program and staff's ongoing professional growth and enhancement.

Kaplan offers a wide variety of professional development topics for Infant/Toddler, Preschool, and School Age educators and caregivers. Professional and experienced consultants will deliver in-service to small or large groups at time and locations convenient to your program!

Topics include, but are not limited to:

- Creative Curriculum Approach
- The Beyond Curriculum Series
- Learning Accomplishment Profile Series
- The Learning Environment

- Conscious Discipline Orientation
- Language & Literacy Development
- Infant/Toddler Development
- *And much, much more!*

To learn more about Kaplan Professional Development, please contact us!
Telephone – 800-334-2014   Email – training@kaplanco.com
Web – www.kaplanco.com/training

Here's what our customers have to say about Kaplan Professional Development

"I learned so much in the last two days and I believe it was because I was able to do the activities to learn instead of just listening to someone talk."
– Teacher, Lac du Flambeau, WI

"{The Trainer} was very insightful and energetic – she made it fun to learn!"
– Teacher, Newberry, SC

"Kaplan did an exceptional job of taking the time to understand our program needs and what we wanted to achieve from our training. In doing so, they provided our programs with a customized and highly interactive training session that was tailored to fit our immediate needs and objectives."
– Director, Hartford, CT

Other Recommended Titles from the Authors

An Industry Standard Endorsed By Early Childhood Professionals Worldwide

Make your classrooms the best they can be!

Kaplan Exclusive

ALL ABOUT THE ITERS-R
A detailed guide in words and pictures to be used with the ITERS-R
Debby Cryer
Thelma Harms
Riley

ALL ABOUT THE ECERS-R
A detailed guide in words & pictures to be used with the ECERS-R
Debby Cryer
Thelma Harms
Cathy Riley

INFANT / TODDLER ENVIRONMENT RATING SCALE REVISED EDITION
THELMA HARMS • DEBBY CRYER • RICHARD M. CLIFFORD

Spiral Bound!

EARLY CHILDHOOD ENVIRONMENT RATING SCALE REVISED EDITION
Thelma Harms   Richard M. Clifford   Debby Cryer

Additional notes for clarification of the rating scales available at www.fpg.unc.edu

Environment Rating Scales
By Thelma Harms, Richard M. Clifford, Debby Cryer. From the Frank Porter Graham Child Development Institute of the University of North Carolina. Evaluates physical environment, basic care, curriculum, interaction, schedule, program structure, and parent and staff education.

All About the ITERS-R
This resource guide should be used with the Infant/Toddler Environment Rating Scale-Revised Edition. It explains why each item is important, what is needed to meet the requirements for all items, and how to score. Over 800 color photographs taken in child care settings are presented in this text of 465 pages.

18-50034	**SAVE! When you buy the set!**	
	(All About the ITERS-R & ITERS-R spiral bound)	**$64.95**
18-11647	All About the ITERS-R *Kaplan Exclusive!*	48.95
18-10308	ITERS-R (spiral bound)	17.95
18-11218	ITERS-R (Spanish)	16.95
18-13599	Video Observations for the ITERS-R (DVD) (with instructor's guide)	58.95
18-50943	Video Observations for the ITERS-R (VHS)	58.95
18-31436	ITERS-R Video Guide & Workbook (for VHS)	4.95
18-14892	All About Diapering Poster *NEW!*	5.95
18-14893	All About Handwashing Poster *NEW!*	5.95

Environmental Rating Scales Materials Classroom List
Kaplan Professional Development has created these lists to correlate with ITERS-R and ECERS-R. *Kaplan Exclusive!*

18-11882 ECERS-R FREE!   **18-11881 ITERS-R** FREE!

All About the ECERS-R
Designed to enable teachers to create developmentally appropriate learning environments for preschool and kindergarten aged children. This manual provides step-by-step instructions on how to design a quality day care environment. Should be used side by side with ECERS-R, the scale used to develop and quantify quality standards in the USA, Canada, and abroad. Includes The "How, What & Why" for each indicator, 7 sub-scale items, step-by-step instructions, and over 700 color photos. 441 pages.

18-50035	**SAVE! When you buy the set!**	
	(All About the ECERS-R & ECERS-R spiral bound)	**$64.95**
18-46796	All About the ECERS-R *Kaplan Exclusive!*	48.95
18-11841	ECERS-R (spiral bound)	17.95
18-46798	ECERS-R (Spanish)	17.95
18-13600	Video Observations for the ECERS-R, DVD (with instructor's guide)	58.95
18-42149	Video Observations for the ECERS-R (VHS)	58.95
18-42150	ECERS-R Video Guide & Workbook (VHS)	3.95

For professional training to fit your needs call 1-800-334-2014

SCHOOL-AGE CARE ENVIRONMENT RATING SCALE
THELMA HARMS • ELLEN VINEBERG JACOBS • DONNA ROMANO WHITE

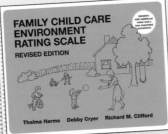

FAMILY CHILD CARE ENVIRONMENT RATING SCALE REVISED EDITION
Thelma Harms   Debby Cryer   Richard M. Clifford

Environmental Rating Scales

18-33503	SACERS School Age Care	**$17.95**
18-33504	SACERS Scoring Sheets (30)	8.95
18-13598	Family Child Care Environmental Rating Scale: FCCERS-R (spiral bound)	17.95
18-84475	FCCERS-R Video Observations (DVD)	58.95
18-84476	FCCERS-R Video Observations (VHS)	58.95

Convenient Order Options

Order Toll Free 1-800-334-2014
Monday–Friday 8 am–6 pm EST
Fax Orders: 1-800-452-7526
Order Online: www.Kaplanco.com

Customer Service: 1-800-334-2014
Monday–Friday 8 am–6 pm EST

Shipping Charges

Order Size	UPS Items	2nd Day Air	Next Day Air	Truck Items
Orders OVER $1500.00	FREE Shipping*	25% of order value. $14.56 minimum.	30% of order value. $36.40 minimum.	15% of order value. $62.50 minimum.
Orders UNDER $1500.00	15% of order value. $5.00 minimum.	25% of order value. $14.56 minimum.	30% of order value. $36.40 minimum.	15% of order value. $62.50 minimum.
All Orders Shipping to AK, HI, PR, VI, & Canada	UPS not available. USPS+ 25% of order value.	30% of order value. $26.80 minimum.	35% of order value. $44.40 minimum.	Contact Total Customer Care for a freight quote.

Note: International orders, call Total Customer Care for shipping quotes: 1-800-334-2014

Ship To:
Name _____
Street Address _____
City _____ State _____ Zip _____
Phone (____) _____
Email _____

Bill To: (if different from Ship To)
Name _____
Address _____
City _____ State _____ Zip _____
Phone (_____) _____
Email _____

Method of Payment: (Sorry No COD's or Cash)
Account Number (if known) _____

   Purchase Order No. _____

   Check or Money Order (enclosed) to Kaplan Early Learning Company

   Visa   MasterCard   American Express   Discover

Card No. _____ Exp. Date _____
Signature _____
Cardholder Name_____
Address _____
City _____ State _____ Zip _____

*Orders over $1,500.00 will receive free shipping on UPS items, but will incur regular shipping charges on truck items.
+USPS is United States Postal Service.
No free shipping to Alaska, Hawaii, Puerto Rico, Virgin Islands and Canada.
Orders shipped complete Alaska, Hawaii, Puerto Rico, Virgin Islands and Canada..

Prices: Prices subject to change without notice.   Terms: net 30 days.
$1\frac{1}{2}$% late fee for past due invoices.

Qty.	Item #	Description	Price Each	Total Price

P.O. Box 609 • 1310 Lewisville-Clemmons Road
Lewisville, NC   27023-0609
Corporate Headquarters: 336-766-7374
email: Info@Kaplanco.com

Subtotal	
Sales Tax: For delivery in AL, AR, AZ, CA, CO, CT, FL, GA, ID, IL, IN, KY, LA, MA,MD, MN, MO, NC, NJ, NY, OH, OK, PA, SC, SD, TN, TX, VA, and WA, please add applicable tax or submit tax exempt certificate.	
Delivery Charges	
Total	